Socrates N' Suits
Book III

Socrates N' Suits
Book III

Jack "Suitcase" Simpson

To order additional copies of this book, contact:
Xlibris Corporation
1-888-795-4274
www.Xlibris.com
Orders@Xlibris.com
32484

CONTENTS

Book III of the SOCRATES 'N SUITS triad is the conclusion of the developing friendship between one of the world's most eminent philosophers and Jack "Suitcase" (Suits) Simpson, fighter pilot, experimental pilot, and business man of 40 years. **BOOK I & II** details when they met and how Socrates' 2500 years of intellectual experience guided Jack through combat and four years of testing two of the USA's fastest fighters. Jack started his business as a $300 a month janitor. Socrates guided him through the myriad of stumbling blocks and recoveries until one day he said, "Socs, after 77 years, it looks like I'm an overnight success."

AN ASSIST IN UNDERSTANDING THE THIRD BOOK OF THE TRILOGY

BOOK III is a synergy; [NL synergia, fr. Gk synergos working together] of the author's hands on experience in the professions of Marketing and Sales with particular emphasis on marketing analysis. An in depth marketing analysis proffers writing of a beneficial marketing and business plan in "the language of and needs of" the customer. Speaking of synergy, an Army or a Corporation cannot capture territory, or market share *in* a territory, without a written plan. However, there is a dichotomy: in one you must know your enemy; in the other, your customer.

The nexus of, or road to, any successful experience is "filling your self full of the problem." You will read, in **BOOK III**, a chapter thus entitled. You also will comprehend my marketing problems being solved in many shapes and forms and in many different activities such as playing golf, while driving a car, the lessons of history, men putting away tools in a warehouse, my pedigree Boston Terrier, a meeting with a USAF General.

This written literary work is not necessarily to be read in sequential chapters. The reader may want to peruse different topics, therefore the offering of problem solving may be the same to these different essays. I did not have in mind writing a best seller. I want only for you to vicariously be there with me while we bring professional success to you and your company.

John J. Simpson
March, 2006

SOCRATES MAN OF ATHENS
MAN OF GREECE
MAN OF THE WORLD

Socrates, 439-399 B.C., was famous for his view of philosophy as a pursuit proper and necessary to all intelligent men. Socrates is one of the great examples of a man who lived by his principles even though they ultimately cost him his life.

Socrates was widely known for his intellectual powers even before he was 40. The oracle at Delphi pronounced him the wisest man in Greece. He became convinced that his calling was **to search for wisdom** about right conduct by which he might guide the intellectual and moral improvement of the Athenians.

Philosophy [Gr.,= love of wisdom], study of the ultimate reality, causes, and principles underlying being and thinking.

THE COLUMBIA ENCYCLOPEDIA
Fifth Edition, 1993
Columbia University Press

MONTH OF OCTOBER IN THE YEAR OF OUR LORD 2005

To the Ladies and Gentlemen reading BOOK III of the Trilogy:

I am using this missive as a venue to introduce myself as an above average friend of Jack "Suitcase" Simpson known to me as "Suits." My name is Socrates, a Greek philosopher from Athens with a view of philosophy as a pursuit proper and necessary to all intelligent men and women.

By the way, I vicariously attended an elegant *d*inner party not too long ago. Suitcase was invited as an honored guest. The party was hosted by a Mr. and Mrs. Christian Drake; a beautiful lady teamed with a Marine buck-ass private. You know how some of these parties go-a lot of brass and a buck-ass! I didn't want to say that but the temptation was overwhelming. I better explain!

"Suits" called me (collect) from gunnery school a little more than 50 years ago. (See **BOOK I**) He was reading Boorstin's *HIDDEN HISTORY* and in discussing Gibbon's *The History of the Decline & Fall of the Roman* Empire, Boorstin said, "Gibbon seemed to speak to me."

Well, "Suits" jumped all over that. He said, "Mr. Socrates, if Jimmy Stewart can talk to a rabbit, and Col. Scott can have God as his co-pilot, why can't I talk to you about flying my wing?" So, after importuning me with numerous reasons why I should say "OK", I accepted his call and the rest is history. In talking to him I learned he was an assiduous reader in the historical aspects of philosophy. He besieged me to fly his wing and teach him about philosophy and how, through the search for wisdom, he could become a better man. We have met a number of times; a very friendly man but a little bit of a wise cracker. I must have picked up on that; therefore the "brass and buck-ass"! Blame it on "Suits."

"Suits" and I discussed the party. Overwhelm is not an exacting word but I know he was affected deeply by the thought that such an august group of great men and women would take the time to meet him. Of course credit goes to Mr. and Mrs. Drake but since I was flying "Suits" wing, I had the sense these great men, regardless of rank, were there to meet the pilot, the author, and the genuine friend of Mr.

Drake, Yes, we discussed Christian Drake. "Suits," told me Chris left Manhattan Beach (See **BOOK I)** in tattered shorts with pockets full of sand. He returned later in "tailor maids" full of gold; well earned through steely self-discipline, hard work, and determination. Credentials for a tough United States Marine!

We also exchanged thoughts on the attendance of the number of bright stars and eagles; not to go unnoticed by "Suits"! He told me although these men of esteemed character knew how to laugh at themselves and with others not to be fooled. "For within," he said, "there lies a band of structural steel that through time, self-assertion, confidence, attained knowledge, and a bit of cockiness, the steel undergoes a metamorphosis into gold and silver. It is then carefully metered and molded for those who earn the right to wear the silver wings as a pilot in the United States Air Force and the gold wings of the United States Navy.

Ah, yes! And the wives! Scintillating, convivial, liking company, well groomed! Leaders all!

I know "Suits" will be, over time, keeping in touch with all of his friends; he always does. He couldn't say enough about his feeling of a very strong emotion in meeting, what he said, were such an honorable group of fighter pilots and their wives.

If you have read any of *SOCRATES 'N SUITS*, you know I will be there for you any time you need assistant. I can be reached in Club Cloud Nine any evening. Just please don't interrupt me if I am in a chorus of Salley in the Alley!

Very personal regards,

SOCRATES
Wingman to a guy named "SUITS"

SPECIAL THANKS TO:

Marvin Gussman, President, THE MARVIN GROUP. He gave me an office, a computer, a printer, bookshelves for all of my research volumes, and word to the Director, Information Systems, to help "Suits" whenever he needs it.

Jim Fish, Vice President, Corp. Operations for all his assistance in cases too numerous to mention.

Every time I yelped for help Bea English, Maria Cazares, Mike McDowell, John Young, Darren Bond, Mike Hershewe, Nick Dale, and Ann Duus were only too happy to help.

Todd Kiyama, THE MARVIN GROUP'S computer graphics designer and photographer.

My wife Dagmar. A woman marked by extraordinary elegance—and patience.

Though he tried to get away with no notoriety, for me that would not do!

Many, many thanks to Bill Allin, THE MARVIN GROUP'S Director, Information Systems. Without his continuous help the *SOCRATES 'N SUITS* trilogy would never have made it to the publisher.``

THANK YOU G.I. "JOE"

Richard T. (Joe) Forman, Lt. Col. USAF (Retired), was, for six years, a Combat Crew Duty officer as a navigator/bombardier on a B-47 and B-52. "Joe" flew a number of combat missions in Vietnam.

Please don't ask me how I, a fighter pilot, became friends with a STRATEGIC AIR COMMAND navigator!

Canadian Marconi was a client of mine when SAC (Strategic Air Command) was searching for a long-range Radio Frequency Navigation System. Joe was serving in the Systems Requirement Division; we became friends during negotiations. We kept in touch with each other and when Joe retired and moved to California we devoted time to become very good friends; our divergent USAF professions not withstanding!

Joe has a Bachelors and Masters in Business Administration and a Masters in Procurement Management; a perfect candidate to peruse **BOOK III** and offer a critical review. He did just that and Joe's learned advice was very much appreciated.

I garnered a lot of respect for Joe. Over the years, we have had many conversations concerning the relationship between the buyer and seller in the modern marketplace. We discussed ideas about the exchange of values as a way to satisfy both parties in transactions. Expectations such as courtesy, credibility, competency, communications, and confidentiality, are the foundations upon which values are formulated.

Joe and I agree that market-place stabilization requires extraordinary skills on the part of the buyer and the seller. Such skills are achieved education, training and experience; no one is born with them.

So! G.I. Joe! Thanks!

TESTIMONIALS FROM **BOOK I & II**

Your descriptions of all the exotic dalliances with "femme fatales" were both graphic an titillating. The book's highlight to me however, was the introduction of **Socrates** as your guiding light and continuing mentor . . . that was pure genius.

Grant A. Gould, M. D.

SOCRATES 'N SUITS chronicles the life of an extraordinary individual during a period of profound change in the technology of jet flight and the application of that technology in modern warfare. The tale reflects the humor, adventures, and philosophy of Mr. Simpson. It is often bawdy, full of hilarious incidents that reflect the lifestyle of a truly unique group of men who lead the development of modern high-speed aircraft. It is sometimes profound, reflecting a value system and approach to life. It is always spellbinding, a tale worth reading.

Dr. Edward Kutchma, Director
Aircraft and Weapons System Evaluation (retired)
Naval Air Warfare Center, Point Mugu, Ca.

Your description of your first mission over Korea was with such frankness and vividness made me feel I was right there with you. I was attracted to the presence of Socrates. I really enjoyed the way he imparted his time-tested philosophy to you. I think that most of us have a traveling companion like Socrates—but not many can fly an F-86!

Walt Braddy, Private Pilot
Retired Aerospace Project Manager

I am in combat—I am in control of this—this "thing," which hurdles through space at speeds that boggle the mind. The earth rises before me as I dive to unleash unheard of firepower on the enemy below. I can see the train, the tunnel, I fire—my

God, I can't pull out quickly enough! I'm going to—THAT'S HOW I FELT! Simpson puts you right in the seat of that jet, both as a combat fighter pilot and as an experimental test pilot. When you're through reading, you feel you've been there! What an exhilarating rush of the senses! Simpson is at once mesmerizing, comedic, unbelievably sad, and yes—even educational. I have never paid much more than a passing thought about philosophy, but I think I'm about to give old "SOCS" a call.

> George M. Houx, Ret.
> Aerospace Executive

Kate Galt, who's father was a Navy fighter pilot and ace, says: I can't tell you how much I enjoyed reading your book. Apart from learning so much about your life (always a mystery to me), I most appreciated seeing into your heart.

You have a tremendous sensitivity and empathy, no doubt developed through the many experiences you've had at the "cutting edge" of life and death. Socrates 'N Suits was a revelation. Dad would have loved it too!.

Jack "Suitcase" Simpson writes like a pro. His conversations with Socrates in his search for the truth is engaging and fresh. His two books are beautiful, tumultuous, and poignant; and very satisfying for those of us in search for the "word" and the "truth" and what is in our inner self.

Perhaps one complaint: it made me want to climb back into the cockpit and do things I did 60 years ago.

> Lee Stanley
> Senior Bureau Chief
> East-West News Bureau

A chance for every fighter pilot to relive his past. The humor, the terror, the great loves and the thought of forever being in the hands of Socrates. A book that is a MUST for anyone that has dreamed of the 'wild blue yonder.'

> Col. Norb 'Red' Gorman
> USAF Fighter Pilot, Ret.
> 180 plus A-1E missions—South Vietnam (mission verbiage by author)

I met "Suitcase" walking down the Strand one early Sunday afternoon, years ago, carrying a box—with vodka, orange juice and ice. He said he was looking for a volleyball game. I invited him to play with our gang and later to a bar-b-que; told him to bring a date. Well, "Suitcase" showed up with a stunning blonde; tall, great figure, convivial, articulate. She was a real heart thumper. I asked her how long she had known Jack. She answered, "Oh,!" as she look at her watch., "about two hours now."

"Suitcase" has written a chef-d'oeuvre, in words, as he says, "that are a fictional re-creations of actual events." His narrative about the loss of the husband of his former Las Vegas girlfriend is heart breaking; his ejection from a crippled experimental fighter heart chilling; and Socrates' calming, comforting words to a broken man after the loss, in a very short period of time, of three more of his test pilot friends; heart warming.

Joseph McNeil
Attorney at Law

Suitcase, I enjoyed your book. And do not think it demeaning to women. I do believe you simply enjoy the company of women and had great respect for those with whom you were involved. You seemed to love "womanhood" and as a single man enjoyed your times with them. The flying was a bit too technical for a layperson such as I, but I'm sure pilots would appreciate and relate to your experiences in combat and your test flying. You have led a very interesting and colorful life—good for you. Keep it up!

Susie Brinegar
(Widow of a USAF fighter pilot—added by author)

In this book, Suitcase has captured vivid recollections as a young combat pilot over the skies of Korea, and later as a corporate test pilot over California, told in a way that will keep you on the edge of your seat. Through it all, Suitcase relied upon the philosophy of Socrates to guide him through the tough times—and, by giving Socrates an active part in his ventures, has masterfully blended fact and imagination into a story that is a must read. In my civilian aerospace position as Manager, Test & Evaluation on a classified missile program, I had innumerable discussions with my work force about many subjects; matters such as honor, human greatness, duty, honesty, reputation, courage—any dialogue that helped form a team effort. It was Suitcase's book that vicariously got me talking to Socrates, and Plato, and Aristotle, and many more philosophers. All it took was a trip to the library.

The lessons of history—powerful stuff!

Gordon Jenkins, Col. USAF (Retired)
Mgr., Test & Evaluation
Northrop Corporation
100 F-105 missions—North Vietnam (mission verbiage by author)

I have known "Suitcase" for 50 years; in pilot training, transition to fighter aircraft, combat, and our civilian lives. In SOCRATES 'N SUITS his descriptions of air-to-ground missions and experimental flight testing are intense, vivid, and compelling. His chilling account of ejecting from a crippled experimental fighter makes you want to be a baggage handler at a railroad station—as far away from the test flying profession as possible. And his relationship with Socrates is warm and rewarding. When I first reviewed SOCRATES 'N SUITS I didn't think fighter pilots would be interested in philosophy—a love and pursuit of wisdom. Hell, I thought fighter pilots knew it all. But many of us went on to productive lives in the business world and one day I found myself in a library—wondering if Socrates and his contemporaries could help me with a couple of problems associated with work. And wouldn't you know! In my search for wisdom I found remarkable words, written over 2000 years ago, they were of immeasurable help. In all due respect to my good friend "Suitcase" it's now SOCRATES 'N GEORGE! And I know a couple of "classic" fighter pilot songs myself!

George Gilbreath, Col., USAF, (Ret)
Managing Director, Warehousing, with a large merchandising company

Thank you so much for allowing me to read (edit) your newest book. I admit that I got so involved in your marvelous storytelling that I neglected to edit very closely! I laughed and cried throughout the book! I did not feel at all you were being derogatory towards women—you just respect and appreciate us and tell it like it is. One of my Caesar salads is on the menu for your next visit to Boulder.

Love,

Nancy (Wife of a of a CEO that hired
me for a particular consulting job)

In reading SOCRATES 'N SUITS, by Jack "Suitcase" Simpson, I couldn't help but think how difficult it would be for another reader, who didn't know him, to believe he had accomplished so many feats, not only with flying jets, but also with women. Since I have known "Suitcase" for over sixty years—through high school, double dating, and as a best friend, and witnessing his attractiveness to the opposite sex, the feats are easily believed by me!

So to those readers who have any doubt—don't!!!

John B. Flynn, MA, Ret.
Psychometrist
VA. VR&C

SOCRATES 'N SUITS is characterized by Jack's experiences as a single engine fighter pilot in combat and an Air Force test pilot and later, a civilian experimental pilot. He also presents an unfolding, dynamic rapport through one-on-one conversations with the brilliant Greek philosopher, Socrates. What do Jack's experiences in war and flying have to do with life's everyday desire to render a dramatic but even-tempered role? I think you will find his approach to the subject truly thought provoking; a dynamic training ground for the impulsive turns of mind and matter!

Bob Hoover
Experimental Test Pilot/Acrobatic Pilot

For a one-word reaction to SOCRATES 'N SUITS, mine would be exciting! Someone who had actually been in combat may enjoy it more than I did. However, I have often been there in my 'WALTER MITTY MOMENTS'. It makes me appreciate the Korean fireworks ending shortly before my USMCR commission. I have never read any philosophy, but I liked Cicero's line, "Nature is the one who has granted us our lives without setting any schedule for repayment." I think that will help me grow old with less trepidation regarding my ultimate demise, even though it will be a tremendous loss to the world. I have to get my bit of levity in here!

My only negative feedback might be on agreeing that some of it may be a little demeaning to women. I have known Jack for forty years, therefore I know it wasn't meant that way. I do not mean to sound prudish and with my past, I would not dare.

SOCRATES 'N SUITS is definitely a man's book.

Rex May
USMC Fighter Pilot/ UAL Captain

Congratulations on your unique and gripping books, SOCRATES & SUITS, BOOK I & II, fusing your real life experiences as a fighter pilot in Korea and subsequent supersonic test pilot, with the dynamics of life outside the cockpit. Instead of a one-dimensional zoomie's tale (WW II lingo for Navy pilots) limited to takeoffs and landings, you have artfully filled in the blanks before the takeoffs and after the landings, and blended them, in many cases, with the dynamics of harrowing flight. Your honesty and integrity in forthrightly describing your foul-up on your first ground support mission in Korea, when you ended up bombing a bush, sets a tone of credibility for all the exciting adventures you later describe. I especially had the feeling of being in the cockpit when you described, second by second, the challenges you faced as you fought to bring in for a landing at LAX an F-100 after a flameout. You add a whole new and different dimension to the books by conceiving and introducing Socrates as your "wingman". In a sense, Socrates is not a fiction, but is a vital element in your stream of consciousness, holding up a mirror to your very real and exciting life.

Suitcase, the combination of your flying adventures at the end of the envelope, the humor and partying life, all joined with a serious measure of cogent philosophy, make S&S, I & II, two terrific books.

George V. Hall
Attorney at Law

I was so enchanted with SOCRATES & SUITS, BOOK I & II, I couldn't put them down; one morning it was three-thirty when I finished, as a critic, BOOK II. The author has made Socrates so believable I was wondering why I never had the chance to meet this guy! Having known Suits for 40 years it doesn't seem fair that he kept Socs all to himself.

I found Suits' love affairs to be hilarious. At first read he might be considered on the sexist side. Not so!! He is just a guy that loves women—and lots of them.

I understand he is working hard on BOOK III. I am looking forward to more adventures with SOCRATES & SUITS.

Mrs. Betty Paul

(As the author, I might add that Mrs. Paul has been reading since her 4th birthday. She has read, on the average, 4 to 5 books a week. Now in her eighties, Mrs. Paul has read over 4000 books—fiction, non-fiction, on love, war, biography, history, a cross section of vocations and avocations. I am happy to know she thinks I made Socrates so believable.)

Suitcase has the exceptional skills to be a learned practitioner in the marketing world. The discipline he achieved through the military and further his time as a test pilot have contributed to his long success and his creation of the Socrates 'N Suits Trilogy.

I am honored to have played a small part in the authorship of this book.

Richard T. (Joe) Forman
Lt. Co. USAF (Retired)

I have finished both books and I really enjoyed them (immensely). Your first chapter in BOOK I was excellent. I don't remember anything I have read that kept my interest as that chapter did.

I was going to tell you that your life reminded me of Howard Hughes without the drill bits and the billion dollars, but I know you were a lot better pilot than Howard.

The biggest surprise in the books was finding out how much reading you have done. I already know how much brass you have and I knew you had bad judgment was i.e. when you insisted on staying out all night on our double date when we had our big game with Nebraska the next day, but I had no idea of your reading habits.

The next biggest surprise I got was realizing how hard you had to work to put those books together. I really didn't think you could stick with it—but you did and you did a great job. I admire you for that.

Tom Gillespie, Fraternity Brother
Marine fighter pilot, test pilot
Vice president, Marketing & Sales

ABOUT GEORGE V. HALL AND THE ORIGIN OF HIS THOUGHTS

George Hall is featured in *SOCRATES 'N SUITS*, **BOOK I**, both as a member of our volleyball gang at 3600 Strand in Manhattan Beach, and as pseudo cross-country runner. The "cross country" came from George's un-canny ability to cover eight city blocks in less than a couple of minutes when we would call and announce, "chicken in the oven". George is the kind of guy that one would rather pay his rent than feed him.

But let's not be fooled; behind George's happy-go-lucky life style is a brilliant and practical mind. He had a Bachelor and Masters in chemical engineering and was, at the time I met him, production supervisor at Chevron Refinery in El Segundo, Ca. He left his engineering position at the refinery to attend UCLA law school. This career change was in partial fulfillment of his emerging dedication to accurately abstract REALITY and re-state it in concrete terms; always with special emphasis on TRUTH and what is RIGHT and GOOD and, particularly, the mechanisms for determining these philosophical and ethical concepts.

Ethics, simply stated, was to George, "The art of determining what is good and right." Ethics lead George to ask the question, "Is their any job where one could make a living that dealt with the subject of Ethics?"

George's answer was practicing law! He took the Law School Admission Test in November of 1955, was accepted at UCLA School of Law in September, 1956, and admitted to the California State Bar in 1960. He successfully practiced law until retirement in 1992.

Throughout **BOOK III of the Trilogy**, I will be quoting George Hall's aphorisms. They come from his brilliant, thought-provoking mind! Although I do not agree with everything George expatiates on, I present his views with a feeling of deference, approval, and respect for his practical points of view. They will not necessarily be applicable to the subject at hand of each chapter but be assured his thoughts are generated by dynamically principlizing his perceptions.

The aphorism presented before each chapter will do what?? They will make us THINK!

EXAMPLES

REALITY & TRUTH

For centuries, Humans have been, and continue to be, swirling around like clouds; they are floating above, and unconcerned with, the solid bedrock of REALITY upon which TRUTH is built!

ON OLD AGE

Too many people allow themselves to become withered flowers in their old age; a time when the Human mind remains capable of producing the most beautiful of lifetime's dreams!

BARBARA CLOSE

HER MAGIC GRAPHICS & CALLIGRAPHY

Ms. Close also proceeded stepwise to reach her pinnacle of her contemporary pinnacle of achievement. From lettering homeroom posters in high school, to an epiphany upon seeing a hand lettered card attached to a gift, inspired her to enroll in a calligraphy class, all of which led her to finally emerge as the polished artist and calligrapher as Ms. Close is today.

JJS/Nov., 2004

DEDICATION
GRANT A. GOULD, M.D.

I first met Grant Gould at a party in Newport Beach, Ca. in the late sixties. He got my attention while playing the keys off a 'jazz' piano with a percussionist and a base fiddle. Man! Those guys were swingin'.

I found out a lot about Grant Gould that evening. He was a brilliant doctor and surgeon; taught himself to play the piano; taught himself electronics so he could repair TV's and radios; and he was an auto mechanic. But the thing that drove me "straight down the middle" to shake his hand was the fact he was doctor to a beautiful, well shaped, blonde starlet that lived in our club about six doors from me. I was ready to be *Mr. CHARMMM—ING*—until I found out she was married.

But we are still friends; have been for over 35 years. And why not? Here's a man who was valedictorian of his senior high school class.

He was president of his graduation class from University of Toronto Medical School, won the president's honor award, and was president of the Toronto Chapter of the Alpha Kappa Kappa Medical Fraternity.

Following internship at Ottawa Civic Hospital he joined the Canadian Navy. After basic training, a surgical residency followed at the Halifax Naval Hospital. Dr. Gould was then posted overseas to serve as Surgeon Lieutenant aboard H.M.C.S. **REGINA**.

In the Normandy invasion, his ship was torpedoed while rescuing survivors in the English Channel. Although blown off the bridge, with a crushed chest, King George VI decorated Dr. Gould for medical care of fellow survivors aboard the rescue vessel. His ship had sunk in 28 seconds.

Grant retired as a Surgeon Lieut. Commander. He established his general practice, in Vancouver BC in 1947. Following preceptorships in general and gynecological surgery, he began limiting his practice to these disciplines that also comprised his practice after moving to Newport Bach in 1965. He served on the emergency staff, Hoag Memorial Hospital, University of California (Irvine) student health center surgical staff, and became a FAA Medical Examiner in 1986. He is now semi-retied, practicing mornings only.

Grant reviewed **BOOK I & II** of the *SOCRATES 'N SUITS* trilogy, and agreed to edit **BOOK III**. Grant Gould has been such a great doctor and friend I have forgotten about the dynamite starlet. Well—almost!!

Thanks, Grant. It's an honor to dedicate **BOOK III** to you.

Let's take a look *backward* over our shoulders before we address the **BOOK III** *forward*!

BOOK I & II
OF THE TRILOGY
SOCRATES 'N SUITS

A real friend of mine, Jay Martin, called me from San Francisco the latter part of April, 2002, just about the time I finished reviewing the galley proofs on **BOOK II**. I say friend. Even though I haven't seen Jay in a few years, when he learned I wrote *SOCRATES "N SUITS,* he immediately found, and read, **BOOK I**. Jay Martin, a brilliant and very successful attorney, called to say, "Congratulations, Suits; after Socrates, please continue to write; you'll be an interesting author to follow. That is a definition of a friend!

Just for a little hack ground; **BOOK I** tells the story of me as a fighter pilot/test pilot in the Korean War followed by an assignment to North American Aviation in Los Angeles, representing the USAF as a test pilot on the development of the world's first supersonic fighter, (MACH I),the F-100 Super Sabre. **BOOK II** continues the story of my flying, but as a civilian experimental test pilot for Lockheed Aircraft Corporation on the unfolding of the world's first Mach II (twice the speed of sound) fighter known as the F-104 STARFIGHTER.

Well, Jay now knows I am presently out of the experimental flying business, having submitted my resignation to Lockheed, but found a much more challenging vocation in the profession of engineering sales and management consulting. **BOOK III** of the trilogy, destined to be published about the 1st quarter of 2006, addresses the *synergy* between philosophy, the lessons of history, the history of war, and free enterprise. It tells the story of what a fighter pilot, turned businessman, learns from well-documented chronological records of past events—and obtaining knowledge and awareness from such exposure. Also, as in **BOOK I & II**, there will be convivial stories about women I had the pleasure of meeting, plus a few laughs, and continuing verbal exchanges with Socrates. **BOOK III** is a presentation—like a buffet—only **BOOK III** will not be about food to eat but food for thought.

THOUGHT! Now here is a powerful word. The action, or re-action from *your* thoughts, control your own universe—the beginnings and the continuing development of your excellent world as you wish to learn it, learn from it, see it, and participate in it. What a position to be in! What a notable challenge!

"Gee! Suitcase," you say, "that seems like a tough path to follow."

Not really! Of course it will be tough, but is any worthwhile pursuit easy? Heck! I've dated a few women, fallen in love, struck out with distinction (as did Babe Ruth,) learned to laugh at myself and with others, and experimental flying extended me the privilege of knowing I've "been there—done that" in spades! I love the companionship of classical music, I continually read about the lives of philosophers, and I have been an entrepreneur for close to 40 years. I have also been a professor of marketing and sales for eight years, and in reference to the lessons of history, I'm right there with Napoleon, Hitler, and the Russian winters. Some of my mistakes were monumental! But, as Carolyn Kenmore says, in *SOMETHING MORE*, by Sarah Ban Breathmach, "If you can learn from hard knocks, you can also learn from soft touches."

It has been my research in these individual disciplines mentioned above that keep getting me excited. And, below, are observations that I hang on to:

1. "He who cannot draw on three thousand years, is living from hand to mouth . . . *GOETHE*
2. . . . the only thing we require to be good philosophers is the faculty of wonder . . . Jostin Gaarder, *SOPHIE'S CHOICE*
3. The composition and orchestration of symphonic music is an art that transcends all socio-political boundaries. Music of the masters is cosmopolitan; it belongs to the world. Classical music reflects culture and character, experience and values. Jack Simpson, *SOCRATES 'N SUITS*
4. As does the study of philosophy . . . ibid
5. A book must be the axe for the frozen sea inside us . . . . *FRANZ KAFKA*

By the way, I have not forgotten the word *synergy*. It's really the nexus of **BOOK III**. Synergy comes from *synergos*—"working together"; combined action or operation. My *ROGETS II, The New Thesaurus*, says, "Joint work toward a common end—cooperation." Synergy proffers, in experimental flying, the epitome of instant cooperation between mind, arms (stick and throttle,) and legs (rudder pedals.) Time allowed for judgment is extremely limited and crucial. Yet, in Carl Von Clausewitz *ON WAR*, his main subjects are broken down into THE NATURE OF WAR, THE THEORY OF WAR, STRATEGY IN GENERAL, THE COMBAT, and THE PLAN OF WAR. A well-defined marketing and business plan also offers the same subjects; is not the fight for market share a war? Both subjects present joint work toward a common end—cooperation. In my opinion, in what seemingly appears to be worlds apart, these five subjects present synergy in action!

I personally think everyone should sit down for a minute or so each day to think, to contemplate legacy and culture, and history, and character and values, and then stretch out and *wonder;* how come, what about, what if, and why? All this could be in terms of thinking about what contribution each of us could make in advancing the dynamics of free enterprise to a more desirable state.

My studies, teaching, and the profession of marketing and sales offered me the opportunity to do this—to THINK. I have been given no choice so I'm sure as hell going to take a look at it! It is going to take a lot of digging. I have learned no matter how inpatient the dig for honest success, the excavation process cannot be rushed. And when we hit bedrock of disbelief and discouragement, the undeniable romance of the treasure hunt will always save the day. How true! How true! The day I had to eject from a crippled YF-104A (the 8th one manufactured) and my parachute opened at 15,000 feet, I was hanging there in *my* bedrock of disbelief and discouragement wondering how this could be happening to me. In time, however, the romance of the treasure hunt was saved the day I observed four young fighter pilots in tight formation proudly flying their production F-104As in close formation over the San Francisco Bay Bridge. It was an absolutely beautiful sight!

There are other reasons for us to begin to think of ourselves, because of the digging, as archaeologists. The qualities that lead excavators to their spectacular finds are the same qualities that we must hone to reach our own breathless discoveries. According to archaeologist Dr. Fagan, archaeologists need sheer persistence, endless patience, and the ability to recognize patterns, keen powers of observation, curiosity, and "a conviction, nay, a passion, that their instincts are correct. An archaeologist's instinct is powerful, compelling, perhaps best described as an overwhelming sense that one knows where to find what one is searching for."

Is there not synergy between an experimental pilot, a vice president of marketing and sales, a successful lawyer like Jay Martin, and an archaeologist? In the very tough job of finding a new fighter's perfect stability and control, we have an overwhelming sense where to find what we are searching for. It is recognizing patterns, powers of observation, and curiosity, because that is what is putting us out there on the edge, and we know what we are hunting for. Finding it is what causes the trouble, particularly at speeds and altitudes never before attained in an experimental jet fighter.

And sales personnel must learn to market and sell "in the language of and needs of the customer." It's not going to be given to us. So we have to have the ability to recognize patterns, have keen powers of observation, and curiosity. It speaks the same language for lawyers.

Gil Rob Wilson said it all in a verse of an experimental pilot's poem. He wrote, "As long as this is a free man's world, someone has to lead. Someone has to carry the ball in thought, and word, and deed. Someone has to knock on doors that never have known a key. And, someone has to see the things that throng would never see."

Mr. Wilson was speaking to all of us; archaeologists, experimental pilots, lawyers, and sales executives.

To me, that's synergy!

I believe in recognizing the lessons of history. I believe if one wants to make a difference, and add stability to the trajectory of their lives, one must combine history with the study of the lives of the great philosophers. I believe the study of strategy and tactics in war, is a study of ones own life and it offers a complement to the honest pursuit of the dynamics of free enterprise. Also, it is important in recognizing that *time* cannot be slowed down, or sped up, will partially assist in the search for the moments that will make that difference. It is up to the individual.

To do that, we need to dig deep: through the assumptions and expectations that have shaped us. Through the successes and failures that have defined us. Through the loves and hates, gains and losses, promises and pain that have bound us. And through the risks and ruins, tumults and triumphs that have set us free.

I have found, by reading what the lessons of the past offer, we will dig up all the perfectly reasonable choices that fulfilled our dreams and, also, we will find ourselves brushing off the dirty linen hiding the half-truths that have hunted us for all these years.

BINGO!!

Jay, my next book after the trilogy will be of a different nature. I didn't realize it at the time I outlined the idea in my mind, that my concept would become "Broadcast News." It is the narrative of a brilliant 'three letter' All American high school senior making a shocking announcement at the Senior Prom that stunned his beautiful cheer leader girlfriend, his family, and his close friends. The paths each followed after graduation, plus an unexpected random event, is *SOMETHING TO THINK ABOUT*—in fact, I just gave you the title of my new book.

Thank you for taking the time to write, Jay.

"In the face of a true friend a man sees as it were a second self. So that where his friend is, he is!"

Cicero, Friendship, VI

A REAL FRIEND IS ONE

WHO WALKS IN

WHEN THE REST OF THE WORLD

WALKS OUT!

WALTER WINCHELL

FORWARD
THE KOREAN WAR; I MEET
JACK "SUITCASE" SIMPSON

On my arrival in Korea, I possessed a set of orders assigning me as executive officer to Colonel Royal Baker, Commander, 4th Fighter Group, Kimpo AFB (K-14). However, prior to my arrival at the 4th, my orders were changed to report to Suwon, (K-13), 8th Fighter Bomber Wing, 35th Squadron, as Squadron Commander. I was ordered to K-13 because of my accumulated hours and varied mission profile experience in the F-86. The 35th Squadron would soon be transitioning from the Lockheed F-80 to the new North American F-86 Sabre. The date was Valentine Day, February 14, 1953.

Thus, my aspirations of becoming a MiG killer were shattered. However, I did score aerial victories in WWII, and over Hanoi in the Vietnam fray. Jack has selected, as the cover to **BOOK III**, a copy of the Vietnam painting of my downing a MiG 17 on St. Patrick's Day, March 17, 1967, some 23 years after my first aerial victory, 29 October, 1944. This is possibly a record for elapsed time between a first and last victory for any fighter pilot.

My first one-on-one meeting with "Suitcase" Simpson was sometime in the middle of April, 1953. I called him to my office at squadron headquarters. After a formal, "Lt. Simpson reporting as ordered, Sir," I gave him an "at ease" and said, "Here, on this piece of paper, is a number 52-4401. It is your assigned new F-86F fighter. Move out to the flight line and make your claim. That will be all, Lt. And good luck!"

Have you heard the statement Tran configuration? Well, this guy "Suitcase" came to my office as a normal, bright, talented kind of guy. After his salute, he was so happy he drifted, on some kind of ether, at some kind of supersonic speed, to the flight line. It wasn't always that way. His dream of having his own fighter, in combat, came true only after nine broken-hearted years.

Many of you may not know that "Suitcase" was sworn in as an aviation cadet in March of 1944 waiting to be called to pilot training in the Army Air Corps.

When he arrived at Keesler Field (Mississippi) in 1945, he was unceremoniously transferred to the infantry where he underwent eight weeks of physically tough, rugged, burdensome and insensitive training for combat. The government didn't need fly boys; they needed bodies for the invasion of Japan. The atomic bomb saved "Suitcase". He returned home after an honorable discharge. He then attended college, majoring in aeronautics with a bachelor's degree, graduated, and with the Korean War waging, entered pilot training. In 1952 he won his pilot wings as a USAF fighter pilot. And the rest is history (**BOOK I**).

Let's move forward! The date was 21 May, 1953. Earlier, I had been directed by 5th Air Force, through chain of command, to lead a secret air-to-ground bombing mission to far northwest Korea. Everything about the flight was to be classified; take off time, the target, the mission profile to the target, return geography, the planning, time on target, radio silence, why, what for, when, etc. Also, the pilots, a flight of four, would not fly their own aircraft. The F-86's to be flown for the mission would be the newly arrived F-86s' not yet assigned to a pilot. There were to be no pilots' names on the side of the cockpit, no art or names of any kind on the side of the fuselage. We were directed to carry 2 each 1000# bombs, and the new 200gallon drop tanks for increased range. I was told, "It is up to you, Colonel, but choose your men carefully."

Although this was to be only his ninth mission, I chose Suitcase as my wingman plus two other pilots of growing stature in the squadron. His performance was flawless; we were in pea soup weather, with altitudes ranging sometimes as high as 35,000 feet to and from the target. Flying wing in conditions such as we encountered takes innate ability and extreme concentration. Our dive-bombing mission was on target and without loss even though the flak was extremely heavy.

I can say today the target was the Suiho power plant, located on the Yalu river, close to Manchuria. This was one of the most dangerous targets assigned to the Sabre fighter-bombers due to the proliferation of AAA sites surrounding it. A large number of jets came home with flak holes in the wings and fuselage, although only a few were shot down.

As the war continued I kept my eye on Suitcase. He moved upward—element lead, flight lead, wing test pilot, chief pilot of the Replacement Training Unit, and by the middle of July he had flown 60 some missions. It was time to make my move. I transferred him to southern Japan to a base where F-86s from all four wings in Korea were literally torn apart and rebuilt. His assignment—test pilot! However he did sneak in a flight from his base in southern Japan to K-13 and asked my permission to fly his last combat mission on the last day of the war. What could I say? You know Suitcase!

After four months in southern Japan he received his new assignment as an acceptance test pilot at North American Aviation in Los Angeles. How this young pilot accomplished the assignment is a story in itself. He was soon assigned, representing the office of the AF Plant Representative, as project test pilot on the

F-100, the world's first supersonic fighter. He was at North American for twenty months.

Upon his discharge, in September of '55, he was hired by Lockheed Aircraft Corporation as an experimental test pilot to fly the F-104. The F-104 "Starfighter" was the world's first Mach 2 (twice the speed of sound) fighter. He was just three years and three months out of flight training.

I had the chance to visit with Jack while he was at North American. In March, 1955 I was one of eight pilots selected to make an attempt to break the official transcontinental speed record. The record total time is a requirement of the Federation Aeronautique Internationale, an international federation responsible for veracity in length of course, proper flying profiles, and speed.

Our aircraft, eight in number, was the Republic Corporation F-84F "Thunderstreak", parked at the North American, Los Angeles International airport facility. The finish line was the tower at Floyd Bennett Field, Long Island. I won the race with an official time of 3hrs. 44min. 53sec. A speed of 650mph!

After that particular time, we lost contact with each other. Jack continued to test fly for Lockheed (**BOOK II**), while I was commanding a fighter wing at Takli, Thailand, during the early fighting of the war in Vietnam. I survived 134 missions.

As fate would have it, after my retirement from the USAF I was working for Republic Aviation at Edwards AFB as a test sight manager on the development of the A-10 fighter-bomber. "Suitcase" had worked for an aerospace company, and in the middle sixties started his own company in marketing and sales. He was visiting a friend, an Air Force test pilot assigned to the A-10, and he happened to mention my name. Jack's home was two hours from mine. So there we were, 30 years later, engaged in a warm, enthusiastic reunion.

It continues to this day; two fighter pilots with 50 years of mutual respect and esteem of for each other.

I would be remiss if I did not note that Jack flew in from Los Angeles to be the featured speaker at the grave sight ceremony during the burial of my late wife at Arlington National Cemetery, 29 February, 2000.

His eulogy was a stirring, sober, response; eliciting strong emotions that helped ease my pain. This is one hell of a guy!!

Col. Robert (Bob) Scott
United States Air Force (Ret)

FORWARD—IA

FOR JACK

My name is Ryan Heafey. Ryan who? It doesn't matter; keep reading. I have only known three Simpsons in my life; Jack, O.J., and of course Homer. Jack is the only one I really know and we call him "Suitcase", but when I was a small child living in Oakland, California with my father, he was "Uncle Squishy Juice".

The first real memory of Suitcase was when I was about 10 years old and Matt (my brother) was 6. My dad had this friend who came over to the house and we were introduced to him as "Uncle Suitcase"; he was young like my father and full of swagger and bravado. He had, what at the time seemed liked huge biceps, which he liked to flex for us kids. He would say, "Hey! you want to see what solid steel feels like?" and point to his bicep. We felt it and it was hard as a rock, but we told him it felt like squishy juice. That's where "Uncle Squishy Juice" came from.

When Jack came over to visit it was bedlam at our house because he flew around like he flew planes, fast and low. My brother and I figured we could take the macho Simpson and coaxed him into a pillow fight in my room. He hit me so hard with that pillow I saw lightning and thought I had been knocked out. I couldn't cry in front of him, so I attacked again and again. Finally, I guess he had enough of toying with us because he grabbed the mattress off the bed and pinned my brother and me under it. We were screaming now fearing he was going to deprive us of oxygen until we died, so we screamed for our dad. Our father ran into the room and started yelling at Jack but Jack countered with, "I'm just trying to teach them how to be men". Oh yeah! My dad was a lawyer and he lived by the book so, Uncle "Suitcase" gave us our life lessons on pain threshold and not quitting even when Matt and I were overwhelmed.

Next time I remember "Uncle Squishy Juice", was when he and my dad were going on a date. (My dad and mother had divorced). In walks, "The Juice" with two drop-dead beautiful women to whom he introduced me. I don't remember their names. I do remember their bodies and faces, though! And I also remember him saying one of them was a Playboy bunny. Gee, I didn't think she looked like a bunny. Besides who needed that! I had the Sears catalog and wanted to check the new bras. Kids now days have it made; Victoria Secret, Venus Swimwear, Fredrick's of Hollywood, etc. Hell, that's not mentioning the inter-net and cable.

I always remember in my dad's office at home there was a picture of Jack and my father at some black tie function and Jack was being his usual self and was leaning back telling a story and everyone around was laughing, especially my father. Needless to say they both had cocktails in their hands and obviously had consumed several prior to the photo being taken. I will always remember that picture PLUS—the first time "Suitcase" got me arrested.

About that arrest! My dad allowed Uncle "Suitcase" to take me to his ranch in Springville, California when I was about 12 or 13. I'd have to check the arrest date to be sure. Anyhow, we went to Jack's "Mums the Word Ranch", in Springville. I was from the city and to me this was BFE (Bum F—Egypt). Suitcase said a friend of his had a daughter and the kids were going to a BBQ later that night and would I like to go. I, of course, asked what she looks like. He told me she was cute so I said I was in. We were introduced and someone drove us to the BBQ, which was bullshit; it was really a county kegger in the middle of BFE. I had never drunk alcohol before (unless you count the wine in the back of the church after altar boy duties; forgive me Lord for I have sinned) so they asked me if I wanted a beer. I said, "I would like a Coke because I'm not old enough to drink." They all laughed like it was a joke and gave me a beer. I drank and drank and drank and the next thing I remember someone was helping me get up off the ground. I was thanking them just as I saw the word SHERIFF as we walked past the car that I was placed in the rear of, with handcuffs, so I couldn't show them my pillow fight tactics my Uncle Suits had shown me. The next day, or actually for several days, I wasn't feeling very well. After "Suitcase" bailed me out of juvenile hall he said my dad was pissed. I remember at juvenile hall they kept asking me were my parents or guardian were so they could call them. I couldn't tell them where my uncle lived and the "Mums the Word Ranch" wasn't in the phone book; neither was Uncle "Suitcase", so they called my dad. My dad called Jack and I'm glad I was in jail and not listening to that conversation. I think we both learned a lesson in hard knocks that day.

Uncle "Suitcase" thought it was odd I became a cop after that experience. But he even came to my hometown several times to ride alone with me on my "beat". I think he was scared even though he would never admit it. He has always been there for me even when I wanted to get out of the cop business and buy a tow truck company in Lake Tahoe. He studied the business and was an advocate and argued for me with my dad. He thought it to be a very good deal. My dad said it wasn't a wise investment, which translated to, "I don't want to tell my friends my son owns a tow truck company". I saw huge potential and for $150,000 it was a good deal.

Anyhow, the deal didn't materialize. I was told by a friend of mine at my father's funeral last year that company just sold for a couple million. We tried to tell him, but you can't argue with a lawyer. Well you can, but at least I didn't have to pay him his hourly fee.

"Suitcase" showed up and took my brother, sister and me to lunch the day my dad died. We all had a great conversation and had fun watching "Suitcase" work his magic on us by taking away our dread for what was about to transpire. We parted with fond hugs in front of the hospital and 30 minutes later my father died. "Suitcase" was always there for us whenever we needed him; now, he is like a father we don't have anymore.

I love to read and expand my mind by always having a book within arms' reach. I picked up reading from my dad and Uncle "Suitcase." Both are avid readers. When I read **BOOK I**, and then **BOOK II** of *SOCRATES 'N SUITS*, I learned about the part of Jack I never knew, and a lot about the part I did know. I felt like a lot of things came together for me—about who I was and why I turned out the way I am. It was in no small part to Jack's love and support that I constantly try to become the beautiful person that everyone likes to see in a man today.

Thanks Jack, for keeping us focused on what life is all about!

FLYING A FIGHTER AIRCRAFT DESIGNED

FOR SUPERIOR PERFORMANCE

REQUIRES STUDY, RIGID MENTAL TOUGHNESS,

PHYSICAL VIGOR AND EXPERIENCE.

THE SAME CRITERIA SHOULD COMPLEMENT OUR AIMS IN LIFE!

WHY DO I SAY THAT! STOP AND THINK!

COMPARE A SUCCESSFUL FIGHTER PILOT TO A SUCCESSFUL
BUSINESSMAN.

INTELLIGENCE, WIT, JUDGEMENT, AND THE OTHER

TALENTS OF THE MIND, HOWEVER YOU WANT TO NAME THEM—

OR COURAGE RESOLUTION, PERSEVERANCE, AS

QUALITIES OF TEMPERAMENT, ARE UNDOUBTEDLY GOOD AND

DESIRABLE FOR BOTH DISCIPLINES.

Bob Hoover, Test Pilot
BOOK I of the Trilogy
SOCRATES 'N SUITS

IF AN UNDERTAKING WAS EASY, SOMEONE ELSE WOULD HAVE
DONE IT!

IF YOU FOLLOW IN ANOTHER'S FOOTSTEPS, YOU MISS THE
PROBLEMS WORTH SOLVING!

EXCELLENCE IS BORN OF PREPARATION, DEDICATION,
FOCUS, AND TENACITY; COMPROMISE ON ANY OF THESE
AND YOU BECOME AVERAGE!

EVERY SO OFTEN, LIFE PRESENTS A GREAT MOMENT OF
DECISION, AN INTERSECTION AT WHICH MAN MUST DECIDE
TO STOP OR GO; A MAN LIVES WITH THESE DECISIONS
FOREVER!

EXAMINE EVERYTHING; NOT ALL IS AS IT SEEMS
OR AS PEOPLE TELL YOU!

IT IS EASIEST TO LIVE WITH A DECISION IF IT IS
BASED ON AN EARNEST SENSE OF RIGHT AND WRONG!

THE GUY WHO GETS KILLED IS OFTEN THE GUY WHO
GOT NERVOUS. THE GUY WHO DOESN'T CARE ANYMORE,
WHO HAS SAID, "I'M ALREADY DEAD—THE FACT THAT
I LIVE OR DIE IS IRRELEVANT AND THE ONLY
THING THAT MATTERS IS THE ACCOUNTING I GIVE
OF MYSELF," IS THE MOST FORMIDABLE FORCE
IN THE WORLD!

THE WORST POSSIBLE DECISION IS TO GIVE UP!

John Chatterton
SHADOW DIVERS
by Robert Kurson

SYNERGY

WEBESTER'S NINTH NEW COLLEGIATE DICTIONARY defines synergy as taken from the Greek word *synergos* working together: SYNERGISM; *broadly;* combined action or operation

However, synergism again from Greek *synergos*, is defined as interaction of discrete agencies (as industrial firms) or agents (as drugs) such that the total effect is greater than the sum of the individual effects

As the reader is well aware, the underlying wording of *SOCRATES 'N SUITS, Book III of a Trilogy,* are, "*The synergy between a philosopher, fighter pilot, the lessons of history, and free enterprise.*"

As an example of synergy, is Carl Von Clausewitz's book *ON WAR* detailing the organizational chart of responsible and accountable warriors from the general to the sergeant. The better the organization, and communication, the more effective he plan on defeating the enemy.

The same thought processes hold true for an organization used to defeat the enemy (competition) in capturing a high percentage of market share.

To my way of thinking, that's synergy! And you will read examples of what I am saying throughout the book!

THE HARDEST THING IS TO GET STARTED,

BUT THE REALLY HARDEST THING

IS TO FINISH.

Yogi Berra
Hall of Fame baseball player

IF YOU HEAR A VOICE WITHIN YOU SAYING,

"YOU ARE NOT A PAINTER," THEN BY ALL

MEANS PAINT . . . . AND THAT VOICE WILL

BE SILENCED.

                    VINCENT VAN GOGH

IF YOU HEAR A NUMBER OF VOICES FROM

THE OUTSIDE SAYING,

"YOU ARE NOT A WRITER," THEN BY ALL

MEANS WRITE—AND THE VOICES WILL

BE SILENCED.

                    Jack "Suitcase" Simpson

ONLY LOSERS PLAY IT SAFE

PLAY TO WIN

That's become the mantra of sports. But as we hunker down to watch the New England Patriots and the Philadelphia Eagles in Sunday's Super Bowl, the upsetting truth is, that in a society that puts a premium on risk-taking and competitive gusto, coaches often take just the opposite approach.

Time and again, an entire season can ride on a field-goal attempt—often beyond the 45-yard line. I know. I grew up a Buffalo Bills fan. I can still see kicker Scott Norwood's 47-yarder in Super Bowl XXV sail inches wide of the right upright.

That's why it's difficult no to pick the Patriots Sunday. Not only do they have one of the clutch kickers in the game in Adam Vinatieri, but he's backed up by Bill Belichick, a coach who rarely plays it safe.

Vinatieri's kick may have won the Super Bowl three years ago, but what's often forgotten is that bold play-calling gave his foot a chance.

At Belichick's urging, with time running out in regulation, Patriots quarterback Tom Brady passed the ball downfield. Such daring put Vinatieri in position for glory!

BEYOND THE SPORTS WORLD

Playing it safe gets you some wins, but rarely does it get you the win. Examples aren't confined to the world of sports:

While President Bush didn't have a mandate after the 2000 election, he ran the country as though he did. He tackled education reform (a traditionally Democratic issue), reformed Medicare (a sacred cow of Washington) and pursued a bold foreign-policy agenda. And he won re-election.

Thanks to the phenomenal success of iPod, Apple owns 65% of the burgeoning MP3 market. But CEO Steve Jobs isn't about to tell his players to drop back into a prevent defense (which sports fans know prevents one thing: winning). Apple recently came out with a low-cost model of the iPod and is also rolling out an inexpensive desktop computer, the Man Mini.

China is turning heads by taking chances. Not only will it host the 2008 Summer Olympics, but the communist country is roaring in business and recently put a man in space—a watershed moment for a country that at one point in its history walled out the world (the ultimate prevent defense). It is now intent on literally giving the rest of the planet a run for its money.

After Martha Stewart was found guilty of lying about a stock sale, she vowed to appeal her five-month sentence. But she soon realized that to win, she needed to make tough choices. Stewart decided to serve her time and forge ahead, tackling her opponent instead of waiting to be tackled. Her decisive actions and optimistic voice said one thing: winner. Her company's value, which had dropped to $489 million at the end of last year, soared to $1.3 billion.

THE WHAT-IF GAME

Coaches readily draw parallels between sports and business, even sports and life. The winning ones will rush out with a tone about how Average Joes should adopt their philosophy or aggressive management style. Yet so few follow their beliefs when it counts they play it safe—and lose.

That's what San Diego Chargers coach Marty Schottenheimer, New York Jets coach Herman Edwards and Pittsburgh Steelers coach Bill Cowher did at crucial moments this postseason. Each will not be able to play the what-if game this Sunday—either in front of the TV or from the bleachers in Jacksonville.

The playoffs are one thing, but even the NFL's biggest stage—the Super Bowl—abounds with coaching miscues and blunders.

Which brings me back to 1991: Norwood's kick went wide by about 18 inches. If he'd been a few yards closer, the Bills probably would've won a championship instead of being remembered as the only team to reach the Super Bowl four consecutive times and lose every time. Fans like me are left to second-guess every plays and loss.

Unlike corporate boardrooms and political "war rooms," though, the white-knuckle decisions of Super Bowl Sunday are open for us to dissect on Monday morning. Just ask Norwood. Or Brady, for that matter! Justice is swift when dozens of cameras are watching, and those who play to win—even if they ultimately lose—have an easier time answering questions in the locker room after the game.

The trophy that will be hoisted in one locker room Sunday night was named after NFL coaching great Vince Lombardi. No one dare ask whether he played to win. He did "Winning is not everything—but making effort to win is," he said.

Such a simple thought—if only followed through.

A contributing writer for USA TODAY Sports Weekly; Tim Wendel is the author of Castro's Curveball and The New Face of Baseball. He is also a member of USA TODAY's board of contributors.

February 3, 2005

IT IS NEVER TOO LATE

TO BE WHO

YOU MIGHT HAVE BEEN.

George Elliot (1819-1880)
Writer

In reference to ONLY LOSERS PLAY IT SAFE,

Bill Cower and the Pittsburgh Steelers

Won the 2006 Super Bowl.

CLEARING UP MATTERS III

I know! The first thing entering your mind when you start to read *SOCRATES 'N SUITS* is, "Why the Roman Numeral III after CLEARING UP MATTERS?

A very good question!

SOCRATES 'N SUITS is the **third (BOOK III)** of a trilogy; the **first** and **second (BOOK I & II)** was published in the 1st quarter of 2002 in combined print and electronic, by **Xlibris,** a strategic partner of **RANDOM HOUSE VENTURES**. They are entitled *SOCRATES 'N SUITS*. The prologue introducing the two books was entitled CLEARING UP MATTERS **I** and **II**. The books offer an exchange of dialogue with Socrates, the brilliant Greek philosopher and me, a fighter/test pilot. Yes, we exchanged the value of clear, decisive matters under discussion; that being philosophy; defined by most as the search for wisdom.

I also learned something else the hard way; Socrates could fly like *JOHNATHAN LIVINGSTON SEAGULL*. The first time we met was over the skies of Las Vegas in a wild dogfight; he kicked my ass! We met, for the second time while he was accompanying Bob Hope on a USO tour to Korea. Socrates even flew my wing on an air-to-ground mission. After careful planning, we went after a train—and caught that sucker with his pants down and his caboose bringing up the rear!

The two bound works entail a narrative between Socrates and Jack "Suitcase" Simpson, flying a fighter in aerial combat, a test pilot in the USAF while stationed at North American Aviation at Los Angeles Int'l. Airport, and as an experimental test pilot with Lockheed Aircraft Corporation, at Burbank, and flying out of Palmdale, and Edwards Air Force Base, California. Also, as a necessary accompaniment, were stories of sex.

My God!?? You say SEX?? Already you speak of SEX?

Yes! Of course! Every fighter pilot holds the belief that one—half the world was created to **try** to make love with the other. Notice I said '*with* the other,' not '*to* the other.' And to be honest, the stories are told to add a little conviviality. One is not expected to address the horrors of war or the heart throbbing agitation and anxiety of experimental test flying without throwing in a laugh or two.

In fact, I have shown a picture of a surgical nurse by the name of Elizabeth Cotton. We dated when we both had a day and evening off about once a month. I would hit her with a snowball and she always threatened to hit me with a fresh apple. I knew I was safe; fresh fruit was a luxury in those early days of making K-13 a permanent base.

And my friend Elizabeth?? She was as fresh as an angel food cake pulled from the oven only a moment ago!

SOCRATES 'N SUITS carried with it the unpredictable manifestations of the life of a fighter pilot—honor and glory, patriotism, fear and death, human greatness, courage, friendship and pain. Socrates and I talked about these independently existing matters. Socrates had high hope (Remember the song 'High Hope' sung by Sinatra—'high apple pie in the sky hope'), that others, and I, would learn by study and doing. "Learn what?" you ask. You learn when the study of philosophy is combined with obtaining knowledge and awareness. In addition, when the results of the lessons of history are taken into consideration, the character of the philosopher, as a man, is inextricably connected with the manner of life he leads. Philosophy, to me, is the never-ending search for love and the pursuit of wisdom.

In addition, Socrates and I talked about how women bring out both the grandeur and misery of man. We discussed the nature and power of love. Philosophy, to me, is he never-ending search for love and the pursuit of wisdom.

I found this search to be a paradox; tenets contrary to received opinion but at the same time emotionally exciting. The closer examination in **business, family relationships,** and with my **fellow man and woman** opened an insatiable appetite to answer the most impossible of questions—why am I here and what am I doing about it?

OK! you say! That covers the first and second of the trilogy, but why, in this book, is a fighter pilot shooting up enemy jets on the cover, when Socrates and this guy 'Suitcase' are going to discuss business? Why Socrates? And a 'Suitcase'! Who is he? A traveling salesman! You gotta' be kidding! I've heard all those jokes! Like the one about the man walking into a clothing store. The manager walks up and says, 'What is your pleasure, Sir?' The guy must have been a fighter pilot because he answered, 'Sir, my pleasure is making love, but I came in to buy a tie!'

Anyhow, who the hell are these guys? And what do they know about business?"

"Well," as your author, I say to myself, "Someone has a good point! The readers have a right to ask these kinds of questions. Why keep them is suspense! So, let's start with Socrates.

I have studied philosophy, and Socrates since early college; I continue to this day. Knowledge of Socrates (he didn't write anything) and his teachings comes indirectly from certain dialogues of his disciple Plato and from the *Memorabilia* of XENOPHON. In fact, the chapter entitled *WHY PLILOSOPHY* offers the reader a limited overview of *my* philosophic reasoning attended by my friend Socrates.

I think a closer look at the man known as the 'Man of Athens, Man of Greece, and Man of the World,' is appropriate.

As you know, ancient Greeks were the first to develop a democratic way of life. More than 2000 years ago, they started the idea that every citizen should take an active part in government. Historians regard them as founders of Western civilization. Greek civilization was far more advanced than any that existed before. The world's first great orators, philosophers, historians, dramatists, and poets, were Greek. Later on in the book you will complement these men by reading of their legacy and culture. In reference to orators and philosophers, Socrates taught Plato. Plato taught Aristotle, and Aristotle tutored a man known for his outstanding leadership, Alexander the Great. Also, the Greeks were the first people to study geometry, medicine, botany, physics, and zoology on a scientific basis. They also held the first athletic games; predecessors to the Olympics. So I hope you can understand why I chose Socrates as my mentor. He surrounded me with history, culture, legacy, truth and the dynamics of study and learning. Yes, he is *my* man of Athens, and of Greece, and of the World.

Socrates was famous for his view of Philosophy as a pursuit proper and necessary to all intelligent men; he is one of the great examples of a man who lived by his principles even though they ultimately cost his life. A particular assiduity of Socrates is characterized by his steady attention and effort in knowing how to face reality; he had the moral courage to brave not only the tyranny of the judges who condemned him, but the mob that could not understand him. Better said, "The mob who would not take the time to *try* to understand him."

Socrates was widely known for his intellectual powers even before he was 40, when, according to Plato's report of Socrates' speech in the *Apology*, the oracle at DELPHI pronounced him the wisest man in Greece. In that speech Socrates maintained that he was puzzled by this acclaim until he discovered that, while others professed knowledge without realizing their ignorance, he at least was aware of his own ignorance.

Socrates became convinced that his calling was to search for wisdom about right conduct by which he might guide the intellectual and moral improvement of Athenians. Neglecting his own affairs, he spent his time discussing virtue, justice, and piety wherever his fellow citizens congregated. Some felt that he also neglected his public duty, for he never sought public office, although he was famous for his courage in the military campaigns in which he served. In his self—appointed task as gadfly to the Athenians, Socrates made numerous enemies.

Socrates' contributions to Philosophy were a new method of approaching knowledge, a conception of the soul as the seat both of normal waking consciousness and of moral character, and a sense of the universe as purposively mind-ordered. His method, called DIALECTIC, consisted in examining statements by pursuing their implications on the assumption that if a statement were true it could not lead to false consequences. The method may have been suggested by ZENO, but Socrates refined it and applied it to ethical problems.

His doctrine of the soul led him to the belief that all virtues converge into one, which is the good, or knowledge of one's true self and purposes through the course of a lifetime.

And so, Socrates' doctrine closed the circle for me. I said in the beginning, Philosophy is a never-ending search for wisdom. In trying to gain knowledge of my true self, I set the course of my lifetime; or lifeline—to Socrates.

I would fly *his* wing anytime!

Socrates was perhaps the most original, influential, and controversial figure in the history of Greek thought. Philosophy, widely defined as the love and pursuit of wisdom, was considered before Socrates as 'pre-Socratic'; he was the 'hinge' or the orientation point, for most subsequent thinkers. And he was the direct inspiration of Plato. As I stated above, knowledge of Socrates comes from certain dialogues of his disciple Plato, a pupil and friend of Socrates, plus another historian of great mental ability, Xenophon.

I MEET SOCRATES
(AN EXCERPT, IN PART, FROM *SOCRATES 'N SUITS*)
BOOK I

The only way *I* knew how to meet Socrates was to ask him!

Daniel Boorstin in his book *THE SEEKERS* said, "Socrates brought the search for meaning down from heaven to earth." I would have been a fool not to take advantage of that. My first thought was, "Gee!, I would certainly his wing, but what if Socrates could fly *my* wing?"

Daniel Boorstin, senior historian of the Smithsonian Institution, the Library of Congress emeritus, and author of *THE DISCOVERERS* and *THE CREATORS*, captures the adventure and scope of events of humankind's development of technology and philosophy. He played a special part in my personal relationship with Socrates. Here's how!

Lady luck came to me in the form of a horrendous thunderstorm and a grounded airliner. I had planned to meet a lovely stewardess friend one early evening flying in from Dallas to Las Vegas (I was in fighter pilot gunnery school at the time.) I received a call from my attractive friend to let me know her flight was cancelled and she would call me later. Funny thing—it was raining where I was also.

Since I had plenty of free time I decided to visit a bookstore. I drove from Nellis Air Force Base to downtown Las Vegas through pouring rain, exited my car, dodged pea size raindrops, and puddles of debris and water. I made it inside.

I gingerly too off my wet raincoat, shook it, folded it inside out, put it over my arm, and slowly walked toward the shelves of books. I stopped to pick up *NEWSWEEK* and *TIME* and spent a few long seconds, would you believe minutes, looking at the cover of some 'girlie' magazine. The girl on the cover was stunning—I think!! I don't remember seeing her face; I was captivated by her beautiful body.

WOW! A girl with a good shape like that young lady is often the reason why a young man like me is in bad shape.

Anyhow—I started down the non-fiction isle—back up the other side—nothing seemed to interest me until I spotted the spine of book—black cover, blue stripe, white printing—a 5x8 paperback. On the spine were four words; *HIDDEN HISTORY*, Daniel Boorstin. I grabbed it!!

I left the store; it was still raining; raining so hard I saw a sparrow putting sandbags around its nest. So I hopped, skipped and jumped to a restaurant four doors away. I ordered, and during dinner perused *TIME* and *NEWSWEEK.* But as I was about to read another article I looked outside and noticed it has stopped raining. I paid my check, walked to my car, and headed toward my pad at Nellis Air Force Base.

Finally in my room I settled in to read my new book.

In *HIDDEN HISTORY*, Boorstin speaks of Gibbon, author of *THE DECLINE and FALL of the ROMAN EMPIRE*. He said, "For Gibbon, while human nature is anything but unintelligible, it remains only partly explicable." For him the menace to understanding was not so much **ignorance** as the **illusion** of knowledge. It is more accurate to insist for Gibbon there are no trivia. Human habits, utterances, exclamations, and emotions are the very essence of his history—not mere raw material for distilling 'forces' and 'movements.' The more vividly we see them, the better we know our subject.

Boorstin continues. "But despite—perhaps, because of—this recognition (of our capacity to grasp) Gibbon was not a pessimist. On the contrary, in his optimism Gibbon seems to be a spokesman for the age of enlightenment. 'He seems, sometimes,' said Boorstin, 'to speak for a faith, burgeoning in his lifetime, that man's uninhibited critical faculties can grasp the world.' I once thought of Gibbon in precisely the same way. He spoke to me from, and for, a **period** of history. But in the years since Gibbon first spoke to me, he has come to say something more. He has become a more personal historian in what he said and what I hear."

I sat straight up, riveted to my chair. My mind was racing. "Spoke to me?" I said to myself! "Back up! Read it again"! Boorstin did say that! What luck! The rain!!. The grounded flight!!. The bookstore!!. And of all the books available, I spot *HIDDEN HISTORY.* And to top it off, it's written by Boorstin!! And on top of *that*!!—he says Gibbon "has become a more personal historian!!! *And* adds, "—since Gibbon first spoke to me.'"

Personal historian!!. Eureka!! I am a modern day Archimedes! That's it!! That's my answer! I have found my wingman!! I had spent more than a few nights studying the dialogues associated with Plato and I kept running into numerous narration and dialogues associated with Socrates. I'm talking about friendship, and courage and social intercourse associated with Protagoras, and Plato's *Apology* representing Socrates' defense of himself at his trial before the Athenian government. I liked this guy Socrates. If by any chance he could fly, he'd make a hell of a wingman.

So I came to a conclusion that helped change my life. If Boorstin and Gibbon can carry on a useful dialogue, why can't Socrates and I do the same thing?

I could ask so many questions—learn so much about philosophy from Socrates and his friends. It would give me a great chance to exchange stories and thoughts on the many aspects of life that I wanted to understand. If I can pull this off, Socrates and I can actually sit down and start discussing, without qualification or exception, the special quality of his thinking—particularly when he says things like, "Wonder is the feeling of the philosopher, and philosophy begins in wonder."

This is my lucky night!!.

I began to think. What the hell!!. Jimmy Stewart had Harvey! After Spencer Tracy crashed a B-25 into an enemy aircraft carrier, in the picture *A Guy NAMED JOE*, he came back to nurture Van Johnson through combat in a P-38: they were both in love with Irene Dunne. And Col. Bob Scott had God as his co-pilot. Can't get much better than that! Well, I don't have to start at the top—but in spite of others' considerations or expectations to the contrary, in *my* mind, Socrates could be *my* personal historian. He and I could be more intimate in our spoken language. We could learn from each other—such as when we raise our glasses on high to give a toast. He could say, "Yasou (that's Greek for cheers!)" I could say, "Cheers ass!" That's fighter pilot language! In English! I could teach Socrates!

As far as I am concerned, Socrates would be leading life of immortality and would provide an abundance of historical legacy through his **experiences**. Knowledge has been defined, at least colloquially, as that which one remembers after he has forgotten everything he has learned. This definition, however, presumes a very important factor; that there is, indeed, something to be learned. We all know, of course, there is always something to be learned, but what generates wisdom? What makes for a collective wealth of knowledge? It is **experience.** Passed from generation to generation, discipline to discipline, person to person. From the knowledgeable to the novice!

Socrates is the knowledgeable; I am the novice. Through his wisdom, he could help me reshape my convictions and improve my performance in life's tests of self-esteem and character.

Boorstin's *THE DISCOVERERS* was a vivid, sweeping, and original history of mans' search to discover the world around him. Socrates and I could discover the world around us in the form of relations with people. The CREATORS was a history of the heroes of the imagination. Will not Socrates be a hero of my imagination? Will he speak to me from, and for, a period of history, including my history?

I was excited. What the heck! I jumped up from my chair and walked to the pay phone outside our officers' quarters, dropped in a dime and called Socrates collect!! I wanted to get his attention!!

The operator on my end said to the information operator, "Socrates, a collect call for Socrates! Silence—No, Not Zoc! *S* like your socks! *No*! For God's sake (excuse the expression, operator,) it's not Z. ABCDEFGHIJKLMNOPQR—*S*! like Sun or er—er—Sock or—Socket—or—Socked in! or even SEX!! Yeah, Sweetheart! That's it! S—for Sex!!"

The information operator said, "Oh! yes, Sex—er I mean Socrates. Here he is—in the gold pages under PHILOSOPHERS! Just a moment, please. I'll connect you."

I waited! And waited! And then—

An enriched, vibrant voice came over the phone. "Hello! Yes! This is Socrates. Who is this?"

I introduced myself and gave Socrates a quick review on why I was calling. I heard him sigh. Silence! Then he said, "OK, operator,

I'll accept the call."

I proceeded to tell him about Gibbon becoming Boorstin's personal historian and talked about my limited studies of Philosophy and history. I then inquired if he would help me combine history with contemporary experiences to see if I could understand and accept the 'more often than not' capricious and whimsical aspects of life. And, I was facing a new dimension, for me, of business and wanted to be able to handle 'the unexpected.' Also, in reference to Philosophy, I asked him if he would please take me further than just defining Philosophy as love of wisdom. "I would appreciate you helping me find mature understanding and insight in exercising my curiosity and intelligence," I stated. "And I want to discuss reality—and truth. I would appreciate it, also, if we could touch on what you know of the great businessmen who impacted our lives—you know, Socrates, men like Carnegie, Rockefeller, Watson, Ford. I don't want any secret paths to success but I believe the schools rammed too many things down our collective throats. Why couldn't we ask questions? Why couldn't we take an opposite view? I want to be more aware, I want not to be afraid to face the truth—and reality, I would lik . . . . "

He cut me short. "Whoa—! Whoa—! Slow down! Easy! Easy! What did you say your name was?"

"Jack—Jack 'Suitcase' Simpson."

"Suitcase?? My Gosh! Where'd you get a handle like that?"

"I was so ugly when I was born they slapped my mother—and then put me in a suitcase. I was so ugly my mother had morning sickness **after** I was born."

Silence . . . .

"Gee, I'm paying for a long distance call and end up having a jokester on my hands," Socrates said. Then he got a little irritated. "This call is costing me a lot of money but yet, maybe, just maybe, I can slip it in to God's SPRINT bill. Most of us use AT&T but He always likes to show off by telling us He can hear a pin drop light years away.

But let me ask you, Satchel, why should I help you? You have been so excited about asking for so much. I—I just don't know. Give me a reason why I should help you."

"Well, Sir, first it's Suitcase, not Satchel. He was a great baseball pitcher. And, Sir, I have read about you. You said that in searching for answers to the kind of questions I'm asking, it is more hopeful if undertaken by two friends, one more experienced than the other."

"Did I say that? Oh! I see! What makes you think we'll be friends?"

"That's a good question! Tell you what; I'll make you a deal! You teach me the practical aspects of Philosophy, since you have the experience, and since I have the experience I'll teach you about the practical aspects of girls—lovely girls."

"What!! You think you're a lover?"

"Not necessarily. I can't define 'lover' but I'll give you an idea of something that matches practical aspects."

"I'm listening!"

"OK! I was out with a girl the other night and after some serious smooching she said, "All right, I'll let you make love to me, but only if you can make me hear bells ringing and see lights flashing."

"So?"

"So I made love to her on a pinball machine."

Dead silence!! I mean silence. "Hello . . . !" "Hello . . . ?"

Finally, Socrates said, "You're crazy, You need help!! Ever think of seeing a psychologist?"

"Well, I have nev—"

No! No! Never mind! I guess I'll be better than a psychologist.

OK! Satch—, pardon me,—Suitcase—whatever! I'll be glad to help. I know what you want. Actually, I am pleased you called. There is a lot of that kind of talent you're looking for 'up here' but we don't get too many calls. I might speak to a few of my philosopher friends and tell them to stand by. I know you are curious and have a love for truth and knowledge. My friends will be happy to comment on any philosophical question.

But remember one thing, Suit—! Wait a minute! W A I T—AH—M I N U T E! Let me think! Let me thin—! Now I remember! Everyone 'up here' with fighter pilot wings knows you only as 'Suitcase.' You'll have to tell me what that's all about. OK! You want truth and reality! I want you to know philosophers, myself included, make mistakes—and we do not necessarily all agree. We are philosophers because of history. We offer help from history; we advance truth and knowledge derived from historical participation or observation; just as the *Declaration of Independence*, the unanimous declaration of the thirteen United States of America—"We hold these truths to be self-evident—," advanced truth and knowledge from historical participation or observation.

And in all due respect to Boorstin, we'll go out and create a history of heroes of our own imagination.

But I was thinking as you were prattling on. If I help you I would like a little something in return. Let's call it a favor, my fighter pilot friend. I'm tired of wearing these damn frazzled, cheap, feathered wings. We have to wear them every time we want to go anywhere. We all agree they are of a beautiful white material. But there are some guys 'up here' that got a dispensation to wear blue. They call themselves

"THE BLUE ANGLES." But, frankly, I'm not interested in either color. Michael the Archangel must have gotten a deal at *COSCO*. Do you have anything in silver—with a star—and a wreath?? Sure would make me proud!!!."

"Of course! Of course! I have access to wings. Socrates, you have a deal!" I said. "By accepting my request to help me, the pleasure of returning the favor will be all mine."

"That would be just great! I need them because there is a special club for U.S. Air Force pilots up here called *CLOUD NINE*. Although I talk to a lot of pilots, including many of your friends, the rules for admittance are very strict. Every member must have a pair of silver wings and they have to know a dirty fighter pilot song so I am not eligible. The Navy and Marines have one of their own. I think it's called *TAIL-HOOKER*, or something like that! They throw a lot of wild parties."

"Yes, Mr. Socrates, I have heard of such parties. The Navy and Marines invite a lot of secretaries to attend. They all type fast and run slow!"

(As a matter of fact, the favor *was* all mine. In *SOCRATES 'N SUITS*, **BOOK I**, I presented Socrates with a pair of silver wings, topped by a silver star surrounded with a silver wreath—the wings of a Command Pilot in the United Stated Air Force. He walked into *CLOUD NINE* singing a risqué fighter pilot song I taught him. They welcomed Socrates with open arms.

And, as I said in the book, Socrates showed up at very critical time for me and soothed my mental state through combat and test flying as NOXEMA sooths a sunburned body.)

"By the way," I said, at that time, to Socrates, "How *will* we go about arranging a meeting?"

"Don't worry about that," Socrates said. "You'll know—and then we'll make our plans from there. I can't guarantee exactly when, but you'll know."

"Socrates, I'll remember this a long time. You said earlier that philosophers offer help from history. And you advance truth and knowledge derived from historical participation and observation. The title of my third book will be entitled *SOCRATES 'N MR. SUITS*. It will address Philosophy and the lessons of history as a gift to free enterprise. And I will have grown up—from Suits to Suitcase. You make me a happy man. Thank you. I'll be patiently waiting.

And Socrates, please take a minute and say hello to Rickenbacker, and Bong and McGuire and two beautiful guys—my brother-in-law and my special friend, Bill Boucek. My bother-in-law was killed flying a P-47 on Okinawa after WWII, and my friend Bill was killed in a P-51 in England after flying 25 missions in a B-24. There are many, many, others but it makes me sad in saying 'too numerous to mention them all.'"

I know who they are, Mr. Suitcase. I know them all. I have been talking to these men; you flew with many of them. They are fighter pilots and experimental pilots. A special breed.

"That's what I like to hear, Socrates. That's great! I'll wait for you to be in touch."

"You'll hear from me. And by the way, you're friends mentioned something else to me."

"OH! What?"

"They said you would never grow up!

Have good day."

Oscar Levant said it right when he said, "Happiness isn't something you experience; it's something you remember."

So, now we have the answer in part of the question of Socrates. As you see, I talked to Socrates on the phone, but how did I originally meet him?

SOCRATES WELL MET
(AN EXCERPT FROM *SOCRATES 'N SUITS*)
BOOK I

Casey Finnegan is a fighter pilot—one of the best. After receiving his wings as an air force pilot he flew F-86's in Germany and then joined the famous North Dakota National Guard—the 178th fighter squadron, also named the **HAPPY HOOLIGANS**. I met Casey in Las Vegas during one of my early 'swings' with the fighter jocks while I was waiting to be assigned to a class in gunnery. He and I met a chorus girl during one of those long, drunken evenings. We didn't get along too well with her highness. She was very conceited; her head was so swollen it had a waist.

Casey called me one day and asked if I would like to go to a dinner party with him and a few of his friends from Fargo. A couple of **HAPPY HOOLIGANS** had flown in to raise some hell and gamble. I said, "Hell, yes!"

The next morning we were sober enough to have Casey invite me to fly one of the guard's T-33's. I hadn't flown since graduation; a six week layoff.

The T-33 was a pleasure to fly again, and an hour at the controls passed quickly. I flew loops, chandelles, cuban-eights, and barrel rolls . . . all of the old maneuvers. Ummmm, I was a bit sloppy at times—but the acrobatics were still in my brain from air force pilot training. Three touch and go landings at home base had worked out well and my confidence in my somewhat rusty skills was reasonably high. With ten being the highest, Casey gave me a seven, nine, and then a ten. Chicken shit!!

My friend Casey was quiet in the back seat as we climbed back up through 20,000. We still had 200 gallons of fuel remaining and I was contemplating what to do next when Casey called out another aircraft at ten o'clock level. As I looked the sun flashed off the aircraft and I could see it was a small airplane headed almost directly at us. We were talking to Las Vegas approach control and they had not mentioned other traffic, so I was curious. I started a left turn and lowered the nose to build airspeed so that the bogey would pass overhead. At 15,000 feet and 400 knots I waited until my target was about a mile ahead. At the right moment I started the nose up to loop in behind the target, which appeared to be another T-33. As I approached completion of the first half of my loop the other aircraft passed just off of our right wing. I rolled upright about 1000 feet above and behind the target and lowered the nose to close the gap. At about 500 feet the other aircraft began to rock his wings in a standard 'join-up' signal. Great!

I overshot the join-up slightly and pulled out to the right until my speed diminished to match the other aircraft. As I moved in to join on his right wing I realized that I was looking at a highly polished, pristine F-80 'Shooting Star' without tip tanks installed. The wing tip had a fairing over the fittings where a wingtip tank, like those on our T-33, was usually installed. "How the hell'd he get away with no tips?" I asked myself. "And wher'd he come from?" The F-80 had no visible exterior markings and was absolutely beautiful—fresh and clean. To my surprise the pilot wore a cloth helmet with goggles. What did Casey and I have here? A WW I pilot with a sudden increase in mental poise and alertness?

We continued our formation flying. I stuck my T-33 in close. He did not look at us so I could not be sure, but I thought I saw a long, gray, beard. I settled in to concentrate on flying close formation. The F-80 pilot seemed to know I was working hard to maintain formation so he made a few easy turns left and right until I settled down. He was flying on my right wing.

Casey said. "I wonder who that sumbitch is?" I shook the stick to acknowledge I had control and continued to descend toward the long runway at Nellis. I checked out with Las Vegas approach control and then called the tower for landing. They had us in sight and requested that we enter a high and wide left downwind for the active runway. I agreed to comply and began slowing to configure for landing. We entered the initial approach to the runway at 1500 feet. I gave the old fart the signal for a 'one-second interval' at break. At the right moment we banked hard to the left, dropped the gear in our turn, turned base leg and rolled out on final approach with the F-80 still in close formation. My landing went well. We turned off the runway at and rolled straight in to the parking ramp with the F-80 still attached to our right wing. After shutdown I walked over to greet our wingman. Casey said he would meet him later. I was startled to see an 'elderly' man with a beard climb out of the cockpit. He had taken off his goggles and cloth helmet and yes, he did have a beautifully trimmed gray beard. He was dressed . . . . he . . . he . . . reminded me of Roscoe Turner the flamboyant race pilot from the 1930's. His boots were pure spit and polish—their brightness enhanced by the reflection of the sunshine. He wore tailor made jodhpurs, a military style double-breasted jacket with belt, and an over the shoulder leather strap. Rickenbacker? Luke? Baron von Manfred Richthofen, the 'Red Baron'? Who the hell is this guy?

I walked up to him. "Hell'uva job of flying," I said. "Didn't make too much of an ass of me. Only beat the tail off me, that's all. I held out my hand. My name is Jack Simpson. My friends call me Suitcase."

"Yes, I know," said the hot-rock stranger. "How are you, Suitcase? It's a pleasure to meet you. Socrates is the name. Philosophy's the game," he said as he put forth his hand to shake mine.

I was dumbstruck! Astounded! Astonished! You name it! I was overwhelmed with surprise. I shook Socrates' hand. I said, "What the hell—? How did you—what are you doing? How come?" I was so thunderstruck, I couldn't ask a simple question.

"Take—take it easy, Suitcase." Socrates said. "You called me. I'm here to help you; but not today. I'm was on my way elsewhere but when I spotted your T-33. Well—as they say, the rest is history! But not to worry, my newfound friend! We'll meet in due time—at the right place. I have some other friends to see and I'll meet you when you may least expect it but my word is my bond."

"Yes, but—but how did you know? How did you get here? And how did you learn to fly so well? I mean, you kicked my ass. I don't even know you and I don't like you already," I said with a smile. I added, "You don't even have wings, unless you were bullshitting me."

"No! No! I was telling the truth. But just because I don't have wings doesn't mean I don't know how to fly. I'll tell you one thing only. All of your friends plus some other fighter pilots up there in *CLOUD NINE* took me aside—you know—your brother-in-law, Bong, McGuire, the Red Baron—they told me about your air-to-air weaknesses. I think I proved today that I am a quick learner."

"Oh! Is that right???" I said. "Well don't worry, Socrates. You teach me to be a better man and I'll teach you to be a dirty old man—with wings! Is that a deal?"

"Deal! I'll see you when I see you. I have to go?"

"Wait! Wait! How are you going to travel? Where will you stay??"

"Don't sweat the small stuff, my friend. That's my worry."

He smiled. And with that, he climbed back into his F-80 cockpit, started the engine, waived goodbye, taxied out, took-off, made a low pass over the field, pulled up into a beautifully executed immelmann, and was gone. And then it hit me. Normally an F-80 needs an auxiliary power unit to start. His did not! Nor did Socrates take the time to refuel!

I thanked Casey and the **HAPPY HOOLIGANS over drinks at the bar** for their hospitality. They invited me for dinner, but I had plans for the evening. I met two of my friends from class 52-E who were already in gunnery class, and three chorus girls from the *Desert Inn*. We had dinner, and danced, and drank Grand Marnier in an 'off the main drag' bar while we listened to a great piano player play anything anyone requested. The three of us sang a couple of 'acceptable' fighter pilot songs—had the crowd laughin' along with us. The girls were dynamite! One of the ladies was exceptional; very pretty, very big busted, and very tall. I'm a little over six feet but with high heels this gal could eat peanuts off the top of my head. She said, "Suitcase, you have to dance with me before you go," and with that she grabbed me by the arm and we twirled to the floor. Hell, I was on tip of my toes hanging on for dear life! When we started to dance I couldn't breathe as my nose was right between two mounds of beautiful flesh and my ears were covered as if I were wearing earmuffs. I thought of the word tittup. Hell, how could I not have! We were tittupping—moving in a lively manner often with an exaggerated action. Hell, I couldn't hear the music but I just relaxed and let her rapidly move those knockers in a lively manner! What a night!

Reminds me of a story. Ashamed of her gigantic bosom, a woman went to Hal Poop Poo the faith healer. He looked her over and told her since faith could move mountains—! Well, you know the rest! She paid him a large some of money and he started to pray. He prayed for hours and hours and, lo and behold, her bosom grew smaller. Her breasts became beautiful, but now she has two giant lumps on her ass!

Anyhow, every guy should have to go to Marine boot camp before college and every girl should have the opportunity to join a Las Vegas chorus line. Something to add to a man's development and a lady's innate beauty and personality. The maturing process is amazing.

One of the guys told a great story. All of Nevada, therefore some towns near 'Vegas', have their share of houses of ill repute. So, my fighter pilot friend says, "The police make one of their periodic roundups of ladies of the evening. In the courtroom, the judge asks the first, 'Are you a prostitute?'

'I was only taking a walk. I'm a chorus girl.'

The second also responds. 'I'm a chorus girl.' The first dozen have the same answer. The last girl saunters up to the bench. The judge asks her, 'What do you do for a living?'

She answers, 'I'm a hooker.'

'How's business?'

'It could be a hell of a lot better if it wasn't for all of these damn chorus girls!'"

The girls loved it.

Well, now you have the story of how I first met Socrates. True to his word, and soon after I flew my first combat mission, (it was a disaster,) he bummed a ride to Korea with a touring USO show featuring Bob Hope. We had our first meaningful visit at the K-13 Officers' Club. From that time on, through combat and test flying, (*SOCRATES "N SUITS*, **BOOK I & II**) he helped me acquire the valued process of gaining knowledge and thinking on how the study of Philosophy would help keep my equilibrium in daily life. He taught me that Philosophy instills the search for wisdom, and history offers a venue. Socrates said, "Jack, it just takes time to sort things out and learn.

I received the report originating from the bar at club *CLOUD NINE* when you flew your first mission; Rickenbacker, Bill Boucek, your brother-in-law, and your good friend, oh! I forget his name. He was killed at Big Spring one night in pilot training."

"Yes, Socs. I know of whom you speak. A magnificent individual by the name of Barfield; 52-F dedicated their class book to him."

"Yes, that's the gentleman. Anyhow, you're right! Your first mission was a disaster! Seeing all that flak would be enough to scare the pants off the proprietor of a haunted house. And having a couple of men blown out of the sky didn't help you keep your equilibrium either. You goofed up because you were scared but as your flight leader said after the mission, 'Join the crowd.' Everyone learned something that day including your ability to tell the truth.

Jack, did you ever have apprehension about taking an important test in college?"

"Of course."

"Why?"

"I was worried about having enough knowledge of the course."

"Bingo! Your first mission was the most important test of your life. You didn't have *any* knowledge of combat, or the enemy. Knowledge, or truth that is attained when we know, is the essential good of the mind, and also a good means to be used in action. Is their anything more realistic than action in combat?"

"I guess not, Socs. I never nearly pissed my pants during a college exam."

"Ah! Ha! Very good, Suits. But don't worry, as you flew more combat missions you gained knowledge by learning it is a relation between the knower and an object known. Right?"

"Right!"

"OK! Now you had knowledge by acquaintance (or knowledge *of*) the enemy. What did I say earlier? 'It takes time to sort things out and learn.'

By gaining experience attending briefings, de-briefings, flying your missions, asking questions, talking to experienced pilots, brain storming with the intelligence officers, etc., you will transition to knowledge by description (or knowledge *about*.) A lot of people know of the Korean War, but since they haven't been there, they have no knowledge about it.

Knowledge about! You have heard the question many times in your life—what about this? What about that! Keep asking! It will save your life and you will become a very good combat pilot.

Now let's talk about wisdom. Remember, Jack, the philosopher must not be thought of as a wise man, but rather as a lover or as a seeker of wisdom. Over all the qualities of mind or character that are known as excellencies, or perfection's, wisdom is, perhaps, the one most universally admired. It is also, perhaps, the one that is generally thought most difficult to achieve. It does not consist in profound knowledge but, rather, the wise man that knows how to manage all the affairs of life well. He offers his life the understanding of what is true, right, or lasting. He has good judgement; and common sense. Are you with me?"

"I'm hangin' in there."

"Good! What is your thought on what I have just said"?

"Well, Socs, I'm not a philosopher or a wise man, but as a seeker of wisdom, which is never ending in my opinion, I'll just have to go out and do things, make mistakes, and learn—and never give up."

"You have the right idea, my friend. My teaching you, Suits, is not a barrier to others, but an opening of avenues. It is essentially a matter of human relations, and of one man passing on the best of his inner visions to others; in this case, I pass my experience and wisdom to you and you to others.

The mere fact of you being able to stop and consider and ask the question, 'Who am I,' is proof of a highly privileged state: a luxury of civilization that is not open to all.

Wisdom will consist in knowing yourself and your **inevitable** surroundings as they are. They are good, relatively at least, for they are part of you, and anyway, they are all you have. A peaceful accounting is needed in these circumstances; a count of your actual blessings instead of a revolt against fate's injustice. Never condemn those who take a negative road: some destinies are so tragic they deserve infinite forgiveness and compassion. I think you will learn that."

THE SUITCASE QUESTION

OK! That takes care of Socrates, for the moment. Now you ask; What does Suitcase know about business, particularly sales?" Good question! My answer is, "I know enough to ask, and read, and learn, and grow through practical wisdom by doing. And I am not afraid to make mistakes. I built my future life's foundation on what I learned from Socrates."

Now let us get back to your other question.

Since my last name is Simpson, my nickname 'Suitcase' came from a well-traveled baseball player, Harry 'Suitcase' Simpson. I played four years of college baseball so my teammates called me 'Suitcase' also. Three men from the team, and I, entered pilot training; they called me 'Suitcase', then it was the group in our officers' quarters, then the flight line, then the Wing, etc. And on top of that, I played left field and managed our Class 52-F fast pitch softball team known as the "Foxy Fliers" We entered the Polk County, Florida, league and won the championship-14 and 1. The league consisted of Class 52-E, the base, Bartow, Winter Haven, and other local communities *plus* Cypress Gardens, home of all the beautiful water skiers. Soon that was the only name I ever had. Of course when I was in trouble, which was often, my senior officers called me *Lt.* Simpson. Even today, 50 years later, my friends still call me 'Suitcase.' I do get variations; Suits, Satchel (remember when I first talked to Socrates,) Briefcase, Uncle Pocketbook, Bookends, Streetcar, Super-case, Sweet-cakes, and Shoelace. However, when creditors call, which is often, they always ask for *Mr.* Simpson. In **BOOK I** and **II** Socrates called me 'Suits' and I sometimes called him 'Socs;' same as in **BOOK III**.

The original 'Suitcase' came from an old eastern U.S. cartoon named *TOONERVILLE TROLLEY?* It featured characters such as The Conductor, the Fat Lady, the Thin Man, the Magpie and 'Suitcase.' They called on him to put out forest fires because of his big feet.

THE COVER

The painting on the cover is a copy of a painting, by Maxine McCaffrey, first hanging in the Pentagon, and later in the Federal Building in West Los Angeles. It displays Colonel Bob Scott, my 35th Fighter Squadron commander in Korea (**BOOK I**) flying his F-105 jet in a dogfight with a MiG in Vietnam; the western edge of Hanoi; Eater Sunday, 1967.

After high school and before becoming a fighter pilot, Col. Scott attended Iowa State University for two years majoring in aeronautical engineering. He joined the US Army Air Corps and received his wings in March, 1942. He first assigned as an instructor but in early '44 was assigned to the CBI (China Burma India) as a pilot in the Northrop P-61 night fighter. Col. Scott shot down two enemy aircraft.

After WWII Col. Scott was sent back to college for 3\1\2 years, followed by fighter testing in Florida and test pilot school at Edwards. I met him as my commander in Korea. He flew 117 missions. Upon returning to the States, he was a fighter bomber squadron commander, was sent to Edwards as a test pilot on F-105 and F-107 fly-off of the Air Force's first Mach 2 fighter-bomber. He then commanded the first F-105 squadron before reporting to Vietnam as commander of an F-105 Fighter Wing. He retired in 1970.

When Colonel Scott retired he later became a very successful cattle rancher in two states—New Mexico and California. A fighter pilot turned successful businessman.

History is full of great men in other professions turning into great businessmen. And it can work both ways. The great writers in the reign of Elizabeth, during which there was such a development of robust life in England, were not literary men according to the modern acceptation of the word, but men of action trained in business. Spenser acted as the Lord Deputy of Ireland; Raleigh was, by turns, a courtier, soldier, sailor, and discoverer. Bacon was a labor lawyer before he became Lord Keeper and Lord Chancellor. It has been said that even the man of genius can write nothing worth reading in relation to human affairs, unless he has been in some way or the other connected with the serious every-day business of life. A fighter pilot with combat experience and a test pilot *is* connected with the *very* serious every-day business of life.

Thoroughly trained men of science, including aerodynamics, and learning, have proved themselves efficient as first-rate men of business. Culture of the best sort trains the habit of application and industry, disciplines the mind, supplies it with resources, and gives it freedom and vigor of action—all of which are equally requisite in the successful conduct of business. Thus, education and scholarship usually indicate steadiness of character, for they imply continuous attention, diligence, and the ability and energy necessary to master knowledge; and such persons will also usually be found possessed of more than average promptitude, address, resource, and dexterity.

Eddie Rickenbacker was a fighter pilot; WWI's leading American ace became president of Eastern Airlines. Paul Thayer, a fighter pilot and test pilot became Chairman of LTV. Corwin H. (Corky) Meyer, was the Grumman senior engineering fighter test pilot for 22 years before being promoted to senior vice president, product operations, with responsibility for 23,000 personnel. Robert A. Mitchell, a Spitfire fighter pilot, is president of Northrop Grumman, Ryan Aeronautical Company. RAdm. Thomas Cassidy, Jr., an Associate Fellow in the Society of Experimental Test Pilots, is President and Chief Executive Officer of General Atomics Aeronautical Systems, Inc. Bill Bettis, flew a cross section of Naval aircraft including fighters is the owner/hands-on operator of *Nieuport 17 Restaurant* in Tustin, California. The food is *par excellence* and his restaurant is widely acclaimed as having the greatest collection of pictures of aircraft and pilots; a virtual review of aviation history.

Exceptional pilots turned outstanding businessmen!

And look at me! When I resigned from test flying, a small aerospace company hired me in an executive position in marketing and sales. Later, my company was amalgamated into a bigger one but it went bankrupt. I was then hired by a large aerospace company but was fired after three years; a maverick; an independent who couldn't get along with the staid, status quo. My fault! The men I worked for were marked by dignity and seriousness. In my opinion, they were too serious. They didn't want anybody making mistakes. It made them look bad!

I was really down; even verbally put down by my 'friends'. "Ha! Ha! Simpson goes from test pilot, to junior executive, to a kick in the ass outta' here!" I found I really didn't have any real friends. One usually learns this, at a particular interval of time that is limited and often crucial. They say nothing; do nothing. They don't want to be tainted. But yet they will buzz about, talk about, and wonder the next move.

But I had Socrates! He said, "Suitcase, I'll be your friend. My experience (condemnation to death) tells me what you are going through. Understand Jack, friendship is different from all other relationships. You and I have that relationship. Unlike acquaintanceship, it is based on love. Unlike lovers and married couples it is free from jealousy. Unlike children and parents it knows neither criticism nor resentment. Friendship has no status in law. Jack, in your new business world, you are learning business partnerships are based on a contract. So is marriage. Parents are bound by the law, as are children. But friendship is freely entered into, freely given, and freely exercised.

Friends never cheat each other, or take advantage, or lie. Friends do not spy on one another, yet they have no secrets. Friends glory in each other's successes, and are downcast by their failures. Friends minister to each other, nurse each other. Friends give to each other, worry about each other, and stand always ready to help. Perfect friendship is rarely achieved, but at its height it is an ecstasy."

No doubt I felt much better after Socrates spoke to me. In addition, Marcus Aurelius, through my friend Socrates, left me with two thoughts: 1.) "(Think About)How much trouble man avoids who does not look to see what his neighbor says, or thinks, or does." And, 2.) "Does another do Suits wrong? No! They can't! Because Suitcase only has to look to himself! Suits now has what the universal nature wills him to have; tell him to do what his nature now wills him to do. As I understand it, he did absolutely nothing to bring disrespect to the company, management, or himself."

What Marcus said was true, but I had to work, so I took a job as a $300 a month janitor. However, I did not forget Socrates' talking about life's test of self-esteem and character. So I took my lowered status; I put myself to the test of self-esteem and character. I knew I had to face reality. I just needed time to sort things out. But there is one saving grace about cleaning floors and scrubbing toilets and bathrooms—it kept me from biting my fingernails! I didn't blame people for laughing at me. That was OK. I had Socrates. He offered me counsel and guidance for facing up to the trials and tribulations of human life. Socs said, "Remember, Jack, with any new path, expect the unexpected!"

And another of Socrates' friends, Friedrich Wilhelm Nietzsche, the controversial German philosopher, sent me a message through Socs. Nietzsche said, 'Mr. Suitcase, remember, *you must carry a chaos inside you to give birth to a dancing star.*'

It took years of effort and long hours; selling the capabilities of my maintenance company during the day, cleaning floors and bathrooms at night. I hired my first employee, then my second, then my tenth. Soon there were thirty-seven. And there were failures and chaos inside.

My first company vehicle was an eight year old Ford station wagon. I was dating a Continental Airlines stewardess. I picked her up from a flight one early evening to take her home before I started my round of cleaning. While going through an intersection, a car zoomed in front of us from the right, running the traffic light. I jammed on the brakes. Mops, buckets, dusters, bottles of polish, cans of wax, and 'dutch' cleanser were promptly jarred from their places in the rear of the wagon and ended up in one pile to the left, right, under, and on top of us. The 'dutch' cleanser enveloped us in a cloud of white powder. We looked like workers in a flourmill. After dusting ourselves off and spitting powder for more than a few minutes, my friend said, "Gee, Honey, I know my uniform needs cleaning after every flight, but this time I didn't expect to be in it."

You talk about chaos inside!

What a great lady! We met not too long ago at a wedding; it had been 33 years. I asked her if she still cleaned her clothes with 'dutch' cleanser. We hugged! And laughed! Life is great!

What did Socrates say? "It just takes time to sort things out and learn." I met a fellow graduate from college who was an engineer at a very successful electro-mechanical actuator company. They needed help at North American Aviation. I had been a test pilot there (**BOOK I**) and knew many of the engineers. I was hired as a consultant. And soon I was consulting to another company. And then another! My net income, as an individual offering professional services in marketing analysis and sales, grew to be more than my service business. So, I had to make a decision. It was time to act and give birth to a dancing star. It was:

THE SIMPSON COMPANY
MARKETING ANALYSIS &
MANAGEMENT/ENGINEERING SALES

Robert Grudin said in his book, *TIME AND THE ART OF LIVING*, the years forget our errors and forgive our sins, but they punish our inaction with living death.

AN ADDENDUM TO
CLEARING UP MATTERS

As I end this introduction into the third book of the trilogy, *SOCRATES 'N SUITS*, I am reflecting on my thirty-five years experience in marketing and sales as an entrepreneur. I had no guarantees, no weekly pay check, no surety of length of contract, no reimbursed expenses, no mileage, no furnished car, no retirement plan, no long term health insurance, no medical, no paid vacation, no sick leave, no overtime, no 401K, no matching of savings, and no—I wouldn't have traded it for anything in the world. Why? Because I have experienced, first hand, the true dynamics of free enterprise. And, although I was on my own, when facing the reality of any enterprise, one never accomplishes anything alone.

I was fortunate enough to realize, early, that entrepreneurship requires the accompaniment of dedicated personnel. I call it 'An Exchange of Value. It boils down to a buyer and seller backed by a number of accomplished men and women in all disciplines.

Although Socrates will offer wisdom, and I, practical experience, **BOOK III**, *SOCRATES 'N SUITS,* is no panacea. I have no remedy for all ills or difficulties in business or any secrets about closing 'a deal.' I can tell you, however, the search for the wisdom (philosophy) and gaining knowledge **about** closing 'a deal' and 'keeping it going' (as a business) is both fascinating and exciting. The chapters FULL OF THE PROBLEM, LESSONS OF HISTORY, YOU CAN'T SELL IF YOU DON'T LISTEN, and WHY COMPANIES FAIL will serve as a guide. I learned the hard way. I was never afraid to make a decision—I just didn't make all the right ones.

In CLEARING UP MATTERS, **BOOK I,** I mentioned the luck I had in discovering another of Philip Caputo's books entitled *MEANS OF ESCAPE.* I learned from him how I could feel good about writing **BOOK I & II** and not worry about people believing my text was full of sophistry. Caputo said his story was "a fictional recreation of actual events." That is exactly what *SOCRATES 'N SUITS* is. Every recounting of past events is true, but time and fog has forced me to use just a little bit of oh!—should I say—finger crossing. I found I didn't have to use any toes; just a couple of fingers—on each hand!

No finger crossing on descriptions of my consulting contracts; just my contact with the ladies!

I am wondering about **Book III,** also. It is a printed and bound work about my valued experience in marketing and sales; in particular marketing analysis, my ken. My work and time was directed, in the most part, for companies of unlike or dissimilar disciplines. Also, as an avocation, I hosted a number of Saturday morning college lecture series, and taught college evening classes as a professor of marketing and sales. I did this for seven, or eight years. I never used a text although I was given literally dozens of texts on the subject matter. It came with the territory. Every publisher gave me a text with the hope I would use it in a particular class. In all due respect, they were all the same—seriously written, straight to the point, this is 'the way it is,' and 'get ready for the test at the end of the chapter.' That is not to say the authors were not learned, bright, and capable of teaching what they wrote, but I often wondered how much experience they had 'in the trenches.' I've been in the trenches; selling encyclopedias door-to-door in order to pay my way back into college; it wasn't exactly a two-martini lunch. I put my students in the trenches. I wanted them to stand up in class and be counted and take on any and all objections to their beliefs on how to solve a particular problem. They weren't graded on being right or wrong. They were graded on the strength of their convictions. I often divided the class in half and gave them a problem that was—say, facing a manager of sales. The class knew all the facts but the pressing question was asked, "The particular company in question forecasts a period of growth. Will the company benefit more by hiring direct sales personnel, or should the company go the manufactures' representative route? How about warehousing distributors"? And why?

One half the class was assigned direct, the other half representation. The class responded with passion and zeal! We had some knock down, drag outs! It was a great learning experience for all, including yours truly.

My concern is *SOCRATES 'N SUITS* is not a textbook, nor is it a printed and bound volume headed for a best-seller list. It is, however, an excellent book of words or of information about all particular fields or sets of concepts regarding the profession of marketing and sales. I say the "profession of marketing and sales" because honorable, upstanding sales, is a calling requiring specialized knowledge and often long and intensive preparation. *SOCRATES & SUITS* does only corral my varied experiences in the business world, but I also talk about women, and other personal experiences; enhanced, I hope, with levity. I also had Socrates! He was the one that told me "you learn by doing". But I have decided, "Heck! I'll tell my story to the best of my ability and then I'll look hard for a publisher."

Today, as in every day, I continue to read; I have a beautiful wife, and friends, but reading fulfills my desire for solitude. THOUGHT! You are never alone when you think! I find myself doing "more of a study" of a book—Tolstoy, Mark Twain,

Boorstin, Darwin, and Lives of Leaders in many disciplines such as Presidents, Generals, and CEO's! Believe me, I am not talking with excessive pride, or bragging. I just like to be in the company of great men and their writings.

Well, I got lucky again! In 1988, Stephen Hawking, one of the most influential thinkers and brilliant theoretical physicists of our time, wrote a book entitled *A Brief History of Time*. Professor Hawking gave us the thought that the ultimate 'Theory of Everything' seemed to be just over the horizon.

I must tell you I was reaching over the horizon on every page I studied, and ended falling over as one very confused individual; like the guy who ran up to Reverend Billy Graham after one of his lectures and said, "Sir, that was great speech and I sure like your crackers!"

That's how far out of tune I was trying to perceive and recognize what the hell Professor Hawking was talking about!

Well, he has written a new book; *The Universe in a Nutshell*. It's driving me nuts—but I seized his introduction and said to myself, "He could be talking about me and what I am trying to create in a person's mind about the widely known and esteemed **profession** of marketing and sales." Professor Hawking asks, in speaking of his 1988 publication, "Has the situation changed (Theory of Everything) since then? Are we any closer to our goal"?

As will be described in this book, we have advanced a long way since then, although too many managers are still making the same mistakes; too many, in my opinion! They do not 'reach back' and learn what history (history of prior managers—their contributions; their mistakes) have to offer. It is an ongoing journey still, and the end is not yet in sight. According to an old saying, "*it is better to travel hopefully than to arrive*". Our quest for discovery fuels our creativity in all fields, not just in science. If we reached the end of the line, the human spirit shall shrivel and die. But I don't think we will ever stand still: we shall increase in complexity, if not in depth, and shall always be the center of an expanding horizon of possibilities.

I italicized 'it is better to travel hopefully than to arrive' because Hawking and his words were an immediate inspiration to me. It means never giving up, particularly in my profession, to a competitor and never allow yourself to arrive at a point where you think you have it made. Quest for discovery of new and better ways is paramount in our profession and it should fuel our creativity in marketing, sales, merchandizing, distribution, quality and service. Hell, Hawking could be talking to us in a lecture series about what it takes to compete. No, we will not stand still, and we will expand our horizon of capabilities. If one does not think so and is not willing to devote his professional life to the mental and physical growth of his sales responsibilities, then it is best to find another profession.

People and companies stand still too much! They end up paying a tremendous price in growth, personnel, dollars, and energy that should have been expended to keep the company in a competitive position in the first place.

Or, they just disappear!

The reason I read is simple; I learn such great deal from others! I have named Caputo and Hawking. In one of the chapters you will be reading the words of von Clausewitz from his classic *ON WAR*. I just changed the titles from General to Vice President, Sales, and the message is exactly the same—a synthesis on how to organize and win! If you are in the profession of marketing and sales, I think it foolish to read only Drucker, or Peters and Waterman, or Stanton (*FUNDAMENTALS of MARKETING*). Expand your horizons and search what you can learn from von Clausewitz, Hawking, philosophers, and many more distinguished **THINKERS**

John Stuart Mill (1806-1873) British philosopher, said, in *On Liberty* II, "No one can be a great thinker who does not recognize, that as a thinker it is his first duty to follow his intellect to whatever conclusions it may lead. Truth gains more even by errors of one who, with due study and preparation, thinks for himself, than by the true opinions of those who only hold them because they do not suffer themselves to think."

Epictetus, A.D. c.50-c.138, wrote nothing (like Socrates), but acquired renown as a teacher. I would like to have had him as a teacher in marketing and sales. Some of his lecture series would be entitled:

1.) *How a man on every occasion can maintain his proper character.*
2.) *Of Contentment—Of Tranquility*
3.) *Of progress or improvement*
4.) *On friendship and freedom from fear*
5.) *What is the matter on which a good man should be employed, and in what we ought chiefly to practice ourselves.*
6.) *What things we ought to despise; what things we ought to value.*

Another lecture series would be entitled "*What Philosophy Promises*"! Here we have a man teaching 1900 years ago and makes as much common sense, to me, today, as he did then. "True good is within oneself," he taught. If salespersons do not take the time to learn that, they have nothing to offer a customer.

Philosophy and the lessons of history (books) offer **a world** of common sense experiences. I am not talking the serious study of metaphysics or epistemology or logic. I'm talking reading of the thousands of years of accumulated experiences leading to wisdom passed on to contribute to one's value of living—within yourself and others—at home and in the marketplace.

Socrates visited me only when he thought I needed a little shove. We had rewarding discussions pertaining to what Philosophy and the lessons of history have to offer sound business practices; they are inexorably tied together. And there is failure. I was on my own; basically under the same circumstances as flying a fighter; no instructor pilot jumping in the cockpit with me; no guarantee of returning alive from a mission or no guarantee of a successful test flight. "But, Suitcase," Socrates said, "in business you must be ready to push forward a solid wall of truthfulness and the assumption of responsibility for the quality, worth, and durability of your words and actions. Providence, nor I, will accept nothing less!"

And on top of that, I discovered Socrates is no softie! Remember the passage from **BOOK II** when he told me he loved me? That may be in only certain circumstances. Why? Because remember he also said, as I was looking at what he had in his hand, "No way, Suitcase! You cannot have my BUD *Lite*."

AN ADDITIONAL SUPPLEMENT!
AN EXPOSITION ON
WHAT I THINK,
AND BELIEVE, AS A RESULT OF HAVING
PHILOSOPHY AND SOCRATES
POINT THE WAY!

I have just finished reviewing "PROPERTIES" on my WINDOWS '98; I was surprised to say the least! I created "Clearing Up Matters" on November 28, 2002; it is now the middle of October, 2004! It has been visited and revised over 200 times, most of the time for a word or two, a line or two, or an injection of a short paragraph or two. I guess it proves the 'old axiom that nothing has ever been written that hasn't been re-written.

Did you ever see the original Declaration of Independence! Or Lincoln's Gettysburg Address! I have! Words scratched out and rewritten! Whole sentences scratched out! And rewritten! Those two brilliant, widely known and esteemed proclamations inscribed with freedom of man in mind, had more scratches than a flea-ridden dog!

It has been 50 years since I first met Socrates, his contemporary friends, and others along the way. My study of philosophy centered more on the time-honored philosophers and what experiences and knowledge they had to offer me. I chose that road rather than philosophy's core: logic, aesthetics, ethics, metaphysics, and epistemology. However, that is not to say I didn't run into the "origins of ideas" as I vicariously met the likes of—oh! let's say!—Voltaire and Hobbes and Locke.

In **BOOKS I & II** of *SOCRATES "N SUITS*, you will find innumerable passages where Socrates offered me love, solace and mental stability in withstanding the impulsive, often illogical turns of my mind. It was particularly appreciated after my completely inferior and appalling first combat mission, due to fear, plus trying to understand how I could effectively fulfill my responsibility while having one's heart in one's mouth!

After the mission, Socrates had put his arm around my shoulder when we walked in the field near my squadron headquarters, as he explained to me in a calm but emphatic way why I must learn by study and accomplishment the difference between 'knowledge of' and 'knowledge about'. "You have knowledge of flying a fighter in combat," Socrates said, "but you don't know a single thing about it! If you want to live, you damn well better learn."

"And," Socrates continued, "don't forget what Plutarch told you in *Caius Marius*! 'The strangeness of things; and Suitcase, what could be more strange than your first mission, often make them seem more formidable when they are not so; and—by our better acquaintance, even things which really are terrible, loose much of their frightfulness.' Just think! Plutarch was born about 46 A.D. Was he thinking about you some 1900 years ago with the words 'better acquaintance'?"

"So where are we?" Socrates asked.

"Looks like better acquaintance takes us back to 'knowledge of' and 'knowledge about', I said with a smile.

"Right on! Suitcase! Right on."

I **damn well** learned! Socrates' esteemed advice kept me alive during 60 additional very tough air-to-ground combat missions. And no, I can't count on my fingers on my right and left hand the number of friends I lost! There are no subtractions in this mathematical exercise! I don't count at all! One number hurts as much as the other! The U.S. Air Force and Naval Air Force counted though! The practical application of Socrates' and Plutarch' advice sowed the seed for "Top Gun" and "Red Flag", where the two air forces trained new pilots using actual opponents' aircraft, hostile pilots, and flying existing tactics of a designated foe.

I also learned to take the attitude of a 4.0 average of a student walking into a classroom prepared to take a tough test. He didn't have time to worry; he was better acquainted and had knowledge about the subject. The same posture grew within me; *I* became better acquainted and had knowledge about the enemy. As a member of the 35th Fighter Bomber Squadron I had a job to do; helping the men on the ground involved in an appalling, dreadful, bloody fight for literally inches of land. I couldn't do them any good if I wasn't prepared—or dead.

I often think about those days in combat fifty-one and a half years ago. Socrates and his philosopher friends affected my life. Since that time I have prepared and made it a point to "know about" as much as possible before every move I made, or presently make. I am the A student. Socrates' help and philosophical thought has been incalculable. There was a nebulous something surrounding us that day we walked in the field! Remember! I described almost the same thing in **BOOK II** when I saw the blackened devil of death! Why were so many fighter pilots killed in combat when I didn't get a scratch? Why were so many experimental test pilots killed when I, as a relatively inexperienced experimental test pilot, lived through two major crashes in addition to all those dead engine landings when so many things went wrong? Is Socrates showing me off? Is he showing everyone, through me, that my searching and learning what philosophy has to offer is a continuing pursuit of wisdom that will tender a general understanding of values and reality? Isn't that what any fighter pilot or experimental test pilot or any businessperson is expected to do? Sure it is! Search! Think! Make Mistakes! Learn! Don't give up!

Maybe it's because I can't give up the search. I have to be around to continue my pursuit of wisdom; and Socrates won't let me down, just as he wouldn't let me let the troops down in Korea.

Socrates soon introduced me to Marcus Aurelius, 121-180, Roman emperor and zealous Stoic, the school of philosophy holding that the wise man should be free from passion, unmoved by joy or grief, and a firm, restrained response to pain or distress. Aurelius also said, in *MEDIDATIONS*, that "in the morning I shall meet with the busybody, the ungrateful, arrogant, deceitful, envious, and unsocial". He said, and I'm paraphrasing, that people become arrogant, deceitful, envious, etc., by reason of their **ignorance** of what is good or evil. Boswell, in *Life of Johnson (1763)*, says that "mankind has a great aversion to intellectual labor; but even supposing knowledge to be easily attainable, more people would be content to be ignorant that would take even a little trouble to acquire it."

Well, I think that's a shame. Like one man says, "So many women, so little time." Too bad more men aren't saying, "In addition to women, so many eminent books, so little time."

It has slowly become apparent to me, through Socrates and Aurelius, and many others, I have been a little less passionate or fervid about things, particularly in joy or grief or shocking happen stance. And in reading about, and empathetically living the lessons of history, I have learned nothing really happens that hasn't happened many times before; only in different dimensions! In it's place, my understanding has taken on a dimension of skew-ness or distortion in the realm of accepting *and* comprehending; no matter what happens I don't get the feeling of any strong emotion.

Mark Twain, born 1700 years after Aurelius, says, "The character of the human race never changes, it is permanent." Circumstances change from time to time for better or worse, but the human race never does.

Let me give you an example or two! My circumstances regarding professional sports have changed. I used to enjoy football, baseball, basketball, boxing, and hockey but they have now become, to me, a gigantean bore.

In football, I tire of the arrogant "look what I just did" displays of players in the end zone and three time losers from drugs back on the field after a slap on the hands and a microscopic relief of dollars from their wallet. In addition, I read where one football player, after catching a ball in the end zone, in a display egregious egoism and pomposity, runs and steps on the rival's logo. An insult to any normal man's intelligence! Of course intelligence is defined as: mental acuteness, or the act of understanding, or the skilled use of reason, or the ability to apply knowledge. This moron doesn't have the mental acuteness or intelligence of a wet brick. I say "wet" because I want to stay as far away as possible from my "dry" sense of humor.

Baseball has become a turbulent display of bean balls, chair and bottle throwing, fans running on the field, and fisticuffs; so much so TV is now showing the many team upheavals as part of a review on the championship playoff series. Wait 'till an irate pitcher throws a 90mph fastball and hits a player in the head so hard it kills him. It's going to happen; count on it!

If hockey keeps up the deceitful, low life guile of deliberate injuries to opposing players it will soon be like watching the Christians vs. the Lions because the consciously unsocial, morally offensive fans will demand more!

A star-loaded basketball team shamefully lost a championship series because of envy extending far from the surface of the court. And the fans, probably the most behaved, until recently, and loyal of any, were the losers. They lost watching a star player because the poor little, 7-footer, thought only of his ungrateful self. And just in the past few days, the newspapers, TV sports shows, plus radio and TV commentators, are "shocked" at the melee between players and fans at the Detroit Pistons-Indians Pacers game. The country is aghast and dismayed with the brawl with its naked display of fear and loathing. Pro athletes, and the fans that watch them, don't like each other anymore.

"I have been on the sidelines at 49ers games for 20 years and I have witnessed the change," says critic Harry Edwards, a San Francisco 49ers consultant. "The resentment is deeply rooted and hard-wired and it has to do with money, race, and class."

Read on! Hal Holbrook/Mark Twain says, ""We're having a greedy love affair with money."

And in reference to boxing, a previous heavyweight champion went from excellence to excelling . . . . in disdainful, haughty, supercilious un-sociability.

Think back to Walter Payton, Lou Gehrig, John Wooden, Joe Lewis, and Wayne Gretzky! The absolute greatest; and gentlemen all!

I feel a sense of impropriety; the acts described totally lack conformity to what is socially acceptable in man's conduct and speech. My former strong emotions about professional sports are now being replaced with reality! I am intuitively aware of their "me first" attitude!

Hal Holbrook, who as a young actor in 1954 began developing a one-man show portraying Mark Twain onstage, calls it "Get Rich" because we're having a greedy love affair with money. "I mean," says Holbrook, "we're forgetting everything. We're just so in love with money, and everything in our society feeds into it, beginning with the television and the advertising and the commercialization of the human being. We have become a product. What a horrible conclusion to come to for a human being."

I recognize, in action, the professionals' excessive and arrogant self-confidence. The terrible injustice is that he doesn't recognize it. Someday, a wind will come along and blow him, his dollars, and his inflated ego away. And he will too stupid to know the reason why.

I have the same cognizance regarding politics; oh God! The misconduct and immorality of it all!

Please don't get me wrong; I am not preaching! I am not indulging in pompous moral reflection! I am not evangelizing! I am, however, aware, to the fullest extent, of the "me first, things are going too good" attitude that, in my opinion, is burying the moral fiber of man.

I vicariously observed a man, married, and President of the United States, deny, in all of his haughtiness, having sexual relations with a young woman who, through his "spin masters" tried to destroy along with several other women. He then compounded his egregious act by lying about it, under oath, in a court of law.

The Majority Leader of the US House of Representatives "received his second admonishment in six days" from the House ethics committee! The Majority Leader response to the complaints was that he was "mistreated" by the panel.

The oil-for-food agreement on Iraq enriched three U.S. firms along with individuals. Since the U.S. Government is looking into possible acts of fraud, I will not name names, although one name goes to the top of the class, or pardon me, I mean the United Nations.

Ex-shuttle inspector faces 166 count indictment; Federal charges say reports on Discovery's condition were falsified. The disputed inspections were scheduled in a period that includes the final flight and fatal crash of space shuttle Columbia.

Atrocities in Sudan have reached the state of genocide.

All of the above "short notes" were taken from a morning edition of a local paper. Aurelius was 'right on' in saying, "In the morning I would meet, among others, the arrogant and deceitful." That was about 1,850 years ago. About 350 years ago, Pascal said, "Human society is founded on mutual deceit; man is only disguise, falsehood, and hypocrisy, both in himself and in regard to others. He does not wish any one to tell him the truth."

Politics outweighed facing the truth in an attempt to impeach the President. "The economy is too good to make a change," so said one commentary!

Republicans beat back the effort initiated by the Democratic Leader for a call for a special counsel to investigate the House leader's conduct. The vote was decided along party lines. The Republicans were afraid to face the truth.

After 18 months of atrocities in Sudan, the international community has yet to take a single punitive action against the Sudanese government; they know over 1.2 million have been forced from their homes and more than 1000 people a day are dying. Opposition to sanctions has come from Arab countries that are sympathetic to Khartoum and from Security Council members, such as Pakistan and China, who are heavily invested in Sudan's emerging oil industry.

It's no surprise that France and Germany and Russia are dawdling, loath as they are to jeopardize lucrative oil contracts. As usual the United Nations is impotent. After all, Sudan is a member in good standing of the UN Human Rights Commission. A few months back, in fact, Sudan was reelected to the commission. Can you believe that!

The arrogance and deceit of it all! Will no one face the truth and deal with the reality that has already killed nearly 2 million?

The above information came from a synthesis, by author, of articles from *TIME*, October 4, 2004 Edition, and *FORBES*, October 18, 2004 Edition, and Boswell, in Life of Johnson, *The Great Treasury of Western Thought*.

The information regarding Mark Twain and Hal Holbrook came, in part, from *MARK TWAIN*, written by G. C. Ward, Dayton Duncan, and Ken Burns.

So, I am aware!

"So what!" and "Suitcase, you don't seem to be able to get it!" say many of my acquaintances. But I stand strong! My reading and thinking have put me in a position to recognize I am still trying to learn more about myself; I will not speak out! But I will write! What did Mill say? "Truth gains more even by the errors of one who, with *due study and preparation*, thinks for himself!"

I owe a lot to my philosopher friends! Socrates told me Will Durant called him the other day and said, "Tell Suitcase to worry not! Tell him to always remember that truth will not make him rich, but it will make him free."

One of Will Durant's great books is *The Story of Philosophy*.

WHY PHILOSOPHY

In *SOCRATES 'N SUITS*, **BOOK I & II**, I spoke of meeting Socrates, the great philosopher from Greece. I wanted him to "fly my wing" because, in my limited studying of the lives of philosophers, I needed someone to lead me in the right direction; the direction which would offer me the chance to better understand myself and my fellow man.

It's really that simple! I knew I had a lot to learn and I picked philosophy to be my intellectual coach.

I believe the chance to roam a bookstore or library with the thought in mind to carefully consider what book would contribute to, or further enhance, my study of Philosophy is an unadulterated gift. Maybe I didn't wish to study, per se, but I would buy a book just to see what more philosophy had to offer.

This is what I found out:

In addition to the lessons of history, philosophy offers a pure endowment of man's experiences that are voluntarily transferred by one person to another—without compensation. The study of philosophy extends to man the chance to learn to love and pursue wisdom.

With this study, one will probably find him or herself a tyro when it comes to pure intellectual investigation. Heck, I did! However, I prepared myself for a great deal of reading and to think through what was gifted to me in book form.

For many, many years I would get out of bed at 5am, brew a cup of hot coffee, sit down in my quiet, dark study and reflect and ponder over what eminent philosophers were trying to tell me. I knew it would take a long time to sift through the never-ending exploration in regards to a general understanding of values; and a continual search for some degree of excellence. It took ten years to write SOCRATES 'N SUITS, **Book I & II**. What I learned **about** philosophy was like the last drop of water from a canteen held to the lips of a thirst craved downed pilot in a one-man raft. As he squeezed with his shaking, bony, sun burned fingers, he kept saying, "There has to be more! There just has to be more!"

It was the same thing with me in *my* particular approach to philosophy. The longer the time of the search, there grew within me an evolved appreciation; and I couldn't let go. Just as the downed pilot couldn't let go of his canteen! In philosophy it becomes a love of the pursuit of wisdom. 'Love of Wisdom.' Beautiful words but be careful—nothing comes easy. It may be better said that philosophy is the 'search for' moral self-discipline. Tough order! And in order prepare to do that, one must read, study, think, love one self, and develop personal self-esteem. Believe me, I'm not preaching. It's just that philosophy, to me, means generating an awareness of how great life and living among your fellow man can be.

What I said in the second line about being an amateur means only my lack of education in the many disciplines of philosophy. Part of my recent studies included a book entitled THE OXFORD COMPANION TO PHILOSOPHY. It's very thick and heavy; I could use it for my bench pressing exercises at the gym. According to the author, Tom Honderich, Professor of the Philosophy of Mind and Logic at University College London, Philosophical inquiry includes, among many disciplines, EPISTEMOLOGY, the study or a theory of the nature and grounds of knowledge. It also includes METAPHYSICS that inquires into the nature and ultimate significance of the inverse. LOGIC is concerned with the laws of valid reasoning. ETHICS deals with the problems of correct conduct, and AESTHETICS attempts to determine the nature of beauty and the criteria of artistic judgment. Well, if you read SOCRATES 'N SUITS, **BOOK I**, all the guys in Manhattan Beach passed AESTHETICS with an A+. With all the stewardesses on the beach, it didn't take us long to determine the nature of beauty and the criteria of artistic judgments. We determined a minimum of a 9 ½, pretty face, scintillating smile, great bust (at least, and I mean at *least* a 36,) plus hips, rear end, and legs to complement the first three.

There goes the moral self-discipline bit!

With all kidding aside, philosophy attracted me by the challenge to pursue wisdom and the search for a general understanding of values and **reality.** I wanted to take on a mental sphere of activity that would allow me to encompass the overall value by which one lives and to try to entertain the calmness, equanimity, and detachment regarded as that befitting a philosopher.

Speaking of calmness and equanimity, I *am* seeing some progress; I am learning that my married partner has become my best friend; we get along beautifully. Most of the credit, however, belongs to her.

Also, you probably noticed above I put a bold face on the word reality. Reality is, quite simply, the quality of being factual; an actuality. In my own little philosophical thought processes I say to myself, "If man grasps the *quality* of reality, he grasps and understands the *quality* of truth. He understands the *quality* of relationships by telling the truth. And truth offers man what? It offers man freedom from deceit or falseness. If something is going on in a man's life that is factual, and only he in his own conscience can determine such, then he can't possibly tell a lie. Man can be deceitful, but then he is only lying to himself. Fools are those who try to impose their own selfish desires on reality.

It takes courage to face reality and tell the truth. The world owes much to its men and women of courage. I do not mean physical courage, in which a man is at least equaled by the bulldog. What I mean is the courage that displays itself in silent effort and endeavor—dares to endure all and suffer all for truth and duty. It is courage that is more truly heroic than the achievements of physical valor, which are rewarded by honors and titles, or by laurels steeped in blood.

I am learning from my studies of philosophy, that it is **moral** courage that characterizes the highest order of manhood and womanhood. It takes courage to seek and to speak the truth; courage to be just; courage to be honest; courage to resist temptation; and courage to do one's duty. In SOCRATES 'N SUITS, **BOOK I** & **II**, I tell of having a hell of time with 'one's duty' on my first combat mission and, later, telling the story of facing hundreds of men glaring at me with fierce, piercing eyes just after I wrecked a jet airplane in pilot training. Yes, Socrates and I had quite a discussion on reality and truth.

If men and women do not possess this virtue, they have no security whatever for the preservation of any tests of moral courage.

Truth and reality are *the* important parts of the evolution of the mind that continually pursues the search for a general understanding of values. And it is the measure of those qualities that determine a man's worth.

Socrates and his fiends speak to me about moral courage, truth and reality all the time. One evening when I was really down, just having lost three of my experimental test pilot friends, Socrates, God bless him, showed up to have dinner with me at the BANTAM COCK, a fine restaurant in the San Fernando Valley. We immediately started discussing the truth about the deficiencies of the F-104 and how it affected my life (see **BOOK II**, Chapter 9). Hell, I knew the truth about the YF-104A but no one in management wanted to hear it. I remember saying to my great friend, "OK, Socs, here comes a chicken or the egg question. Which comes first, truth or ethics? In other words, if I speak the truth am I ethical, or am I ethical because I speak the truth? And, while you are looking at me with your quizzical stare, answer this also, can you *teach* truth? Can you *teach* ethics?"

He looked at me for at least thirty seconds; stroking his beard as was his usual countenance while thinking. He then surprised me a bit by asking, "Do you have time for another glass of Merlot?"

"Sure do!" I said. "We'll just finish the bottle and order another if we have to."

After I poured each of us a glass he said, "Thanks, Suits. The taste of fine wine makes me think of woman and song but in answer to your question, I'll diverge a bit! You know me by now that my discourse moves in two directions—outward to objective definitions, and inward, to discover the inner person, the soul. I believe the soul to be the source of all truth. No, the search for truth among man cannot be conducted at a series of weekly lectures, for it is the quest of a lifetime. I ask myself a lot of questions that I am hardly ever able to answer. Nevertheless, my query has to continue—for a lifetime. You are aware of my dictum, 'The unexamined life is not worth living.' I cannot possibly give or teach my disciples the truth. Each of us must find it out for ourselves. The history of philosophy is enveloped with statements of brilliant men trying to define truth but you'll find no one wanting to specifically teach it. I am talking about Aristotle, Plato, Aquinas, Gibson, Boswell and Emerson. Even Emerson said that truth is such a flyaway, such a sly-boots, so un-transportable and un-barrelable a commodity that it is as difficult to catch as light.

Who can teach that?

John Locke, in addition to gaining fame with his essay *CONCERNING HUMAN UNDERSTANDING* wrote *A LETTER CONCERNING TOLERATION* in which he said, "The truth certainly would do well enough to shift for herself. She seldom has received and, I fear, never will receive much assistance from the power of great men, to whom she is but rarely known and more rarely welcome. She is not taught by laws, nor has she any need of force to procure her entrance into the minds of men."

"So, no!" my friend Socrates said. "I think truth is too fleeting to teach. Have I answered your question?"

Socs savored sip of his Merlot.

"Of course it does. Thank you." I said. "Now the next question: Can ethics be taught? I have a friend of mine working for an aerospace company and one of the mid-management executives got caught in a payoff scandal. The president of the company is now making all executives attend a class on learning ethics. I think he is going down the wrong road. I don't think you can teach ethics or, as it is said, 'More formally known as moral philosophy'!"

"I agree! I don't think ethics as it stands alone can be taught. But let's ask this question. What is ethics?"

"Well, Socs, as you have made me aware, ethics is the discipline dealing with what is *good* or *bad* and with *moral* duty and obligation."

"You're right! And I remember the night we were having dinner—oh! someplace—you said the church was shoving the TEN COMMANDMENTS down your throat and you were extremely angry because the nun said, "God gave them to us, so follow them.' You were young then. What did the TEN COMMANDMENTS tell you?"

"Told me not to miss church on Sunday, not to steal, not to kill, don't take another man's wife, honor my mother and dad, not to—"

"So you knew what was *good* or *bad*. Can you *teach* good or bad?

"No Socs, I don't think so. I can *learn* by knowledge about. I know by *common sense*; I *learn* what happens to others when they kill or steal. I know you can make people aware of duty and obligation. But, *morality* among men! It is up to the individual! I don't think you can *teach* "good"! And in all practicality I don't think it 'bad' to miss church on Sunday."

"Suitcase, you answered your own question. Now are we going to get another bottle of Merlot or not?'

(I am lucky! I have an assiduous critic; a man characterized by his careful and exact evaluation of **BOOK III**. He said, in using the words underlined above, "There is insufficient evidence to support my premise. You fail to define "good" or "bad". Or, "Where does common sense come from?" We were at lunch. After I called to the waiter and said, "Separate checks!" we got into a heated, but edifying, discussion. Please see the last page as to the results."

Gee! I sure do miss Socrates; the old fart! But he'll show up one of these days. Enough of that discourse!

EPOSTOMOLOGY, METAPHYSICS, ETHICS and LOGIC makes for extremely interesting study, but individually, these particular disciplines do not interest me. In studying philosophy, with practical learning experiences from Socrates as detailed in **BOOK I** and **BOOK II**, I was more interested in learning about self-knowledge and self-love. Also, an offer of the general recommendations for the conduct of life! That would entail honor, friendship, fear, characteristics and conditions of human nature and knowledge, morality, truth, courage, values and happiness.

BOOK III continues my learning. Socrates and I meet more of Socrates' friends. They speak of free enterprise—trade, commerce, and industry. I meet Adam Smith, Karl Marx, and J.S. Mill; others contribute ethical, political, or historical comments.

According to my *OXFORD COMPANION*, Honderich says, "Philosophy, the search for wisdom, brings together, first of all, the work of the great philosophers. As that term is commonly used, there are perhaps twenty of them. By anyone's reckoning, this pantheon of philosophers includes Plato, Aristotle, Aquinas, Hobbes, Spinoza, Leibniz, Locke, Berkeley, Hume, Kant, Hegel, and Nietzsche."

But I say, "Where the hell is my pal Socrates, or 'Socs' as I called him?" I was ready to jump all over Honderich but then I remembered what he added. "Socrates, teacher of Plato, is one of the most significant yet enigmatic figures in the history of philosophy; significant because his relation to Plato was crucial to the development of the latter, and thus indirectly in the development of much later philosophy. Socrates was enigmatic because he wrote nothing himself, and therefore presents the challenge of restructuring him from the evidence of others."

I discussed how we learned **of** Socrates in *CLEARING UP MATTERS* as pertaining to **BOOK I & BOOK II** of the TRILOGY. I quoted Daniel Boorstin in his brilliant book *THE SEEKERS* who said, "Socrates brought the search for the meaning of philosophy down from heaven to earth," I also said, "I would have been a fool not to take advantage of that".

We learned through Xenophon, and in three of Plato's works; the *APOLOGY*, an idealized version of his defense at his trial. Crito, gives Socrates' reasons for refusing to take the opportunity to escape. And *PHAEDO*, a moving re-creation of his final hours, containing first a Platonic treatise on the philosophy of life, death, and immortality and then a description of the ideal philosophic death.

In one of his thirteen books on philosophy, *THE EXAMINED LIFE*, Borden Parker Browne, Professor of Philosophy at Boston University, states, and I quote, "Plato and Xenophon affirm that Socrates turned away from the natural science that engaged him in his youth. He brought philosophy down from his contemplation of the heavens, caused it to enter into the cities and houses of men, and made it concern itself with human beings."

Browne and Boorstin are on the same path.

THE EXAMINED LIFE has 35 excerpts form the philosophers who shaped Western thought. Augustine, Machiavelli, Locke, Rosseau, and Dewey, among others, discuss thought, culture, beauty, capacity of man, wisdom, and need for open-mindedness. I mean, how more fortunate can we get to be able to use these great minds to learn to be better persons. You pick up a book and start thinking about what you can do to know yourself better, learn to be more open-minded and enjoy a better world that you will, subliminally, be contributing to.

I have read *CRITO*, *PHAEDO*, and the *APOLOGY*. And, in addition a best selling novel entitled, *THE TRIAL of SOCTATES*. Here's a guy, well respected, who was, in practice, a loyal citizen, served with distinction on the battlefield (Peloponnesian War,) and adhering strictly to his ideals of legality and justice. Once under the democracy he was alone in opposing an unconstitutional proposal. And once under the tyrannical regime that briefly ousted the democracy at the end of the war, he refused an order to participate in the arrest, and subsequent death, of an innocent man.

None the less, his association with notorious anti-democrats, led to his accusation on vague charges of impiety and corruption of the young, and to his condemnation to death.

Socrates is my kind of man; a man of character, truth, moral strength, honesty, dignity, and integrity. And he taught me about the influence of reading books! "It builds character while learning," he said.

Socrates told me man is usually known by the books he reads, as well as the company he keeps. He said, "There is a companionship of books as well as of men; and one should live in the best company, whether it be of book or of men."

"Companionship of books as well as men!" Socrates continued. "Keep the two in mind; temper those words. Although genius always commands admiration, character most secures respect. The former is the product of brainpower, the latter of heart-power: and in the long run it is the heart that rules in life. Men of genius stand to society in the relation of its intellect, as men of character of its conscience; and while the former are admired, the latter are followed."

You know! Socrates is right! A good book can be among the best of friends. The way Socrates talked, it is the same today as it was way back in his time—almost 500 years before Christ. So it will probably never change. I find a book the most patient and cheerful of companions. It does not turn its back upon me in times of adversity or distress. It always receives me with the same kindness; it is always ready to speak to me; fill me full of information. And I control the conversation! It's not like being married. I guess you heard the one about the judge who said, "I understand that you and yours wife had some words."

The defendant said, "I had some but I didn't get a chance to use them."

Ah marriage! The cooing stops with the honeymoon; the billing goes on forever!

Socrates also said, "Men often discover their affinity to each other by the mutual love they have for a book—just as fighter pilots bond by the mutual admiration of what they accomplished."

"Suits," he said to me, "The book is a truer and higher bond of union. Men can think, feel, and sympathize with each other through their favorite author."

Socrates also suggested that books possess an essence of immortality. They are by far the most lasting products of human effort. Temples crumble into ruin! Pictures and statues decay! But books survive! Time is of no account with great thoughts, which are as fresh today as when they first passed through their authors' minds, ages ago. What was then said and thought, still speaks to us as vividly as ever from the printed page. The only effect of time has to sift and winnow out the bad products; for nothing in literature can lone survive but what is really good.

The great and good do not die, even in this world. Embalmed in books, their spirits walk broad. The book is a living voice. It is an intellect to which one still pays attention. Hence we will ever remain under the influence of the great men of old. You're under the influence Suits, of Plato, Aristotle, Epictetus, Aurelius, Gibbon, Darwin, Tolstoy, etc. You mention their names in your studies. They become your silent partners in war, flying, business, friendships and love.

The imperial intellects of the world are as much alive now as they were ages ago. Homer still lives; and though his personal history is hidden in the mists of antiquity, his poems are as fresh today as if they had been newly written. Plato still teaches his transcendent philosophy; Horace, Virgil, and Dante still sing as when they lived; Shakespeare is not dead: his body was buried in 1616 but his mind is a much alive in England now and his thoughts as far-reaching, as in the time of the Tudors."

I hope, now, those who read "WHY PHILOSOPHY" are content with my answer!

My mentor told me of insufficient evidence to support my premise (middle of page 4) regarding the following:

> You fail to define "good" or "bad".
> What is moral?
> On what basis do we judge "good" or "bad"?
> Where does "common sense" come from?
> How does one obtain 'common sense"? What is it?
> You mention the TEN COMMANDMENTS! Why were they handed down?

Well, I don't agree, or disagree, with my mentor. But my **BOOK III** is not a printed and bound work about the tenets of philosophy. It reviews, sometime in great detail, my experiences as a marketing and sales executive, in teaching, from lessons of history, my learning process about philosophy, free enterprise, study, and the rewards of thought.

I did the examination! I opened my mind, like a parachute, to exposure! I participated in or partook of personally as much information as possible to learn to be a better man. And I appreciated, in depth, what I learned from a great number of philosophers including the American born, Ralph Waldo Emerson, (1803-1882), Boston, Mass., who said, "In every man there is something I may learn of him, and in that, I am his pupil.

I know what "good" or "bad" is. My life is based on the fact that I know the difference. It is due to being exposed plus "been there", "done that". It is my responsibility to know and act accordingly.

I know "common sense" is the unreflective opinions of ordinary men like me. I know it is *sound* and *prudent* but often unsophisticated judgment. That is all I have to know! I know from the experiences of doing, in a particular discipline, whether a man or woman is making "common sense". If *I* think good, that's good. If not, I have the ability to determine "if there is something I may learn of him," If there is something I *may* learn, I'll stick around. If not, I'll leave.

Moral, in my writing on page on page 4, is, to me, relates to principles of right or wrong in behavior. *I* make those judgments and accept the responsibility of my ability to make sensible decisions in these matters.

The TEN COMMANDMENTS, according to the Bible, is the summary of divine law given by God to Moses on Mt. Sinai. They have a paramount place in the ethical system in Judaism, Christianity, and Islam.

Most Christians know, or can recite, what the COMMANDMENTS teach. If one believes, good for him. If not, it's his business. I act according to my beliefs. I don't kill, or steal, or commit adultery, and I loved my great, warm, loving father and mother. The TEN COMMANDMENTS didn't tell me to do what is mentioned above. They COMMAND by fear. I am not surrounded by fear. I am surrounded by love—of myself, and by that I have learned to love others.

HISTORY & PHILOSOPHY

Ah! What Rare, Pure, And
Exemplary Gifts To Man

I was going through some notes the other day; I wrote them the night Socrates and I had, what I consider, a great brainstorming session about the importance of history. We had been skiing at Big Bear Lake most of the afternoon. Remember! That was the day I met, by chance, Marilyn Chambers, the queen of porn starting with her first picture, *BEHIND THE GREEN DOOR*. I say "by chance" because when I ended one fast run, I whizzed right into the open line yelling "single" and the lift attendant guided me into the slot next to a beautiful ash blonde with a smile that could brighten the Grand Canyon at midnight.

It was Marilyn and, as I found out, the current, and soon to be the former, model for the liquid Ivory Soap ad on PROCTOR & GAMBLE bottles. We got along great! I told her I had never kissed a girl that was 99 & 44/100% pure. In fact, I told Marilyn that French kissing her would be like bathing my tongue in holy water!

We laughed—a lot!

Marilyn told me about the changing of her careers. When I asked her how would I know about the movie and when would I see it, she flashed that smile that could melt the snow we were about to disembark on and said, "Don't worry my new found friend. You'll know! You'll know."

Marilyn was right. I was in Philadelphia visiting fiends about two months later and they took me to see it. Very different! New! Exciting! Avant-garde! Triple-X rated, and certainly an intelligentsia that developed a new concept in the arts for me. Did I think much of the new arts? Naw! I only saw the movie about ten times.

Let's see! Where was I? Oh! Yes! My notes!

"War," said Socrates is basically armed conflict between states or nations (international war) or between factions within a state (civil war), prosecuted by force and having the purpose of compelling the defeated side to do the will of the victor. Sometimes the victor will order persecution, imprisonment, or death. In your Civil War, General Grant told General Lee at Appomattox Courthouse to take his men and go home.

"—I, Grant, wished to express it clearly, so that there would be no mistaking it. As I wrote on, the thought occurred to me that the officers and soldiers (of Lee's army; parenthesis by author), had their own private horses and effects, which were important to them, but of no value to us; also that it would be an unnecessary humiliation to call upon them to deliver their side arms."

"—The whole country had been so raided by the two armies (most of the men in the ranks were small farmers) that it was doubtful whether they would be able to put in a crop to carry themselves and their families through the next winter without the aid of their horses they were then riding."

The above quotes extracted from *Personal Memoirs*,
by Ulysses S. Grant,
THE MODERN LIBRARY, NEW YORK, 1999.

Socrates continued. He told me he thought history, in its broadest sense, is the story of humanity's past. "It also refers to the recording of the past," he said. "The sources of history include books, newspapers, printed documents, personal papers, (like the personal papers of your Presidents) that are much in demand. I think we could also count on other archival records, artifacts, and oral accounts. And speaking of oral accounts, I saw a book in your library not too long ago entitled, *LEND ME YOUR EARS*; GREAT SPEECHES IN HISTORY. The speeches were selected by William Saffire, considered by many to be the most political columnist in America. If I remember correctly, some of the speeches were: "Lenin Defends Proletarian Dictatorship," "Mussolini Justifies His Invasion of Ethiopia," "Hitler Declares Germany's Intentions," and I, your friend Socrates, "Condemned to Death, Addressed My Judges."

"You are right, Socs, but also included in *GREAT SPEECHES* is Khrushchev tearing down Stalin, Nixon rallying 'the Silent Majority' to the 'San Francisco Democrats.' Socs, I understand the historical aspects, but I couldn't see anything friendly or respectful about people 'tearing down' or 'blasting' people. Also, I didn't appreciate Nixon pumping sunshine up peoples' rear ends about death and debacle in Vietnam. I personally don't think there is anything positive to be learned about the lessons of history here."

I continued. "Don't get me wrong, my friend. We have discussed history as the recording of man's past, and I fully understand guile or deceit but I can't buy those as being the *GREAT SPEECHES IN HISTORY*.

Yes, Socs, I enjoyed reading most, but not *all* of the passages. Why? Because in the back of my mind I would be thinking, vicariously, 'Am I standing here listening to someone delivering actual birth to truth? Or was the discourse written by a speechwriter or even another specialist in oral communication affiliated with a particular crusade; generated to persuade patronage for notoriety, hostility, votes, or selfish self-aggrandizement?'"

"Well, Suits, I can't argue with your thinking. Plato, in his *REPUBLIC, II*, quoted me in saying, 'Because we do not know the truth about ancient times, we make falsehood as much like truth as we can, and so turn into account. Plato said that about 400 years before Christ. And Suits, ancient time (meaning the 400 years as an example) is upon us; nothing has changed. The fiction, the canards, the falsehoods, and the misrepresentations by politicians today, particularly in today's time when seven or more men and women are looking for most votes or delegates to represent a particular political party, is disturbing and agitating.'"

"You're right on, Socs. I thought many of the speeches were rhetoric and sheer sophistry! All the reasoning is fallacy because it's directed on a personal basis and not all on historical fact. People can do to speeches the same as CPA's can do to balance sheets or profit and loss statements. They manipulate the numbers to their own, and managements' liking."

I reached the point I was struggling hard to make. "But enough of that! Tell me more, Socs, about your thoughts on history and what can I do to absorb it?"

"OK I'll try but I can't give you an exact answer, but I *can* tell you some quotations from philosophers and others who have thought about the **character** of history as an intellectual discipline and as a distinct branch of human knowledge.

Let me start with early history. It included quotations from eminent historians—oh! let me think—men like Herodotus and Thucydides, Plutarch, and Tacitus, Hume, Gibbon and Toynbee.

These brilliant men reflected about the art of writing history and about the task of the historian as a reporter and interpreter of the past. But let me back up a bit and talk a little about these eminent, distinguished men. I have my reasons!

As an example, Herodotus, 484-425 B.C., a Greek historian, is called the Father of History. I won't go into a lot of details about his travelling the coast of Asia Minor to the northern islands and to the shore of the Black Sea; but he also spent time learning and writing during his visits to Mesopotamia, Babylon and Egypt. By 447 B.C. he was in Athens, and in 443 he seems to have helped found the Athenian colony of Thurii in S Italy, where he probably spent the rest of his life completing his history. That classic work, the first comprehensive attempt at **secular** narrative history, is the starting point of Western historical writing. Herodotus was the first writer to evaluate historical, geographical, and archaeological material critically.

The focus of his history is the story of the PERSIAN WARS, (500 B.C.-449 B.C.,) a series of conflicts fought between Greek states and the Persian Empire but the extensive and richly detailed background information put Greece in its historical perspective. He discusses the growth of Persia into a great kingdom and traces the history and migration of the Greek people. Among his grand digressions are fascinating histories of Babylon, Egypt, and Thrace (SE Europe, occupying the southeastern tip of the Balkan Peninsula and comprising NE Greece S. Bulgaria, and European Turkey.) He also studied details of the pyramids and specific historical events. The value of his work lies not only in its **accuracy**, but in its scope and the rich diversity of information."

"Do you want to say something, Suits?"

"Yes, I do, Socs. When you were discussing the value of Herodotus' work owing to his accuracy, but also his scope and rich diversity of information, a U.S. contemporary (he died in 1986) was Theodore H. White and his series of books *The Making of the President*. He covered the presidential campaigns in an astute, dramatic reportorial style, and in 1962 he won the Pulitzer Prize for general nonfiction. Seems he and Herodotus had something in common; accuracy and rich diversity of information. Boy! That kind of reporting is refreshing to me!"

"Also, Socs, if I may continue—"

"Please do!"

"OK! How about Stephen Ambrose from *UNDAUNTED COURAGE;* Thomas Jefferson, Meriwether Lewis, and William Clark about the opening of the American West. He was also, I thought, a great author about conflicts of war—*CRAZY HORSE and CUSTER*, and *D-DAY*, June 6, 1944, the Climatic Battle of World War II. Ambrose also wrote, later, a TV series, BAND of BROTHERS: E Company, 506th Regiment, 101st Airborne from Normandy to Hitler's Eagle's Nest. So Herodotus writes about the Persian Way and Ambrose writes about WW II.

God! Socs. History presents particularly excellent study but *THE LESSONS of HISTORY,* in far too many cases, seems to be inexplicably ignored. Anyhow, thank you for letting me interrupt."

"Well, Suits, you are right about the lessons of history. In too many cases they *are* ignored. In examinations of the chronological records of past events, and we'll use as an example, war, egocentricity of command leads to serious blunders. In 216 B.C. Hannibal handed the Romans a crushing defeat at Cannae, Apulia, SE Italy. Hannibal's troops assumed a crescent-shaped formation to meet the Roman troops, which were especially concentrated in the center; the Roman commander had won battles by his center concentrations in the past and refused to adopt to the situation by having his troops move to meet the crescent shape. As the Romans advanced, Hannibal, by brilliant strategy, managed to encircle he entire Roman force and cut it to pieces.

The battle of Tannenberg, ((NE Poland, WWI) is a central event in Aleksandr Solzhenitsy's novel *August 1914* (1972). Russian armies under generals Sammsonov and Rennenkampf had invaded East Prussia from the south and east, respectively. German strategy was to fall back in crescent shaped front and at the proper time "managed to encircle Samsonov's forces"; 90,000 Russian prisoners were taken and Samsonov committed suicide. The German strategist said he had learned from history the story of Hannibal at Cannae.

Kursk, is the capital of the Kursk region, W European Russia! Near Kursk during WWII, in 1943, the Germans and Russians fought the greatest mechanized battle in the history of war. The Germans attacked with overwhelming forces of tanks and mechanized guns. The Russians fell back until, with superior communication, strategy and tactics, moved laterally at the proper time and angle encircling the Germans and forcing irreparable damage. And so began the Russian advance on the Eastern front!

And speaking of Germans, and Russians, and France and ego, Napoleon's decision to invade Russia marked the turning point of his career. Napoleon gathered the largest army Europe had ever seen. The *Grande Armee*, some 500,000 strong, including troops of all the vassal states and allied states, entered Russia in June, 1812.

. . . . with his troops decimated, his prospective winter quarters burned down, his supply line overextended, and the Russian countryside and grain stores empty, Napoleon began his fateful retreat on October 19th. Stalked by hunger, the *Grand Armee* was not 1/5 of it's original strength; a loss of 400,000 men. Just think! 400,000 men!

Hitler's invasion of Poland had begun WWII; June 22, 1941. In December, 1941, he assumed personal command of war strategy. In his plan to attack Russia, history has shown his unthinking boldness and haste. He had to beat the Russian winter. A poor defense strategist, he refused to admit defeat after the battle of Stalingrad (now VOLGOGRAD) and in pursuing the war, although his supply lines, like Napoleon, were overextended, brought death to vast numbers of German troops. He learned nothing from history and Napoleon's defeat and as the tide of war turned against him, Hitler's mass extermination of Jews was accelerated, giving increasing power to Himmler, and the dread SECRET POLICE, the Gestapo and SS (Schutzstaffeel).

Hitler's legacy is the memory of the most dreadful tyranny of modern times!"

"Well, Suits, pardon my stretch, but it is getting late and as much as I love to "brainstorm" with you, I have to get back to my friends. No! No! don't worry! We'll be together again. In the interlude, I think you are intuitively aware of war and the lessons learned from history. I see you are "aware" because you are reading General Grant's *Personal Memoirs*. The introduction by Caleb Carr is very interesting, is it not? Fits in exactly what we are talking about. Not only were you in two wars yourself but your continuing research by reading the variety of topics in this venture of learning will be of constant topic for thought and learning. Go ahead! Introduce your readers to Carr's *INTRODUCTION TO THE MODERN LIBRARY WAR SERIES*. He is, after all, the series editor."

Stick with Cicero, and Plutarch, and Titus, and Livy. They are marked by sharp forceful activity and are very knowledgeable. And they will guide you as I. Heck! Jack, look behind you. I see in your bookshelves at least 100 books in your personal library with the titles *GREAT BOOKS & HARVARD CLASSICS*. In addition you have a treasure in your 1771 page *GREAT TREASURY of WESTERN THOUGHT*. You don't need me other than to deepen your thoughts about the big difference between "knowledge of" and knowledge about". Remember the discussion we had in Korea when you messed up on your first mission. I think that exchanging of your views at the time vs. mine, plus Captain Coffin's experienced input kept you alive during the rest of your 60 close air support missions. Talk about war and the lessons of history. Our conversations were the genesis, or initiation, of what is known today as **TOP GUN & RED FLAG**."

"You know, Socs, you don't know how right you are. I am a lucky man to have met you. Caleb Carr's introduction made a significant impression on me in that maybe I'm not so square after all, not that in mattered. And in reading bits and pieces of Plutarch I learned he was not so much interested in histories, but lives. I have been saying all along I was not interested so much in the discipline of philosophy comprising as its core logic, aesthetics, ethics, metaphysics and epistemology, but of the lives of the men who brought forth those subjects as a nexus for me to learn about *them*."

"Good thinking! Shake my hand and give me a hug my great friend. And I'll send you a couple of more thoughts about the importance of history in the words of my great friends. And wipe that frown off your safe. You will receive the info. Peace and love."

And with that, Socs was gone!

Well, what am I going to do? First, Socs did mention my reading of Caleb Carr's introduction to General Grant's *Personal Memoirs* and he thought I should pass it on to the readers of **BOOK III**. So, here goes:

The term "military history" has always been a bit of a problem for me explains Carr as it has, I suspect, for many other students of the discipline. The uninitiated seem to have a prejudicial belief that those who study war are an exceedingly odd lot: men who at best have never outgrown boyhood and at worst are somewhat alienated, perhaps even dangerous, characters. Of course, much of this general attitude was formed during the sixties and early seventies (my own high school and college years), when an interest in the details of human conflict was one of the most socially ostracizing qualities a person could have. The tarnish has never quite disappeared: In our own day the popular belief that military historians are somehow, well, *off*, endures in many circles.

By way of counterargument let me claim that enthusiasts of military history are often among the most committed and well-read people one might hope to encounter. Rarely does an important work of history go out of print; and those who know war well can usually hold their own in discussions of political and social history as well. The reason for this is simple: The history of war represents fully half the tale of mankind's social interactions, and one cannot understand war without understanding its political and social underpinnings. (Conversely, one cannot understand political history or cultural development without understanding war.) Add to this fact that military history very often involves tales of high adventure—peopled by extreme and fascinating characters and told by some of the best writers ever to take up a pen—and you have the actual secret of why the subject has remained so popular over the ages.

The new Modern Library War Series . . . . illuminates so many aspects of a particular people's experience and character. Francis Parkman's *Montcalm and Wolfe*, for example, not only shows how very much about the psychology of pre-Revolutionary leaders one must understand in order to grasp the conflict known in North America as the French and Indian War, but is also the work of one of the great American prose stylists of the nineteenth century. Ulysses S. Grant's *Personal Memories* (which owe more than a little to the editorial efforts of one of Grant's champions, Mark Twain) contrast the remarkable humility of their author with the overwhelmingly dramatic circumstances into which Fate flung him, and that he struggles so hard—in the end, successfully—to master. Theodore Roosevelt's *The Naval War of 1812,* too long neglected, was the first work to reveal the prodigious intellect, irrepressible character, and remarkably entertaining style of this future president consistently made a good part of his income through writing. And finally, we have *A Soldier's Story,* the memoirs of Omar Bradley, "the G.I. General," who, surrounded by a sea of prima donnas during World War II, never stopped quietly learning his trade, until he became, during the conquest of Germany in 1945, arguably the most progressive and important American commander in the European theater.

To read any or all of these books is to see that military history is neither an obscure nor a peculiar subject, but one critical to any understanding of the development of human understanding. That warfare itself is violent is true and unfortunate; it has been a central method through which every nation in the world has established and maintained its independence, however, makes it a critical field of study. The fact that the personalities and stories involved in war are often so compelling is simply a bonus—but it is the kind of bonus that few academic disciplines can boast.

While I was studying and copying Mr. Carr's discourse on "military history" for the reader, Socrates kept his word and forwarded to me, by e-mail, the following cerebration of some of the minds of great philosophers.

They are as follows:

"To remain ignorant of things that happened before you were born is to represent and remain a child. What is a human life worth unless it is incorporated into the lives of one's ancestors and set in an historical context?"

Cicero, *Orator, XXXIV* (106BC-43BC)

Marcus Tullius Cicero, greatest Roman orator, famous also as a politician and a philosopher. He studied law and philosophy at Rome, Athens, and Rhodes.

"The study of history is the best medicine for a sick mind. In history you have a record of the infinite variety of human experience plainly set out for all to see. And in that record you can find for yourself and your country both examples and warnings; fine things to take as models, and, base things, rotten through and through, to avoid.

Livy, *Early History of Rome*, I, 1 (60 BC-17AD)

Titus Livius Ivy, Roman historian. The breadth of his education is apparent in his evident familiarity with the ancient Greek and Latin authors.

"It was for the sake of others that I first commenced writing biographies; but I find myself proceeding and attaching myself to them for my own; the virtues of these great men serving me as a sort of looking-glass, in which I may see how to adjust and adorn my own life.

Plutarch, *Timoleon* (46-120AD)

Greek essayist and biographer, Plutarch lectured in philosophy in Rome and Athens. His great work is *The Parallel Lives* comprising 46 surviving biographies arranged in pairs. (One Greek life with one comparable to Roman.) ## see below

In the next few days, or weeks, some of you will start reading my **BOOK III** of the trilogy. It is a discourse involving Socrates and what he and I think is synergy between philosophy, the thoughts and experiences of a test pilot turned businessman, the *lessons* of history, and free enterprise. It addresses the subjects with pure certainty for me, but in the past I received many (vocal and written) adverse responses to my selection of Socrates as my mentor in writing *SOCRATES 'N SUITS*, **BOOK I & II**. The books detail my experiences in aerial combat, test flying in the USAF and as an experimental test pilot for Lockheed.

They all said, and I am synthesizing:

"Great book(s);"

"Hell, I'm right there in the cockpit with you;"

"Can't believe you lived through so much in combat, and crash landings, and ejecting from your crippled experimental fighter when the tail came off."

But, they also said, "You're a hell of a writer but forget the Socrates bit;' Suitcase, you have a talent for writing but why all the philosophy sophistry?"

Why?

Well, first Socrates was my man of the hour; my hour! In studying his life I discovered, in Socrates, a "shit-kicker" just like me. He was as man of Athens, a man of Greece, and a man of the World.

Also, I wrote the books as a challenge because I said to myself, "I am going to do it." It took me ten plus years but what kind of a man would I be if one of my friends asked one day, "Hey Suitcase, how's the book(s) coming?"

And my answer could have been, "Oh! It got a little tough with my business and travels, and all that studying, and reviewing history, and all the books, and libraries, and writing, and re-writing four or five or ten times; hell, I decided to give up on it."

If that is what you think that could have happened, well—you just don't know me. For those who read **Book I** remember, in 1945 I fell to my knees in the hot Mississippi sun crying when they told me I was no longer an Aviation Cadet, and "welcome to the infantry." Well, when I regained my composure I looked up at those three guys (in the Blessed Trinity) and said, "Is this the way you treat someone when he asks for a favor? All I wanted to do was fight for my country. OK! Go ahead, God, or the Son, or the Holy Ghost or maybe the Three of you, keep shooting your best shot, but you will NEVER, NEVER again get me down or get me to give up. Nor will I ask a favor. Yes, if I can help someone that is praying to you, I will. But *I* will never ask again!

I think I scared them so much, five years later they started the Korean War just so I could learn to fly as a fighter pilot. I earned my fighter pilot wings in September of 1952 followed by ten weeks of gunnery, and then went directly to K-13, Suwon,

Korea, 8th Fighter Bomber Wing, 35th Fighter Bomber Squadron. In February 1953, my commanding officer called for me to report to him. "Lt. Simpson reporting as ordered, Sir," I said as I saluted.

"At ease, Lt.," he said as he was shuffling a number of slips of paper. Finally he handed me one of the slips and said, "The number on that paper is 52-4401; it's a pristine F-86F. That is your fighter. Go out to the flight line and say hello."

I was stunned! I notice he said "fighter"! I said, "Yes Sir! Thank you, Sir!" I saluted, did an amazingly quick "about face" and floated to the fight line. The time was 4 months shy of eight years when I fell to my knees crying in the sands of Biloxi, Mississippi, but I had my fighter. I named it *Suitcase's Appleknocker.*

NEVER! NEVER! Give up!

Socrates would still be the one in which I would learn so much but we would have never talked about flying nor would I have had the chance to teach him a dirty fighter pilot song and pin his Command Pilot wings on his proud chest. Notice the cover of **BOOK I**!

Will Durant, in his book, *The Story of Philosophy,* says there is a pleasure in philosophy, and a lure even in the mirages of metaphysics (a division of philosophy that is concerned with the fundamental nature of reality and being), which every student feels until the course necessities of physical existence drag him from the heights of thought into the mart of economic strife and gain. Most of us have known some golden days in June of life when philosophy was in fact what Plato calls it, "that clear delight"; when the love of a modestly elusive Truth seemed more glorious, incomparably, than the lust for the ways of the flesh and the dross of the world.

Philosophy, to me means the pursuit and love of wisdom. I want to avoid the thought, that Durant touches on, "That so much of our lives is meaningless, a self-canceling vacillation and futility; we strive with the chaos about us and within; but we would believe all the while that there is something vital and significant in us, but we could decipher our own souls."

Philosophy tells me there *is* something vital and significant in me, and philosophy helps me decipher my own soul. It teaches me to know myself and love myself. I can't learn to love anyone else until I learn to love myself. Schopenhauer, (1788-1860) said, in *Further Psychological Observations*, "Why is it that, in spite of all the mirrors in the world, no one really knows what he looks like?" In my opinion, no one knows what he looks like because they do not take the time to learn. Plus, it's surprising to learn that once the step is taken, there begins an overwhelming flow of self-confidence and awareness of beauty from within. "Seek ye first the good things of the mind," Bacon admonishes us, "and the rest will either be supplied or its loss will not be felt."

I find philosophy a great way to spend my free time searching—searching—for something that will give me the opportunity to learn more about others and myself! Just think for a second! After I goofed badly on my first mission Socrates explained to me the difference between "knowledge of" and "knowledge about". He said, "Suitcase tell me about Paris, France."

"Well," I said, "you have already told me Paris is in France. I know the famous Eiffel Tower is there and the Seine River runs through it; not the Eiffel Tower, but Paris."

"You always were a wise guy."

"Who me?"

"Yes, you! Please continue!"

"OK! On the right bank of the Seine is the ARC DE TRIOMPHE, the LOUVRE, and the BASTILLE. The left bank houses the CARBONNE and the FRENCH ACADEMY. And oh yes! Paris has the famous Follies Brassiere!"

"Suitcase! For gosh sake! A brassiere is a woman's close-fitting undergarment with cups for breast support. In the *FOLLIES BERGERE*' ladies do not need support. If you'll excuse the expression, they 'let 'em all hang out.' I can tell by that expression on your face you said that on purpose. But enough of your foolishness!

I must say, however, your knowledge of Paris is pretty good for an APPLEKNOCKER. Now tell me, how you would get from the Eiffel Tower to the French Academy."

"Hell, Socs, I wouldn't have any idea."

"That's my point, Suits. You may know *of* Paris, but you don't know anything *about* it."

"Suits, after all of your training and gunnery school and getting to know your new friend (I see you named her *APPLEKNOCKER*) you definitely have knowledge **of** flying a fighter and combat but you don't know anything **about** the enemy, or flying a fighter in war, or how good, or bad, you can be. You have new circumstances in which you will have to learn about yourself and your fighter, about how the enemy thinks and acts, what is expected about a potential leader, how to fly a successful mission, how to get home with one or two of your wingman in trouble, how you plan, how you listen, how you are tuned to what the briefing officers tell you about the tactics of the enemy depending on the mission profile, etc., etc. You learn "about" by listening, doing, getting in there and taking the fight to the enemy, not by "hell bent for leather" but by outwitting and out thinking him. It is impossible to do such with a crowded mind full of scare and worry. An 'A' student enters a test with a clear, confident mind. Learn to fly your missions the same way. You are in a deadly game, Mr. Suitcase; learn about flying to live and win."

I just sat at my desk—for a long time—just thinking about many things but mostly about my luck in my life—in war—in test flying—in meeting Socrates. I was thinking about how much better our lives would be if we could devoid ourselves of so much unhappiness and misery if we learned more about "knowledge about"? Would you be better off in business, sports, friendships? How about marriage! Fifty percent of married couples divorce after seven and a half to eight years. That is because they married without knowing about each other. Marriage is, at best, a struggle—disparate thinking, money, family interference, live in in-laws, a troubled child. We marry without any tests, nor, unlike in combat, we are not drilled in how to keep the marriage alive by constant, intelligent, first hand briefings, by those who have "been there!" What is needed is a marriage counselor version of **TOP GUN** (see below). Marriages last for those who learn to give and take. Fighter pilots live because wingmen learn to protect and give their lives if needed. Married couples do not think like fighter pilots. They can't! They haven't been trained to think as a whole for protection of the marriage and family. How do you do that? I don't know and I don't think marriage counselors can do much either. None of them think the same. And priests and ministers don't have the experience. They haven't "been there" "done that". "Been there" "done that", with proper, experienced training, is how the transition is made from "knowledge of" to "knowledge about".

The Air Force and Navy learned how to do a better job. They now have **RED FLAG and TOP GUN!** They collected experiences from air combat from WWI, WWII, Korea, and Vietnam. And then they had proven fighter pilot **experts** digest the material and come up with a pattern of thought on how to keep new pilots alive instead of losing them during their first five missions. Mormons have a very low divorce rate. Why? Because they are like fighter pilots! They all come from the same school—with experience in protection and constant learning on how to "fine tune" the information gained from "knowledge about". The territorial divisions of the Mormon settlements are wards and stakes. Each ward has a bishop and two counselors; five to ten wards compose a stake. Significant characteristics of the Mormon creed include the emphasis on revelation in the establishment of doctrines and rituals, the interdependence on temporal and spiritual life, tithing, and attention to community welfare. Mormons believe in "celestial marriage," whereby individuals marry for all eternity.

There is a definite synergy between the school of thought in **TOP Gun** and Mormon Bishops! It's combined action; it's working together for a single purpose—pilots to fly again and kill; married couples to love again and procreate!

I wrote the above two paragraphs—oh! I don't know—months ago. Just the other day, on June 22, in *Life*, SECTION D of *USA TODAY*, there was a front-page article entitled, *Hearts divide over marital therapy*. It states, "New registry evaluates counselors' 'values'". The article goes on to say:

"Couples who are trying to patch up a troubled union often turn to counseling as a last-ditch effort to keep the marriage intact. That's what marital therapy is all about, right?

Not necessarily.

Most couples probably don't know there is a long-standing debate among practitioners over whether therapists should actually try to save a marriage or whether they should remain neutral or treat the couple as two individuals for whom divorce possibly could be the best outcome."

Can you imagine a **TOP GUN** instructor or a Mormon Bishop being neutral? What the hell can you learn from that? And you don't treat a flight of fighter pilots as "two individuals". You can't! They depend too much on each other. Married couple should be taught to depend on each other also. In order to stay alive, fighter pilots and married couples must learn to give!

A veteran marriage and family therapist at the University of Minnesota, is among those who take the marriage-saving view. He believes therapists have been too neutral and have focused on the individual. He blames the period for the trend that he believes has rendered therapists so neutral that they are sabotaging marriages.

He also is among those who say that too many therapists aren't sufficiently trained to counsel couples and that the profession isn't regulated consistently, so consumers don't know what they are getting.

Try passing that on the commander of **TOP GUN** or the council of Mormon bishops. Be prepared to duck!!

Socrates suggested I "look in" some more on Plutarch. We spoke of him earlier. I think Socrates knew that if I kept searching I would find something that would tie Plutarch's historical writings, about A.D. 100, to a particular angle to which something is considered in *my* life.

Well, Socrates hit it!

About ten or fifteen years ago I asked my doctor (**BOOK III** is dedicated to him) what he thought of cosmetic surgery?

He thought about my question for a short while and then answered thus: "I think if a woman would be made to feel better about herself—give her a little more self confidence—give her a chance to enhance her real beauty—a little tuck here and there— eyes, chin, maybe a little to the breasts—would be fine. But it's the men I worry about."

"Why is that?" I asked.

He said, "Because in my opinion, a man that allows a knife to change his face, no matter how little, destroys the innate CHARACTER of the individual; it destroys his countenance; his facial features that should convey his *true* meaning, feeling, and mood—are destroyed."

In Adler's (editor in chief) *GREAT BOOKS OF THE WESTERN WORLD*, BOOK #13, addresses Plutarch. Plutarch, writing of ALEXANDER, said, "It being my purpose to write the lives of Alexander the king, and of Caesar, by whom Pompey was destroyed, the multitude of their great nations afford so large a field that I were to blame if I should not by way of apology forewarn my reader that I have chosen rather to epitomize the most celebrated parts of their story, that to insist at large on every particular circumstance of it. I must be born in mind that my design is not to write histories, but lives. And the most glorious exploits do not always furnish us with the clearest discoveries of virtue or vice in men; sometimes a matter of less moment, **an expression or a jest, informs us better of their characters and inclinations, than the most famous sieges, the greatest armaments, or the bloodiest battles whatsoever. Therefore, as portrait-painters are more exact in the lines and features of the face, in which their CHARACTER is seen, than in other parts of the body,** (bold face by author) so I must be allowed to give my more particular attention to the marks and indications of the souls of men . . . . "

About 1900 years separated my doctor friend and Plutarch. Yet, both men fully appreciated the strength of a man's character as seen through his face. It's amazing to me—this constant learning in what history has to offer.

I have said again, and again, I am not studying philosophies, but philosophers. I am spending time, as Durant says, "With the saints and martyrs of thought, letting their radiant spirit play about us until perhaps we too, in some measure, shall partake of what Leonardo called, 'the noblest pleasure, the joy of understanding.'" Each of the philosophers I have talked to or studied in the *SOCRATES 'n SUITS Trilogy*, has some lesson for me, if I approached him properly. And the lessons are "about", not "of", the subject matter. History says the philosophers have "been there," "done that." Why in the name of the good Lord would I not listen? Great men speak to us only so far as we have ears and souls to hear them.

So let us listen to these men, ready to forgive them their passing errors, and eager to learn the lessons that they are so eager to teach. "Do you then be reasonable," said old Socrates to Crito, "and do not mind whether the teachers of philosophy are good or bad, but think only of Philosophy herself. Try to examine her well and truly; and if she be evil, seek to turn away all men from her; but if she be what I believe she is, then follow her and serve her, and be of good cheer."

There was another "Suitcase's Appleknocker" in my flying career. As you have read in my biography, my initial USAF test flying career started at North American Coroporation where I tested the first supersonic fighter, the F-100. After my discharge, honorable I'll have you know, Lockheed Aircraft hired me to experimentally test the first MACH 2 (twice the speed of sound) fighter, the YF-104A. My ground crew Captain named it "Simpson's APPLEKNOCKER."

Everything went well for over 100 hours and about 160 landings until one day I was fooled in an attempt to simulate a "dead-stick" (without power) landing. The picture tells it all! I was lucky that day; I survived. But the "Appleknocker" died. So did, as you read the accompanying story, my guide "Suitcase" Simpson.

You view another "picture" painting; the sixth YF-104A. It is a lifelike image of me ejecting, upwards, upside down, at 25,000 feed, when the tail came off during what is known as "a lateral-longitudinal" test.

The reader may wonder why I compliment the end of the chapter HISTORY AND PHILOSPHY with a continuing thought on the evolution of the aircraft I flew. First off, I mentioned in the chapter how I was assigned F-86 #52-4401, which I named. From that day on, for five years, every combat or test flight was, to me, considered upfront and personal. Review what Bob Hoover said about a successful fighter pilot and successful businessman. I simply think I was blessed to be given the time to gain behavioral and intellectual discipline that paved the road toward a successful business career.

LISTEN! LEARN! THINK! PREPARE! THEN SELL!

My first job in marketing and sales after my career in experimental flight-testing Lockheed's YF-104A, was representing a small, technically and economically competitive aerospace company headquartered near Manhattan Beach. My responsibility was "the Bay Area," San Francisco east to Sacramento and south to Sunnyvale, Palo Alto, and San Jose. It took time and hard work but I soon developed a bond, both professional and personal, with the purchasing and engineering professions. The company I represented specialized in hydraulic actuators and three axis (pitch, roll, and yaw) gyros. Roughly, a gyro is a wheel (or disc) mounted to spin rapidly about an axis and also free to rotate on one or both of two axes generating torque . . . , etc., etc.

It is a self-evident or universally accepted truth, particularly in a sales territory, that 80% of your business will come from 20% of your customers. I soon learned most of my client's dollar volume would be generated at Lockheed Missiles & Space, in Sunnyvale. The company was in the initial development phases of the POLARIS, A-1 missile. It was to be fired from a submerged submarine. My boss, who offered me the job, was a former North American test by the name of Dick Chapin, a very serious test pilot with an extremely keen, discerning intellect. He was hired away from North American to accept the responsibility as Vice President, Marketing and Sales. One of his immediate accomplishments was meeting the technical and economic requirements of a hydraulic actuator that was designed to supplement stability and control of the POLARIS weapons' system.

Dick approached me and offered me the responsibility of marketing and selling our company's engineered product(s). It would also be my duty to make sure our company delivered a quality product, on time! Dick said, "Every entity associated with an engineering discipline of advancing the state of any art, when it comes to design, manufacture, test, quality, and/or delivery, runs into problems. You and I know that first hand with the problems North American had on the F-100. Hell, it was the world's first supersonic fighter. You don't walk through the speed of sound without paying one price or another.

There are two secrets to solving any problem. One is facing reality and the other is doing something about it. Right?"

"Right!"

"If we have a problem here at BSFX, you tell me and I'll jump on it. And what will you do?"

"I'll go to the buyer and let him know and ask for his verbal inputs and engineering assistance."

"OK! Good," Dick said. "In addition, keep your eyes and ears open. When the engineers move, you move, because they are probably working on the advanced versions for what we know will be, in the future, POLARIS A-2 and A-3.

Stop and think a second, Jack! Your experience in flight testing the design, fabrication and performance properties of those values determining the characteristics of stability and control in the F-104A weapon system, and we're speaking **values**, are not different in the Polaris Weapon Systems. Think in terms of value as degrees of excellence. That's what you and I want! High degrees of excellence in anything we do! Am I starting to sound like Socrates?"

"Common sense, Dick! Socrates is synonymous with what he would call 'sound and prudent but often unsophisticated judgement.'"

I was also directed to work through purchasing and engineering with the mind set for analysis in determining new requirements for hydraulic and/or mechanical servo systems. A servo system is an automatic device for controlling large amounts of power by means of very small amounts of input and automatically correcting performance of such systems.

Our company, BXFS, was gaining a reputation for quality, delivery, and value. That was good news for Lockheed and BXFS, for the present, but two things had me concerned. One, more and more competitors were on the scene telling Lockheed how high-grade their actuators and other servo systems were. And two, companies were 'buying in' at low price (hoping for ECP's—engineering change proposals) thereby using this tactic, or strategy, to gain more dollars and at the same time becoming a contractor on what the aerospace professionals knew would be a long term missile program.

I gave each subject a lot of thought. I was determined to defeat my competition on selected bids of my choosing. I analyzed the combin-ation of BXFS' intelligent engineering, state-of-the-art cost saving manufacturing machinery, incisive analysis of the design controlled drawing and specification; and management. And by management I meant both companies engaged in what I called the "proceeding;" a **natural** phenomenon marked by gradual changes or operations conducted toward the end result of more technical and economically sound business growth. I was determined to **out think** my competition and prepare for better **value**.

I remembered one night in the past when Socrates and I were talking about my combat and test flying experiences. I was at Lockheed at the time; having just been assigned the responsibility for the #1 YF-104A, so it must have been when I ran into him while skiing at Big Bear. (That is also when my ski lift partner, by chance, happened to be a beautiful porn star—see **BOOK II**). Gee! What a ride that was!

Now where was I? I'm thinking!! I'm thinking!! Oh! yes, Socrates asked, "Suits, do you think you are a better pilot than most of your contemporaries? I'm speaking of your flying in Korea, or now, as an experimental pilot?"

"Gee, that's a hell of a question, Socs," I answered. "In fact that's sorta' a rhetorical question answered only by comparing mission profiles and experience. Flying a proven fighter in combat is one type of a difficult and burdensome task. Test flying a new experimental fighter is a certainly difficult and burdensome and also recondite with an added awesome responsibility. Yes, flight leaders had responsibility in performing the mission and bringing his wingman back alive but I would consider that **after** the fact. An experimental pilot has horrendous responsibility that I would consider **before** the fact. You can't lead men in combat and stay alive without the right kind of platform. We, in experimental flying, proved the F-104 was **not** the right kind of platform.

So, yes, to answer your question I think I was a better combat pilot than most of my contemporaries. I answer with no thought of self—aggrandizement; I believe I was better because I worked harder to fulfill a responsibility. In reference to my experimental flying the XF and YF-100A and the XF and YF-104A, I believe it's too early to tell as I did not have enough accumulative experience to say I had complete control of my emotions."

"I know I didn't raise a lot of hell in Korea when the guys would get together and drink and sing and talk about women. I did a few times but I elected to put in a lot of quiet time thinking through the mistakes I made during my missions and how I could do better and, when directed, become a more complete flight leader. I spent time trying to learn the art of thinking. Remember what Emerson said when asked, "What is the hardest task in the world"

He answered, "To think!"

You know, Socs, we talked about it. During one of our discussions you were saying, 'Who does not feel the charm of thinking that the moon and apple are, as far as their relation to the earth goes, identical. Also, of knowing respiration and combustion to be one; of understanding that the balloon rises by the same law whereby the stone sinks.' In between all that chicken you were eating at the cabin, you mentioned the use of the powers of the mind, as in conceiving ideas, making inferences, and making judgements.' And I think about the mess I made of my first mission and making a judgement against it."

"You're talking about Capt. Coffin helping you gain knowledge about yourself and the North Koreans."

"Yes, Socs, plus the fact I was soon flying as an instructor in the Replacement Training Unit and flying test missions early in the morning. I learned a hard lesson in pilot training; I couldn't drink and fly the next day. But you already know that story. So, I think it would be ill advised if I said I was, or am, a better pilot but I had the opportunity to surround myself with the right kind of input."

"Makes sense to me," Socs said. "Can you sum it up in one word"?

"No! But I can make it in two words."

"Two words?"

"Yes. Dumb shit!"

"Jees! Suitcase! What does that mean? At times you *are* a dumb shit! You know that! Stop and think! I'm not asking about your first mission or that beautiful brunette and your bourbon snow cone caper, I am asking about surrounding yourself with what you said, 'the right kind of input.'"

"I was just putting you on, Socs. Boy! You're getting to be a grouch! The right kind of input offered me wisdom—good sense and judgement. You taught me that—accumulated philosophic or scientific learning. You helped me become a better combat pilot, Socs."

I was laughing to myself as I was thinking about Socs. Also, I am still wondering when he is going to show up again. Anyhow, after we chatted I was thinking about my bourbon snow cone mischievous act. (**BOOK II**) I remember telling Socs the story about two drunks that found themselves on a roller coaster. One said to the other, "We're damn well making great time, but I'm not sure if this is the right bus."

Oh well! Let's get back to the present in reference to my **thinking**. I remember Socrates telling me that one man's superiority over other learned men consists chiefly in what may be called 'the art of thinking'; the art of using his mind. "Thinking," said Socrates, "is a certain continual power of seizing the useful substance of all that a man knows, and exhibiting it in a clear and forcible manner; so that knowledge, was, in him, true, evident, and actual wisdom. And remember also, what Aristotle once said in *Ethics*, 'The pleasures arising from thinking and learning will make us think and learn all the more'."

"So, Jack," my friend Socrates said, "your constant pursuit of one or more means by which you will think, and learn, and act as a man, will, by osmosis, keep you in a continuous circle of extreme gratification."

After a week or so, I got an idea. I was going to revolutionize myself from a salesman to a catalyst, an agent that stimulates or precipitates a reaction! And I was going to listen! I wanted, as Socrates said, "to seize the useful substance of all that I knew and exhibit it in a clear and *forcible* manner." As I perceived it, the normal way my competition was selling wasn't going to be the most effective anymore. That is, the normal process of receiving a specification outlining in written form the **function** for an actuator or servo system accompanied by a drawing **outlining** size, weight, material, dimensions, operating parameters, etc. These specifications were always forwarded from engineering to the buyer. BXSF's competitors would then design the actuator and/or system to fulfill what they thought Lockheed engineers had in mind. They would then price it and send the completed bid to the buyer on the date of bid closure.

The "seizing of the useful substance" for me was learning that competitors were not receiving a contract for reasons that would be most important for me. What would I learn to my advantage? Once again I listened. A contractor's bid would be rejected because Lockheed engineering did not understand what the *contractor* had in mind with their submitted bid, or Lockheed felt the competitor did not fully understand what *Lockheed* had in mind. Too many questions! Wonder why they went that way? Why this material vs. another? Why no suggestions about reducing weight? Don't they have any experience in manufacturing engineering? Wonder why no mention of quality control?

Good questions, all!

Also the bids were either too high or uncommonly low in price. No purchasing agent or buyer is going to pay for a system where they think the companies involved have a communications breakdown with the prime (contractor)—no matter the price.

This is how I reacted:

> After receiving the bid, BXFS's team of hydraulic engineers, manufacturing engineers, shop management, quality engineers, etc., would study the bid and then engineer a design. I would then, with permission from purchasing, bring the engineers from BXSF and Lockheed together to convert Lockheed's needs—the written word in the form of specifications—and transformed the "technical publication" into an engineering design, and with LMSC's engineering inputs and blessing, into an acceptable product. BXSF's engineers would sit down in a Lockheed conference room and review every detail of the written spec. and engineering drawings. We wanted to make sure we knew what engineering design Lockheed engineers wanted and at he same time they wanted to be sure our company was qualified to meet their needs.

After the meeting I always briefed the buyer what had transpired. We never discussed price during the engineering discussions.

About a week before the sealed bid was due, I again received permission from the buyer to review with the Lockheed engineers our company's particular design based on our past mutual exchange of information. Naturally, we were not allowed to discuss price. The Lockheed engineers would review our drawings, and suggest a number of small and varied changes. We *listened* to what they had to say! I again briefed the buyer, and after returning to the plant where the Lockheed suggestions were followed, my company submitted the bid on its due date. My company gave Lockheed a design based on the language of, and needs of Lockheed. I also made it a practice to know my competition; if anyone asked me about the company or companies I always had something positive to say. I would not, as an individual, be the determining factor in the competitive process so why not? My company didn't have to be low priced. Why? Because we offered, in everyone's mind, something of value!

We were successful; we won quite a number of contracts.

But I (we) couldn't rest on our laurels. Competition is always tough and to continually stay on top takes more than engineering drawings and prices. It was at this personal stage of my life I decided the word profession meant paying the price of time, more education, exposure and experience. If I wanted to be a successful salesperson, I couldn't pick a single arena like hydraulic valves and gyros. I had to enter the arena of people. If I wanted to consult in the profession of sales, I had to be prepared for all classes of professional people in an assortment of circumstances and learn, over the long run, the value exchanged between those professionals who buy and those professionals who sell.

Dignity and Truth

BXSF's actuators sometime failed during the operational suitability testing. Sometimes we failed at a higher temperature than the specification required in cold testing, or lower temperature the spec. required in high temperature testing. The actuators were not performing during the operational suitability tests (in the BXSF lab) as we had envisioned. I kept the buyer informed and if it appeared the problem(s) would impact schedule, I went personally to the purchasing manager through the buyer. I said, "Mr. So and So, we are having some problems with the Such and Such actuator; it may be a small aberration in the design that our engineers missed or it may be in the manufacturing process. Could you send a couple of men to BSFX and let's nip this thing in the bud?" A purchasing manager has high standing, and standards, among others, and when he signs a purchase order he expects performance and truth.

The next day a manufacturing specialist, a design engineer, and I, were on our way to the plant. It took a few days of hard thinking, ideas, and work, but the problem was solved.

What did we gain here? Well, we gained a solid rapport with Lockheed. The next bid on the actuators would be won by BSFX as long as the price was fair—not necessarily low. Lockheed would not spend the large amount of man-hours, and money, solving our collective problem and then chance other problems by giving it to another company because of a lower price.

What else did we (I) gain? *The Arts of Teaching and Learning!* BSFX was exposed to the art of listening and we were **taught** by Lockheed the nuances of space age design.

Socrates was an extraordinary teacher. Perhaps the most illuminating passage on the subject of learning is one which Socrates compares himself to a midwife who does nothing more than to help the mother give birth to the offspring. So the teacher helps anyone wishing to **learn** give birth to ideas. The primary activity is in the learner, not the teacher, as it is in the mother, not the midwife.

The primary activity was in the learner, as it was in BSFX, not the midwife, Lockheed.

I think you are now in a position to understand why I wanted having Socrates and his friends helping me along the serpentine path of life. In this juncture, as a neophyte salesman, the little example of BSFX and Lockheed, combined, collectively, with thinking and learning, plus the help from Socrates and Aristotle gave a tremendous boost to my learning process. Socrates, living in an era 400 years before Christ; and Aristotle, about 350 years, played the *key* role in helping me, **this particular day,** match contemporary management to understand the gratification of thinking and learning which led both parties to honor dignity and truth. It's such an easy way to do business; to honor man and his institution. You are bound to get the same thing in return. I remember Socrates pushing me about learning about myself (see chapter entitled 'Exchange of Values'). I am now, be it through BSXF and Lockheed, or direct exposure to buyers and sellers, or even osmosis—in the daily process of absorbing the language and deeds of men that surround me. Socrates said, "Suits, the individual man should seek to know himself for what he really is and should esteem himself for his true worth and make inevitable his desire to be known and esteemed by others according to his merits. Honor is the name that ancients like me gave to the good that satisfies this natural desire; and we prized it highly among the goods that a virtuous man should seek; higher than wealth or sensual pleasure."

Good man, my friend Socrates. I'm lucky.

The "virtuous man" words uttered by Socs struck an accord with me; an accord that would give me a guideline marked by firmness and determination to compete, on particular specifications, with other qualified corporations, and be a winner. Socs handed me an innate number of virtuosos; men for me to think **with** them and **through** them. They would combine their outstanding talents and experiment and investigate what techniques and advancement in the sciences would be needed to technically and economically advance the "state of the art" in producing the new POLARIS' A2 and A3. We are talking years here! And guess who is going to stick with them like binoculars on a back stage Las Vegas showgirl dressing room.

You got that right!! ME!! Well, considering I'm not in jail!

As each engineer, through his technical knowledge and experience, was promoted to the A2 design team, I asked the engineer, after I cleared it with purchasing, if I could visit at the times so as to determine what important new designs and technology would be implemented in advancing the "state of the art". What were the engineers planning in order to meet the more stringent specifications of the A-2? Should BEFX plan on the possibility of new materials and the fabrication thereof, including what new machinery was available to add efficiency to the process? Would the structural integrity specifications change? How about the performance parameters associated with new warheads? How about weight, wall thickness, power requirements, electrical, hydraulic, electro-hydraulic? What new disciplines should BSFX consider entering? I basically lived with engineering and at this stage

I "listened, learned, thought, and planned." Also, every time I visited engineering I kept the buyer informed. The selling? I was selling every day by just being there. When the design specifications were ready to release through purchasing to BSFX and other competitors we were ready to speak Lockheed's language.

And over the years, BSFX won a lot of business.

In addition to what was just described I strengthened BSFX's technical and operational rapport with Lockheed's testing lab. The laboratory testing BSFS's actuators. I found out from the engineers who was responsible in the lab, met the gentleman, and discussed if there was much difference between the way their lab did their testing vs the testing procedure at BSFX. Yes, there was a difference, although small, but I thought it could make a big difference if each company didn't follow the same procedures and use the same type of test machine. "It is in this way," I said to the chief technician, "we could make sure, by following the same pattern, BSFX was designing and manufacturing to specifications and if not, why not? On the other hand, if BSFX sent Lockheed what we thought was a perfectly good actuator but your technicians detected a flaw, we could determine, in the shortest period of time, why they detected it and we did not."

I asked the chief technician at what time they reported to work. He said, "Well, we all usually meet at the coffee truck between 6 and 6:15AM and we are in the lab by 7." I said, "Good, I'll call you next time I'm here." Imagine his surprise when the next morning at 6:15 AM when I asked a gentleman if there was a Mr. Rafferty present. When he pointed him out I walked up to him, introduced myself and said, "Match you for the coffee," as I dug into my pocket for a coin. From that day on, for two years and two months, BSFX never delivered a malfunctioning actuator. And when I made an appointment with Mr. Rafferty I always said, "Thanks! I'll see you at the truck at 6:15AM." I was never, never, a minute late!

What did BSFX have now? I think we had a platform for continued success. Both companies—engineering, manufacturing, quality, functional testing—everyone **communicating** and working toward a single goal. The delivery of a quality product, on time, on cost! Life became a lot easier. Nothing was "yucky" anymore!

Reminds me of a story I read some time ago.

A little boy sat in the kitchen with his grandmother while she prepared cake batter. As they talked, the youngster talked about how "yucky" everything in his life was. School was yucky. Soccer was yucky. Even Mommy and Daddy were yucky.

Grandma listened closely to his tales of woe. Then she asked if he'd if he'd like a snack while they baked the cake.

"Sure!" he replied.

First she offered him some raw eggs.

"No, they're yucky."

"How about this nice flour?"

"Grandma, that's yucky, too!"

"There's always the shortening."

"Yucky! Grandma, everything you want me to eat is yucky!"

"Well, yes, by standing alone all the ingredients taste yucky," she said to him. "But mix then all together in the right way and they make a terrific-tasting cake. Isn't that right?"

"Yes," the little boy said.

"Life works the same way," said his grandmother. "Sometimes everything seems "yucky" but when you put it all together life is really a wonderful treat!"

BITS & PIECES
Lawrence Ragan Communications, Inc.
316 N. Michigan Ave
Chicago, IL 60601

The beginning of the end came slowly but it came just the same; in a period of about fifteen months. One of the owners of BSFX was killed in the crash of his own plane while landing at a private airport in Arizona. His partner was a CPA; very good at crunching numbers but he knew nothing about managing the kind of shop his partner had developed. Also, in all due respect, he couldn't comprehend accountabilities and responsibilities. Things soon got out of hand and he sold the company to a large chemical milling and machining company. They knew nothing about us and we knew nothing about them.

There was no synergy! The management of our new association (it was the beginning of the "fashion" of the business world; conglomerates) knew another word for conglomerate! It also means ACCUMULATE. That is exactly what they were doing in a helter-skelter fashion.

In all due respect they offered me a heck of a deal; salary, expenses, car, bonus. They wanted to keep the Lockheed account sound. I turned them down because I knew it would never happen. They had no management capable of understanding our (BSFX) particular discipline.

I reported what I thought would happen to the Director of Procurement and Engineering at Lockheed. I suggested they keep their eyes on things; I did not say anything that could even be construed as being detrimental to the company. I also told the gentlemen I was going to tender my resignation.

In sixteen months BSFX was no longer in business. In four and a half years the conglomerate was no longer in business. The owners of the companies amalgamated into the corporate structure resigned. They had their money and it was, as is true today, almost impossible to find management capable of taking on the responsibilities of others in a short span of time in order to meet pre-planned schedules.

In the meanwhile, I got lucky. I was invited to a reunion of my college, class of 1951. One of the attendees was a very bright engineer who I had gone to dinner with after one of our student council meetings. He was now working at NORTH AMERICAN AVIATION and while swapping stories he told me HOOVER ELECTRIC COMPANY was looking for a sales engineer. HOOVER had most of the electro-mechanical actuators on the F-86, the F-100, the SABRELINER, the A3J, and various new missiles being tested for future introduction into inventory. He told me a Mr. George Sullivan was the man I should call and that he would call him first and let Mr. Sullivan know who I was and at the same time, give him a short history of my background. A very nice thing for him to do!

HOOVER ELECTRIC was owned, singularly, by Dr. Veno A. Hoover. He was a Ph.D. graduate from California Institute of Technology in three separate disciplines—electrical engineering, physics, and mathematics.

Later, (I was hired) as I got to know Dr. Hoover, I was amazed at his brilliance. A man of exceptional mental ability! Dr. Hoover went after all the toughest engineering requirements. His creed was HOOVER ELECTRIC was to rate the highest in any engineering contest with no thought of production. His shop was strictly R&D; production was to be sub-contracted. That was OK by me because what *I* loved most about the man was his excellent sense of humor.

Soon after I came aboard as a consultant in marketing and sales engineering, I met another bright individual, Charles "Chuck" Weideman. Chuck was hired in 1954 as an acceptance test technician while in Santa Monica City College majoring in electronics. This was the day of vacuum tube. The transistor had not yet been invented, there was no instrumentation for flight testing, and no computers for presaging parameters for aircraft such as stability and control. I had experience in that arena. It was one of the factors that led to the destruction of the #8 YF-104A (**BOOK II** of the Trilogy.)

Chuck and I got to know one another pretty well when he was promoted to the R&D test lab.

I remember one Wednesday Dr. Hoover told Mr. Sullivan he wanted to see Chuck Weideman and me in a meeting. Mr. Sullivan called and asked if I could meet with Dr. Hoover at a particular time on Friday morning. I said, "Yes, of course," so the face-to-face arrangement was set.

Dr. Hoover got right to the point. "I want to supply actuators on the NASA (National Aeronautical and Space Administration) shuttle. Think you gentlemen can do anything about that? Mr. Simpson!"

"Yes, Sir, we can. I hope Chuck doesn't mind but he and I were talking just the other day and I know from friends, in particular a former test pilot, that North American is looking for companies that can design, fabricate, and qualify their product(s) under a space environment."

Chuck followed with, "I agree with Jack, Doctor. But keep in mind that Hoover, although already renown from the aircraft division, is not known at NASA. We will have to qualify under stringent NASA requirements for such disciplines as management, quality assurance, production/manufacturing, subcontractor management, qualification testing, finance, etc., etc. This information will have to be presented in writing, in separate volume form, all for the purpose of source selection. Jack and I have no doubt that Hoover will always be number 1 in engineering but all of these other parameters are just as important."

"So!" Dr. Hoover said.

"Well, Sir," we can do it. I just wanted you to know—"

"I know NASA will be tough Charles," Dr. Hoover said. "And I also know you gentlemen can do it. Mr. Simpson can get us the carefully chosen actuator bids, engineering and I can do our part, and Mr. Sullivan and you can handle the rest. Isn't that correct, Gentlemen."

All three of us looked at each other and then at Dr. Hoover and said in unison, "Yes, Sir!

Thus began the evolution of Hoover Electric, North American, NASA and an amateur (me). That is, compared to Dr. Hoover and Chuck Weideman. I must say, it took time and proper planning, but, in the end, never has a marketing plan and the concomitant business plan worked so beautifully although much easier said than done! (please refer to the chapters on details of an actual marketing and business plan.)

After meeting Dr. Hoover I started talking to myself. "This is big league stuff Simpson. It won't be like BSFX where Dick Chapin started things for you. But you're not the new kid on the block anymore either! The POLARIS actuators were for one flight. The shuttle goes into space and returns and it will require quite a number of different kinds of actuator in reference to form, fit, and length of function. The Polaris actuators were all the same. This will be your first test in adding 'function' to the writing of the Hoover marketing and business plan. It is the nexus for future development and every detail must be thought through. Chuck Weideman and you will have to "cherry pick" the actuators. But relax! You'll be OK since you'll probably be working closely with him."

The meeting with Dr. Hoover thus put me in a position to put into practice what I had been learning from books, and magazines, and articles from the *FORTUNE and THE WALL STREET JOURNAL*. I remember reading in *FORTUNE* a few years ago something to hang my hat on. The article said, "Behind every successful man you will always find a great planner."

Hoover Electric gave me an excellent platform for **BOOK III's** treatise on such consequential significance as PLANNING, TIME & THE LESSONS OF HISTORY!

I went to my apartment and took out two books I had read recently. In his book, *A ROUND OF GOLF*, Tommy Armour the veteran golf pro tells us to use our brains and not our brawn. He reminds us that **planning** and thinking through every shot will permit us to play a scientific game. He says planning reduces strokes, errors, and tension with the game. Mr. Armour suggests that it will be more fun for others to play with us when we have a planned game.

Professor Joseph Thompson in his text *SELLING* states, "Any professional plans his efforts."

A professional must think his way around a golf course, a territory, a boxing match, and by all means an experimental test flight. In the same way, sales effort must be planned effort. And regardless of ability, a salesperson cannot effectively sell by the seat of their pants—or girdle. Today, in the new world of marketing and sales, the salesperson is a manager. The person manages their time, their sales effort, their market, and their customer; the salesperson duplicates at the territorial level, top management's management effort.

I see a world of synergy here; planning for success! Tommy Armour plans! Professor Thompson plans! Mohammed Ali plans! General Tommy Franks plans! CEO Herb Kelleher plans! The vice president of Toyota's North American manufacturing operations plans! Dr. Hoover plans!

In most cases, whenever you meet a truly effective salesperson, you will meet a planner; a person who thinks ahead and decides in advance what he or she is going to do, as well as why, when, where and how the task will get done.

I know exactly what must be done, or better said, how Hoover Electric will win its share of profitable actuator business on the NASA shuttle. A definitive plan and purpose has been identified! Our goal has been set! At this instant, the most important question! How much time is available? Its sagacious management is now the vanguard!

In his wisdom God gives to each of us a limited, finite number of hours in a year in which to achieve our goals, both material and spiritual. He gives us these hours in sequence, day-by-day, month-by month, year-by-year. If they are wasted, however, they are not repeatable or refundable. He gives the same amount to the rich and to the poor and to the young and to the old. Whatever success we may achieve in this life will come from the purpose to which we put God's priceless gift—**TIME**.

A salesperson's time management is important because the structure of the territory demands pre-planned frequency of calls not only due to the of selling present products but plans must be made for growth of the territory by increasing demand and expanding geographical boundaries.

It takes time to figure the route of a salesperson's car or truck; as golfers should do for the route (flight) of their ball. Time in understanding the needs for each customer relates directly to the number of calls per day, time left for cold calling and frequencies for call back.

Taking the time to plan and the best use of time is the point I am trying to stress. Good planning is the secret to understanding how well one is doing a particular activity or achieving a specific goal in the shortest period of time. If things are going wrong one is able to make corrections in your "game plan." In any competitive atmosphere a game plan is of the utmost importance because one can strengthen his or her position in the marketplace by learning sooner than your competition what faults appear in your plan. Competitors make mistakes too! We all do! The secret to success is learning sooner, making corrections for the better; learn more, think more—and sell more!

One might wonder why I continually bring up the thought about what books have to offer; what do they do for me? Well, it is because history books parallel what I have learned in "*my* lessons of history" from the companies I have worked with. I have seen plans, inexorable plans, based on false and misleading information—executives who steadfastly stick to original plans when information from the territory dictated a change. It's okay to be wrong. Plans are based on information available at the time, since it is impossible to predict the future. The purpose of planning is to manipulate the present systematically in order to be prepared for the future. Systematically is the key! However the future may be now! Marketing and sales management must be aware of what information is available from the territory to allow for adjustments. In WWI French General Joseph Joffre, was intractable in his belief in Plan 17, and would not change or even allow his commanders to alter plans even though they had first hand information and experience with the German attacks through Belgium. Is there a difference between management's planning under false pretenses trying to get something done in business and a chief of staff's personnel planning under false pretenses trying to get something done in war?

As far as I am concerned the answer is **no.**

Business is a form of war; albeit less deadly in the form of carnage.

In his book, *MANAGEMENT*, Drucker has this to say about planning and getting things done:

These three prerequisites, (1) productive work, (2) feedback information, and (3) continuous learning, are, so to speak, the planning for worker responsibility for job, work group, and output. They are, therefore, management responsibilities and management tasks. But they are not "management prerogatives," i.e., things management does alone, by itself, and unilaterally. Management does indeed have to do the work and make the decisions. But in all these areas the worker himself, from the beginning, needs to be integrated as a "resource" into the planning process. From the beginning he has to share in thinking through work and process, tools and information. His knowledge, his experience; his needs are a resource to the planning process.

The worker, or field commander, if felt to be a resource, will readily feed back experienced information to the commander in chief or marketing manager. The experienced information is gained from talking to the customers.

Is there a difference between sucking up lives at the rate of 5,000 and sometimes 50,000 a day (WWI) and sucking up $5,000 and sometimes $50,000 dollars a day due to bad planning and blocked avenues of information needed for the planning process?

Again, an emphatic no!!!

Now let's talk about understanding **TIME**. Anything worthwhile takes time. When we see the most famous equation of the 20th century, e=mc2, the relationship between energy and inertia, we immediately think of Einstein.

It was around 1871 that, most scientists like Maxwell, Faraday, and Ampere, agreed that light was a form of electric and magnetic interaction, but no one could understand how it got from place to place. Everyone believed that some sort of medium, or substance, was necessary to support the fields. This substance was the famous luminiferous aether that was to occupy some physicists for the next 40 years. Until Einstein did away with it all! Einstein explored the aether puzzle with his friends for 10 years, first at the ETH (Eidgenossiche Technische Hochschule) in Zurich from 1895-1900, and then at the Swiss patent office in Bern from 1901 to 1905 when he proposed relativity.

Einstein didn't do it alone. He worked with friends like Maurice Solovile, Conrad Habicht, and along with Mileva Maric, Marcel Grossman and Mike Besso. Einstein also studied Michelson, and Morley, and Mach and Galileo. And he also benefited from the lessons of history through algebraic notation, logarithms, analytic geometry, calculus, and system of equations.

The point I am trying to make is one must understand that anything worthwhile takes time. I know, as does Dr. Hoover, Chuck Wiedeman and the chief engineer Jim Ballast, that we must all establish a professional rapport with our like professionals, including purchasing at North American on the shuttle program. And we won't do it overnight. We all must take time to think problems through, and should be smart enough to call on other professionals for help. Book research offers other thoughts to learn from the lessons of history. Einstein did, Truman did, Ludendorff did at Tannenberg (WWI) and Patton at St. Lo., (WWII).

Are we any different when it comes to accountabilities and responsibilities? Again, a resounding no!

"Descended from the apes! my dear, let us hop that is not true, but if it is, let us pray that it will not become generally known." That was stated by the wife of the Bishop of Worcester after she heard about "the origin of species." But Charles Darwin, the gentle Englishman who studied barnacles, orchids, and earthworms, was used to being unappreciated. Before the journey that was to change the field of biology (40,000 mile journey on the BEAGLE from 1831 to 1836), the way Michelangelo changed the ceiling of the Sistine Chapel, Darwin's father, a respectable medical man, wrote to him: "You care for nothing but shooting dogs, and rat-catching, and you will be a disgrace to yourself and all your family."

When I read about Darwin, I said to myself, "Hell, I have heard like things said about Hoover Electric. What do they know about the shuttle? Hoover is good on airplanes but this is space," they would say.

Well, when we took our time and followed our business and sales plan, as Dizzy Dean used to say speaking as an announcer for the ST. LOUIS BROWNS, "The Browns scored 'dem ten runs so fast, Chicago never knowed what hit 'em."

Darwin's "natural selection" had been in the air waiting to be born. So was Dr. Hoover!

I think I have an awfully good point to make. We'll let the lessons of history—past performance—and the value of experience speak for itself.

Copernicus studied early Greek records. Galileo couldn't accept the teachings of Aristotle. Einstein modified Newton's formulas. Darwin studied Lamarck and Geoffrey Saint-Hilaire, and Dr. W.C. Wells, and many other papers written in the middle 1800's. Edison, in his quest for "the birth of the bulb" had studied the possibility considered by scientists ever since Jobart had, in 1838, heated a carbon rod. J.W. Starr, an American from Cincinnati, had patented an incandescent lamp in England, as far back as 1845. Dr. J.W. draper constructed a platinum lamp shortly afterward. W.E. Stairs did the same in 1850 and was followed by E.C. Shepherd, in 1858.

There was, thus, no shortage of men trying to break the near monopoly that gas exercised in the lighting industry. Yet, all were faced with the immense gap between theory and practice. Edison said, "I speak without exaggeration when I say that I have constructed 3,000 different theories in connection with the electric light . . ." The experiments of 21 and 22 October, 1879, proved that Edison was over the hump. "I think we've got it," he said.

No one at Hoover had to be an Einstein or Darwin or Edison. But one can not very well contribute to the state-of-the-art or to the growth of a company like Hoover unless he or she studies and gathers the plethora of information available in libraries and in the territory that will help formulate marketing theories or plans.

And who says the first plan has to work? Did Edison's? The plan will certainly cone closer to fruition sooner if we at Hoover recognize what is available from the mouths and experiences of purchasing agents, buyers, engineers in various disciplines, manufacturing processes, configuration management systems, and quality practices and procedures. Why not sell "in their language?" North American is the one that is going to buy. History dictates it—read Plato's *PHAEDO*.

But all of the above planning takes time—and awareness—and perception. Einstein—10 years and Darwin 22 years—why should we, or any sales manager, think we can come up with a successful plan overnight?

Time is a great teacher, a great healer, a great legalizer and leveler; it stands still, slips away from us or flies past us. We can save time or lose it, spend time or waste it. Even, beat it or kill it!

What we cannot do, oddly enough, is define it. As businessmen, we do not have to. We just want to understand what time means to Hoover Electric in our thinking and planning.

The ability to gain confidence in decision-making takes time, or should I state, it takes experience through time to have confidence in decision-making.

In his book, *CHARACTER*, Samuel Smiles says, "The results of experience are, of course, only to be achieved by living; and living is a question of time. The man of experience learns to rely upon time as his helper. "Time and I against any two," was a maxim of Cardinal Mazarin (Jules, 1602-61, cardinal of the Roman Catholic Church; made himself valuable to Cardinal Richelieu).

Time has been described as a beautifier and as a consoler; but it is also a teacher. It is the food of experience, the soil of wisdom. It may be the friend or the enemy of youth; and time will sit beside the old as a consoler or as a tormentor, according as it has been used or said, and the past life has been well or ill spent.

Patience is the wisdom of time, the only channel through which time's expansiveness and quiet power can become properties of human will. The patient worker controls the most extensive dimension of mind and can achieve a kind of greatness even if the mind's other dimension are narrow, (as with native weavers of rugs). The spider, whom works minutely and slowly, weaves a giant image of herself and becomes a mighty huntress in time.

Robert Grudin,
TIME AND THE ART OF LIVING

"It were good . . . that men in their innovations would follow the example of time itself, which indeed innovateth greatly, but quietly and by degrees scarce to be perceived."

BACON
OF INNOVATIONS

One more thought! Management—almost alone—has to live always in both present and future.

A military leader, too, knows both times. But traditionally he rarely had to live in both at the same time. During peace he knew no "present;' the present was only a preparation for the future war.

During war he knew only the most short-lived "future"; he was concerned with winning the war at hand.

But we at Hoover (management) always must do both. We must keep the enterprise performing in the present—or else there will be no Hoover or any enterprise capable of performance, growth, and change in the future.

My first personal call at North American, Downey, was to the senior buyer, electrical/mechanical, buy the name of Anthony (Tony) Maricopa. I had made an appointment for 9:00 A.M. and after introducing myself and presenting him with my Hoover card I told him I appreciated his punctuality. He said, "That's no problem; as a matter of fact, a number of buyers and engineers and I were wondering when Hoover Electric was going to call. Dr. Hoover has quite a reputation at North American, Inglewood, (the aircraft division). Actually NASA is the powerhouse here and my first question, Jack, is will Dr. Hoover be prepared to meet the almost frightful number and degree of specifications NASA is imposing on us and all of our vendors?"

"Actually, Mr. Maricopa, that's the reason I am here. Our management, engineering and quality—"

"Pardon the interruption! Forget the Maricopa bit! Call me Tony."

"OK, Tony, I'll do that! Anyhow, yes, Dr. Hoover is ready to start at the bottom, and work through purchasing, that would be you, and—well, what the heck, I might as well show you our business and marketing plan and you tell me what you think. Do you have the time?

"I'll take time. Let's see what you got!"

And so, at nine o'clock on that September morning, Tony Maricopa and I laid the foundation for what would become an extremely tough year for Dr. Hoover and the great Hoover Electric Company. It was agreed that purchasing would send us a package (request for quote) with design-controlled drawings and specifications plus NASA requirements for particular actuators (we were sent five over a period of 7 months) and Hoover would compete with other companies. Maricopa, and engineering, processing, quality, configuration management, production/manufacturing, handling of proprietary data, and certifications, and all related personnel would de-brief our company of the pros and cons of our proposal. Dr. Hoover, Chuck Weideman, and Hoover's engineering manager attended every meeting. We learned we had a lot to learn about NASA requirements. But, we also aware the North American engineering was chomping at the bit as Dr. Hoover submitted some brilliant designs but he was being held back from a purchase order "until all concomitant NASA requirements" were met.

Tony Maricopa was one tough, purchasing executive; but he was also very fair. He was always at the plant with the right personnel edging us on, cajoling, coaxing, wheedling, blandishing, soft-soft-soaping, driving us crazy—but with a purpose.

One day, in our ninth month, he said to me, "Jack, I think Hoover Electric is ready. Dr. Hoover's engineering has been brilliant, but remember, competition is tough. Here's the scoop! We have an electro-mechanical actuator, (there are four of them) which will be responsible for opening and closing the huge shuttle bay doors; payload bay doors. This will be one tough specification as it calls for lubrication, in space of course, but lubrication that must hold its properties for innumerable operations plus many launches into space."

Eureka! I had an idea! It was in embryonic form for about a week before it exploded right in front of me daring me to grab. For some inane reason or another, all week long I was thinking about Russia's first satellite and the night I pulled off the highway to try and spot it. I was in Pasadena for an LA Symphony presentation. I got back in the car thinking—brilliant engineering plus the words, "lubrication in space". All of a sudden I said, "That's it!" "That's got to be the key to Hoover's success." So, after spending nine months LISTENING! LEARNING! THINKING! PREPARING! I thought we were on our way! A USAF general was the second in command in managing the JET PROPULSION LABORATORY. I personally knew him from our mutual membership in The Society of Experimental Test Pilots. "I'll give him a call," I excitedly said to myself, "and ask if he could help Dr. Hoover with a potential problem of lubricating in space since JPL had many successful mission profile satellites." My general friend said, "Sure, Suitcase, come on over. We will be happy to share with Dr. Hoover what we know."

The rest is history. Our day, through learning and preparing (takes time and patience; we had actually been selling since the first day I walked into North American's door) had arrived. Our systematic methods allowed Hoover to win that particular purchase order and seventeen more including centerline latch actuators, umbilical door actuators, radiator latch, and "Canadian arm" hold in place actuators.

I had dinner with Chuck Weideman just last week. Dr. Hoover's designs, after these many decades, are still number one in NASA's requirements for performance. Chuck still handles, with engineering excellence and first-class communications, every NASA need!

I can't say it enough. Selling in "the needs of—and language of" the customer. But you "hafta" fill yourself full of the problem first. And above all—don't be afraid to dream!

SOURCE SELECTION INFORMATION
NASA's REQUIREMENTS IN ADDITION TO
1st CLASS ENGINEERING
CAPABILITY

MASTER TABLE OF CONTENTS

VOLUME I—EXECUTIVE SUMMARY

TABLE OF ORGANIZATION
EXECUTIVE SUMMARY
The Right Company
The Right Management
The Right Team

VOLUME II—MISSION CAPABILITY

VOLUME III-COST
(Not Required)

VOLUME IV-CONTRACT DOCUMENTATION

VOLUME V-PAST PERFORMANCE

TABLE OF FIGURES

COMMON SENSE

Common sense has a variety of labels; some define it as reason, others, intelligence, and yet others speak of instinct and sometimes intuition. Additionally, there are those who have lease on this remarkable quality are usually those who praise it so highly, believing, mistakenly, that they have a large share in their own character.

Common sense is often distorted into meaning a very low grade of reason; in other words, the sense that is common to practically everyone. This is totally untrue. Common sense is one of the most rare traits of character there is to be found. Common sense consists of being able to see facts clearly, without interference because of prejudice or personal interest, and consequently take action in tune with established facts. When I study the word "experience" in the dictionary I am mentally tuned to two explanations: 1) practical knowledge or practice derived from direct observation of, or participation in, events, and: 2) the conscious events that make up an individual's life. Therefore, I personally belief one must gain experience before achieving rewards, through common sense, in business or personal life.

Common sense is a dual trait of character. It first consists of seeing facts and then, second, acting upon them. To see facts and not acting upon them is to play the part of an ignorant individual, and to act without understanding the facts is pure folly.

The reason why I have chosen the term "common sense" for a chapter in **BOOK III** is because practically all reasonably intelligent individuals can actually see and understand, in time, the facts about most of the problems of life. When they fail to do so it is usually always injurious because of their personal prejudices, selfishness, or a desire to evade responsibility in failing to understand most problems are created by the individual his or her self. They willfully blind themselves in such cases to what they could readily understand if they were seeking only the truth. And by truth in this stead I mean absolute confidence in words and actions; a willingness to step forward and be heard without trepidation. What usually occurs, however, is those not reasonably intelligent by reason of trying to compress time, rush to believing half-truths or they cannot accept the responsibility of facing reality. It is not, therefore, actually practiced sufficiently to be called common.

We can liken the average individual to a baseball player of great ability in hitting who merely stands at the plate and watches the ball, but makes no attempt to hit it except in spasmodic intervals and then in only a half-hearted manner. How much success a man can make of his life can be readily estimated by the success that would attend such a ball player if he acted in the manner described above. It doesn't afford common sense. This is probably one of the most potent reasons why so few individuals actually attain success, from the standpoint of respect and good will of their fellow men, as well as financial and business standing.

Many salespersons have great ability to hit for a high average in sales closures, but they give up easily or, in most cases, do not use common sense to overcome what seems to them as an insurmountable problem when, by using their head, they could easily overcome and gain respect and good will of their fellow men, as well as financial and business standing.

I'll give an example of what I consider using one's common sense but I'd like first to paraphrase what I learned from a book entitled *CHARACTER*. The book was written by a man by the name of Samuel Smiles. He had this to say about common sense:

We spoke earlier of knowing one's self. And what better position for a salesperson because as Smiles says, "Contact with others is a requisite to enable a man to know himself. It is only by mixing freely in the world that one can form a proper estimate of his capacity. Without such experience, one is apt to become conceited, puffed up, and arrogant; at all events, he will remain ignorant of himself, though he may heretofore have enjoyed no other company."

Swift once said, taken from the *GREAT TREASURY OF WESTERN THOUGHT*, "It is an uncontroversial truth, that no man ever made an ill-figure who understood his own talents, nor a good one who mistook them." That is common sense! Many persons, however, are more ready to take measure of the capacity of others than of themselves. That makes sense too!

A due amount of self-knowledge is, therefore, necessary for those who would *be* anything or *do* anything in the world. It is also one of the first essentials to the formation of distinct personal convictions. My father once said to a young friend who was bragging about his accomplishments, "You know only too well what you *can* do; but until you grow older and put yourself to the test more and have learned what you *cannot* do, you will neither accomplish anything of moment nor know inward peace."

Anyone who would profit by experience will never be above asking help. He who thinks himself already too wise to learn of others, will never succeed in doing anything either good or great. We have to keep our hearts and minds open, and never be ashamed to learn, with the assistance of those who are wiser and more experienced than ourselves.

The man wise by experience endeavors to judge correctly of the things that come under his observation, and form the subject of his daily life. What we call common sense is, for the most part, but the result of common experience wisely improved. Nor is great ability necessary to acquire it, so much as patience, accuracy, and watchfulness. Marvin Gussman, one of my clients for 28 years (and continues to be so), always thought the most sensible to be met and read are intelligent men and women of business and of the world, who argue from what they see and know, instead of spinning cobweb distinctions of what things ought to be.

We often read about, talk about, and hear people speak of the lessons of history. President Truman never looked back on any decision he made, because as he said, "I think I am using common sense when I am just applying current thought to the lessons of history."

In Miller's book about Truman, the one thing prevalent was that every time Truman quoted some lessons from the past, Miller knew that Truman knew what he was speaking about. Why? Because he had checked with the Library of Congress, and was amazed at the number of books that were checked out and read by Truman over the years as a Representative, Senator, Vice-President, and President.

You may wonder whether or not the lessons of history plus applying common sense would be applicable to your own life. I think paralleling the possibility of applying the lessons of history is accompanied by the word 'opportunity.' Opportunity does not present itself to a person very often. But when it does, one must have the awareness to recognize opportunity, apply past lessons of history and experience, and take immediate advantage. Let me give an example:

One morning I was having breakfast at a club where I was a member. The president of a large real estate company came in and sat down with me to have breakfast. He slammed the *WALL STREET JOURNAL* down on the table, and said, "It seems as if people will never learn that the price of land, and labor, and material, and money will never be as it is today. History dictates these costs continue to rise. But yet, they always want to wait to see if fate will deal them a better hand."

I don't know what brought that man to my table, as we were not necessarily close friends, but we always had a wave and a smile for each other; we had a friendly relationship. And I can't, at this moment, tell you what prompted me to say what I did, and follow through with what ended up becoming a very successful marketing program for the real estate company, and financial reward for me—unless it was subconsciously recognizing opportunity.

Let me start off by saying that I do not have a real estate license, I've never been in a real estate office, and I know nothing about selling real estate. But I do know how to sell and plan, and in this particular instant of time, grabbing at "The lessons of history." I said to the president of the company, "Instead of sitting here slamming the *WALL STREET JOURNAL* down and complaining about what people *don't* know, why don't you take the time to go to those people you feel qualified to purchase and tell them what they *should* know in order to add value that knowledge and turn it into a sale for your company?"

He said, "What do you mean?"

"OK!" I said, "I am going to lay it on the line. Right now you probably have two or three salespersons sitting in models waiting for potential customers to come in and look around. The moment they open their mouths the sales personnel are talking to someone they have not taken the time to determine their qualification. Yes, they have read the newspaper ads and have seen all the pretty flags flying but that is not good enough. When the sales personnel open their mouths, it puts your company in the same category as all the others selling tract homes or condos. It's a total waste to time, money, and talent particularly in a buyer's market.

Instead of standing around like your salesmen are probably doing at the tract in which you speak of, why don't you use a little common sense and go forth and find the people that are qualified to buy your townhouses. Cut your advertising; you don't know how cost effective it is anyhow. Bring them to the tract by appointment only, and fulfill their pre-qualified needs."

Of course, the president thought I was crazy; no one had ever talked to him like this in the past, and he had absolutely no idea what I was talking about. So rather than expound more at that particular time, I said, "Pull some of your salesmen, your sales manager, and vice-president of sales of your company together, give me a call, and I'll meet with them and lay out a thought process. If it sounds good, hire me to help you. If they don't think it makes sense, we'll drop it and I'll meet you again for breakfast next week and you can slam your *JOURNAL* down again, if that makes you feel any better."

I was invited to meet with the vice-president of marketing and several sales managers of tract homes in their corporate office the following day. When we had the niceties of introductions and coffee out of the way, I stood up and said, "Gentlemen, for whatever it is worth, this is my thought, and here are my plans. If you accept it, hire me to complement your activity until we sell all of the homes in the particular tract we speak of. If you do not buy my plan, I, at least, must thank you for being open-minded enough to invite me here to be with you."

"Here's what I would do: First of all, I would close the sales office at the tract, and I would stop all advertising. I would stop the printing most of the brochures about the sales tract, and I would release all the personnel that are in the tract office. I cannot comprehend a person calling himself a salesman, sitting in a tract office, waiting for someone to come in that would potentially buy a house, because in the first place, that 'someone coming in' has not been pre-qualified, and secondly, it is impossible to develop a sales presentation around someone without first knowing what their needs are. All selling must be planned in "the language of" and the "needs of" the people. The needs in this particular case being, location, affordable price, payments, and the desirability of a one, two, or three bedroom home. In addition, since the main stumbling blocks of your sales has been the price of labor, material, land, and money you must overcome these objectives *before* the person walks on the tract. They may have the greatest desire in the world to live in the biggest, most beautiful house in the tract, but if they can't afford to pay for it, there is no reason for them to be there. In addition you are not hired to give a lesson in Economics 102. You are hired to sell homes!

I continued. In the summer of 1950 I had to drop out of school because I ran out of GI Bill money. I researched a number of jobs in the St. Louis area, and decided that I could make the most money to get back in school the next semester by becoming a commissioned salesman. The total of commissions being directly proportional to the amount money I needed to re—matriculate and the amount of work that I was willing to do. So, I went to work for Encyclopedia Britannica selling books door to door. I worked very hard, and listened, and loafed with the best salesmen, and learned. Not only did I made enough money to pay for the rest of my education, but actually took a few days off to fly back home before the fall semester started again. I am going to apply the lessons of history and sell your homes by the Encyclopedia Britannica method."

Silence! Dead silence. I am sure these "knowledgeable" sales personnel were saying, "Who is this dumb shit? The Encyclopedia Method? He has got to be kidding! Etc, etc."

Let me jump to the end of our meeting now, and say that the company was open mined enough and enhanced by the thoughts of what we could do. Hell, they weren't selling anything anyway.

They hired me!

The sales plan that lead to the sales of all units was as follows:

One, I called the corporate office for Encyclopedia Britannica in Chicago, and found the man that I thought was best capable of putting together a psychologically sound presentation as to why, although the cost of labor, and material, and land, and money was escalating, it was now time to purchase a home. I wanted the presentation in the form of a canned speech, exactly the same way Encyclopedia Britannica sold books door to door, because we were going to use the lessons of history, and use their particular method of sales to accomplish our goal. Let's face it, it's nothing more than a numbers game. You make so many house calls, get so many appointments, make your presentation to so many families, and X number of families will buy. The secret was finding those qualified people. At any rate, through the help of Encyclopedia Britannica, we put together a magnificent presentation showing the location and attractiveness of the homes, the advantages of buying that particular home, the history and performance of the builder, the sound thought processes behind handling the objectives of labor, land, money, et cetera, and had it presented in a format, from open to close, with the same psychology that Britannica uses in selling an encyclopedia.

Also, I asked the salesmen and sales manager to give me a list of 25 or more of every objection that they ever encountered, and how those objections were answered in a positive note. This was accomplished.

The next thing I did was put an ad in a paper for licensed real estate salesmen that had door-to-door sales experience. And after interviewing an untold number,

I hired five salesmen that had the kind of experience I speak of. I then took those salesmen to a remote resort for three days, and we did nothing but review in minute detail the sales presentation, and along with that, every objection that could possibly be conceived and what the answers were to be given in a positive vein. I speak here of a canned presentation, or, as most salesmen say, a canned speech.

In my opinion there is absolutely nothing wrong with a canned speech. A sales manager knows, as a result of a canned speech, that all of his sales personnel are presenting their case in the best possible vein, and are answering all objections in the same way. It allows a salesman to present every particular positive point regarding a particular product and it gives him the confidence to know that no matter what objections may arise, he is not only capable of handling the objections, but can continue on with his positive presentation. If a sales manager knows that all of his salesmen are presenting a case in a particular method, by reviewing results after a number of presentations, he can tell how effective the opening or close may have been. In other words, if his sales personnel come back and say that I was doing quite well until I reached the portion regarding the cost of money, I ran into a number of objections that we had not thought of. And if several sales personnel are saying the same thing, the sales manager immediately knows where he must strengthen his presentation. Also, if a number of objections are basically the same, it allows the presentation to be presented in the language of the people who are being called on, so that this objection will not come up again.

At any rate, after three days, the five salesmen were eminently prepared to make the presentation to a qualified buyer.

Now the secret! Who was that qualified buyer? It only made common sense to me that the most qualified people would be those who were presently paying rent in apartment houses that matched what their monthly payments would be once they had moved into the home. And it was almost a parallel qualification, people living in one and two and three bedroom apartments, would be those people who would buy a one, a two, or a three bedroom home. I won't go into too much detail now, but to make a long story short, we got the address and phone number of every person living in apartment houses within a 15 mile radius of this particular tract area.

Again, speaking of history, I know, or I knew that insurance salesmen made presentations in homes as a result of telephone calls by qualified personnel, in this case mostly women, who would call a housewife during the day, introduce themselves, and psychologically make a presentation over the phone as to why it is sound for an insurance salesman to call. I did the same thing. I researched a number of insurance companies in this particular city, found a number of people that made these kind of calls, hired them, and had the same type of call made to the apartment houses to set appointments for our salesmen to call. And that's exactly what we did. We made appointments; the salesmen called at the apartment house in the evening, made a "Britannica type" presentation as to why it was now time for that particular person to apply the money that they were spending on rent to the investment in a new home. Next, an appointment was made to show that particular home, at a particular time, on a Saturday and Sunday. The tract was open on Saturdays and Sundays, by appointment only, through the particular salesmen who would accompany these personnel to the home. In the meanwhile, because of the knowledge we would gain of these people, we had a contract prepared for them. And when they showed up at the site on a weekend for the appointment to see a particular one, two, or three bedroom home, the contract had already been made out, and the salesman, at the right time, would pass the contract to the husband as he showed the wife the recreation room and the children the swimming pool, et cetera.

And low and behold, it wasn't long before the tract was sold out.

To me this sales campaign was a result of two experiences: lessons of history and application of common sense.

The case history that I just spoke of is an example of using your head or common sense. It is imperative to understand, though, that common sense is not the ingredient that would lead to a purchase order and it should not be used that way. It is used in this case to do something a little different which opens a communication link to a potential buyer. That action *then* allows the salesperson to develop a personal and business rapport.

We spoke in an earlier chapter about character and work. A salesperson's occupation is darn hard work and because of its personalized nature many additional traits of character must be prevalent in addition to common sense and courtesy.

A salesperson must know his or her self, be trustworthy, truthful, disciplined, reliable, patient and have an abundance of self-control.

Smiles, in his book on *CHARACTER*, speaks of these many attributes throughout his book and I'm going to quote a portion that sounds as if it were written as a salesperson's creed:

Talent is by no means rare in the world; nor is even genius. But can the talent be trusted? Can the genius? Not unless based on truthfulness—on veracity. It is this quality more than any other that commands the esteem and respect, and secures the confidence of others. Truthfulness is at the foundation of all personal excellence. It exhibits itself in conduct. It is rectitude—truth in action, and shines through every word and deed. It means reliability, and convinces other men that it can be trusted. And a man is already of consequence in the world when it is known that he can be relied on—that when he says he knows a thing, he does know it—that when he says he will do a thing, he can do, and does it. Thus reliability becomes a passport to the general esteem and confidence of mankind.

In the affairs of life or of business, it is not intellect that tells so much as character—nor brains so much as heart—not genius so much as self-control, patience, and discipline, regulated by judgment. Hence there is no better provision for the uses of either private or public life, than a fair share of ordinary good sense guided by the quality or state of being correct in judgment or procedure. Good sense, disciplined by experience and inspired by goodness, issues in practical wisdom.

MORE COMMON SENSE

I had moved from the club mentioned above (I had purchased a home), but while still there I met a very nice man by the name of Mike Ballen and his wife Jackie. He lived at the club also. I didn't know too much about him at first but we seemed to "hit it off" because he was from Cleveland, Ohio, and knew a few doctors from the same hospital where my sister had graduated as a nurse. Also, we were both early risers and liked singles tennis. So, about three mornings a week my tennis adversary was Mike Ballen. He was very competitive; a tough match. We had been playing against each other, or with each other in doubles matches, for a three months or so when he asked me to have lunch with him on a particular Saturday afternoon. It was at this lunch when he told me he knew, other than what I had told him, I was a successful sales representative and a professor of marketing and sales at Orange Coast College and that he was looking for someone with sales and marketing experience to sit on his Board.

I was rendered helpless for a minute or so, wondering where he had gotten his information, but I recovered and said, "Mike, I would be honored." He said that would be great. We talked details for an hour or so and he said he would be getting in touch with me a give me *all* the particulars.

"Well," I said to myself while driving home after lunch, "you're now going to be on his Board representing the marketing and sales division of The Ballen Group, a group of insurance disciplines specializing in Auto, Boat, Health, Disability, Fire, and Credit Life. My responsibility will be Credit Life, the kind of insurance that covers, let's say, the head of the household who has decided to build an additional room on his house, build a bigger garage, a patio, or a swimming pool. If the head of the household died before completion, his Credit Life policy would cover the cost of completion. It would protect the lender, the contractor, and the credit rating of the family. The lender could be a bank, a savings and loan, or a corporate credit union.

Mike was very successful with his enterprise, but in talking with him about a myriad of subjects he seemed to be always dissatisfied with the less than normal performance of the Credit Life division. Over ensuing weeks I had in mind a pretty good idea what was wrong but at the time, I didn't know enough of the details to comment.

Now, I still didn't know enough but Mike put me on the Board to come up with some answers. I had already made up my mind about one thing. The sales reps were not sure how much potential business was "out there" in each of the four categories. Common sense told me if they didn't know where the construction money was, and what financial institution was the lender, they could not determine what percentage of the market they could plan on capturing. If they knew, as an example, how much money was being spent on, say swimming pools, the lessons of history (past performance of the reps) would tell the rep(s) how many sales dollars in insurance

(Credit Life) they would expect to capture for the company and what amount of dollars they would make on commissioned sales.

Remember! When I had to make 'X' amount of dollars to matriculate back to school, Encyclopedia Britannica gave me a territory and said, "If you knock on 'X' number of doors, you will get 'X' number of appointments, and from there you will be given the chance to offer 'X' number of sale's presentations, and from that you will sell 'X' number of units. That 'X' number of units will pay your way back to school."

And they were right! I knew how many dollars I would need to return to school so I knew how many cold calls I would have to make and "down-loaded" from there. It wasn't easy but door-to-door sales offered me great lessons in principles, how to think on my feet, and a combination of emotional, intellectual, and moral qualities. And the lessons were free! I followed what Encyclopedia Britannica had to say. I paid my way back to school!

But, be that as it may, I was back to "filling myself full of the problem" again. The problem was simple enough. How do we find the number of dollars being spent and on what projects? Sure, the sales reps could continue to call on the financial institutions and ask about dollars being spent but that is what I call 'lack of the driver's seat communication.' A salesperson must be in the driver's seat by knowing he or she has something to sell that would enhance the buyer's company (needs). But particular needs must be learned first. We didn't know anything! By that I mean concrete evidence (information) on which to build a sales plan.

As the days turned into weeks and the weeks into months I was learning credit life insurance was a tough sell. The insurance was easy to sell because of the protection but finding where to sell it effectively by getting the most return for time and energy expended wasn't easy.

And then one day, it was in the evening, I got lucky! Some person who, by the way, I never had a chance to meet, was building a house on one of the streets where I walked my dog. So Jake and I would walk up the driveway and into the garage and from there into what was to be a bath, the kitchen, what appeared to be the dining area, etc. On the way back to the sidewalk I noticed the wind had picked up and a "flapping" sound got Jake's attention. I said, "What's that, Jake?" as he stood frozen, three feet on the sandy apron, one folded at his ankle, rigidly moving his head with five degrees of azimuth side by side, hair raised on his shoulders and back. His ears were moving from straight up to low along his black, tinted with a gray, forehead. His head was cocked! Jake was trying to "tune in" the sound. A beautiful specimen of an uneasy, anxious pedigree Boston Terrier! He was growling, telling me he didn't like what he was hearing. Jake looked at me, and then at a 4x4 that was holding, with a nail, about an 8x6 card that was oscillating with the gusts of wind. "I see it, Jake! I see it!" I said, as I observed the 4x4 also.

Jake continued his deep, reverberating sound, poised, ready to strike anyone or anything that might bring harm to me. I said, "That's OK, Jake. Good dog! I see what is bothering you. Let's go investigate," and he jumped as I slowly picked my way through the sand toward the post. Jake had calmed down a bit, but couldn't get the leverage in the sand as he missed couple of tries to catch the "flapper" in his teeth. "No sweat, Jake," I said. "I'll grab it before it rips off and cover it with one of those red bricks over there." Jake seemed to agree as he stepped back and watched me take the card and partly cover it with the brick at the base of the 4x4. As I was covering it I saw two words, in big print, **BUILDING PERMIT.**

I was stunned! Paralyzed! Eureka! Jake found my answer!

I was Archimedes, one of the great mathematicians of antiquity! I was Gell-Mann, vicariously receiving the Nobel Prize for physics! I was Genda, jumping from a streetcar in Tokyo! I was with the laborers at the junction of Hwy. 15 and the 10 free way. My mind was racing; charging toward a goal where I already knew the way to the answer; plan, hire, test, distinguish, write, communicate, structure, analyze, responsibility, accountability, growth. My outstanding dog, my best friend, had solved my insurance problem in the form of a card about to be covered with a red brick!

I stood there, helpless, but my racing mind gave me stability. I needed that to think! Why? Why a card in the wind?

Found by my dog? How irrational! Absolutely ZERO relationship to what I needed. "How come?" I said to myself. "It couldn't be presaging. I offered no indication of something in advance! I couldn't give a reason for expecting anything! Filling ones-self full of the problem doesn't guarantee a thing other than, maybe, gray hair. There was no prescience or vision here!" But it was here! Or there! A flapping card with two words that ended up bringing, in time, The Ballen Group a spectacular increase in profitable sales.

Jake knew! He and I leaped and skipped about playfully as we played with his favorite ball all the way home.

I sat down at my desk as soon as I returned home; my thoughts were still circulating my feeble mind. "First," I said to myself was 'plan.' I continue writing notes. A new Business Plan does not necessarily command attention to new product development or new markets. The first order of business is concentration on, and development of, the present product that is the backbone of Ballen's business. Ballen offers many disciplines of insurance; your concentration will be Credit Life with particular attention to building permits for swimming pools. Answer the questions, "How many new swimming pools, in Orange County, will be built in Ballen's fiscal year (May 1 thru April 30)? Where are they located? How much money is being spent? Who is the contractor? What is the name of the lending agency? How many pools are they financing? Do they provide their own insurance or do they use a broker? What insurance company? Building date? Completion date? Excellent information for planning! Etc., etc

Hire! You have a friend of yours who was recently laid off because of a publication company closing their doors and moving to the Seattle area. He makes a good appearance; good in cold calls. Hire him at a fair wage to visit all cities in Orange Country and get copies of all swimming pool building permits.

Test! After receiving the first five permits or so, using the same sales rep, start analyzing the quality of information garnered from the owner, the builder, and the financial institution. How effective are the questions? Where are we making mistakes in planning? What entity is the most rewarding? The most negative? Start processing all information into a rough marketing plan.

Distinguish! Webster's dictionary defines the word: to perceive a difference in: to separate into kinds, classes, etc. As more building permits yield more and more information, sales management must perceive the difference between the knowledge that would strengthen the marketing plan and information that would be of no use. For example, what information was most useful and effective in closing a sale. It's like an experimental test pilot writing the first tenants of what is called the DASH 1, the pilots operating handbook. He must distinguish what information is trustworthy against what is possibly deadly. You sales personnel are gathering information on, or for, the evolution of the swimming pools' contribution to the growth of Ballen in the form of profitable dollars from Credit Life sales. The DASH 1 is continually enhanced; as should the Ballen marketing plan.

Write! Write the marketing in as much detail as is possible as the continuing information from the permits and reps is received. What information feeds a successful sale. What information causes a stumbling block; and why? You are starting with, like a new fighter, an "X" model. The next is a "Y", the first production followed by the "F" for production. Start with a "X" marketing plan and with additional, new information, go to the "Y' followed by the "F".

Communicate! Talk to one another. Work in unison until time dictates the assignment of specific territories with specific dollars that should be captured from specific customers.

Structure! Organize, on paper, the organization chart depicting the geographical area assigned to each representative.

Analyze! Analyze how effective the organization is with the concomitant potential sales dollars obtained by each representative. Continuing updating the marketing will assist in determining the affectivity of the plan.

Responsibility! Detail, in writing, a course of action demanded by the one in charge; in this case, the director of sales.

Accountability! A measure, in writing, of those qualities that will determine merit, desirability to the marketing organization, usefulness to The Ballen Group, and the sales representative organization, plus the importance of the individual in becoming part of the growth of the company.

Growth! Continual perception, consciousness, and awareness of the significance of quality as needed in a marketing plan as the nexus for growth for all aspects of ANY company trying to compete for contemporary well-defined business, plus continual, precise upgrades for unremitting, profitable, market share.

The sales of credit life insurance took off like a home sick angel. The same type of information was available on building permits for new patios, new bedrooms and baths, and additions to garages. But the most important consideration of any person responsible for growth, is determining in advance (through analysis) what a territory should produce in sales, and assigning responsibilities and accountabilities to sales personnel. Marketing and sales management should lead taking no excuses for not capturing a defined market share.

THROCKMORTON MORGANTORY

JAMES J. "DOC"

(as registered)

ALIAS

JAKE

"HE ALSO TRANSFORMED MERCEDES FROM
A COMPANY WHOSE ENGINEERS
SHOVELED PRODUCT TO CUSTOMERS
TO ONE THAT FIRST LISTENED TO WHAT CUSTOMERS
SAID THEY WANTED TO BUY."

DIETER ZETSCHE, PRESIDENT
CHRYSLER, DAIMLER-CHRYSLER
TIME, DEC. 4, 2000, SPEAKING OF
THE NEW PRESIDENT, USA

THE QUESTION FOR STAPLES WAS
HOW DOES A FAST-GROWTH COMPANY
GROW UP FROM ADOLESCENCE TO BE A LITTLE
MORE OF A MATURE COMPANY?
"Less Is **MORE!**"
WHEN ASKED ABOUT THIS BOLD
MARKETING APPROACH, CEO RONALD SARGENT
SAID, "WE STARTED WITH CUSTOMERS AND ASKED,
WHAT'S IMPORTANT TO YOU?"

TIME, **INSIDE BUSINESS**
FEBRUARY, 2005

KNOWLEDGE / RESPONSIBILITY

The word knowledge in the *GREAT TREASURT OF WESTERN THOUGHT* is broken down into two hundred different ideas on the subject. It is discussed by such influential and distinguished men as Boswell, Aristotle, Locke, Kant, Dante, Plato, Bacon, Santa Yana, etc.

Most of these learned men tend to be in substantial agreement; that knowledge, or truth that is attained when we know, is the essential good of the mind; that it is both good in itself, to be loved for its own sake, and also good as a means to be used in action and production; that, while man aspires to know all that is knowable, human knowledge at its best is imperfect and limited; and that knowledge is a relation between a knower and an object known.

This will certainly not be a philosophic discussion on knowledge. But in everyday language of the marketing and sales profession we hear the same mundane expressions—"one must have knowledge of the product, knowledge of the territory, knowledge of the competition, etc." That sounds good, and it is essential to know those things, but there must be more to it than that. I'm not saying "must" meaning demanding. I am saying that there has to be more to learn of knowledge when applied to the profession of marketing and sales. It is sure to give a person more insight and food for thought which will help understand those oft repeated, mundane expressions better. If we understand better, we can communicate better.

I know one thing already. To become knowledgeable take time; and far too many managers do not take the time to think, plan, learn, communicate—everyone seems to be in a rush and everyone takes too much for granted.

In my research, though, I have found two arenas that, "Philosophically Speaking," should be discussed; and I feel they should be of some value to a manager in the decision-making process:

1. The difference between knowledge by acquaintance (or knowledge by familiarity) and knowledge by description (or knowledge *about*. For example, A manager of a sales territory can be more effective in planning a sales campaign with knowledge about a territory than just being familiar with it.

2. The difference between speculative knowledge, as in conceiving ideas, and practical knowledge, as resulting from experience. In Russell's *Theory of Continuity*, he speaks of the confusion between acquaintance' (being familiar with) and knowledge about. Acquaintance, which is what we derive from sense, does not, theoretically at least, imply even the smallest "knowledge about," i.e. it does not imply knowledge of any proposition concerning the object with which we are acquainted. It is a mistake to speak as if acquaintance had degrees: there is merely acquaintance and non-acquaintance. When we speak of becoming "better acquainted," as for instance with a person, (or a territory—added by author) what we must mean is, becoming acquainted with more parts of a certain whole; but the acquaintance with each part is either complete or non-existent. Thus it is a mistake to say that if we were perfectly acquainted with an object (a territory or a product) we should know all about it.

"Knowledge about" is knowledge of propositions, or something put forward for consideration. To know that two shades of color are different is knowledge about them; hence acquaintance with the two shades does not in any way necessitate the knowledge that they are different.

Management must take the time to discuss in detail what is expected from a territory if they are acquainted with it or have specific knowledge about it. I can say one thing! A company cannot possibly write an effective marketing plan based on acquaintance or speculation.

Aristotle says we are experts because we possess knowledge in some particular branch. I think the problem in many corporations is that they have their share of experts, but communicating that knowledge to others, enabling them to fulfill particular needs, is a problem. Communication can't be just handed down. It must be handed back up in the form of complete understanding.

And another thought! I think this lack of effective communication (and communication is not only words, but observation) is one of the reasons an expert salesman in the field will not necessarily make the best sales manager. In my opinion, it is not necessarily the knowledge about a territory showing increased sales that makes one eligible for sales manager. It is how to communicate performance, and accepting responsibility for continued updating and strengthening of the marketing and business plan. The experience of having been responsible for a territory is important, but a high number of dollars in sales is not the number one criteria for the making of a sales manager.

Now, back to Aristotle:

"Knowledge, as a genius, is explained by reference to something else, for we mean knowledge of something.

But particular branches of knowledge are not thus explained. The knowledge of grammar is not relative to anything external, nor is the knowledge of music, but these, if relative at all, are relative only in virtue of their genera (common characteristics); thus grammar is said to be the knowledge of something, not the grammar of something; similarly music is the knowledge of something, not the music of something. (Increasing sales is the knowledge of something, not the sales of something) by author.

Thus individual branches of knowledge are not relative. And it is because we possess these individual branches of knowledge that we are said to be such and such. It is these that we actually possess: we are called experts because we possess knowledge in some particular branch."

We are called sales managers because we possess knowledge in some particular branch (of business.) Knowledgeable sales managers must have, or show, intelligence of a high order.

In reference to my thoughts a few pages ago about sales management's responsibilities and accountabilities, I would like to quote Peter Drucker from his book on management. He speaks of middle management—my thoughts are in terms of sales management.

"Middle management has not disappeared, as was predicted. Indeed not even the traditional middle manager has disappeared. But yesterday's middle management is being transformed into tomorrow's knowledge organization.

This knowledge requires not only restructuring individual jobs, but also restructuring the organization and its design. In the knowledge organization, the task, all the way down to the lowest professional or managerial level, has to focus on the company's objectives. It has to focus on contribution, which means that it has to have its own objectives. It has to be organized according to assignment. It has to be thought through and structured according to the flow of information both to and from the individual position. And it has to be placed in the decision structure. It can no longer be designed, as was the traditional middle-management job, in terms of downward authority alone. It has to be recognized instead as multidimensional.

Traditionally, middle-management jobs have been designed narrowly. The first concern has been with the limits on a middle manager's authority. In the knowledge organization we will instead have to ask, "What is the greatest possible contribution this job can make?" The focus will have to shift from concern with authority to stress on responsibility."

Aristotle, in his discourse, *POLITICS*, says, "Every man should be responsible to others, nor should anyone be allowed to do just as he pleases; for where absolute freedom is allowed there is nothing to restrain the evil which is inherent in every man."

Man should be responsible to others; and man should look forward to assuming a responsibility, but, for some reason, things do not seem to work out that way.

I once heard some manager say, "Some people grow under responsibility, others merely swell." I have been associated with two very large organizations—the U. S. Air Force and an aerospace company. It seems to me that those who were given a responsibility because of seniority or promotion used their new office as a steppingstone for their next move. Responsibility didn't enter their mind—that is responsibility to the organization, their fellow employees or officers and to the public at large. Responsibility seemed to be measured in office furniture, use of the executive dining room and salary. Everything seemed to be done to show how good *they* were—how smart the company was in promoting *them*. Everyone seemed to take responsibility for themselves only.

And, also, as I have worked my way through life, I have met others in many professions who say—and they all say the same thing—"Hell, they asked me about that position, but I don't want the responsibility; I'm satisfied where I am."

Owen D. Young understands it better than I. He said:

"There is a single reason why 99 out of 100 average businessmen never become leaders. That is their unwillingness to pay the price of responsibility. By the price of responsibility I mean hard driving, continual work and the courage to make decisions, to stand the gaff—the scourging honesty of never fooling yourself about yourself. You travel the road to leadership heavily laden. While the nine-to-five-o'clock worker takes his ease, you are 'toiling upward through the night.' Laboriously you extend your mental frontiers. Any new effort, the psychologists say, wears a new groove in the brain. And the grooves that leap to the heights are not made between nine and five. They are burned in by midnight oil."

And I would like to add—don't be afraid to make a mistake.

Owen D. Young (1874-1962) was an American lawyer and corporation official. He graduated from Boston University Law School in 1896. He lectured at Boston University (1896-1903) and practiced law in Boston. Mr. Young moved to New York City in 1913, became general counsel for the General Electric Company, and later served (1922-1939) as Chairman of the Board. The creation of the Radio Corporation of America was chiefly the result of his efforts and he was associated with other large corporations. With Charles G. Dawes, he was a United States representative at the Reparations Conference of 1929. As chairman of the Reparations Conference of 1929, he forwarded the *YOUNG PLAN*, which made Reparations a financial, rather than a purely political matter.

My discussion so far has addressed individual responsibility and my thoughts concerning such. Personally, I think responsibility is a blessing—a consciousness that gives one the opportunity to see how well one can handle the decision-making process, knowing all along no matter how good one is in a position—mistakes are going to be made. Assuming a responsibility allows one to see how well he handles failure; therein lies the judgment of man by his peers.

Anyhow, let's speak of the responsibilities of management.

Peter Drucker in his book, *The Practice of Management*, says,

"The responsibility of management in our society is decisive not only for the enterprise itself but for management's public standing, its success and status, for the very future of our economic and social system and the survival of the enterprise as an autonomous institution. The public responsibility of management must therefore underlie all its behavior. Basically it furnishes the ethics of management."

To me, it is like a cop putting on a uniform. It's responsibility; but it is also a trust.

In the profession of sales, I often wonder if management realizes their responsibility. Not too long ago I had a student come to my lecture series on "An Analysis of a Territory". I spoke about how a salesman systematically analyzes his territory to obtain the most dollar return for time and energy invested. The student was an engineer in a medical instrument manufacturing facility and his president was "Mr. Everything Else."

Business expansion was on the president's mind and since the president had to spend more time in the plant, the engineer I speak of knew the product "real good." He, in a directive from the president, was now the sales manager.

As of this writing, I have been teaching, or guest lecturing, sales and marketing for fourteen years and every class has ten to fifteen students (personnel in the business world) who are in class because the boss told them one day that he was "Going to put 'em in the field to sell and maybe they ought to take some classes or something." And 90% of the time the boss had never been in the field himself.

Or the boss will walk into a top salesman's office one day and say, "Mr. #1 Salesman, old Mr. Bones ain't coming back, so you're the new sales manager."

The president of the instrument company telling the engineer that he is now in sales and the boss telling the #1 salesman that he is the new sales manager have absolutely no idea of their responsibilities; and to compound things, the instrument salesman and sales manager are so new in their positions that they could not possibly know their responsibilities either.

Bank of America is known for its hiring of competent personnel, its training, its continued educational process, its personnel promotional activity and its methodology of spotting up and coming managers and administrators.

A. P. Giannini, Bank of America, says, "I leave everything to the young men. You've got to give youthful men authority and responsibility if you're going to build up an organization. Otherwise you'll always be the boss yourself and you won't leave anything behind you."

Giannini can say what has been stated above because he has seen to it that his company is structured properly and responsibilities are assigned as a matter of time, training and performance.

Performance of a company depends on sales, and management must learn responsibility to understand what it takes to grow internally and externally.

Responsibility is demanding and in order to compete in the market place and grow, management must be familiar with the *demands* of the market place. The two men I mentioned earlier came to work one morning and didn't even know the demands of their own company. They were lost, management was lost, responsibilities undefined. Both companies are now a thing of the past.

The demands, according to Drucker are:

1. Manage by objectives
2. Take more risks for a longer period
3. Make strategic decisions
4. Build an integrated team with each member capable of managing and measuring his own performance
5. Realize the task (responsibility) in developing managers equal to the task of tomorrow
6. Be able to communicate information fast and clearly
7. Be able to motivate people; be able to obtain the responsible participation of other managers.
8. Must be able to see his business as a whole and must be able to relate his product and industry to the total environment.

A new type of management is required in this new business era—one that realizes that responsibility begins rather than ends when the goods reach the shipping platform. First of all, such management will concern itself primarily with the knowledge and manufacture of customers rather than the manufacture of the product alone. Management must resort to logical analysis more than to precedent. A keen understanding of human beings will permit management to secure unusual results.

-Howard E. Blood

"You can't escape the responsibility of tomorrow by evading it today."
-Abraham Lincoln

I wrote earlier of the Credit Life Insurance Company. The problem with the president was that he was too successful. It was basically a sales-oriented company, and he had a number of salesmen in the field. Since he was so successful as a salesman, he thought that the other men could go out and do the same thing he had done. The reason that he failed to establish the goals, and then communicate the establishment of those goals, is the fact that since they had different kinds of credit life insurance to sell—automobile, homes, new patios, pools, extensions, etc., the man in the field was left without a rudder. They had no knowledge of stability and control. They had no one effectively communicating with them as to what the goals of this particular company were and how responsibility was going to be assigned in order to meet the goals.

Failure of the chief executive officer to establish and communicate major corporate goals is a never-ending problem. The problem with many chief executive officers is the fact that their companies are singularly owned and, in most cases, family-oriented. In actuality most of these men, or women, who are in charge, have grown with the company. As they grow and attain positions of stature, sometimes they forget that no matter what the business is, they must have knowledge of basic good business principles and practices. Why? Because the company must be structured for success! Also, in numerous circumstances, personnel will agree to be hired by the owner thus joining the company; and the owner assumes right off the bat that because he has attained success, all new employees are supposed to automatically understand what the business is all about and what their responsibilities are.

It's Monday night, and I want to turn on ABC football, but before I do, I want to leave you with a thought. Do you think that Tom Lasorda had great communication with the front office, O'Malley of the Dodgers? Do you think Lasorda has great baseball knowledge and in turn has great communication and assignment of responsibilities with his coaches in reference to the success of his baseball team? Do you think the same thing was true with Tex Schramm and Tom Landry with the Dallas Cowboys and his coaches? Do you think the same thing is true with Art Rooney and the former coach of the Pittsburgh Steelers, Chuck Knoll? Just count the World Series and Super Bowl rings! Year after year after year you know them in terms of success.

Why not your company?

NEVER MISTAKE KNOWLEDGE

FOR WISDOM.

ONE HELPS YOU MAKE A LIVING;

THE OTHER

HELPS YOU MAKE A LIFE.

SANDRA CAREY

AN EXCHANGE OF VALUE

The composition and orchestration of symphonic music is an art that transcends all socio-political boundaries. Music of the masters is cosmopolitan; it belongs to the world. Yet, it reflects the culture and character of the composer's native land—the territory of his or her experiences and values.

My knowledge of symphonic music is limited, yet I deeply appreciate all that goes into bringing carefully orchestrated, sonorous music to *my* being.

When I attend a symphony (The Philharmonic) I comfortably sit and think back centuries to the genius of such great composers as Beethoven, Mozart, Haydn, and Tchaikovsky. Then, as I listen and look at each member of the orchestra playing his or her instrument, there sets in a deep appreciation because I know many years of hard, tough practice were spent to reach what is not yet their zenith of ability or desire. This is because the best always try to become better. They want to add a measure of those qualities that determine merit, desirability, usefulness, and importance. The musicians want the orchestra to have *value*.

At then I look at Mehta, or Giulini or Chung, and watch these accomplished maestros bring together, into a united whole, all the individual notes and individual personalities and individual instru-ments into a masterpiece of beauty and sound.

For the price of a single ticket I can sit in a concert hall with pleasurable ease and watch literally hundreds of men and women take from the past and give me, at present, something of value—an exchange, as it were.

In my way of thinking, this exchange is not what Mozart was taking in the form of praise as a child prodigy. It is not what each member of the orchestra takes in the form of a paycheck; it is not what Giulini takes in the form of his photograph for *PEOPLE* magazine. Any time the orchestra plays to an appreciative audience it is not what they individually *take*, but what they collectively *give*.

It is not what sales personnel *take* from a territory that makes them successful. It is what they *give* to a territory, in the way of determining merit, desirability, usefulness, and importance (to the growth of the company represented,) that allows the salesperson to fully appreciate what an exchange of value is. The value is not something you grasp or assign a commission to. It is the subtle process of appreciating the territory's *character*; a character that specifically matches the man or woman responsible for its development. If done professionally a territory brings forth truth, and that which is good, and that which has intrinsic beauty.

I remember one time Socrates talking to me about truth and goodness. He said, "The most challenging expression in anyone's vocabulary are three words that name the universal values that elicit respect and evoke wonder. They are truth, goodness, and beauty—or the true, the good and the beautiful. These three values pertain to the three dimensions of human activity."

As a professional salesperson, thinking in Socrates' terms, the reward and value exchanged with a buyer is knowing you have delivered quality, dealt with him under the highest code of ethics, and told him the truth about cost and delivery.

Socrates continued (speaking of man the philosophical animal), "In the sphere of making, we are concerned with beauty or, to say the least, with trying to produce things that are well made. In the sphere of doing, as individuals and members of society, we are concerned with good and evil, right and wrong. In the sphere of knowing, we are concerned with truth."

The vice-president of material directs his buyers; the vice-president of sales directs his sales personnel. Both want to orchestrate truth to each other and goodness and beauty in product. It is in this atmosphere of EXCHANGE OF VALUE(S) that we have a solid method of contributing to the dynamics of free enterprise—with integrity and amity at both ends of the spectrum that transcends all socio-political boundaries.

I consider one of the distinguishing attributes of the profession of marketing and sales is that of offering a subliminal exchange of value between the one who buys and the one who sells. Subliminal to me means being just below the threshold of conscious perception; I perceive a sale, in time, subconsciously, every time I meet a buyer. And value is a standard or quality I regard as worthwhile or desirable. Without this conscious perception or standard of quality, brought together by the catalyst of time, the buyer and seller will see themselves in the business of merchandising. A sale may be made in a short time if the salesperson has the right product, at the right time, at the right cost, at the right delivery time (either on the shelf or fast warehouse delivery) and sold to the right person. But that is not selling or marketing; it is merchandizing.

How many red-hot products are still on the market from last Christmas? Not many; if at all! This Christmas, even before Thanksgiving, shoppers will stand in line for hours and will bowl each other over, and even steal, for hot 'merchandise.' I mean if one kid is going get something 'hot' the kid next door has to have it too! Next Christmas there will be more lines, with personnel charging through doors at 5am, and fighting each other for position to purchase another 'hot product.' We should, shamefully; name this material oriented sudden charge the 'skewed spirit of Christmas.'

I call this revolution of charging and fighting, ephemeral excitement. This kind of action offers insufficient time to add intrinsic value, in the world of marketing and sales, to the triad of product, buyer and seller.

Intrinsic value means, to me, thinking in the long term as to what the professions of sales and purchasing can contribute as a **team** to the foundation for economic and technical growth of a company(s). I mean long-term growth in a conscious effort to know the nature of my values and emotions, my company's values and emotions, and those of the personnel I would be calling on.

I decided that the word profession meant paying the price of time, education, exposure and experience. If I wanted to be a professional sales person I couldn't pick a single arena such chemicals, or valves, or paper products. Of course, they could be a start but I decided that if I had to enter the arena of understanding intrinsic value I had to start by understanding people. And to do that, I first had to take the time to understand myself.

As I said, TIME is the catalyst—TIME to learn of One's self, One's company, and TIME to plan and undergo a marketing analysis to identify the customer. TIME is essential to develop and test product. TIME is necessary to manufacture a quality product and TIME to develop a marketing and sales plan based on a detailed marketing analysis. And also TIME for the buyer and seller to recognize and achieve an 'exchange of value'—which I further define as selling, servicing, and offering product in the 'language of' and 'needs of' the customer.

If you wish to achieve the goal of the marketing and sale of a multi-million dollar contract, or even the goal of writing a few books, or the painting of several pictures, we learn our goals are indeed drawn out and demand cumulative individual efforts. You will also learn goals are greater than the individuals who produce them, if we view these individuals at any single point in TIME. For no one can, in a single moment, recall the multitude of shapes his mind took during the course of the work. Nor can the individual revive the various intensities of passion and calm that injected itself into its production, or glow with the incremental power built up by weeks or months of care. The work resembles not the partial man, alone within the minutes, but the whole man, incorporate in TIME.

On Friday, December 8th, 2000, *USA TODAY* carried two features I found very interesting: 1.)**The disappearing popular songwriter**, and 2.)**Once upon a time, there were 12 troubadours.**

A synthesis of the articles is as follows:

1.) "Solo artists still sing in their own words—but is **anyone listening**?" And:

2.) "Brief sketches of our featured troubadours and how their **fables unfolded**."

Why isn't '**disappearing**' and '**once upon a time**' associated with the works of Mozart, Beethoven, Haydn, Shubert, Tchaikovsky, and many others? Talk about songwriters! Ever hear anything more beautiful than *Beethoven's Ninth*? Or Mozart's brilliant opera, *The Marriage of Figaro*? How about Verdi's *La Traviata*?

On this Saturday afternoon as I write, I'm taking time out to think of this coming evening. All over the country the classical orchestras' of Pittsburgh,

Chicago, St. Louis, San Francisco, Los Angeles and other great cities will be performing symphonies composed by these brilliant self-enriched, self-respected men. I also think of the superb conductors: Esa-Pekka Salonen, the Los Angeles Philharmonic, Vladimir Spivakov, the Russian National Orchestra, Carl St.Clair, Pacific Symphony Orchestra, and others as famous like Eugene Ormandy, the Philadelphia Orchestra, and Leonard Bernstein, of the New York Philharmonic. These accomplished men have been guiding, and will continue to direct, masterpieces of music over long periods of time that have been loved, and valued, by tens of millions over hundreds of years; an en-richening exchange of value. They are enriched through TIME, self-discipline, failures, determination, and test of character.

And so too the soloists! Did you ever hear Murray Perahia play the piano in Beethoven's *Piano Concerto No. 1?* How about Alexander Pervomaisky playing Mozart's *Violin Concertos?* Or Peter Jancovic and his flute playing Mozart concertos? It is, simply, awe-inspiring!

Did any of these men try to compress TIME for speedy recognition? Not possible! Were they not determined? Did they not face failure? And did they not possess steely self-discipline to succeed?

Do you think a professional salesperson should get off any easier?

I don't see the words Xerox, or IBM, or MacDonalds, or Marvin Engineering **"disappearing"** or being considered "**once upon a time**". Why? Because management and marketing and sales appreciates TIME, and tests of character, and failures. In addition, collectively, there is the never ending quest for knowledge about self, and the determination in trying to understand the states of pain and anguish throughout life that tests one's resiliency, mettle, and personality.

The last time I was with Socrates was soon after I resigned from my test flying position at Lockheed. He came to my apartment to wish me well in my new 'adventure' into the world of business. As we toasted to my success he told me of a Greek philosopher, a friend of his by the name of Lucius Seneca. Socrates told me to look him up during one of my trips to the library.

Well, I did just that. I learned that success will come to the ordinary individual, even to those with ordinary ability. But triumph over the disasters and fears of human life is only granted to great men.

I learned that if one is always content with the thought of 'having it made' and to pass through life without a qualm or compunction, that person is ignorant of half of nature. People may think someone to be a great man, but if Fortune doesn't give him a chance to demonstrate his merit, how is Jack Simpson, or any other person, to know his greatness? If a man is to know himself he must be tested. No one knows what he can accomplish except by trying.

If a man is to know himself, that task should be the cornerstone for youth in school. It should be the cornerstone for the business community. It is also, above all, a wise statement of observation for all those determined to succeed, with honor, no matter the endeavor.

If man is to know himself, there *will* be **millions listening**! And, there will be *no* **fables unfolded**!

The foundation for an exchange of value can be the same for a sales person and buyer as a composer and conductor. The buyer composes the requirements; the salesperson conducts the evolution of a sale. The salesperson writes the 'music' for the sales presentations, and the buyer conducts the 'movements' for the evolution of the purchase order. If you do not think so, there will soon be a '**disappearing**' salesperson or a '**once upon a time**' territory manager.

An exchange of value should be built on self-enrichment and self-respect between the buyer and the seller; self-enrichment being the process of developing or augmenting one's mental facilities about knowing one's self, the company represented, the product, the valued procurement needs of the company and the professional responsibility each carries. In time, accompanied by a record of performance, this augmentation will *earn* self-respect, character and superior conduct. We are back again to what?? Truth! Goodness! And Beauty! The three dimensions of human activity!

I remember two other statements of truth that Socrates spoke to me. "The character of the philosopher as a man, is inextricably connected with the manner of life he leads," and "the philosopher as a seeker of wisdom is the wise man who knows how to manage all affairs of life well."

Since at least one-third of a salespersons' life is selling and one-third of a buyers' life is spent in purchasing, it is a good place to start managing all affairs of life well.

The manifestation of the value we (the buyer and seller) set on one another is that which I call *honoring and dishonoring*.

To value a buyer or salesperson judged at a high rate is to *honor* him or her; at a low rate is to *dishonor*. But high and low, in this case, has to be understood by comparison to the rate each man or woman sets on himself or herself.

AS SOON AS YOU STOP CLIMBING,

YOU ENTER A ZONE OF RISK

OF FALLING!

GEORGE HALL

THE DIGNITY OF MAN

Emmanuel Kant, (1724-1804) was a German metaphysician and one of the greatest figures in philosophy. He said all objects except man have exchange value, a price for which they will be sold. Even an object of great sentimental value will be sold (consider a Heisman Trophy, a World Series winner's ring, a Super Bowl winner's ring, or Wimbleton Trophy) if the offer is high enough. But man possesses dignity (infinite intrinsic value) and is therefore priceless. To charge that 'every man has a price' Kant would reply that any man who sold himself for money would be cheated out of his rightful due, for man is above all price and possesses infinite worth.

Kant said it best—men and women must learn to exchange 'intrinsic value' offered out of sheer dignity. Men and women must be in a position to receive, and give, the chance for priceless professional and personal friendships. In my way of thinking, the search for wisdom, (philosophy,) combined with the lessons of history, is an overture to the business world and the profession of marketing and sales offers that bonhomie!

But in order to develop the professionalism, and confidence in oneself, while gaining the knowledge of others, the salesperson must first gain cognizance *about* his or her self and learn the limits of their own worldly wisdom.

I wondered how I would start to go about accomplishing this never ending task?

I started thinking—then it hit me. "You dumb jerk," I said to myself. "You were just talking about 'Seneca' and 'Fortune giving man a chance to demonstrate his merit—but only through trying.' You found Seneca in the library. He left a message for you over 1900 years ago—1900 years! Hell, that's way much older than your mother-in-law! Well, would you believe a little bit! Also, Socrates told you to spend more time in the library. He said, "Suits, I love you, but I'm not going to give you all the answers. You do the groundwork and then I'll help with 'a little push' when I think you need one."

"Also," Socs said, "You and I talked at one time about Descartes. Do you remember Rene Descartes? He was the great French philosopher, mathematician, and scientist whose methodology was a major influence in the transition from medieval science and philosophy to the modern era."

"Yes, Socs, I remember us talking about him." He's the man who said, '*Cogito, ergo sum*—I think! Therefore I am.'"

"Very good, Suits. I too think! Therefore I think you are getting to be a good student."

"OK! Here is what he had to say about going to a library and doing research. Descartes said, 'The reading of all good books is indeed like a conversation with the noblest men of past centuries who were the authors of them, nay a carefully studied conversation, in which they reveal to us the best of their thoughts.'"

"Simpson," I said to myself, "it's simple. You *are* the man; the cornerstone and the foundation. These brilliant men, Seneca, Kant, Descartes and Socrates are talking to you! Get off your rear and spend some valued time in the library."

So—I suddenly realized I was the foundation and my blueprints were books in the library. I wanted to examine more closely this 'exchange of value.' If I didn't know how to value myself I couldn't exchange it with anyone else because I wouldn't understand how it applied to my needs. I asked myself a lot of questions. What could I gain if I looked deeply into learning more about life, about people, about me? I determined two things; 1.) I had to learn more about me and 2.) I had to seek a way to learn from the lessons of history and to appreciate the practical aspects of philosophy.

When I was test flying, I started by spending many free afternoons and evenings in the Burbank library. I ran through a lot of 'how to' books. Dr. Donald Laird was one author. He wrote about attaining self-confidence, self-reliance, self-respect, etc. He was very good for me; made a lot of sense. And a former third baseman for the St. Louis Cardinals told about how he raised himself from a weak image of a salesman to a very successful insurance sales executive.

But I wasn't satisfied; and I didn't know why I wasn't satisfied. "Well," I said to myself, "Socrates isn't going to help you. Why don't you go to the section on philosophy and see if you can find anything in reference to contemporary business or at least something about learning more about yourself. So far, you are reading about the success of other people; you are not learning about yourself.

"Yeah! Yeah! I know!" I was still talking to myself. "You were a successful paperboy and you paid for your last year of college (when your GI Bill ended) by selling encyclopedias' door to door, but you had no idea what philosophy, the lives of philosophers, and the lessons of history had to offer.

Remember Seneca said, 'If a man is to know himself he must be tested.' See if you can find something on knowing yourself and then wrap yourself with the language of learned philosophers. Just read and make mental note. Remember when Socrates asked you one day before a combat mission what your most important piece of personal equipment was? You said, 'My parachute.' And he said, 'You're right! If it opens it saves your body and soul. Attach an open parachute to your mind. All kinds of thoughts will enter. Then, at the right time, you will be able to pick the right thought that fits the occasion.'"

I continued talking to myself, "It sounds 'far out,' but what do you have to lose?"

About halfway through one particular afternoon I 'ran into' a guy by the name of Plotinus, 205-270AD. He was born in Egypt but ended in Rome teaching philosophy for the last twenty-five years of his life. He talked about learning about your self.

Plotinus spoke about withdrawing into yourself and taking a look; and if you did not find yourself beautiful at the beginning, act as the creator of a statue that is to be made more beautiful. He cuts away here, he smoothes there, and then he makes this line lighter, this other purer, until a lovely face has grown upon his work. So I should do that too!

"Well, Plotinus, Sir, you shall be remembered by me as the 'Great Reminder.' Plotinus, Marcus Aurelius, Emerson, and many other philosophers spoke *through* Socrates to me for several years during my combat and flight test career. I recorded much of what I learned in the first two books of my trilogy, SOCRATES 'N SUITS.

I have learned to accept, without contempt, the disdainful. Emerson told me that in every man there is something to be learned of him so therefore I should be his pupil. That was a little tough because of the number of assholes (pardon me) I have met in my life, but through Emerson I learned to open my mind. If I found the situation too tough, rather than fight it, I have learned to move on. As a fall out, I do not purposely speak ill of any man, or woman, anymore.

Aurelius, in his brilliant book *MEDITATIONS*, taught me that no matter the unhappy, unlucky, sad, and unfortunate circumstances in my life, what happened to me has happened to man millions and millions of times in the past. And, when I thought about it, the animosity was, in most cases, my fault so I have learned not to run to others but to think and read and allow time to straighten things out by myself.

And, through Plotinus, philosophy has taught me to love—women. No, I'm kiddin'. To understand the love of my fellow man, the pilots I flew with in combat and test flying, and the boys I raised through 'Big Brothers'. When I tell a man I love him it's just—well, it's just there. I don't have to explain, or excuse, or reason. It's so honest; the communication of love and respect percolates like water in a spring stream or the bubbles spewing upward in a percolating pot of coffee over a campfire.

But I still have an awful lot to learn, and control, and accomplish. I have to learn to be more forgiving. I must learn to live with members of my wife's family—and control my short—lived temper in that I am always berating myself when it would be easier to 'count to ten.' And I must achieve the personal satisfaction that I am on the right path to knowing more about me, and what philosophy and the lessons of history have to offer.

There is an old fighter pilot expression that states, "No guts, no glory."

It was time for me to make the move—get into the cockpit—head for the battle zone (the study of philosophy; the lessons of history,) buy the granite and start to chisel. St. Augustine said, in *CITY of GOD*, XVI, "For the most part, the human mind cannot attain to self-knowledge otherwise than by making trial of its powers through temptation, by some kind of experimental and not merely verbal self interrogation."

HEADED TOWARD THE BATTLE ZONE

Philosophy's concern with the central problems of the meaning and significance of human experience presupposes an acquaintance with the widest range of facts, and the possession of the conclusion of all types of knowledge, as materials on which to reflect. But 'meaning and significance' is an affair of more than mere knowledge: it raises the fundamental questions of importance, or relevance, and of relative value. In this sense, philosophy is often called an interpretation of knowledge or of human experience in the light of available knowledge.

'Philosophy is an interpretation of knowledge!' Socrates said, when I first called him. Socrates also said he and other philosophers make mistakes and they often disagree. It makes sense to me now. Knowledge comes through experience and a philosopher's different background can effect his impression about the same experience in a different way. It doesn't make him wrong. In fact in studying this 'interpretation of knowledge' I think one becomes more aware of the potential for intellectual growth through honest discord and an open mind.

The best way to study philosophy is to approach it as one approaches a detective story: follow every trail, clue and implication, in order to discover who is a murderer and who is a hero. The criterion of detection is two questions: Why and How! If a given tenet seems to be true, why? If another tenet seems to be false—why, and how is it being put over? You will not find all the answers immediately, but you will acquire an invaluable characteristic: the ability to think in terms of essentials.

Nothing is given to man automatically: neither knowledge, nor self-confidence, nor inner serenity, nor the right way to use his mind. Every value he needs or wants has to be discovered, learned and acquired—even the proper posture of his body. "In this context," says Ayn Rand, "I have always admired the posture of West Point graduates, a posture that projects man in proud, disciplined control of his body." Well, philosophical training gives man the proper *intellectual* posture—a proud, disciplined control of his mind.

To be a philosopher is not merely to have subtle thoughts, nor even to found a school, but to love wisdom as you live, according to common sense and courtesy, a life of simplicity, independence, magnanimity, and trust. I am quite sure that if we can find wisdom, (it will not be given to us) more and more things else will be added. "Seek ye first the good things of the mind," Francis Bacon (1561-1626) admonishes us, "and the rest will either be supplied or its loss will not be felt." Truth will not make us rich, but it will make us free.

Remember Descartes—we met him on the way to our 'battle zone.' "Good books—like a conversation with the noblest men—reveal to us the best of their thoughts." Well, evidently Descartes knows what it takes. He and Bacon were contemporaries! I have learned good books will give you great 'things of the mind' and the rest will be supplied because it put my mind in an aura or atmosphere of surrounding wisdom.

One thing I discovered early on is illusion and self-deception always stand in the way of an honest, penetrating, and fearless self-appraisal. Though it would appear that we have access to the innermost core of our individual being, the self remains an elusive object of knowledge and understanding.

There have been many passages quoted on self-knowledge and self-love—and many attempts have been made to define both—particularly love; it's nature, kinds, and power of love. But the proper objects of love are God, other human beings, one's country, and such ideals as truth, beauty, and goodness. Yet, one of the most famous of all statements about love—the Christian Precepts of Charity—commands us, first, to love God, and second to love our neighbor as ourselves. The same injunction is implied in Aristotle's conception of the ideal friend, as an alter ego—another self. Self-love is, in a sense, the basis of true love of another.

OK! Let's take a few minutes and see if we can't make a transition. A shift from the fact that if I know and love myself to the best of my ability, maybe I can just go on and know my fellow man better. And by knowing my fellow man better I might just make room to know and appreciate his or her profession better. I mentally exchange their contribution, their value. Therefore I go full circle; self-knowledge, self-love, love and appreciation of another. Taking time to understand another's job—and his or her contribution—helps me understand and appreciate their profession much more. The Gods help him who helps himself—by taking the time to study, learn, understand, contribute and think. An open mind between us all offers what? A dynamic exchange of values

Plato said, in *CHARMIDES*, "Self-knowledge would certainly be maintained by me to be the very essence of knowledge, and in this I agree with him who dedicated the inscription, 'Know thyself!' at Delphi." He also said, speaking for Socrates, "The wise or temperate man, and he only, will know himself." Pretty high-powered statements from two prestigious philosophers! Knowing your-self is the essence of knowledge!

In learning about myself, I realized everyone has the obligation to ponder his own specific traits of character. He must also regulate them adequately and not wonder whether someone else's' traits might suit him better. The more definitely a man's own character is, the better it fits him.

The injunction first uttered by one of the seven wise men of ancient Greece, "Know thyself," gets repeated in one form or another century after century. In the book, *PHILOSOPHIES of PEACE and WAR,* Gallie speaks of Clausewitz on the nature of war. He reminds us that it is difficult to believe that the hardship, shortcomings and disappointments of his career did not serve him well when he (Clausewitz) set about systematizing his ideas on the general conduct of war. In this task he showed a dedication to the maxim 'Know thy trade' that is comparable to that which the greatest philosophers have accorded to 'Know thyself' or, 'Know the limits of thy knowledge.'

Smart man, this Clausewitz!

So I said to myself, "Go forward, my friend, into your battle zone, your sales responsibility, your territory, with the potential fulfillment of meeting great men and women. Wrap your arms around knowledge through the experience of great men and exchange what you learn for a more rewarding life for others, which will, in TIME, offer value to your own."

ALL OUR DIGNITY CONSISTS . . .

IN THOUGHT.

BUT WE MUST ELEVATE OUSELVES,

AND NOT BY SPACE AND TIME

WHICH WE CANNOT FILL.

LET US ENDEAVOUR, THEN, TO THINK WELL;

THIS IS THE PRINCIPLE OF MORALITY.

PASCAL, *PENSEES, VI*

MAN AND THE ORGANIZATION

FOR WHAT REASON?
THE CUSTOMER!

When Robert Bies wants his business students to understand the nature of power, he sends many of them off on a real-life case study—to visit the homeless. It's no "gut" course!

In suburban Evanston, Ill., not far from Northwestern University's J. L. Kellogg Graduate School of Management is where Bies teaches. The problem of homeless people is a complex, highly politicized issue. Bies's organizational-behavior students confront it head-on: they study how local government, business and citizens' groups have tossed the problem around like a football; how sound financial decisions—such as tearing down transient hotels to build high-rises—have had the unintended social effect of displacing people. Bies's primary goal is to draw parallels to the man trade-offs of corporate life—but student Bill Anderson, 27, got so involved that he even volunteered to work at a shelter one night a month. "They begin to see that being a manager means more than numbers," Bies says.

Few people do business well who do nothing else.

Lord Chesterfield

The new president of the United Way of Los Angeles said Monday that he wants to improve the charity's image in light of last year's loan problems and get its lagging campaign back on track.

THE LOS ANGELES TIMES

Leo P. Cornelius, who recently headed Philadelphia's United Way, has taken over the Los Angeles job on the heels of last week's announcement that the charity fell $8.6 million short of its $90-million campaign goal for the year.

"This community ought to be raising $200 million, and we are going to pursue it aggressively." Cornelius, 53, said at a new conference at United Way headquarters.

"A $200-million goal would be feasible if United Way attracts more volunteers and goes about fund raising differently," Cornelius said. "The charity has to find ways of reaching more small businesses, he said. Traditionally, the United Way has focused on contracting large companies because it is the least expensive way of soliciting donations."

I am going to touch on something I read that I think fits in with what we will learn about personnel in corporate America. It is a synthesis of John Stuart Mill's review of *Democracy in America*, written by Tocqueville. Mill is writing:

"It has often been said, and requires to be repeated still more often, that books and discourses alone are not education; that life is a problem, not a theorem; that action can only be learned in action. A child learns to write his name only by a succession of trials; and is a man to be taught to use his mind and guide his conduct by mere precept? What can be learned in schools is important, but not all-important. The main branch of the education of human beings is their habitual employment, which must be either their individual vocation or some matter of general concern, in which they are called to take a part.

The private money-getting occupation, of almost everyone, brings but few of his faculties into action, while its exclusive pursuit tends to fasten his attention and interest exclusively upon himself, and upon his family. It makes him indifferent to the public, to the more generous objects and the nobler interests. Balance these tendencies by contrary ones; give him something to do for the public, whether as vestryman, a juryman, or an elector; and in that degree, his ideas and feelings are taken out of this narrow circle. He becomes acquainted with more varied business and a larger range of considerations. He is made to feel that besides those interests which separate him from his fellow citizens, he has interests which connects him with them; that not only the common weal is his weal, but that it partly depends upon his exertions . . . . "

Talk about the lessons from history! Mill probably wrote that review in mid-1800. Was Mill pre-sagest—wise to the problems of United Way?

I will talk more about the United Way, but first a thought process regarding a bond between Aleis de Tocqueville, let's say in 1837, and Leo Cornelius in 1987.

Also a synopsis from John Stuart Mill's review of Tocquevilles (1805-1859) *Democracy in America*.

A leader is a person of individual qualities skilled as a coach or nurturer to attain a major goal; and it is done through ability to influence, in a positive manner, people.

Did anyone ever think of matching Leo Cornelius' desired to raise $200 million with de Tocqueville's thoughts of giving a man in a corporation something to do for the public?

Doesn't this make common sense? Fund-raisers always go to heads of corporations who dictate their mundane, pump full of sunshine, memorandums about "How we want to contribute and look good." The problem is the CEO of the corporation wants to look good; usually at the expense of some very petulant employees.

No wonder United Way fell $8.6 million short.

I say management is missing considerable opportunity to take time and personally outline, to select potential leaders throughout the organizational structure, the responsibility of corporations to the community (United Way).

It is then up to the individuals selected in the corporation to raise funds, in their own Department or Group or Division. Forget the conventional, banal, trite memorandum from the CEO; give the latent leaders the chance to demonstrate communication and leadership skills.

Mr. Cornelius says, "The charity has to find ways of reaching more small business." That makes for common sense too. But isn't it also common sense in that there is no difference (people) between small business and small departments in a large business.

The heads of these small departments could become influential men because "he becomes acquainted with more varied business and a larger range of considerations. He is made to feel that besides the interests which separate him from his fellow citizens, he has interests which connect him with them."

"Throughout the modern world, at all levels of rank and wealth an in just about every walk of life, there are millions upon millions of men and women who share a common fate. Whether they are factory workers or accountants, bishops or colonels, teachers or nurses or government functionaries, they have committed their lives and part of their identities to one of the vast, powerful, complex and impersonal organizations that produce and distribute goods, that explore the frontiers of science, that inform and educate, and govern mankind.

To avoid anarchic chaos, organized actions must be governed by a set of rules. "The system," which specifies how each operation is to be performed and assigns it to a particular member of the organization, not by individual name, but by job category or role. Any one of many qualified individuals can be given the role, for it is the role that matters more than individual qualities, even at very high levels." The British governmental system, to take one example of a large and durable organization, calls for a Monarch. This role can be filled admirably by a man or a woman, who can as different in personality as Elizabeth I was from George VI.

Man and the Organization
Rafael Steinberg

I can't agree with much of what Steinberg has to say.

The sentence, "Anyone of many qualified individuals can be given the role, for it is the role that matters more than individual human qualities, even at very high levels," seems to me, to be controversial. That is because of his use of the words qualified and qualities.

The qualities of an individual are the basis for job selection in an organization. "Role" matters in very few instances. The Monarch in the British governmental system is by inheritance—handed down from family member to family member regardless of qualities. The Monarch fulfills a role.

But the British Prime Minister is elected by the voters to function as first in rank and authority. The Prime Minister is judged not so much as the technicalities of role-playing but on understanding through experience, intelligence, and wisdom that special duty or performance required in the course of term in office.

From my studies of the *Great Treasury of Western Thought*, I realize that history's legacy leaves us with the reflection that certain philosophers are at pains to distinguish reason from understanding, or intellect from intelligence. But all of these words have this common thread of meaning: they designate the power of ability by which men solve problems, make judgments, engage in reasoning or in deliberation, and make practical decisions. There is absolutely no role-playing here.

Steinberg says, that many live the organized life out of necessity. For many, the organization provides financial security and social status, and they are happy playing out their assigned roles.

Today, however, for an increasing number of organizations, people at every level in the hierarchy, the material rewards and social comforts of the organized life are not enough.

They talk of the "rat race," complain about being cogs in an impersonal machine, and sometimes wear lapel buttons that read, "I am a human being. Do not fold, spindle or mutilate." They seek a measure of personal satisfaction that the organization is unable to provide. And they feel that they have somehow lost their freedom on the organization's treadmill, because the organization commands their work, molds them to its needs, shuffles them around like pawns on a chessboard, and attaches to them the labels and values by which they are known to the world.

I feel that if people are satisfied playing out their "assigned roles" they should do so with respect for themselves and the organization. However, if they (people) seek a measure of personal satisfaction that the organization is unable to provide, they should either resign and then complain or continue to work with the company and do something about seeking lofty targets. A person in the state of self-determined growth (and I'm thinking growth with a corporate organization) needs, as a preparation for a useful and satisfying life, a measure of accepted or even self-imposed austerity. Some forms of hardship must be received and endured, not as ends in themselves, but as a systematic training in view of some higher goal.

Joseph de Vinck, in *The Yes Book*, pointed out that our incorporated world would become less and less tolerable unless there is a tide of revolts against regimentation and conformism, a resurgence of the spirit of creative freedom, and originality.

And management should recognize this and assist. So, the organization has to "ease up" and allow creativity—and mistakes; and personnel must stop the complaints and subliminal revolt and work hard and sacrifice in preparation for accepting more responsibility and accompanying accountability.

How is this attained??

Organization and personnel must teach each other—follow Emerson—"in every man there's something I may learn of him—."

Management says, "We send people to seminars all the time."

I think it is the department manager's responsibility to bring everyone together and discuss what is expected of each one; and what each one expects of the manager (leader). Problems cannot be solved unless they are brought out into the open and nothing will be accomplished without effective communication—not from the top down but from the bottom up. An experienced manager should know how to "walk the floor." This management style allows for consistent *conceptions* for better work methods, personnel rapport, innate increase in quality of corporate life, and product and personnel with exacting *perceptions* of the reasoning behind communication directives. It is a communication of *responsibility* with the concomitant acceptance of *accountability* from ground up. It is pure TQMS (Total Quality Management System) by evolution.

I say, "You are going about it the wrong way. You are *sending* a cross section of people from *different* departments to some unknown Guru when you should be bringing an experienced Guru to a cross section of people in the *same* department; but only after the department determines the Guru can help them fulfill their particular needs; speaking their particular language. What is it in the department that is lacking? Who is the best in the particular discipline where it has been determined help is needed?

Corporations are all excited over "quality circles"—for insubstantial things like cars and TV sets. Why not quality circles for personnel in a department? A company should be spending time and money on marketing analysis in order to speak the language and needs of the customer. How about spending time and very little money (in comparison) on the language and needs of department personnel?

And speaking of qualified personnel, a manager should not be promoted by a body of persons in authority. I know it has to start somewhere, but personnel promotions should come from within a department with the department manager being responsible for picking his or her successor; and steps up the corporate ladder should be judged on the department manager's ability to choose a successful successor.

In a "Marketing Analysis and Information Systems" lecture series years ago, I often said that business seminars were a waste of time and money. I quote from the San Francisco Examiner:

"Business Seminars Get Low Marks"—NEW YORK—Half of all business conventions and seminars attended by America's executives and their employees are a waste of time and money, a survey of 100 top U.S. corporations concluded.

The study, conducted by personnel recruiter Robert Half International, found top executives attend an average of 6.4 out-of-town and four local conventions and seminars a year. When asked what percentage of all business conventions or seminars they thought were genuinely worth the time and expense of attending, the respondents answered: "49 percent."

Executives aren't getting their worth because of what I call the "broad-side approach"—most seminars trying to cover too broad a range of subjects to too broad a range of personnel.

Peter Drucker is renown in his writings on specific areas of management. If I have a problem I can research his numerous writings on a particular subject matter. Then it would be just Drucker and me! His book—me in a black leather reclining chair—me thinking through the written message!

But Drucker's seminars are terrible—too rambling, too discursive, too many people asking too many different questions.

It's OK to have seminars—but for individual reasons—CPA's to more fully understand specific changes on particular amendments to new tax law—divorce lawyers on new California law—criminal lawyers on the RICO Act.

"OK," management says, "we'll be more circumspect in selection of our seminar/ personnel planning, but as I now see it, you want each department manager and all personnel in the department to—encompass everything you speak of—this so called growth within by better understanding time, and communication and learning of ones-self, and thinking and accepting responsibility, etc."

Management continues, "Isn't that paradoxical because of the innate frailties of people and their different reasons for coming to work?? How are they going to manage?? They seem to always be worried about their job."

These are good questions. I use them to address concerns of mine—wondering if department managers would take time to understand themselves and their personnel. I say let them worry; it's good therapy.

"It appears that efficient problem solvers 'creatively worry' and carry a problem around with them even while doing other tasks. Brief episodes of mulling over a problem or creatively worrying about it is a precursor to insight, or the 'aha' experience. What appears to be a sudden solution is actually the result of days or weeks of creative worry, detailed thoughts, incremental changes, and critical evaluations—all adding up and eventually allowing the solution of 'pop' in."

Perry Buffington, Ph.D.
SKY Magazine

Isn't that, also, what Gell Mann said! (Read about Murray Gell Mann of "Full Of the Problem" chapter)

Managing Ambiguity and Paradox
In Search of Excellence

Paradox: a person, situation, act, etc., that seem to have contradictory or inconsistent qualities.

"Similarly, the world of management seemed easier when we draw parallels with the military, most people's metaphor still for management structure in the twentieth century. But, again, the parallels broke down when we tried to understand anything more complex, than, for instance, a regiment under fire. There are arguably problems even in that unambiguous imagery. William Manchester, in *GOOD-bye DARKNESS*, tells of Marine vets laughing derisively at the untested zeal and orders of young OCS lieutenants who would lead them into withering enemy fire. Many a young officer ended up going over the wall alone, and not coming back. So, as any seasoned hand well knows, the crystal-clear so-called military model—give an order and get instant compliance doesn't even hold for the military. We need something better if we are really to understand. Unfortunately, better isn't easier at first blush, although it may turn out to be easier as understanding improves. As we shall see, the new wave of management thought leads us to an ambiguous, paradoxical world—just like the world of science. But we think its tenets are more useful and ultimately more practical. Most important, we think the excellent companies, if they know any one thing, know how to manage within a paradox."

I don't think we need something better than the military if we are ready to understand. I read *GOOD-bye, DARKNESS*. The vets laughing were not officers and the OCS graduate lieutenants were there for a reason—to lead. Departments or organizations or regiments are formed to do a specific job. Iwo Jima, the battle of Leyte Gulf and Tarawa were the ultimate tests of leadership without the benefit of time allowing even the best of minds to sort out contradictory or inconsistent qualities. Nothing is crystal-clear in a battle; it is in itself a paradox.

Nothing is crystal-clear in life; it is in itself a paradox.

Nothing is crystal-clear in management or in a department. It is in itself a paradox because it is made up of people who lead paradoxical lives.

We don't have to have "numerous schemes elaborated to describe the evolution of management." All we need is common sense and knowledge of ourselves, our departmental personnel and the customer, so that the proper strategy and tactics may be devised to enhance our own innate capabilities and in time—market share.

Hickman and Silva, authoring *CREATING EXCELLENCE* said, "Strategic thinking and culture building work in tandem. Actions that are based on strategic thinking must effectively satisfy customer needs, gain a sustainable advantage over competitors, and capitalize on company strength. Actions aimed at corporate culture building instill a collective commitment to a common purpose, foster distinctive competence among employees to deliver superior performance, and establish a consistency that helps attract, keep, and develop leaders at all levels."

All firms follow some kind of strategy and function with some form of culture, but most do this only halfheartedly. Sometimes a company develops a strategy it can't implement. When Exxon tried to run its new office systems business like an oil company, it lost millions of dollars to more agile high-tech rivals who knew their business. When Quaker Oats moved into toys and restaurants, it almost destroyed a once invincible food marketing culture. Some senior executives attempt to correct problems in the culture with confusing and alienating policy memos and dictums. Jim Edwards reorganized Bausch & Lomb's instruments group overnight into new reporting relationships, governed by IBM-like operating policies, such as a matrix-style structure that had people reporting to more than one boss. However, the Bausch & Lomb crew didn't respond the way Edwards's IBM experience had taught him they should. Confusion skyrocketed, earning crashed, and Edwards resigned. Roy Ash of AM International lost his job the same way when his seemingly brilliant strategy failed to launch the company into the high-tech future. It was too much—too fast! How many Hollywood personnel that became overnight sensations soon failed because of too much—too fast?

Let me deviate a little here. How many times have you read, or heard "Too much! Too fast" when speaking of a Hollywood actress? How about an athlete just out of college being given millions of dollars for a bonus just to sign a contract? You know what I am talking about! They crash cars, get drunk, smoke grass, take drugs, impregnate women! They can't assimilate, or absorb the necessary time demanded of evolutionary, not revolutionary, growth through mental, physical, and socially proven, through time, parameters. They lack any set of the physical or mental properties whose values determine their character and behavior.

There is synergy here! Synergy between corporate culture, responsibility, and growth, over time, and that of a Hollywood actress and a young athlete!

Let's keep in mind IBM and AM International as we move forward!

By sharp contrast, Hewlett-Packard has instilled a sense of shared purpose and a striving for technological innovation in its organization by encouraging rather than stifling an entrepreneurial spirit. The company has successfully kept entrepreneurs within its ranks, while many rival companies lose theirs to start-ups. The consistency of this purpose has outlasted its founders. H-P's strategy depends on innovation to satisfy customer needs, better products to gain advantage over competitors, and individual entrepreneurial spirit.

Nordstrom's department stores have culture. They cultivate their relationship *with* customers; they constantly refine their internal and external communications *for* customers.

North American Aviation in the 1950's had culture. They could build what the customer wanted; the CEO knew the customer and his employees. And North American had a dynamite field service/product support organization—designed to service the customer.

Many executives wonder why a company fails to live up to its expectations after it being purchased by a larger company. The company may have spent millions making changes in trying to make it better—in the eyes of management. What about the eyes of the customer!

But the management of the parent company didn't understand that even though changes were made on the inside, nothing on the outside changed. Purchasing agents and buyers and quality personnel remained the same. What had been a subtle development of culture over a long period of time was now being cracked or fractured by the new management; and they didn't even realize it.

New management was so busy internally that they forgot customer externally. In the eyes of the buyer the company lost it aesthetic value—its culture. I witnessed this happen to a corporation (let's call it MNO Corporation) that bought a smaller aerospace company let's say AFS, Inc.) that captured, over the years, 75% of an important fuel system on CESSNA, PIPER, and BEECH aircraft.

I was sitting, with my Wichita representative, in the office of a purchasing manager when the secretary announced two visitors from MNO Corporation. The purchasing manager said, "Sit still, Ben and Suitcase. This should be good." And sure enough, the two men, dressed in their New York best, came in to announce their purchase of AFS, Inc. and said something to the effect that "MNO will now be responsible for the purchase orders."

The purchasing agent was very professional and convivial but he looked at the two men and said, "All I know about your company is that it has three letters and I will be the one who decides where I will place my orders."

How ill advised, dumb, or disrespectful can a company get? How often have I said, "Sell in the language and needs of the customer." Remember! It's a two way street! A buyer has to know your company through YOU! YOUR performance! YOUR experience! YOUR technical and economic capabilities! Just because a company is purchased by another means absolutely NOTHING until the buyer accepts the other company's ability to perform. Those two New York "Appleknockers" (look it up) did more to destroy a professional rapport in two minutes that it took AFS 20 years to build.

If I were given the responsibility to purchase a company, the first thing I would do is call on the purchasing personnel from CESSNA and BEECH, in Wichita, and brief them on what I would like to do and ask them for their opinion. The strength and growth from any corporation comes from the companies it is doing business with. Of course, strength also comes from the personnel inside the purchased company but with 78% of a discipline (fuel system), the company must be doing something right.

Everything you do in life should be as professional as possible. I remember once when I was really excited about dating a beautiful girl. I was told one night that she and her current boy friend had broken up. I knew her suitor at the time so I called him and asked if it would be OK if I gave her a call. He said, "Jack, I very much appreciate the call but I would appreciate it if you would hold off to see how this thing plays out."

I said, "I hope it works out well for you."

Just think if Jackie and I had a date for dinner and George walked into the restaurant and saw us. Everyone would have been embarrassed! Life is hurtful enough without adding insult to potential injury.

By the way, the manufactures' representative, Ben, was hired to cover Wichita. I met Ben because he was recommended by a number of purchasing personnel I talked to, asking the question, "Who serves you the best?"

Hell, many went to school with Ben. Many went to the same church! They also belonged to the same Legion Hall, and hunted and fished together.

Speak about honesty, and integrity, and selling in the language of the customer!

YOU WILL MEET A CHAPTER
"FULL OF THE PROBLEM"

We use a definition by social psychologist Theresa Amabile, who says creativity is "both a novel and appropriate, useful, correct or valuable response to the task at hand, and the task is heuristic, meaning to discover; *or* serving as an aid to problem-solving. It is deemed heuristic rather than algorithmic." The first part of her definition is pretty common. You're doing something new that solves a problem. But the heuristic part is really profound. It means that the task—the situation—isn't completely defined. There isn't a rule of thumb; there isn't a step-by-step law leading to discovery. An algorithm, on the other hand, is a complete mechanical rule for solving a problem or dealing with a situation.

"Remember, we want to deal in a novel and appropriate way with a heuristic, that free-form situation. Ted Nierenberg, founder of Dansk International Designs, Ltd., says he becomes creative by working in his garden. He says he just puts his foot on the shovel and suddenly the answer comes to a problem he's been working on for weeks, months, even years. Suddenly there's this tremendous rush, "this joie de vivre." At this point, he not only knows he can solve that problem but thinks he can solve ten other problems and gets ideas for these."

PSA MAGAZINE
February, 1987

What is the hardest task in the world? To think!

Emerson,
Intellect

Real life is, to most men, a long second-best, a perpetual compromise between the ideal and the possible; but the world of pure reason knows no compromise, no practical limitations, no barrier to the creative activity embodying in splendid edifices the passionate aspiration after the perfect from which all great work springs. Remote from human passions, remote even from the pitiful facts of Nature, the generations have gradually created an ordered cosmos, where pure thought can dwell as in its natural home, and where one, at least, of our nobler impulses can escape from the dreary exile of the actual world.

Russell, Bertrand
A Study of Mathematics

Meditation is a powerful and full study for anyone who knows how to examine and exercise himself vigorously: I would rather fashion my mind than furnish it. There is no occupation that is either weaker or stronger, according to the mind involved, than entertaining one's own thoughts.

"The greatest minds make it their profession, to whom living is thinking," says Cicero. Thus nature has favored it with this privilege, that there is nothing we can do so long, and no action to which we can devote ourselves more commonly and easily. It is the occupation of the gods, says Aristotle, from which springs its happiness, and ours.

The pleasures arising from thinking and learning will make us think and learn all the more.

Aristotle
Ethics

Earlier in the chapter I related the thoughts of Hickman and Silva on strategic thinking and culture building.

They also say that individual leaders, not organizations, create excellence. Hickman and Silva state, "Excellence doesn't happen miraculously but springs from pacesetting levels of personal effectiveness and efficiency. Great business, government, and nonprofit organizations owe their greatness to a few individuals who mastered leadership skills and passed those skills on to succeeding generations of executives and managers."

Excellence and leadership and management skill is an evolutionary growth—a metamorphosis—through exposure and opportunity to participate. The entrepreneurs at Hewlett-Packard are part of an organization. Managers are not afraid to let them think—they grow, the managers grow, and the company grows. I importune management to look to them-selves and allow entrepreneurial spirit in every department.

It is not through Gurus, or EST, or X, Y, Z or management; creative excellence comes from within, through study and practice and patience.

Of the three varieties of mental excellence, intellectual, practical, and moral, there never could be any doubt in regard to the first two which side had the advantage. All intellectual superiority is the fruit of active effort. Enterprise, the desire to keep moving, to be trying and accomplishing new things for our own benefit or that of others, is the parent even of speculative, and much more of practical, talent. The intellectual culture compatible with the other type is of that feeble and vague description which belongs to a mind that stops at amusement, or at simple contemplation. The test of real and vigorous thinking instead of dreaming dreams, is successful application to practice—.

Mill
Representative Government, III

And practice makes perfect—but that is what any practice is for—to learn from mistakes.

Managers must walk around and ask—what if—what about—how come—what do you think—?

And then there is never a specific answer. If it is only through subtle knowledge, honed through experience, that you understand your abilities and a desire to understand those around you; and in time, a rare, consciousness of esteem, will envelop your organization and suddenly those around you will manifest respect.

The greatest baseness of man is the pursuit of glory. But it is also the greatest mark of his excellence; for whatever possessions he may have on earth, whatever health an essential comfort, he is not satisfied if he has not the esteem of men. He values human reason so highly that, whatever advantages he may have on earth, he is not content if he is not also ranked highly in the judgment of man. This is the finest position in the world. Nothing can turn him from the desire, which is the most indelible quality of man's heart.

Pascal, Blaise
Pensées, VI

How many star athletes, when recognized for major contribution to a sport, say, "First, I want to thank my coach." I wish we could have just as many company personnel say, "First, I wish to thank my department manager." Too many personnel move to other companies because management will not take the time or effort to recognize employees of distinction. They only recognize mistakes because it may affect them (managers) in the eyes of others. What an abominable shame!

Also, growth in a department or corporation comes from understanding time does not wait. Management must be constantly aware of their responsibility to pass on and discuss their acquired knowledge and improved capability.

The passing of knowledge and capability is simply accomplished by **constant discussion** among all management and productive personnel. Even Peters and Waterman attest to that.

The most fruitful and natural exercise of our mind, in my opinion, is discussion. I find it sweeter than any other action of my life; and that is the reason why, if I were right now forced to choose, I believe I would rather consent to lose my sight than my hearing or my speech.

The study of books is an activity that gives no heat, whereas discussion teaches and exercises us at the same time. If I discuss with a strong mind and a stiff jouster, he presses on my flanks, prods me right and left; his ideas launch mine. Rivalry, glory, and competition, push me and lift me above myself. And unison is an altogether boring quality in discussion.

As our mind is strengthened by communication with vigorous and orderly minds, so it is impossible to say how much it loses and degenerates by continual association and frequentation with mean and sickly minds. There is no contagion that spreads like that one. I know by enough experience how much it is worth per yard. I love to argue and discuss, but in a small group and for my own sake.

Montaigne, Michel de
Essays III, 8
Of the Art of Discussion

As I often do, on my way out the door to catch a flight, I grab a different book (this time: *GREAT* BOOKS, edited by Mortimer Adler) from my library to "sorta" bring me up date on what history of the "earlier world" was learning. I do this just to broaden my knowledge of "things". This particular book's *General Contents* was devoted to Philosophy and Religion.

Well, I got lucky—for the umpteenth time! When I opened the book, there, right in front of me, were these celebrated, famous men ready to settle in (sorry gents, I'm flying coach) and discuss with me such topics as Pragmatism, William James; Science and the Modern World, Alfred Whitehead, The Problems of Philosophy, Bertrand Russell, and one, after a casual review, that I jumped all over, *Experience and Education*, by John Dewey, philosopher, theorist, and reformer of education, 1859-1952.

Earlier we talked about books and the imperative responsibility of management to discuss new ideas and to increase the act of thinking with his employees as he, or she, "walked the floor". While I was experimental test flying and later working for three different aerospace companies (two went bankrupt) that "walking the floor" was a bunch of baloney. When you were hired, you were on your own. So I said to myself, "OK! If that's the way it's going to be, I'll just go ahead and make decisions and if I am recognized I'll get promoted, or I'll get fired! Well, I was recognized, then I was promoted, and then I got fired!

Although Dewey talks about preparing the young for future responsibilities and success in life, I can vicariously see me with a manager brain storming with his employees doing the same thing—preparing the young (in experience) for future responsibilities and success in life in the corporation, in the home, and the neighborhood.

Dewey goes on to say that learning here means an acquisition of what is already incorporated in books and in the heads of elders. Moreover, that which is taught is thought of as essentially static. It is taught as a finished product, with little regard either to the ways in which it was originally built up or to changes that will surely occur in the future. It is to a large extent the cultural product of societies that assumed the future would be much like the past, and yet it is used as educational food in a society where change is the rule, not the exception.

Is that what you want your company to be? Do you want it to an association of men and women that is static with "little regard to changes that will surely occur in the future"? When you "walk the floor" today with the right idea in mind, you are the future of the company and its employees. And let them talk! Let them be heard! And for God's sake, let them make mistakes!!

Management should love to allow personnel to argue and discuss, but within a small group in their own departments for their own sake.

I have given the name of this chapter much thought. I've probably changed the title fifteen times trying to ensure that someone would be interested in reading it. I finally said to myself, "Look, tell it the way you see it." One must have some kind of organization to sell and service a customer even if it is that of a singular entrepreneur—with an organized mind.

Do you start with customer first! Followed by a detailed (as possible at the time) business plan followed by a detailed marketing plan! Then followed by an organization designed by understanding the responsibility and accountability of the personnel for whom the positions (squares) were designed.

If you do not understand what is written above, you do not have an organization!!!!

THE DATING GAME
SELLING IN "THE LANGUAGE OF THE CUSTOMER"!
IT WORKS MANY WAYS

After I resigned from my experimental flight test career at Lockheed and entered the world of competitive business, I met a number of men who were all former military pilots now flying for the airlines, namely United, TWA, and American. Nice guys, all! Most of them were single which meant most of them loafed at Panchos; sitting around pumping sunshine up the ass of many stewardesses and bull shi—ing each other about breaking 200' ceilings with minimum visibility. Some evenings I would sit down and match their wits in the stewardess arena but I couldn't match their flying skills when it came to weather. Since all my flying was in the "X" discipline, my weather had to be viewed as CAFB or "clear as a fu—ing bell."

One evening soon after I sat down, one of the guys said, "We have been talking it over, Suitcase", and we decided to put you to the real test. We submitted your name and address to *THE DATING GAME.*" (It was about 9 months old then—creating quite a stir on TV.) "We have some pretty good money bet here, pro and con, as to whether or not you would accept the challenge."

I didn't say a word! The waitress came to the table, with a facial expression indicating to me she was in on the deal, and said, "Good evening, Suitcase. What will it be?"

I looked up at her and with a smile said, "Come off it Barrie. You know I always have a dry vodka martini before dinner. You hurried over here to find out what my answer would be to the challenge these pseudo intellectuals just threw at me. Well, I'll tell you! I accept their act of taunting another, namely me, to do something intentionally provocative." And as I turned toward my friends I added, "And I expect to win! And when you bring me my drink, I will raise my glass on high to the ones that bet 'pro'. The others, well, I don't know what to say except they are going to lose their money."

And they did! I survived the "weeding out" process at the studio and soon thereafter received word, by registered mail, the date, time, and instructions—acceptable wear, appearance, demure, (reserved, modest, serious—up to the individual,) importance of personality, being yourself, stuff like that!

When I arrived at the studio I was given a briefing, along with the other contestants (three men at three intervals—you know, time set aside for commercials) the background of the lady the winner would be "dating," (our blind date was a dancer from Canada on her way to the New York stage in a production starring John Raitt, or Robert Goulet, or some other male of notoriety. We were also told where we would be seated (on high chairs), the lady's location—behind a curtain, etc., etc. Everyone was very friendly, social, companionable, and we were free to make ourselves at home until a few minutes before "ON THE AIR."

While walking around the front of the seating arrangements for the audience, I noticed three girls in the front row of the studio. They seemed to be having a good time, laughing, gesticulating, and showing some strong feelings about something they were laughing about. It was at that time something hit me. I was struck with an idea on how I could win!

I walked over to the girls, introduced myself as a contestant, and asked if they would help me win.

"Win!," one of the girls said as she looked at her friends. "How could we do that?"

"Well," I said, "this is the way I would like to see it work. With your collective help, of course! Our blind date will be separated from the three of us with a curtain. She will ask us, on an individual basis, about three questions and her choice of her "date" will be made only on how well she feels we answered her queries plus the response of the audience. With the exception of the curtain, all of us will be able to see each other; our date and the audience, the three of us men and the audience. When our lady friend asks me a question, I'll answer by acting as if one of you in my date and I'll answer in such a fashion that will make you feel good and happy. After all! That's what a good date does! What do you think?

They looked at each other, smiled, clapped their hands with a state of joyful exuberance and said, "Sure! We'll help! It will be fun!"

My "competitors" were: a dancer from the same stage in Canada where our blind date was from; he actually escorted her to LA for the game. Nice guy but I think he was a little light in his tennis shoes. The other gentleman was big, gruff looking, but well mannered; an insurance salesman.

Lights came on, a man warmed up the audience, the Master of Ceremonies jumped out with all the smiles of a jackpot winner, and then took the time to introduce us—the three contestants. And then the rumble of the drums and the introduction of the attractive, beautiful, made of qualities that delight the eye, a dancer from the lovely city of Quebec, Canada, Miss Dianne, behind the curtain, Druckner. Yea! Yea! Clap! Clap! Clap!!!

"All right, Ladies and Gentleman, let's get started. And the first question Dianne is directed to who?"

"Contestant #1; can you hear me?"

"Gees," I said to myself, "that's me!" I looked at my three girls out front and said to them, "Yes, Dianne, I can hear you and I am sure you are as pretty as your voice."

The three girls liked that. My date was a little startled but gained her composure and said, "Number 2! What would you do if you and I had just met and found ourselves marooned on a warm, Pacific island?"

Number 2 was quick with a pretty good answer. "I'd grab you hand and we would explore the island."

"How about you Number 3?" He fumbled the ball. I think he tried to sell her insurance or somethin'"

"And how about you No. 1?" I immediately said, "I'd grab your hand, put it around my waist and worry about the island later. I'd explore you! Your hair, your eyes, your lips, your figure! And with that I took my two arms and made an hourglass figure while looking straight at the girls!

That did it! They went crazy, the audience loved it, and by the time our thirteen minutes of fame expired she had picked No. 1! I jumped from the stage and hugged the three girls. I sold myself "in the language of the customer."

I met a lovely lady. She and I made plans with the studio to meet about a week later. We went to dinner at a great restaurant in Hollywood and then danced the night away at a place called "Shelley's Manhole." I invited the chauffer to join us, and the two of them danced like Gene Kelley and Ginger Rodgers.

All in all, a truly great night! A great experience! I love competition! My pilot "friends" didn't say a word. A great lesson to be learned here also! Not one of them said a simple "congratulations"; even from the ones' that made money. I think their recognized standards of conduct are limited to a "check list."

LEADERSHIP AND MANAGEMENT

As long as this is a free man's world
Somebody has to lead.
Somebody has to carry the ball in word and thought and deed.
Somebody's got to knock on doors that have never known a key.
Somebody's got to see the things that the throng would never see.

These lines, penned many years ago, were dedicated to a very select group of talented individuals comprising a close-knit fraternity of professionals.

As an exercise during a recent lecture series, I asked my students to make a guess as to the profession alluded to in the poem. Their responses were as varied as they were interesting: insurance, marketing research, engineering technology, the clergy, science, and planning. None was correct.

In September of 1955, after spending 4 ½ years in the United States Air Force as a fighter pilot and test pilot, I joined an aerospace firm as an experimental test pilot on the development of a new, high-speed fighter. I became an active member of the Society of Experimental Test Pilots, and at one of our annual symposiums' years ago, Gil Robb Wilson, a noted writer and poet, dedicated a poem to us; the first verse of which is quoted above. I have used only the first few lines for a specific reason: No matter what profession a person pursues, the words of the poem apply: particularly to those who take their profession seriously and strive to do their best. And in doing so, minds will open for opportunity. To seize that propitious moment offers the chance to lead!

If you read **BOOK I** of the trilogy you know how I made a fool of myself on my first air-to-ground mission. The irony of it all! It was on April Fool's day, 1953. You may remember I went to an experienced pilot and we started from ground zero and he taught me, by discussions and flying with me, knowledge **about** flying the jeopardous and treacherous missions of close-support. He told me one day that I was ever on a mission flying element lead, and for one of many reasons the leader had to abort, do not, and I repeat, **do not**, waste a micro-second. "He said, "Call

WATCHCASE (the ground radar station) and tell them you have assumed the lead and will continue the mission."

Well, it happened one day on a mission to "THE HOOK," a virulent hunk of interlaced trench warfare where the only way to kill the enemy was to burn them out—with napalm. I immediately put #4 on my wing and told #2 to take position on number 4's wing and that we would continue our mission. I took over and managed according to the mission profile. I was a flight leader from that day on; it was my 19th mission. The secret???

How did HONEYWELL chairman Larry Bossidy turn the company around? He focussed on just one thing—execution!

The responsibilities of exploring the performance capabilities of a new flight leader, or a new fighter, are no different than those of a marketing executive's in exploring and determining the performance of a salesperson or sales territory. The lines of the Mr. Wilson's poem apply to the successful fighter pilot, experimental pilot, and the successful marketing executive. Each must possess two common denominators: leadership ability, and management of others and self. These are the keys – an aptitude for gaining knowledge through proper vision and the ability to grasp significant facts or elements that escape the throng, plus an innate desire *and* capacity to accommodate handily anything on the other side of the door.

It is inconceivable that an experimental pilot would allow himself to be strapped in the cockpit of a single-seat, single-engine, new experimental fighter and attempt to take off with the intent of determining its "designed" performance without first making himself fully cognizant of, and then managing every detail of thought and action before, during, and after flight. There is first the assimilation of all of the technology and experience *that has gone before*. That is, designs based on years of experience of aeronautical engineers, computer analysis, wind-tunnel tests, development and use of mock-ups, and operational laboratory testing. This is the information that is synthesized into what is called a "mission profile" as to what is expected in performance from takeoff through landing.

The first flight is only the beginning. Many tests must be performed; stability and control, power-plant (engine) and performance, stability and control, armament and radar, structural integrity, spin characteristics, emergency procedures, etc., etc. These tests are meticulously planned to broaden the flight envelope as soon as possible without sacrificing pilot and/or plane, yet, at the same time, anticipating the long range when someone's young son will be flying the finished design in hopes of becoming a war hero and "ace."

What is now the "value" of the proven design to the young fighter pilot? It is a design based on the latest state-of-the-art science and technology. It is often held that philosophy is to be distinguished from science in that it is concerned with 'values,' whereas science is not. Whereas philosophy has always been very consciously interested in the relative value of different ideas and aims, it is by no means clear that science is not also.

The scientific idea behind designing and building a new fighter is to establish a relative value between mission and role and tactical responsibility. The relative aim is simple – establish air superiority.

Should not the same hold true for a marketing manager in reference to the performing of his designed territories and sales personnel? Should not a marketing manager take into account all that has gone before; an in depth marketing analysis, the technology and experience with the product? Also considered should be the designs or packaging based on years of experience of engineers, art directors, advertisers, statistical analysts and market samplers? When it comes to leadership, there is no difference between preparation to conquer new airspace and ground space (territory).

Leadership entails all thought processes and details should be meticulously planned to broaden the company's position in the market place – without sacrificing personnel and/or profit – while at the same time planning for long-term growth to contribute to the dynamics of the company and its personnel. It takes a manager (leader) to do this.

To be a manager (leader) requires more than a title of flight leader or Vice President with a big office and other outward symbols of rank. It requires competence and performance of high order. A leader has two specific tasks. The first is creation of a true whole that is larger than the sum of its parts, a productive entity that turns out more than the sum of the resources put into it. The second specific task of the leader is to harmonize in every decision and action the requirements of immediate and long-range future. He cannot sacrifice either without endangering the enterprise. He must, so to speak, keep his nose to the grindstone while lifting his eyes to the hills.

Experimental pilots who fail to manage every detail of every flight are soon lost. So are territories, products and management positions when the same sound management isn't applied.

Douglas Sherwin, in a chapter of *THE HARVARD BUSINESS REVIEW* entitled *Strategy for Winning Employee Commitment*, states, "When we think about leadership, we usually think of special qualities that make managers more effective. So leadership is conventionally regarded as an ingredient of good managing. There is, of course, no 'right' view, but I find it helpful to turn the relationships around – to think not of leadership as an aspect of managing, but managing as a tool of leadership. To look, not to the qualities of leadership, but to the requirement of follower-ship:

We can give managing new meaning and importance by conceiving it as a *tool* of leadership to achieve an organization's purpose. Managing in this view becomes art, technique, systematization, method, and economics. And where leadership is emotions, feelings, spirit, and purpose, managing is cool, impersonal, objective, and imaginative; it connotes professional *action* for getting results, including follower-ship. If we embrace this view, we think of ourselves at every level of management first and primarily as leaders – (as long as this is a free man's world, someone has to lead) and then as practitioners of the art and science of managing.

A flight leader and an experimental pilot, managing all aspects of a combat mission and a flight test is cool, impersonal, objective and imaginative – and he is the epitome of professional action for getting results. And so it is with a professional business leader—sales manager!

Does the best fighter pilot make a good test pilot? Does the best salesman in a territory make a good sales manager or business leader? In both cases the answer is no for two valuable and distinct reasons – recognizing the importance of knowing oneself and that management is a separate and distinct skill. In the pages that follow you will read where a fighter pilot loses his life on a flight test he shouldn't have been on and a salesman promoted to sales manager almost lost his company because he was in a position he shouldn't have been in.

In both cases whom do you blame? I would say the responsible "leaders" that put both men in their untenable positions. They were not managing with skill. If they didn't know themselves, how could they know of others?

MAJOR RICHARD BONG
THE LEADING AMERICAN ACE OF WORLD WAR II:

Dick Bong saw his first combat in the last part of 1942. By the second week in January 1943, he was an ace. Always eager for a fight, Bong would plough his P-38 into an enemy formation of any size. By ones and two his score increased; and, when sent home on leave in November 1943, he had scored 21 victories. Returning, he was assigned to Headquarters V Fighter Command and allowed to pick missions that promised action. Soon he had exceeded Rickenbacker's score of World War I and became America's top scorer. He was then returned to the states and underwent an instruction course in gunnery!

Possibly he did benefit from the course, for upon going back into action, he quickly added 12 victories in 30 missions. Free-lancing, so to speak, Bong could assign himself to any mission he wanted; which helped to keep his score moving up. As his tally climbed higher, he was under some pressure to avoid the risk of further engagements, but he continued and ran his score up to 40 before being sent home again.

Dick Bong was killed in a takeoff accident in a Lockheed XP-80 on an experimental test flight on August 6, 1945. He was a Medal of Honor winner and America's greatest air ace.

CAPTAIN JOSEPH MCCONNELL
THE LEADING AMERICAN ACE OF THE KOREAN WAR:

America's leading ace in the Korean War was Joe McConnell of the 51st Wing. McConnell, who served in World War II as a B-24 navigator, demonstrated his skill as a Sabrejet pilot by knocking down one MiG after another. After claiming his ninth victory, however, he was shot down. He ejected, landed in the sea, and was soon picked up by a helicopter rescue team. He went back into combat almost immediately to claim his tenth kill.

His success continued and, when he was rotated out of combat, he held 16 victories, a record that was not to be exceeded during the war. McConnell did not long survive the war, however. He was killed in 1954 in the crash of a modified F-86 while on an experimental test flight.

During the experimental testing of the XF-104 and F-104A, many aircraft were lost, as were the lives of too many great pilots. As one of the first experimental pilots, I was deep in the development of the airplane and survived two accidents; a crash landing in the first F-104A manufactured – and a successful ejection from the No. 8 aircraft manufactured when the tail was ripped off during a test flight.

I was called to Baltimore, through Lockheed management, by the Commanding General of the Air Research and Development Command and asked what I thought was causing the loss of so many aircraft and pilots. I told the General it boiled down to two things – the Lockheed new weapon system program (F-104) had no leader (flight) and the U.S. Air Force F-104 System Project Office did not have a leader who knew how to manage properly. During the course of our somewhat frictional exchange of thoughts, I told him I had spent 20 months in the Air Force as a test pilot on the development of the first supersonic fighter, the North American F-100. Although we had many problems that were killing test pilots, the contractor, the System Project Office at Wright Field, and the Air Force plant representative's office all had qualified leaders and managers that pulled together as a team to solve those problems.

I told the Commanding General that the antithesis was true for the F-104 project. I said that my own company's flight test engineering department was weak and vacillating, that the Systems Project Office had no qualified personnel, and that the Air Force Plant Representative's Office hadn't been near the flight test division in months.

I made a big mistake, the mistake of telling it exactly as I perceived it. But I have always been that way. If a person asks me a question, I have never failed to face the reality of the truth, as I see it.

The General told me that the F-104 was no different than other fighters – only a little faster – and that I didn't know what I was talking about. He, at the same time, told me the meeting was terminated and for me to leave his office at once.

I stood up, embarrassed, but said, "Yes, sir, I'll go; but I want to leave you with one thought. One of these days, soon, one of your (the Edwards Flight Test Facility, Wright Field test facility, Lockheed, General Electric and other aerospace corporations were under his jurisdiction) renowned test pilots will be killed in an F-104 for some inane, insipid reason, and then you will remember every word I said."

The GRIM REAPER overheard what I was telling the General but was a little confused so in the span of several weeks my words rang true; he killed three pilots in the F-104; one from Edwards, one from General Electric, and one from Lockheed. The Air Force test pilot was a fighter ace, and a personal friend. So were the other two!

I never heard from the General. You know why? Because he didn't have the guts to say he was wrong. It takes a leader among men to say, "You were right! I was wrong!"

Is there any difference, really, between an ill-managed flight test program killing a pilot(s) and an ill-managed sales program killing a company? I had said earlier that the F-100 program "had qualified personnel that pulled together." The program had a leader. The F-104 program did not have that quality of team effort.

It would, therefore, seem appropriate to stress that the first criterion in identifying those people within an organization who have management responsibility is not command over people. It is responsibility for contribution. Function rather than power has to be the distinctive criterion and the organizing principle.

Could Bong, or McConnell, or my test pilot friends, really assume a responsibility for contribution to the development of a new fighter just because they were leading aces? Not without the leadership of management, they couldn't!

Was not function, as a distinctive criterion, the missing ingredient of the management of the F-104 program?

Socrates said:

"To know oneself, that is to know oneself completely, ones conscious and unconscious self, makes for power, self-control, leadership, and success. Individuals encounter difficulty only because they do not truly know themselves; their natures, limitations, abilities, motives, the entire gamut of their personalities. They need a psychological mirror enabling each person to see his spiritual self as it really is, including all its shortcomings, strengths, and potentialities."

A leader who truly knows himself will succeed, by doing, making mistakes, admitting them, and learning from them. For he will know precisely what is within his capabilities, and the area in which to apply them, whereas the person who does not know himself will constantly blunder, even to the point of ruining his life. (or killing himself).

Management is a separate and distinct skill; it is an art in and of itself. As such, it should not be confused with technical operating skills. Leadership ability, managerial skills and operational capacities are not automatically interchangeable. A good salesman is not necessarily a good sales manager. Conversely, an outstanding administrator may have only modest success as a technical operator in his field.

Because leadership ability is a distinct skill, it is adaptable to various jobs. The ability to plan, direct, organize, and evaluate human efforts is equally useable whether the executive is working for an automobile manufacturer or an appliance maker. Military leaders have become business executives, business executives have moved to college presidencies, college presidents have moved into administrative positions in other fields.

Alexander the Great, or Alexander III showed his talent for leadership by quieting the restive cities of Greece, then putting down uprisings in Thrace and Illyia.

Adolf Hitler, as a corporal in World War I, received the Iron Cross (first class) for bravery. Hitler's astute use of his frenzied yet magnetic oratory, and a superb master of Machiavellian politics was the nexus for his rise to leadership. Hitler took action for getting results—including follower-ship!

General George Patton was given command of the 3d Army, which spearheaded, with him in the front, the spectacular sweep of U.S. forces from Normandy through Brittany and N. France. He relieved Bastogne, in a 90 degree turn of his 3d Army (believed to be impossible), crossed the Rhine and raced across S. Germany into Czechoslovakia. He was a brilliant leader!

There is a difference between leadership and management. The leader and the men who follow him represent one of the oldest, most natural, and most effective of all human relationships. The manager and those he manages is a later product with neither a romantic or so inspiring a history. Leadership is of the spirit compounded of personality and vision – its practice is an art. Management is of the mind, more a matter of accurate calculation, statistics, methods, timetables, and routine – its practice is a science.

Leaders are essential! Managers are necessary!

LEADERSHIP (CONT'D)
BREEDS SUCCESS

Success comes from
culture & core values

Perhaps few companies have devoted so much time, energy and effort on culture and core values as the food services company, RTM.

In the spring of 1967, founder Russ Umphenour began working as a counter person at an Arby's restaurant in Flint, Michigan. Russ worked in the unit three nights a week, at $ 1.50 per hour, to supplement his income as a special education teacher. Three months later, Russ was promoted to Night Manager. Reluctant to see Russ return to teaching in the fall, management offered Russ a position as Assistant Manager. Sure enough, he decided to go full time with Arby's and hard work and positive thinking brought success quickly.

By June 1972, Russ had formed RTM (Results Through Motivation) by trading his stock for eleven Arby's operating units in Georgia and belief in people, positive thinking, good business practices, hard work and patience, his management team turned the stores around. Russ then began acquiring additional units, year-by-year, and state-by-state. Today, 37 years his part-time gig, Russ Umphenour leads the RTM Restaurant Group, which operates 915 restaurants in 24 states and 43 markets. Annual sales are $800 million. The entire company employs 25,000 people, and is privately held by management.

Values drive every decision at RTM. Speak to any director, Umphenour, chairman Dennis Cooper, president Tom Garrett, a member of the executive committee, or any unit operator and each can recite the company's six **core values**. Those include: Dream big, work hard, get it done, fair play, have fun, make a difference. It doesn't get any simpler-or more elegant.

Timothy S. Mescon, Ph.D. copied, in part, *Arrivals, AirTran Airways* magazine, August, 2004

RUSS CHEW 101
FAA's chief operating officer
introduces the bureaucrats
to private-sector principles

Choose your metaphor. Russell Chew is trying to turn an aircraft carrier 180 degrees. He's trying to raise the Titanic! He's trying to tame a feral, cunning bureaucracy that would like nothing better than to chew him up—no pun intended—and spit him out.

His assignment is to make the FAA's Air Traffic Organization (ATO) "performance-based," accountable for productivity and responsive to air traffic control users. However you look at it, he has a hard job and it will take years to evaluate how well he does.

Chew, a veteran of American Airlines flight operations, became the ATO's chief operating officer on Aug. 1, 2003, after snail-paced recruiting by the FAA and less-than-patient watching and waiting by Congress' aviation community, which has pushed for a decade toward ATC cost and performance accountability.

Chew discussed his first year on the job and the management principles he's trying to follow with Aviation Week & Space Technology (**AW&ST**) Senior Transport Editor David Bond.

AW&ST: What has your first year been like?

RUSSELL CHEW: When you go through a change, you have to be concerned about the confusion you throw the organization into during transition period. You want to minimize that as much as possible. On the other hand, you're trying to move the whole organization in a different direction. So reorganization has a confounding effect in terms of confusion, but it has a beneficial effect in helping to influence the future. You look at any business the same way.

The reorganization has created something very different. Something as basic as who is the customer was not a well-understood, consistently agreed-upon principle inside the different air traffic organizations. While there were lots of restructurings before, in terms of changing lines and boxes, three was still a fundamental lack of definition around the customer. So we introduced a service model built around a balance between customers and owners and employees. That is basic to defining performance, but getting it understood by everyone was no small task.

AW&ST: Is it understood now?

RC: I think it's beginning to be. I think they can understand it conceptually, but what that means and how they conduct business is not yet understood.

We had a very strict hierarchy here, and it was split up. Acquisition was separate from operations. A basic part of the reorganization was to put those two things together, to make sure that acquiring a capital asset was closely tied to the operating side, both in production of service and also its cost. Government budgeting doesn't require that, and in fact it leads you away from that. Capital programs are handled differently by the government process than operating budgets—the way they're justified, the way they're managed. So tying acquisition and operations together is more challenging than just tying the budgets together. It starts by putting on executive in charge of both the acquisition side and the operating side for each line of business.

There's no such thing as the perfect organization, especially in an operation as complex as ours, because there's always the requirement to move across lines of business. But it's fundamental for any service business to align your activity around the service you're producing, as perceived by your customer. And so we've realigned the businesses of the ATO against the service we produce.

When you have 38,000 people, they lose their way, especially at headquarters, because headquarters is the most isolated from the actual business. An air traffic controller knows exactly what he's doing. A technician fixing a facility or a system knows exactly what he or she is doing. They may not understand exactly why it's important, and having the grander picture supposedly is the value of management.

After you've decided you're a service business and you've realigned your business, you broaden your **leadership**. We created an executive council. The idea was to avoid embedding major decision-making into a single person, because if that person changes, then the direction and continuity of the business is lost. The executive council is akin to a corporation where an executive is responsible for the health of the entire organization, beyond his or her own line of business. In the private sector you do that with things like stock options. But we in government have something that the private sector doesn't have—public service. Our executives have a commitment to something larger than the organization itself, and that's the country. So I don't think the culture works against this concept.

If you broaden **leadership** and the authority to make decisions, you have to define performance. You have to define the services in very great detail and define producing a good service. That's where we introduce the concept of **value**. **Value** is defining the unit of what you produce over what it costs to produce it. The more what you produce is a commodity, the less people are willing to pay a premium for something better, once the standard is good. So we can't view any part of our service, even safety, as having unlimited value. Every decision we make has a cost, so cost becomes the common point of comparison for everything we do. Introducing ideas of unit cost and productivity is the basis for establishing a **value system**. That **value system** has to be embedded into the way performance is measured.

LEADERSHIP CONTINUED

I want to continue the **LEADERSHIP** discussion by taking another view; or I should say **offering** a couple of other views. One is from a powerful businesswoman, Carla Fiorina, Chairman, and CEO of HEWLETT-PACKARD, and Andrew Grove, another former CEO, and now Chairman of the Board of INTEL. He arrived in the USA, from Hungary, with $20 dollars in his pocket.

You have read about a President of the U. S., a United States Marine Corps General, a successful and experienced combat fighter pilot, the thoughts of philosophers, free enterprise (good and not so good) and the lessons of history. In the sub-title of **BOOK III**, I address the synergy of these disciplines. Synergy, from the Greek word *synergos,* means working together. I think the definition, from *WEBESTER*, "working together" speaks from the minds of each of the individuals.

These individuals hold a collective functioning that fits just below the threshold of conscious awareness. It is a vicarious experience; something realized through imaginative or sympathetic participation in the experience of another. It is the understanding that leadership is bred through readiness, experience, knowledge, knowing ones self, the ability to change, truth, self-discipline, love of your fellow man, courage, and principle. They all know, without speaking to one another, first hand, these attributes about each other. It is not good enough to know attributes **of**; it is to know attributes **about.**

It is exactly the same thing in that I know, first hand, the physical and mental strengths of a complete stranger wearing the silver wings of a USAF pilot. The pilot may be flying fighters, bombers, or transport aircraft; makes no difference!

Remember, in **BOOK I**, Socrates and Capt. Coffin taught me, first hand, the difference between knowledge **of** close air support and knowledge **about** close air support. It saved my life!

The same thought process applies in reference to a President, a General, a CEO, a Chairman of the Board. Remember! A company can die in a war for market share the same as a pilot can die in a war for giving his life—so executives have the freedom to compete for market share.

CARLY FIORINA
KEYS TO BEING A GOOD LEADER

What are your principles of leadership? What's the key to being a successful leader?

There are some basic principles that I have learned that continue to instruct me to this day and guide me in both business and in life.

The first is that values matter and character counts, and that no matter how much things change, fundamental values shouldn't. I think in many ways the scandals we have seen in the past few years are about a failure of fundamentals—fundamentals such as a CEO's job is to manage the company, not the stock price; fundamentals such as it is a CEO's job to balance the short term and the long term, irrespective of the pressures of Wall Street. It may not be easy, but it is what we're paid for.

I think leadership takes what I call a strong internal compass. When the winds are howling and the storms are raging and the sky is cloudy so you have nothing to navigate by, a compass tells you where true north is. I think when you're in a difficult situation, a lonely situation, you have to rely on that compass to tell you if you're doing the right things for the right reasons in the right ways. Sometimes that's all you have.

The second principle is that leadership is not a destination. Leadership is a journey. The only constant in any of our lives, whether you're running a company or running a family, or perhaps running a country, is change. And change has never been as constant and as fast as it is today.

To me, the dividing line between what will separate those who truly make a difference and a contribution in the 21st century from those who don't is the line between those who embrace change and those who run away from it. It will be between those who seek to lead change and those who find refuge in the status quo.

As leaders, we can never forget that people want to do a good job. They want to be treated with consideration and respect. They want to feel a real sense of accomplishment in their work, to have their ideas considered and their achievements recognized. People want to feel like they're part of something larger than themselves—to be a part of the larger vision, the direction and the goals that an organization is working toward.

Who played the strongest roles in your professional development?

I have been privileged in my position to meet a great many people all over the world, and I know I am extraordinarily lucky to be able to say that the greatest role models that I have even known are my father and my mother. My mother was a painter and an extraordinary woman. My father is a justice on the 9th Circuit Court of Appeals in California. They both were—are—people defined quintessentially by their character. Both were—are—totally authentic people, and that's a lesson I have carried in my life.

I have thought often—probably all my life, but particularly in the last several years when I have been at the helm of HP—about the lessons I have learned from my parents. I learned that there is no substitute for hark work. Talent will not substitute; opportunity will not substitute; hard work is required.

I also learned that I could do or be anything I wanted to. I don't remember as a girl ever feeling limited because of my gender. And when I think back to that, being a girl growing up in a traditional family in the 1950s, that was not such a usual way to feel.

I learned a sense of "to thine own self be true." I learned from my parents never sell your soul. In the end, they taught me the most important thing you have to be proud of is what you've done and how you've done it. My parents lived that day in and day out. They taught me authenticity.

And perhaps more than any other thing, the primary lesson that I have learned is that the best people are known not just for their capabilities but for their character; that as much as our world changes, there are fundamental values that never do; that responsibility still counts; that integrity still matters; and that honesty counts. And I have carried, I hope, that understanding that it is both character and capability that matter throughout my life and throughout my work.

When it comes to day-to-day business, I think leadership starts by deciding that building diverse teams is a necessary business objective, and making expectations clear that a team is going to be diverse to be truly effective. I think HP has been in many ways a very laudatory meritocracy long before I arrived in terms of building diversity and promoting women and minorities. And yet, it was also true as we looked at our numbers relatively recently that we hadn't made enough process.

So one of the things we decided to do was to track diversity the same way we track other business goals, by measuring and inspecting it—not so that we were sacrificing our standard, because you don't need to sacrifice your standards to have a diverse work force—but we had to inspect it so that people understood the requirement was real.

What's most important is an understanding that having a long-term commitment to diversity isn't an option: It's a requirement. It isn't something that you can turn on and turn off. It has to be built into the fabric of the business. Diversity is a business objective with real payoff, "not a nice-to-do." As soon as people get it into their heads that diversity is a "nice-to-do", I think it's the kiss of death.

Diversity is the right thing to do, but it also is an imperative for business that intends to be successful over the long term. So you do it because it's a have-to-do. taken in part from:

CARLY UNPLUGGED by Tim Talevich
The Costco Connection
June 2004

COMPETITION STAYING ON TOP

Many months ago—actually as I review my notes, it was years ago when I was perusing business oriented magazines and newspapers for **BOOK III**. LEADERSHIP was on my mind for a chapter but I also thought a leader must always be aware of—and must stay on top of—his company's competitive position. In my research I came across an article entitled COMPETITION from *FORTUNE*, February 22, 1993.

Maybe INTEL can, but it won't be like falling off a log. Our corporate mission is to be the preeminent supplier of building blocks to the new computing industry. If we develop the right building blocks, we'll win. If we are wrong, we fail. There's no competitor around who can do as much damage to us as we can do to ourselves.

Technology can make you lose, but it can't make you a winner. First, you have to start with a better product than the other guy's. Second, it has to be better in a way that your customers can appreciate. And third, your customers have to know it's a better product in a way they can appreciate.

Intel's transformation has to continue, we've got to become more than a microprocessor company. We see three distinct ways to market out building blocks. One is selling the basic microprocessor. The second is selling other types of chips-those that control the disk drives, or process video, or do other auxiliary tasks in or around the computer-to PC makers.

The third way is where I believe our future may lie. It consists of selling products to individual users that make your computer more capable, such as fax modems or network boards. Looking ahead to the to the world of electronic meeting, we see big opportunities both in powerful processors and in other products that turn the world's 100 million-plus PCs into multifaceted communication devices.

We'll keep on investing in the capacity to produce our leading-edge chips in quantity. As those chips become available in large volumes, we'll do some not-so-gentle nudging on price to encourage people to migrate on to the next generation.

THE NEW COMPUTER INDUSTRY

The breakup of the old computer industry is what gave Intel it's chance and made the mass-produced computer possible. The old computer industry was vertically aligned; each company sold a completely integrated product based on it's own proprietary technology. Companies like IBM and Digital Equipment designed and built their computers from the bottom up—silicon chips, software, disk drives, everything. These vertically integrated companies would compete against other vertically integrated companies, and buyers had commit to the whole package of one manufacturer or another.

A new horizontal industry model is replacing the old vertical one. In the PC age, everybody's products have to work with everybody else's products or they don't sell.

Intel's processing chips will work in any IBM-type personal computer, no matter who build it. The operating software that enables the PC to work is also standard. Application programs are sold in stores. Like CDs or books, and when you install one, you expect it to work.

Business competes for market share within each horizontal specialty. Intel is up against companies like Motorola in the basic silicon architecture. In operating systems it's Microsoft vs. Apple vs. IBM vs. Novell. Borland competes with Lotus and scores of other companies in all the varieties of applications software, like spread sheets and word processors. And then many others making and selling the PCs. The old competition based on the advantages of one proprietary technology over another has been replaced by one in which you win by providing basic value.

The new computing industry may be the best example of what I call an industrial democracy. It resists central guidance. Nobody can tell anyone else what to do. You PC might have a processor from Intel, a display from Sharp, a hard disk from Conner, memory from Toshiba, a modem from U.S. Robotics, an operating systems from Microsoft, application from four different vendors, and yet it all works together. If it didn't, none of these products would sell. Industrial democracy is brutally competitive, and it can get very messy, but it enables technology to move very fast.

SPEED

These changes in industry structure aren't happening only in PCs, they're happening everywhere. In any industry, as you go from vertical to horizontal, the customer isn't locked in anymore. And when companies lose their proprietary advantages, speed seems to be what matters most.

In all businesses, to provide value, you've got to do whatever it is you do fast and with immense efficiency. Why do you thinks everybody is buying computers? It's not that they render you more productive, in the sense of more physical output per hour. They permit you to make decisions and produce results faster. The whole leveraged-buyout wave of the 1980's was made possible by Lotus1-2-3 running on PS's possible without computers.

In my own little corner of the universe, a lot of other people can build microprocessors. If we hadn't kept moving the technology rapidly-from the 8088 chip in the original PC with 30,000 transistors, to the 486 with 1.2 million transistors, to the forthcoming Pentium chip with over three million—we wouldn't have an advantage. Already a competitor has taken over 50% of the market for 386s. We're focusing on the 486, which no other company is selling yet, and the Pentium chip, which we plan to release this quarter. And we're already beginning to invest hundreds of millions of dollars in the generations that will follow.

The pace of work these days isn't easy to live with, but welcome to the Nineties. Intel didn't create this world, we're just supplying the tools with which we can all work ourselves to death. Exhausting as it is, it's highly preferable to being unemployed.

STAYING ON TOP

Staying on top, and leadership run parallel paths. Keeping defined parallel paths in a climb to success demands awareness of the scope of the market place, including competition, and complete cognizance and comprehension of what it takes to compete both economically and technically.

I researched what I thought would be a good synthesis of what it takes to be a leader. I got lucky as I was, at the time, beginning to read *Who Says Elephants Can't Dance* by Louis V. Gerstner, Jr., (HarperCollins Publishers, New York, 2002) Inside IBM's Historic Turnaround. According to Mr. Gerstner, IBM's LEADERSHIP COMPETENCIES are:

Focus to Win
>   Customer Insight
>   Breakthrough Thinking
>   Drive to Achieve

Mobilize to Execute
>   Team Leadership
>   Straight Talk
>   Teamwork
>   Decisiveness

Sustain Momentum
>   Building Organizational Capabilities
>   Coaching
>   Personal Dedication

The Core
>   Passion for the Business

SAVING THE BEST FOR LAST
CONVERSATION WITH A GIANT

Peter Drucker was born 95 years ago—can it be possible? Now confined to a walker and nearly deaf, Drucker stopped giving press interviews about a year ago. But in late October he granted an exception to FORBES, 13 Dec., 2004 edition), thanks to the urging of Dr. Rick Warren, the founder and head of the Christian evangelical Saddleback Church in Lake Forest, Calif. (The Drucker-Warren relationship may surprise many readers, but it goes back two decades, when the young minister came to Drucker for advice.) We met at Drucker's surprisingly Spartan home in Claremont, Calif. on a recent morning. Drucker's comments on leadership follow.

Ask What Needs to Be Done.

Successful leaders don't start out by asking, "What do I want to do?" They ask, "What needs to be done?" Then they ask, "Of those things that would make a difference, which are right for me?" They don't tackle things they aren't good at. They make sure those necessities get done, but not by them. They are not afraid of strength in others. Andrew Carnegie wanted to put on his gravestone: "Here lies a man who attracted better people into his service than he was himself."

Pick the Important Things.

I've seen a great many people who are exceedingly good at execution but exceedingly poor at picking the important things. They are magnificent at getting the unimportant things. They have an impressive record of achievement on trivial matters.

Avoid Popularity Traps.

Leaders are purpose-driven. They know how to establish a mission. And another thing, they know how to say no. The pressure on leaders to do 984 different things is unbearable, so the effective ones learn how to say no and stick with it. As a result they don't suffocate themselves. Too many leaders try to do a little bit of 25 different things and get nothing done. They are very popular because they always say yes.

Learn to Abandon.

A critical question for leaders is, "When do you stop pouring resources into things that have run their course?" The most dangerous traps for a leader are those near successes, where everybody says if you just give it another big push it will go over the top. One tries it once, one tries it twice, one tries it a third time. But by then is should be obvious this will be very hard to do.

Get a Secret office.

When you are the chief executive, you're the prisoner of your organization. The moment you're in the office, everybody comes to you and wants something. And it's useless to lock the door. They'll break in. Get a secret office elsewhere.

How Organizations Fall Down.

Organizations fall down when they have to guess what the boss is working at, and invariably they guess wrong. So the CEO needs to say, "This is what I am focusing on." Then the CEO needs to ask of his associates, "What are you focusing on?"

Ask your associates, "You put this on top of your priority list-why?" Make sure that you understand your associates' priorities, and make sure that after your have that conversation you sit down and drop them a two-page note: "This is what I think we discussed. This is what I think we decided. This is what I think you committed yourself to within this particular time frame."

The Transition From Entrepreneur to Large-Company CEO.

Again, let's start out discussing what not to do. Don't try to be somebody else. By now you have your own style. This is how you get things done. Don't take on things you don't believe in and that you yourself are not good at. Learn to say no. Effective leaders match the objective needs of their company with the subjective competencies available to them. As a result they get an enormous amount of things done fast.

How Capable Leaders Blow It.

One of the ablest men I ever worked with—this is a long time back—was a German pre-World War II democratic chancellor, Heinrich Bruning. He had an incredible ability to see to the heart of a problem. But he was very weak on financial matters. He should have delegated those tasks, but he wasted endless hours on budgets and performed poorly. This was a terrible failing during a depression, and it led to Adolf Hitler's rise. Never try to be an expert if you are not one. Build on your strengths, and find strong people to do the other necessary tasks.

Charisma Is Overrated.

Once of the most effective American Presidents of the last 100 years was Harry Truman. He didn't have an ounce of charisma. Truman was as bland as a dead mackerel. But everybody who worked for him worshipped him because he was absolutely trustworthy. If Truman said no, it was no, and if he said yes, it was yes. And he never said no to one person and yes to the next one concerning the same issue. The other effective President of the last 100 years was Ronald Reagan. His great strength was not charisma, as is commonly thought, but his awareness and acceptance of exactly what he could do and what he could not do.

If we stop and think about what I have written on LEADERSHIP, I feel every competent leader would find a sentence, a paragraph, and/or a chapter that would affect particular needs as outlined by the brilliant, experienced, and **knowledgeable** men and women introduced to you in this chapter.

LEADERSHIP, CONT'D

Lessons from the Reagan years

Ronald Reagan, described as one of the greatest presidents, might say greatness can be boiled down to two words: "Well! **LEADERSHIP!**"

What makes a great leader? That question is complex enough to keep an army of business consultants employed. As Regan is laid to rest, *USA TODAY* went looking for the leadership lessons of the 40th president.

Start with a moral foundation.

Regan was called the Teflon president because criticism didn't stick. Why was that?

Alan Axelrod, author of leadership books about several leaders including Gen. George Patton and president Harry Truman, said it's because Reagan was "a decent person with high character," contrary to the "selfish pig" impression exuded by many CEOs.

Reagan saw right and wrong. To him, communism was evil, and the human craving for freedom was good. Experts say most people forgive mistakes made by leaders who have conviction and a good heart.

The vision thing matters.

Vision and strategy have fallen out of favor as companies focus on the nuts and bolts of slashing costs, elimination of errors and executing. But vision is the North Star for any organization, says Wess Roberts, author of *Leadership Secrets of Attila the Hun.*

Reagan had a grand, long-term vision to end the Cold War and block intrusive government. He articulated a direction, says Al Vicere, executive education professor of strategic leadership at Penn State.

Take the heat.

Those who transform the world, or a company, make tough calls such as Reagan firing the air traffic controllers, says Noel Tichy, director of the University of Michigan Global Leadership Program. Great leaders have several qualities. One is making tough decisions!

If Regan were a corporate CEO, he would be a combination of Herb Kelleher of Southwest Airlines and Jack Welch of General Electric, Tichy says.

Be comfortable in your own skin.

So what if Sam Donaldson shouts embarrassing questions? Have a jellybean! Joke about being friends with Thomas Jefferson. (Or having Socrates fly my wing as discussed in **BOOK I & II**!) That does not mean making light of the importance of your job.

The most powerful tool is the ability to make people feel like what they do matters, say Paul Argenti, director of Dartmouth's Tuck Leadership Forum.

But leaders who are at home in their skin give the OK for others to feel at home in theirs. That's when things get done.

Unlike former CEOs such as Al Dunlap of Sunbeam, Reagan demonstrated leaders do not need to be mean to be tough, says Jeffrey Sonnenfeld, associate dean of executive programs at the Yale School of Management.

Reagan was secure enough to surround himself with former opponents, including his vice president, George Bush, and Treasury secretary James Baker, Sonnenfeld says.

Maintain a sense of humor.

At all times! Even during a nuclear arms race. "I have left orders to be awakened in case of national emergency, even if I'm in a Cabinet meeting," Reagan said.

Be a great communicator.

Maybe more CEOs should start out as actors because they need to show more emotion and passion.

Where it comes to vision and strategy, "say it well, say it often, say it simply and say it passionately," says Michael Useem, director of the Center for Leadership and Change Management at the Wharton School, University of Pennsylvania.

Successful leaders take a simple message and repeat it endlessly, Tichy says.

"The absence of knowing what's going on, and why, creates a toxic environment where distrust, suspicion, and fear overpower confidence, camaraderie, and courage," Roberts says.

Delegate.

Get out of the way of talented people. Reagan didn't immerse himself in detail as did workaholic presidents Richard Nixon and Jimmy Carter before him.

"It true hard work never killed anybody, but I figure, why the chance?" Reagan said.

LEADERSHIP & LIFE

Thoughts from Tony Zinni

General, U.S. Marines (Ret.)
as taken from *BATTLE READY*
by Tom Clancy

You can't lead unless you love those you lead. That's principle **number one**! All other leadership principles flow out of it. Too much leadership training focuses on the leader and not enough on the led. Your charges are your family. In professions that are true callings, you have to have that. In my profession, guys put everything on the line and can die for it. We have to care about these guys. They have to mean something to us. We must know what makes them tick; who they are; what they want and need; what motivates them.

I remember talking to Prime Minister Meles of Ethiopia a few years ago. Before he became leader of his government, he was a fighting general in a twenty-year-long revolution. He knew his troops. They'd lived and fought together for two decades. One day during the fighting, his troops had to pass through a minefield, without any of the mechanical devices we use for our protection. He had no choice. He had to send troops ahead of everybody to find lanes. Many of them died, but his forces successfully made the passage.

When he told me the story, tears were in his eyes for the troops he'd lost. If you don't or can't feel that, then you shouldn't lead.

The **second principle** is to know yourself. Few leaders are as good as they think they are. And commander develop skills in finding measures of success that make them look good, such as body counts. What's that real measure of success? You get it from truly understanding the conflict and by seeking feedback from the guys with boots on the ground. They're there; they know. An ego can be bruised by feedback, but it's critical truly to know how you stand as a leader. True leaders seek feedback regardless of the new. They learn from it.

All people come in three parts: body, mind, and spirit. No one is complete unless all three are developed and tended to. As a leader, you need to care for these in yourself and in those you lead.

Each leader needs a code to live by. That code can be formed by many factors. Our family, our schooling, our faith, our friends, and our calling in life can all be counted among those factors. My daughter once asked me what I would die for. I thought about that a lot before I answered her. I knew the answer would truly define me. I told her I would die for my faith, my family, my friends, my freedom, and my flag-the five "Fs," a simplified expression of my code. But a code is worthless unless you live it. Words like integrity, ethics, honor, etc., need to be lived and not just uttered.

You never stop learning unless you decide to. I have an unquenchable thirst for knowledge. It is an obsession for me. My sources for learning are all around me. When I make a mistake of fail, I have to know why. I need to know what makes things and people tick. I am amazed at how much people miss by not observing the world around them with an open curiosity.

I have learned more from sergeants than I have from generals. The troops relate to a leader by testing him or her to see if they relate to them, to see if they're open to them and listen to them. They want to know if they're fundamentally honest with them. This is not a "buddy" thing. Leaders can't be buddies with the led. But the troops want to be able to say: "I can talk to this captain. He listens." If you don't listen, they will be polite, but you can forget about their respect . . . or about getting the truth where the rubber meets the road. You want them to tell you: "Sir, this is not working." Or: "It is working," Or: "Yeah, it's working okay, but it could be better." When you know such truths, and can do something about them, that's when you have real success.

I love to teach. It is a principal function of leadership. My teaching philosophy is based on two principles. The first has to do with the mission of the teacher. His role is to provide the students with the facts and with a clear articulation of the varying views, opinions, and options on a given subject. His purpose, after he has provided this framework, is to then teach the student how to ask the questions that really count and not how to give answers that satisfy conventional wisdom and long-fossilized received opinions. If you know how to ask the right questions, the best answers usually follow . . . though it may take time.

The second principle (knowing one's self) deals with the foundation of thinking. It must have a set of values at its base. This requires teachers to emphasize the importance of a values-based thinking process without imposing personal interpretation of those values. The values will be more powerful in a student's life and in his way of thinking, his decision making, and in how he defines his ethical code if he has discovered and defined them on his own.

(Thomas Hobbes, in *Leviathan*, I, 10,—"To value a man at a high rate is to *honour* him; at a low rate is to *dishonour* him. But high and low, in this case, is to be understood by comparison to the rate each man setteth on himself.) by author!

The greatest enjoyment for a teacher is to see that moment of discovery or that moment of doubt that wasn't there before, but now presents the student with a spur to reason.

Learning is guided discovery. The guide is the teacher. His scholarship provides the factual basis for the student's journey of discovery; and his leadership, personal example, and mentoring skills provide the moral basis. A teacher's competence, therefore, comes in two inseparable parts. He must be expert in his subject and he must be qualified in his leadership ability. Technical competence alone is not sufficient. Leading and teaching are synonymous. You cannot assume to do one without the other. As a teacher, I strive to meet the obligations articulated in this philosophy. It requires me to develop in myself the mental, physical, and spiritual qualities I desire to impart and instill in my students.

Over time these dynamic beliefs settled into three categories: those that I was absolutely sure were right; those that I was pretty sure were right; and those that were up for grabs. It was an even split, with new ideas coming and some old ones going; they were in a constant state of morphing over time. I called these my "Combat Concept." To me they were a mechanism for continuous learning.

The particular concepts themselves don't matter as much as the process. This process was so important to me that I extended it from war fighting to other areas—leadership, and team building. I kept asking myself: "What makes people tick? What do they want in life? What makes teams tick? How can I bring them together more strongly and effectively?"

I'd write down my thoughts on these things, but they were always open to challenge and to change. I wanted always to be able to keep examining my core. I learned long ago that when you stop examining your core, you can really be shaken when you take a hard hit.

SHERMAN COFFIN
TEACHING ME THE MEANING
OF TRUE LEADERSHIP

An excerpt from SOCRATES 'N SUITS **BOOK I**
After my first combat mission on April 1st! 1953

After a couple of Jack Daniels and water followed by a steak sandwich I excused myself, thanked Jim (my flight leader) for the lunch and moral support, and headed for my sack at ROGER flight. I was bothered; even though it was my first mission, I had done a piss poor job of flying—**combat** flying. "As of now," I said to myself, "You're undependable as a pilot and wingman. This is war, Suitcase. You can't possibly let that happen again. You *must* do something about it! But what?"

When I got to my cubbyhole next to my sack, I looked through a couple of the history and philosophy books I brought with me from stateside. After about an hour of research on the simple word "fear" I found a couple of interesting thoughts. Aristotle in *Rhetoric*, said, "Fear may be defined as a pain or disturbance due to a mental picture of some destructive or painful evil in the future. We do not fear things that are a very long way off. For instance, we all know we shall die, but we are not troubled thereby, because death is not close at hand. From this definition it will follow that fear is caused by whatever we feel has the great power of destroying us, or harming us in ways that tend to cause us great pain."

"Thanks, Aristotle. You have me thinking," I said to myself.

After reading Aristotle, Plutarch came along, in *Caius Marius*, with "The strangeness of things often make them seem formidable when they are not so; and, **by our better acquaintance** (bold print by author) even things which are really terrible loose much of their frightfulness."

"I'll be damned," I said to myself. "It's right in front of me. I was afraid of getting shot down and being killed because I was along for the ride and had nothing to contribute. So get off your ass and go see the guys at JOC (Joint Operations Control) and get yourself **better acquainted** with the war and see if you can ditch the frightfulness that Plutarch so eloquently addressed. Learn how best to stay alive."

The next time I was free I went to see a particular individual, Captain Sherman Coffin, an experienced combat pilot who had flown 135 missions and was now, while waiting to go home, operations officer at JOC. He was on duty several nights a week. I asked him to help me 'fly through' my pre-briefed and close air support missions, and flak, and show me 'what I needed to learn to keep the scare factor at a minimum and become a more reliable pilot and leader of men.'

Captain Coffin was flattered that I would ask and he said, "Not only will we talk, we'll grab a couple of planes and actually fly you through simulated missions. The secret to success is preparation—know all there is to know—about yourself, your own limitations, the airplane, your crew chief, your wingmen, and the enemy. You *must* know the enemy better than he knows himself. How?? Spend time with the intelligence officer. Take him to dinner a night or two. Ask him a lot of questions. Think through what he has told you then go back and ask him more questions. And go to de-briefings. Put yourself in position to become acquainted (there's that word again—from Plutarch) with every aspect of a combat mission. You want to be a leader! Learn, Lt. Simpson. Learn! Learn! Learn!"

"I'll teach you navigation to and from the front lines—the shortest distance between two points saves time, fuel, and lives. I'll teach you proper radio procedure—how to pick up the air-to-ground controller, the focal points and, how to 'get in and out' of the combat sphere of activity in a hurry."

"There are men on the ground in fox holes, bunkers, hiding behind rocks—anything to stay alive, yet they are taking the fight to the assholes who are hell-bent on killing them. The gooks will kill you too!! That is our job, here in the 8th, to provide effective close air support. And when you have three other pilots with you, and they have to go in on the target one at a time, you can't dilly-dally, or someone, needlessly, will be shot down. Don't think for a second that the enemy isn't tracking every move you make. Remember, the enemy hates your ass. You piss the enemy off. If they see an opening—you and your wingmen are dead!!"

"And remember, Simpson, a leader in any endeavor, but particularly a flight leader in combat, has a tremendous responsibility. If you can't pick up your front line controller after several tries, do not—I say do not—fuck around with indecision. You'll be wasting fuel, time, possibly a ground pounder's life, and in the meantime, you'll be putting your whole flight in danger. If the air-to-ground controller has been shot down that's tough shit; you can't do anything about that. You must develop a rigid, mental toughness. If radio contact is lost, you can't hang around while someone tries to figure out what went wrong. You assume the responsibility of a leader and make the decision to go north above the 38th Parallel and hit targets—pre-arranged targets. That is why you are here; that is what smart flight leaders do. Just radio WATCHCASE and *tell* them what you are going to do. Your decision has to be quick and decisive. Let them know that you know what you are doing. So many, actually too many, dim wit, dumb shit, supposed flight leaders ask WATCHCASE what would they suggest. If I were in charge, I would tell the flight lead I suggest he go back to home base and turn in his wings. Would you want me or another commander to tell you that? Do you think this is a picnic?"

"No Sir."

"Cut the Sir shit. And by the way, don't you go by the name of Suitcase? Oh, yeah! You're the guy who set a bush on fire. (**BOOK I of the Trilogy**) You aren't related to Moses are you?"

"Yes, Sir, I'm the one. And no, Moses would be too hot for me to handle."

Captain Coffin smiled. "I hope you fly better than you make jokes. You gained a lot of respect by telling the truth. McDivitt tells me you are really down on yourself. So you made a mistake. If I told you how many I made we would be here all day. But I learned! Lt. Suitcase, if you want to recover from the misfortune of screwing up, get on friendly terms with your mistakes. Henry Ford said, 'Even a mistake may be the one thing necessary to a worthwhile achievement.' The benefit of mistakes of every dumb move you make, is they can teach you the effect of your actions. Don't be too busy beating up on yourself to learn the lesson you have already paid for. The secret, and I'm going to help, is to draw wise conclusions from foolish choices. Henry Ford was right but in combat we don't have many chances to right a wrong."

"So you were scared. So was I. Let me tell you something, Lt. Suitcase. There is only one universal passion: fear! Of all the thousands of qualities a man may have, the only one you will find as certainty, from the most inexperienced fighter pilot to me, is fear. It is fear that makes men fight: it is indifference that makes them run away; fear is the prevailing current in war."

"You aren't an indifferent man, Simpson, otherwise you wouldn't be here with me. It's guys like you that make the difference."

"You know where that statement on fear comes from? Not from me; except I took a little liberty and substituted the word fighter pilot for soldier and me for Napoleon. I wanted to make it more contemporary."

"No, Captain. Coffin, I don't."

"Shaw! George Bernard Shaw. He wrote *THE MAN of DESTINY*. He was talking about Napoleon. Napoleon talked about fear from the youngest drummer boy to himself. So, if Napoleon recognizes fear and is man enough to admit it, hell, I guess you and I can too!"

"Do you know the name Goethe? Johann Wolfgang von Goethe, Simpson?"

"Yes, I think so, Sir. Give me a minute. I'm thinking! Didn't he write a poem about Faust?"

"He did. His art and thought are epitomized in his great dramatic poem *Faust*. Goethe said, 'How closely linked are luck and merit, is something fools have never known.' Now I ask you, will you be lucky in combat or will fate play a role? Luck is coming upon something desirable by chance. Well, you evidently aren't taking a chance because you came down here to see what you could learn. Merit is credit held to be earned by performance of righteous acts and to ensure future benefits. We here at 'JOC' will do the best we can to teach you the performance of righteous acts and ensure future benefits—like staying alive. In philosophy—I'm Georgia Tech, by the way. How about you?"

"St. Louis University."

"Oh yeah! 'Easy Ed' McCauley."

"Hey, Captain Coffin, I like you already."

"We'll like each other better if we can keep you alive. Anyhow, in philosophy we discussed the early notion of fate is that of an inexorable and blind necessity governing everything that happens. In the Christian era, the notion of fate tends to that of Divine providence. So when you think about what I say, maybe someone 'up there' likes you; and you will never be a fool in that regard."

"Good thoughts, Captain. No one can attract, or should I say be associated with, luck, merit, or fate until he puts himself in a position to accept the outcome. With me, I look forward to it being all good."

Captain Coffin continued talking about WATCHCASE (radar station controlling all flights in and out of the battle zone) in the event a flight leader decides to go north. (The front line, along the 38th Parallel, ran from east to west. Captain Coffin was teaching me if you can't hit your target as called for, have another target north of the line in mind.)

"What the hell does WATCHCASE know?" he asked. "They may call for 'targets of opportunity' but that's bull shit because if you decide to go north, you should have already prepared yourself to know what target is important enough to hit. And you must plan. How is it protected? Machine guns? Anti-aircraft? Maybe nothing!! That's why you should go to briefings whether you are scheduled to fly or not. You have to have command of yourself and the battlefield which runs all the way north, and east and west across North Korea. You don't want to fly into any battle as a weak-dick stranger. And you have to do all this by pre-planning; distance, time, altitude, fuel, anti-aircraft guns, direction of attack, etc. Will you break up into elements, spread formation, in trail? And above all, you must give yourself time to get home. Are you with me?"

"Yes, Sir."

"Pay attention to the briefings and, as I said, attend any number of them, even if you aren't scheduled for combat. Find out where the action is. Why? Because if you lead a flight and have to cancel a particular close-support mission, have a alternative plan in mind as to what you are going to do. What rail juncture, or road, or staging area would you go after? Fuel management is essential. The lives of your men are imperative. And as I said, go to de-briefings. Find out what's working the good missions—the piss-poor missions. Ask yourself about leadership? Assume responsibility. Be prepared to face live and death situations. Some of these so-called flight leaders can't bull shit me. They talk a good mission over a scotch at the bar. Some of these guys aren't doing their job. They haven't taken the time to learn or become acquainted with daily enemy activity. They are flying scared because they aren't prepared. Therefore they're totally fucking ineffective. They think of themselves only. Learn about armament! Flak! Fuel! Lack of top cover! Inexperience! Listen and learn. Pay attention to the men in the squadron. You'll learn by listening to the flight leaders. Who is and who are not living up to combat pilot standards. I don't care how many missions a pilot has, some of them never learn, nor do they have the potential to lead. You read philosophy?

"Yes, Sir, I do."

"Good! Plato, in REPUBLIC says, and he's quoting Socrates, 'A tyrant is always stirring up some war or another, in order that people may require a leader.' We are in a war Simpson. Prepare yourself to step up and fill the void!"

"If you are leading a flight of four with number 2, 3, and 4 having already been assigned to you on a close air support mission, know who they are and what kind of experience they have. If it turns out you can't pick up your controller and you make the decision to go north and you think #2, your wingman, should take the element, put him there and put #3 on your wing. Don't hesitate. Everyone will live longer!!"

"As far as flak and any other kind of enemy fire, I can't help you other than to say it's like preparing for a final exam—the one that will make or break your 4.0. If you are prepared, you don't have the time to worry about your damn grade point average because you'll be concentrating on the test. Lt. Suitcase, just prepare for every mission as if you were looking toward a 4.0."

I went to visit Captain Coffin two nights a week, went to briefings, de-briefings, asked him a million questions.

Captain. Coffin and I flew simulated missions all over Korea—day, night, weather—high altitude, low altitude, he leading, me leading. He would make me calculate every mile we went—and where every pound of fuel would go. But he would first take me high and south of the bomb line and point out the significant landmarks like the ones I needed to identify in a hurry during a close support mission. He pointed out geographical points like the Bull's Nuts and the "M" carved in the mountains by the Imjin River, Pork Chop, Bloody Ridge, the Hook, Chorwan, Kumhwa—where the railroad started north, etc., etc. We flew instruments, night formation, formation acrobatics, and night navigation tests. He would put me under the hood in a T-33, maneuver for thirty minutes over the pitch-black Korean landscape, pull the hood and say, "Find your way home. Remember, Lt. Suitcase, knowledge of radio procedures, the way you handle yourself while in communication with ground control or tower, and intelligent use of navigation aids will keep you alive. There are many air force and navy night missions up north all the time and an uniformed, inexperienced piss ant of a fighter pilot that gets lost and gives any indication of panic can ruin many a mission and that could lead to death. Is that clear?"

"Yes, Sir."

On other nights he would keep me under the hood and say, "OK! Find your way home. I don't want you out from underneath that hood (in the rear seat of a T-33) until you are on final approach."

God! he was tough as hell on me but he taught me what war was all about doing your very best to stay alive. I belived that this was the kind of approach any potential leader needed to inject himself into the main stream by taking knocks and learning from them. I should have been killed on my first mission; Captain Coffin made me poignantly aware of a powerful word. PREPARE! PREPARE! PREPARE!

How can you not love the guy. I took notice how he quoted from Plato and spoke of Socrates, my favorite philosopher.

I became very acquainted with the air war. I became an aware and sensible combat pilot.

What I learned from Captain Coffin is courage is knowledge. My confidence grew. I was able to think and act in the face of fear and transitioned from stooge to sage because of Captain Coffin. I now had the tools to prove to myself that I had the ability to persevere and perform to the fullest extent.

Time would tell if that would hold true.

EFFECTIVE COMMUNICATION

Our own mind is strengthened
by communication with
vigorous and orderly minds!

Of the Art of Discussion
Montaigne, *Essays*, III, 8

Effective communication is the thread that holds a company together. Instead of a group of filaments twisted together, it is a group of informed, self-confident, accountable personnel talking together.

And the together talking (discussion) has to be of a quality of active mental force—fullness, lively, emphatic and subject to both enlightenment—and mistakes.

Michel de Montaigne (1533-1592) in essays, *Of the Art of Discussion*, said, "The most fruitful and natural exercise of our mind, in my opinion, is discussion. I find it sweeter than any other action of our life; if I discuss with a strong mind and a stiff jouster, he presses on my flanks, prods me right and left; his ideas launch mine. Rivalry, glory, and competition, push me and lift me above myself. Our mind is strengthened by communication with vigorous and orderly minds."

Michel Eyquem, seigneur de Montaigne, was one of the greatest masters of the ESSAY as a literary form. Montaigne wrote three *Essais*, which were trials or tests of his own judgment on a diversity of subjects, show the change in Montaigne's thinking as **examination of himself** (bold print by author) developed into a study of mankind and nature. His last essays reflect his acceptance of life as good and his conviction that humankind must discover their own nature in order to live with others in peace and dignity.

Montaigne gives you, through me, an answer why I "entwine" so much philosophy in this book. I proceed on this repeatedly curving course because, as far as I am concerned, philosophy is a continuing pursuit of knowledge. Montaigne said, "Humankind must discover their own nature." I am in a search for a general understanding of values and reality. The search is generally by speculation rather than by observing but what difference does it make as long as you continually search to learn, to know—about yourself and others; to try to understand what others in the past would have done, or did. Philosophic thinking is a ceaseless search to obtain awareness. It is also action of something not known before—and decision making without fear. The increase in confidence level will make oneself a better communicator and a superior leader in discussions. You will also, though probably functioning below the threshold of conscious awareness, be a person living and acting a new way of life.

"Philosophy *is* a way of life—an essential way—that consists precisely of living according to certain knowledge," according to Julian Marias in his text *History of Philosophy*, Dover publications, N.Y., 1976.

The opening section of Aristotle's *METAPHYSICS* answers the question, Why did man begin to philosophize? According to Aristotle, "All men desire naturally to know. It is because of awe that men begin to philosophize."

I stand in awe of what history has to offer us. Awe is the beginning of wisdom. I stand in awe of what companies like Wal-Mart, the new IBM, and LOCKHEED MARTIN can do with effective communication internally and with customers. I can learn and gain wisdom from their experiences.

Drucker, states, in his book, *MANAGEMENT*, "Communication is perception." He goes on, "An old riddle posed by the mystics of many religions—the Zen Buddhists, the Sufis of Islam, and the Rabbis of the Talmud, asks, "Is there a sound in the forest if a tree crashes down and no one is around to hear it?" We now know that the right answer to this is "No." There are sound waves. But there is no sound unless someone perceives it. Sound is created by perception. Sound is communication.

This may seem trite; after all, the mystics of old already knew this, for they too always answered that there is no sound unless someone can hear it. Yet the implications of this rather trite statement are great indeed.

First, it means that it is the recipient who communicates. The so-called communicator, the person who emits the communication, does not communicate. He utters! Unless there is someone who hears, there is no communication; there is only noise. The communicator speaks or writes or sings—but he does not communicate. Indeed, he cannot communicate. He can only make it possible, or impossible, for a recipient, or rather, percipient—to perceive.

GUMPS, PLATO & CHRISSINGER

The above three words are very thought provoking regarding additional expressions about communication.

GUMPS stands for *G*as, *U*ndercarriage, *M*ixture, *P*ropeller and *S*houlder harness.

PLATO was a Greek philosopher and, CHRISSINGER, Thomas, was my instructor in basic pilot training. All three subjects, GUMPS, PLATO, and CHRISSINGER, have something in common. Let's see what the commonality is.

In the process of knowledge, Plato, the teacher of Aristotle, made a fundamental contribution. In human thinking, the general, or universal, takes the form of a concept. And what is the role of concepts in knowledge? Without concepts, Plato emphasizes, we should have, not knowledge, but only sensation. Sensation is merely the exercise of the sense on outward objects; it is merely animal grasping of *relationships*; it implies not merely feeling, but *understanding*.

Sensation is of particular things; knowledge is of the character of things. In sensing, we touch this or that table, taste this or that apple; in knowing, we think of tables as a kind of thing, a form or furniture, of apples as a kind of fruit. Or to put the matter in another way, knowledge takes place when we are able to communicate or use language, to be articulate or to think by using *symbols*.

GUMPS, to me, is the grasping of a relationship. I remember it, and its relationship to flying, as if I learned it yesterday. Yesterday was over fifty years ago. I was in BASIC pilot training. When entering the landing pattern in our training aircraft on a pre-determined heading, at a specific altitude, GUMPS related to preparing the airplane properly, for landing; in a very explicit manner. First the *G*as selector on the proper tank; then the *U*ndercarriage (wheels) down and locked; then the *M*ixture to full rich; then the *P*rop lever forward; then the checking of the *S*houlder harness to make sure it was locked.

My instructor, Chrissinger, in the back seat of our BASIC training aircraft, the North American T-6G, was not Plato; but when he saw me prepare for landing by relating the GUMPS *symbol* in my mind to proper functioning, he knew (knowledge) that I was grasping the relationship correctly and he was holding me accountable.

We both, therefore, had the understanding that I was communicating to him. I had the knowledge of what it took to get us both on the ground in a safe landing configuration.

I was able to communicate discipline versus confusion; and Chrissinger had the knowledge to know the difference between the two.

John Henry Newman (1801-1890) said, in his *Idea of a University*, "The communication of knowledge certainly is either a condition or the means of that sense of enlargement or enlightenment. It is equally plain, that such communication is not the whole of the process. The enlargement consists of the mind's *energetic and simultaneous action* upon, and towards, and among those new ideas, which are rushing in upon it. It is the action of a formative power, reducing to order and meaning." (GUMPS)

As my instructor pilot, Chrissinger was being held accountable to determine my ability to fly. Before allowing me to solo, Chrissinger had to have the knowledge or my enlargement and systematization, but it was my responsibility to communicate that state of mind to him.

The above thoughts on communication are a bit to swallow but GUMPS offers a means to an end in understanding. I researched it only to try to apply an experienced, practical analysis between what Plato and Newman were trying to state. An intense study of both men would not be easy without practicality. As you notice, I didn't even have to communicate directly to Chrissinger; GUMPS did it for me.

But symbols do not necessarily apply in the every day world of business, and in the profession of marketing and sales, the instructor (sales manager) cannot go along on every sales call.

I think an experienced manager's first measure of accountability is to be able to communicate and measure productivity as a result of said communication. The first requirement is that the communication be thorough and complete.

Communication encompasses the skills of listening and getting all involved and actively participating in decisions. Communications are a continuing problem and one not capable of casting a solution.

In Peter F. Drucker's book, *MANAGEMENT*, he said when NASA first came into being, the scientists who dominated it then believed that controls, and especially, computer-based information, would run the system. They were soon disabused.

One constant theme of the Sayles-Chandler** dissertation about managing large systems is the crucial importance of face-to-face personal relationships, of constant meetings, and of bringing people into the decision-making process, even on matters that are remote from their own assignments.

And the Sayles-Chandler theme is not only related to NASA, 1975, but in any business in any year. (** I read the Sayles-Chandler discourse somewhere, at some time, and took note, but I don't remember.)

I offer another example, 10 years later; chapter five of Peters-Waterman, *In Search of Excellence.*

"We were trying to depict to an executive responsible for project management coordination how it might be possible to radically simplify the forms, procedures, paperwork, and interlocking directorates of committees that had overrun his system. We said, quite off-handedly, 'Well, at 3M and TEXAS INSTRUMENTS they don't seem to have these problems. People simply talk to each other on a regular basis.'"

He looked at us blankly. Our words hardly sounded like exotic advice—even helpful advice. So we said, "You're not competing with 3M. Let's go to St. Paul for a day and take a look. You'll be surprised."

Our friends at 3M were tolerant of the excursion, and we observed all sorts of strange goings-on. There were a score or more casual meetings in progress with salespeople, marketing people, manufacturing people, engineering people, R&D people; even accounting people were sitting around, chattering about new product problems. We happened in on a session where a 3M customer had come to talk informally with about fifteen people from four divisions on, 'How Better to Serve His Company.' None of it seemed rehearsed. We didn't see a single structured presentation. It went on all day—people meeting in a seemingly random way to get things done.

One of the biggest faults of most managers I have known through business and teaching is they take for granted that just because *they* know what *they* desire and verbalize such to their personnel, they, the personnel, are supposed to understand. Most of the verbalizing, sad to say, is in the form of one-way directives. Personnel, in most cases, do not understand their managers' explicit needs and desires and how they are to be held accountable.

Why is this? In any society, the nature of interpersonal relations depends in large measure upon the effectiveness of interpersonal communications. Certainly, in business in general, and assigning accountability in particular, the effectiveness of the system is related to the effectiveness of the communications. To go one step further, within each department the planning activity is basically an exercise in communications. If an executive understands something of the theory of communications, he should be able to better manage responsibilities to his firm and accountability to his *personnel.*

"When you communicate, you are trying to establish "commonness" with someone through the use of verbal or nonverbal signals. (GUMPS again). You, as the source, send a message through a channel to a receiver in an effort to share an idea, attitude, or some other kind of information. Fundamentally, a communication process requires only three elements, a message, a source of this message, and a receiver. A final element in the process, feedback, tells the sender whether the message was received and how it was perceived by the destination target."

One of the biggest failures of managers is the understanding of communication and perception. It is easy for an experienced manager to tell his personnel or write a memo outlining what he wants. The experience may come in knowing the company and the department but the real experience would be knowledge of, and fully understanding of, how the personnel perceive what the manager wants. Managers cannot comprehend that it is the recipient who communicates. Long ago, in paying attention to what Drucker wrote, I went from communicator to utterer until I said to my employees or students, "Now, tell me exactly where I am coming from" If they could tell me, exactly, I was effectively communicating. All it takes is a little extra time; and in addition, you genuinely get to know what your people expect from you rather than what you expect from them.

In Plato's *PHREDO* which, among other things, is also the earliest extended treatise on rhetoric (the art of speaking, or writing effectively), Socrates points out that one has to talk to people in terms of their own experience, that is, that one has to use carpenter's metaphors when talking to carpenters, and so on. One can communicate only in the recipients language or in his terms. And the terms have to be experienced-based. It, therefore, does very little good to try to explain terms to inexperienced people.

They will not be able to receive them if they are not terms of their own experience. They simply exceed their perception capacity.

To communicate a concept is impossible unless the recipient can perceive it, that is, unless it is within his perception. A person must be able to perceive how management is giving him responsibility before he can rightly, and justly, be held accountable.

My hope is that after reading the past few pages on communication, someone in responsible and knowledgeable positions in management, will realize the importance of assignments. And, in particular, marketing management must realize the importance of selecting those who will represent their company.

To me it makes only common sense that everyone must be knowledgeable of the company, the product, the territory, the potential, and the need for planning, training, and proper communication. Also, they must be knowledgeable of themselves and the customer.

All front line combat situations are, in simple terms, a matter of life and death. In my combat experience as a fighter pilot, I knew that the highest losses were with those fighter pilots on their first few missions. When you report for duty to a fighter squadron in a combat zone, the flight commander, or squadron commander, knows you have "the right stuff" and have been through the finest flight training the world can offer. But experience, in combat, a life or death situation is lacking.

In order to live, we look to those who are experienced enough to know how to communicate on what it takes to stay alive; how to put past training to good use, and how to be most effective and proficient in using the tools of the trade. **BOOK I** details this in a "true life" adventure (my first combat mission).

And all the while the communication process is taking place, one listens— hard—because this experienced communicator is—what did Drucker say? "Making it possible for a recipient, or, "percipient" how to perceive how to stay alive. I don't know what could be worse for a fighter pilot in combat. Getting shot down for lack of perception on how to stay alive, or being fired, "shot down", for being an inexperienced communicator? Someone in a knowledgeable and responsible position must bear a heavy heart and soul.

But a lot of companies do not realize what I just said, or what we have learned from the above. They don't know how to win; they just hope to win. They don't know how to assign accountability; they just hope they have selected the right person. They don't know how to train, or plan, or hold persons responsible; they just hope they have selected the right person and that things are going right. But, if something happens to show up wrong, it will be a patchwork theory on what to do to fix it.

How can management gain the proper experience to communicate to others under those set of circumstances? They wake up one day and market position is lost, shot down, death in combat for market share, and they don't even know the reasons why.

In their books on American business, *In Search of Excellence*, Peters and Waterman write, "The excellent companies require and demand extraordinary performance from the average man." They labeled it "productivity through people."

Attaining and fine-tuning productivity is impossible without proper communication. It must be remembered that this effective communication must be a two-way street. It would be ill advised, to say the least, if a company had a one-way policy of communication from the top down and didn't allow for feedback from those very experienced people it went to the trouble to hire in the first place. You can be a sure a flight leader knows communication must be a two-way street. The responsibility of a wingman is to protect the flight leader from being shot down. Losing effective communication results in death. Death in combat, death in business! There is nothing more final than that!

"No matter how an organization chooses to systematize the flow of its communications from the top down, memoranda, mass meetings, bulletin boards, employee handbooks; the system must also provide for 'feedback,' communication from the bottom up."

Communication evolves from the Latin word communis, which means common or communal or a synonym, familiar. Thus, when you communicate you are trying to establish "commonness" with someone; you're trying to get familiar. Common sense says the more you have in common with someone the more simple and effortless the relationship becomes, even if the relationship is limited to effective communication. Management must learn "commonness"!

Too many companies are of themselves repressive and cultureless; they have no commonness with their employees. They rule without helping and command without leading, and their employees are in such despair.

We adults in business must shed the image of self-importance and old cronyism and pomposity. I saw too much of that in my 40 years of representation. I could name names of some of the most outlandish. But, if one is to consider the young, inexperienced employees with less time in office than you, remember they could use your wisdom and experience. Drop around once in a while and see what you can do to help and ask, "How you're doing"? Walk the floor! Connect again! It may not lead to circle dances, but your knowledge and effective communication would do well toward leading quality circles.

ETHICS/HONESTY

In *ROGET'S II,* The *New Thesaurus,* **ethics** is defined as "the moral quality of a course of action." An ethical person's activity in business, relationship to others, and self-conduct should be in accordance with principles of right and good behavior. **Honesty,** as defined in the same *Thesaurus,* is being marked by uprightness in principle and action; moral or ethical strength. The word **honesty** is the word applied to truthfulness of statement, to fairness in dealing with others, to keeping one's promises, to trustworthiness, and to a general rectitude of intention and action. Such things as lying, deceiving, cheating, and committing **fraud,** are—obviously—instances of dishonesty.

Alighieri Dante, was a man of intense study of classical philosophy. We know him from D*IVINE COMEDY* fame, one of the greatest of literary classics. Dante originally entitled the classic *Commedia*; the adjective *Divina* was added later. It recounts the poet's journey through Hell, Purgatory, and Heaven. He gave us in *Inferno*, (Hell) a philosophical thought; "Because **fraud** is a vice peculiar to man, it more displeases God."

In introducing the word **fraud** here, I do some injustice to the title of **BOOK III,** because in this book I introduce men of great stature and merit—Socrates, Plato, St. Augustine, Emerson, Col. Bob Scott, Dr. Grant Gould, Bill Bettis, etc., etc. **Fraud** disallows me to account for the synergy between free enterprise and philosophy. Hell, synergy is identified as "work toward a common end." The antithesis of "toward a common end" is **fraud.** But before I launch or usher in my constant reasoning as to why the study of philosophy complements a man's desire to be an honest and ethical person, I can't help but think about the employees and stockholders from ENRON and WORLDCOM and ADELPHIA and TYCO INT'L, etc. Here are stories of senior managers cheating hard working, devoted employees investing their trust and money in corporate officers who fraudulently used off-balance-sheet deals used to hide debt and inflate earnings. WORLDCOM used improper accounting of God knows how many billions were charged to inappropriate accounting expenses; ADELPHIA gave the Rigas family $1 billion in *hidden* loans. And the CEO of TYCO misused company money to buy art and other brazenly expensive, ego building objects just to make him look good in the eyes of others who fill their lives full of "keeping up with the Jones' articles of ephemeral rapture.

Man learns his trade (or discipline) by constant hard work and devotion. He also obtains knowledge or awareness not known before; that it takes time to know and love him self, therefore learning the *value* of knowing and loving others. A man of stature and merit would not allow such corrupt things to happen to *valued* employees. A man who does *not* take the time to know and love himself and learn to lead to serve others is made of pillars of self-serving greed and self-aggrandizement, the pillars being constructed of children's sandbox material or "what the cat left behind". These men cannot hold a rigorous and inelastic candle against honest men of free enterprise. Why? Because their characters are made of melted wax!

If you read **BOOK I** of the *SOCRATES 'N SUITS* trilogy you learned of my first combat mission. Talk about melted wax! I was a disaster! Why? Because I had not thought enough about taking the time to know more about me, and in addition, more about the enemy I was trained to fight. Sure, I flew 130 hours in the T-6; 60 hours in the T-28A, and won my fighter pilot wings in advanced training after additional hours in the T-33 jet trainer. And then followed 80 more hours in gunnery flying the F-80 and the F-86 Sabre. Hell, I had knowledge of what it took to fly a fighter. In fact, I was a damn good pilot—until I was put to the test—on my first mission. I failed miserably—until I became aware of the synergy between a pilot (and his fighter working together toward a common end) and philosophy (Socrates.) There *must* be that same synergy between an honest CEO and hard working employees. We are talking life of a company here; the same life as a pilot in combat!

Socrates sat me down and said, "Suits," the reason you failed is what philosophy teaches a man is to know the difference between 'knowledge of' and 'knowledge about.' You said you had knowledge of what it took to fly a fighter. Big deal! Your problem is you did not have knowledge about yourself **and/or** your fighter under combat conditions. Nor did you have knowledge about the enemy!

(**BOOK I** tells the story, in part, how I learned to overcome my failures associated with my first combat mission. Philosophy, the lessons of history and "getting out and learning by doing, as an element leader and flight leader," changed the way I approached leadership, responsibilities, and accountabilities.)

In war, learning to know one's self is by nature a hurried, revolutionary event. Its circumstances demand a quick account of knowledge about a man and his innate ability to seize the situation at hand, then lead or command. He quickly learns to be honest with himself! Can he grab authoritative charge and lead the way? Is he right in risking thousands of men to capture his objective. Gettysburg, Verdun, Iwo Jima, Inchon, Vietnam?

Everyday business offers an evolutionary process; it is never ending. A man that does not know himself will try to compress time and soon his losses will match the causalities of war. His move will be to cover up, to be dishonest at all costs. What are those costs? Character! Honor! Reputation! Love! Human Greatness! Moral Obligation! Courage! Honesty! and the chance to gain Wisdom! And then, the deepest wound of all—the loss of respect of your fellow man.

Dostoevsky says, in *BROTHERS KARAMAZOV,* "The man who lies to himself and listens to his own lie comes to such a pass that he cannot distinguish the truth within him, or around him, and so loses all respect for himself and for others. And having no respect he ceases to love, and in order to occupy and distract himself without love he gives way to passions and course pleasures, and sinks to bestiality in his vices, all from continual lying to other men and himself—."

I was under contract for an aerospace company (it was my second such contract) "to assist the Vice President of Strategic Sales and Planning in overcoming a serious lack of communication between his company and a prime contractor."

Communication between parties was getting along nicely when I was told I was to be terminated. Why? Because another representative of the company, in Washington, D.C., was caught in a pay-off scandal with Navy personnel! It was embarrassing for both parties. The president decided immediately that all sub-contract sales personnel would be dismissed and all executives of the corporation would report to executive headquarters for ethics classes on a particular day—once a week.

What could I do? Nothing! Particularly when the man I reported to was an extremely ethical executive, as was the president of the company. I was teaching at the time; after I told the class what happened, I told them to think over what the president had done, and did they agree with his solution(s).

The following week we had some very interesting discussions and we all agreed that firing a person in my position, who had nothing to do with the situation and his process, was more of a re-action than an action showing thought and cerebration. And we all agreed that one can not teach ethics to grown men and women. Ethics is not nuclear physics or chemistry. Ethics, in my opinion, is a discipline dealing with knowing what is good or bad *accompanied* with moral duty and obligation. Pick a year—three, seven, twelve, fifteen! Every cultured person that grows in the company of men and women knows what is ethical. Not too many grow up with the answer to the question of what NaCl is or what E=mc2, represents but each knows the difference between right and wrong. There is no half right. There is no half wrong!

Anyhow, the more I thought about our class discussions the more I thought about what I would do as the president of a company. I would make arrangements to attend, along with every employee and spouse no matter their position (it wouldn't bother me a bit to sit next to a machinist or janitor,) a series of classes—on philosophy. The atmosphere in the learning process would innately jell the company together in the "consideration of man—of human nature, human life and the human condition." Together they would discuss such topics as:

SELF KNOWLEDGE & SELF LOVE

The injunction uttered by one of the seven wise men of ancient Greece in "Know thyself!" That commandment gets repeated in one form or another century after century, as a counsel of perfection or as a key to wisdom. Clearly, the task to be performed is not an easy one, since by implication it is one that few men discharge adequately. Though it would appear that we have access to the innermost core of our individual being, and that there is nothing in this world with which we are on more intimate terms than our own self, the self remains an elusive object of knowledge and understanding. Why is it so, in spite of all the mirrors in the world no one knows what he really looks like?

Schopenhauer, asked that question in his *Further Psychological Observations.* Arthur Schopenhauer (1788-1860) also speaks about Education, On the Wisdom of Life, Our Relation to Others, to Ourselves.

Other philosophers' thoughts and reason are to be discussed. Plato, Cicero, the great Marcus Aurelius, Augustine, Bacon, Emerson—so much to be discussed—so much fun in this search for wisdom!

Can you imagine this—this variety of ideas and thoughts—this search for wisdom—shared by the great men and women of your company. Even differences of opinion would coalesce, or bring together the employees into a united whole.

HONOR & REPUTATION

The individual man or woman should seek to know his or her self for what he or she really is and should esteem themselves for their true worth makes inevitable their desire to be known and esteemed by others according to their merits. Honor is the name that the ancients gave to the good that satisfies this natural desire; and they praised it highly among the goods that a virtuous man or woman should seek.

In a company's desire to build strong foundations for growth with legacy and culture in mind, would anyone dare to think, after discussions with their colleges about honor and reputation that he or she would give or take money for contracts all for the selfish reasoning of personnel self-aggrandizement?

One of the most interesting of questions brought before the employees could be, "Is man bound by duty or moral obligation to act or refrain from acting in certain ways by "duty" or "obligation?" Some employees might assert that there are certain things that a person ought or ought not to do if one is going to act rightly, or certain things that a person ought or ought not to desire if one is going to seek real, not merely apparent goods. Would the class then be making points in the context of discussing virtue and excellence rather than duty or obligation? I believe it would lead to employees discussing these vital points over a lunch table or taking the place of a bridge game for one night. That is the format many night school colleges are using today—round table discussions as part of homework.

FAMILY

The institution of the family is inseparable from the marriage rite and all that it entails; the *relation* of husband and wife results from marriage and is fundamental to the institution of the family. The parental care and direction of children is primary as is their collective respect for the free enterprise system from which the breadwinner gathers his wages. A contented worker from a happy home should be the focus of management as much as the balance sheet.

INTELLIGENCE & UNDERSTANDING

There are a large number of names for the human faculty, ability, or power that could be the subject of this discussion. Sometimes it is simply called "mind" sometimes "intellect," sometimes "reason", sometimes "wit." Each of these words has a somewhat different connotation; certain authors are at pains to distinguish reason from understanding, or intellect from intelligence. But all of these words have this common thread of meaning: they designate the power or ability by which men solve problems, make judgments, engage in reasoning or in deliberation, and make practical decisions. An admirable topic for management and labor to discuss!

While teaching a cross-section of marketing classes I had a number of GIs returning from the war in Vietnam. One class had to do with solving management problems. A few were high school graduates; most had a GED. They often asked if they could sit in the class and listen, to learn, what course(s) they might like to take to give direction to their vocation. "Of course," was my response, "and don't be afraid to speak up if you have any thoughts to contribute."

Talk about "GI Ingenuity"! To my surprise and admiration, many times, over a period of years, these men came up with many practical decisions and reasonable thought processes. Management should play heed!

EDUCATION

Education, broadly conceived, covers much more than schooling, or the period in which the young are under tutelage. It embraces every activity by which an individual grows mentally, morally, and spiritually. Whatever contributes to the development of a human person or the fulfillment of his potentialities should be regarded as educative.

The development may be an improvement of the person's mind through acquired knowledge or skill; it may be an improvement of his character; it may be an improvement in the use of his body. For that improvement to be a stable and relatively permanent acquisition, and not a momentarily transient one, must become habitual. "On the job" training should be developed and discussed by management and labor.

FREEDOM IN SOCIETY

This subject treated is not freedom in general, nor liberty in all its diverse forms, but the individual's freedom of action within the social group and the company in relation to other individuals. This freedom is variously described as freedom from coercion, impediment, or duress; freedom to do as one pleases or wishes; the liberty to live or act as one chooses; or the liberty to act according to one's own rules or directions subliminally approved by family, company, and friends.

BOOKS & READING

The discussions would center on the writing and reading of books, the collection and enjoyment of them, and the pleasures and pretensions of the literary life.

The discussion group would discuss praise and dispraise of books, criteria for distinguishing good books from bad, enduring from ephemeral literature, and wise counsel about the books to be read or about the amount and character of the reading one should do.

It would also be good for all to be aware of what Descartes said in *Discourses on Method*, I, "The reading of all good books is indeed like a conversation with the noblest of men of past centuries who were with the authors of them, nay a carefully studied conversation, in which they reveal to us none but the best of their thoughts."

The group could also learn from *Books and Reading*, the thoughts of Bacon, Montaigne, Swift, Plato, Voltaire, Thoreau, Tennyson, and Mark Twain. What an exciting, dynamic way to learn!

My thoughts about discussions as part of a company educational program only touches the minimal—what I consider would be of substantial help in turning a company into a dynamic organization. There could be many additional subjects such as:

Honor and Reputation
Friendship, Charity, and Love of Country
Intelligence and Understanding
Truth and Honesty; Moral Obligations and Courage
Justice and Injustice
Freedom of Thought and Expression
Equality and
The Nature of Life

And last but not least, by any means, Philosophy and Philosophers

Speaking of *human* greatness, the company would grow to be great. The evolutionary process would come about by *thought* followed by superb actions.

Each employee and spouse would be, by openness to the flow of verbal experience, acting out his or her realization that man has unique properties or attributes that differ him from everything else and with him carry the knowledge that his company has unique properties or attributes that differ it from every other company. A solid foundation for legacy and culture!

As the title of this section indicates, the quotations included here deal either with the nature, scope, and value of philosophy as a discipline or with the character and the virtues or vices of the philosopher as a man. Only some of the passages that consider philosophy itself regard it as a body of knowledge, a mode of inquiry, an intellectual discipline or way of thinking; many of them speak of philosophy as a way of life, as a vocation that sets certain men apart from others, just as a religious vocation does. When philosophy is thus considered, the character of the philosopher as a man is inextricably connected with the manner of life he leads. To be philosophical in this sense is to take a certain attitude toward life or to adopt certain rules of conduct rather than to profess certain beliefs or to promulgate theories about the nature of things.

It is only in the latter sense that philosophy is the object of both praise and censure-accorded by some an honorable place in the sphere of human inquiry, and ridiculed by other human undertakings or professions-law and medicine, for example, have been the objects of satirical attack or derisive comment. But philosophy is uniquely distinguished by the fact that many of its detractors, and often the most abusive, are persons who have called themselves or would be regarded as philosophers. The readers will also find that the philosophers quoted seldom agree with one another about the definition of their subject, the scope of their discipline, the method to be employed by them, or the claims that can be made for their conclusions.

Nor do they agree about whether it is necessary for a man to have certain moral virtues in order to be a philosopher; whether he is a man of wisdom or only a lover of or seeker after wisdom; and weather the history of philosopher shows evidence of any progress in the development of philosophical thought.

However, on three points, the reader will find a certain measure of agreement. One is that, whatever its positive values or contributions may be, philosophy does not build bridges, cure diseases, or result in new inventions: it has no technological applications whatsoever. A second point is the concern common among philosophers about the relation of their discipline to religion or theology, on the one hand, and to mathematics and science, on the other. Closely connected with that is the third point; namely, that philosophy, like religion and unlike the natural sciences and mathematics, extends beyond the consideration of what is to what ought to be-to considerations of good and evil, right and wrong, and the ultimate values that constitute the ends or objectives of human life.

LEGACY AND CULTURE
PRIME DRIVERS IN MANAGEMENT

The acquiring of culture is the
developing of an avid hunger for
knowledge and beauty.
Jesse Lee Bennet

It's been said that the toughest feat in sports is to hit a baseball on the major league level. Yet for 56 consecutive games in 1941, Joe DiMaggio of the New York Yankees did just that, resulting in a baseball record that many believe will never be broken.

Joseph Paul DiMaggio joined the New York Yankees in 1936 and played his entire career with the Yankees; he retired in 1955. He was known as a "Thing of Beauty" for his versatility, fielding talent and hitting ability. He was elected to the Baseball Hall of Fame in 1955.

Theodore Samuel "Ted" Williams joined the Boston Red Sox in 1939 and played continuously (with exception of military service) for the team until his retirement in 1960. Williams was one of the greatest natural hitters the game has ever known; he attributed his prowess to his detailed knowledge of the strike zone. In 1941 Ted Williams won the American League Batting Championship with a .406 average; a record most experts believe will never be broken. He was elected to the Baseball Hall of Fame in 1966.

The older of the two baseball leagues, the National League, was organized in 1876. In 1900 the Western League regrouped as the American League and three years later gained recognition as the second major league. Although earlier rules existed, the American and National Leagues adopted joint playing rules in 1904.

The Committee of Baseball Executive appointed, in 1921, Judge Kenesaw M. Landis to the new post of Baseball Commissioner. Landis replaced the three-man National Commission, which had ruled professional baseball since 1903. Landis governed for 24 years.

Why a brief synthesis on DiMaggio, Williams and baseball history? Because it is my firm belief that legacy and culture are interlinked with stability, time, and therefore, concomitant performance; accompanied by a cornerstone of customs, ideas and attitudes shared by a group and transmitted from generation to generation.

Think about what has been said; joint playing rules since 1904, Judge Landis governing for 24 years; Joe DiMaggio and Ted Williams were given the platform of stability that enabled them to perform over a period of time that gave birth to their legacy. Joe DiMaggio didn't play by one set of rules and Ted Williams another. Joe DiMaggio didn't play for the Yankees one year, the White Sox the next, the Cincinnati Reds the next, and so on. The same with Ted Williams!

In the present day atmosphere of free agency and business short-term planning, constant instability of cohesive strategy and un-relentless emphasis on the bottom line, I see a pervasive lack of awareness by corporate executives of understanding the appreciating legacy and culture. Culture, not economics, is the cornerstone of corporate stability and growth. There is no culture or legacy with the Yankees anymore. Dollars have taken over their winning ways.

John Stuart Mill said in 1851, "The grand achievement of the present age is the diffusion of superficial knowledge." To me, the grand achievement of the 1990s was the diffusion of superficial management.

"Culture" in a society as a whole, is "a general state of intellectual, material and moral development."

And what is a society? It is a group of people united for the promotion of a common aim. In the process of thinking through my reasoning on management's lack of understanding culture, I vicariously joined this "group of people" and brought together our collective material, intellectual and moral development into a corporation. We are supposedly united for a common aim. Is management leading us? Is management seeking the chance to look at all aspects of this collective material, intellectual and moral development before making decisions? I don't think so.

In "culture" we speak of the material, intellectual and moral development as a way of life; but that doesn't satisfy me. I also want time, maturity and legacy (continued superior performance) considered. Let us reflect for a minute on Bennett's observation on the acquiring of culture. To develop *anything* takes **time**, and if one's energy and aim is directed toward gaining knowledge and beauty, there is an accompanying gain of development and maturity. With maturity there is an understanding of one's self. Also, there is value to be gained by sharing the experience of attained knowledge and beauty with family, friends and business colleagues.

Whitehead said, in *AIMS of EDUCATION*, "Culture is activity of thought and receptiveness of beauty and humane feeling. Scraps of information have nothing to do with it. A merely well informed man is the most useless bore on God's earth. What we should aim at producing are men who possess both culture and expert knowledge in some special direction. Their expert knowledge will give them the ground to start from, and their culture will lead them as deep as philosophy and as high as art."

In a corporate environment expert knowledge shared and exchanged over a period of time creates an atmosphere for giving birth to legacy.

I think that it would be fair to say that Henry Higginson developed a specific culture in the Boston Symphony Orchestra. The orchestra's legacy has been handed down through a period of **time**. It is strengthened through famous conductors, Symphony Hall, The Berkshire Festival, and the Boston Pops Orchestra.

Tom Watson, Sr., developed an acute no-nonsense business atmosphere and culture at IBM and handed it down to Tom Watson, Jr.

C. R. Smith created a culture of reliable and charismatic business travel at American airlines and passed it on to Robert Crandall.

"OK," you say, "I can't find argument with you about your definitions but how do legacy and culture relate?"

That's a fair question but the answer will not be an easy one. You have to think in terms of both words. The secret is: the *recognition* and *appreciation* of expert knowledge (CULTURE) and the *determination* to continue or hand down (LEGACY) generally accepted works of value and intellectual excellence. It's "recognition— appreciation—determination." It's the Boston Philharmonic—IBM—American Airlines! It's your company!!! To uphold your company's position, strength, and customer satisfaction in the marketplace, you must have all three. You can't have one or two without the other. At the same time, as a company continually strives for knowledge and value, it must develop the ability, character, leadership and personal esteem of employees.

Individuals, not organizations, create excellence. With their unique skills they lead others and prepare corporate strategy for the future and pass on a vibrant culture.

Families possess culture. In a family, parents develop children by caring for, and educating them. Parents set standards for propriety of speech, appearance, behavior, and educational excellence. As the children grow older they recognize and appreciate the family legacy and pass on to their children what they have come to learn and esteem.

Today, though, sadly to say, there are exceptions. With both father and mother working, or a single parent, plus easy access to "fast food", parents do not have the time or take the time to sit down to dinner to discuss propriety of speech, appearance, behavior and educational excellence.

A corporation is a big family. Management should take time to develop its employees and train them to complement the strategies and goals of the company in its competitive growth. Goals and standards for excellence are set. Every member of the organization, from the CEO to the lowliest clerk and janitor share responsibility; and through proper communication, accepts accountability for the organization's products and services. (See Chapter on ETHICS)

Time begins to highlight and distinguish unique patterns with which companies manage and control. Time distinguishes a company from its competition. To perpetuate the culture, each manager and employee passes valued features of quality along to succeeding personnel. The manager and employee possess both culture and expert knowledge in some special direction.

I earlier mentioned IBM and American Airlines. Another fine company, Nordstrom, the department store chain, fits, in my opinion, the pattern of recognition and appreciation of culture and determination to carry it on.

I lectured, teaching "Entrepreneurship", at the Fashion Institute for Design and Merchandising in Los Angeles for three years. One of my graduating class projects was an analysis of the philosophy of management and customer service at Nordstrom. This was a "hands on" analysis—personal interviews by the students with top management and department heads and buyers. I allowed the students time off from class to visit management personnel so they could do the analysis correctly. I reimbursed them for expenses such as lunches, phone calls, parking, etc. My objective was to have the students discover first hand through practical experience what they had previously studied in class.

Several years before I started teaching, I studied Nordstrom, a public company run by the Nordstrom family with many department stores in the western United States. I prepared myself by studying *CREATING EXCELLENCE* by Craig Hickman and Michael Silva.

Nordstrom's "culture" won high marks over that of many other department store chains for three reasons: employees share an unrelenting commitment to superior CUSTOMER SERVICE, management strives to hire and KEEP good people, and employees themselves enforce a high standard of PERFORMANCE. Nordstrom's "culture" has been PASSED ALONG so consistently to so many succeeding generations that no one who works for the family can escape it. If a new employee doesn't suit Nordstrom's culture, fellow employees, not a manager, remind them to perform or resign. Nordstrom's standards and expectations bring non-performers to the company's notice quickly, and Nordstrom's management doesn't waste time getting rid of employees who won't, or can't, adapt.

I would imagine most companies honestly strive for good customer service and they try to hire and keep good people. But that's not good enough! Management must realize the only reason they are even needed or the reason for the corporate entity itself is to perform in the needs of the customer. The communication of determination to excel must permeate the entire organization and it is this philosophy, when passed to succeeding generations, that nurtures culture and legacy. How? They Listen! Listen! Listen! To the customer's needs!

Nordstrom is extremely economically successful. Their corporate stability and growth nurtures their success.

Customer satisfaction is the ultimate objective of every business. In truth, satisfaction is the only product or service. A home tool and appliance maker once thought it was in the business of selling one-and-a-half inch drill bits when it realized that its customers didn't really want one-and-a-half inch drill bits. All they wanted were one-and-a-half inch holes."

There is a proliferation of management changes today. It seems to be the thing to do; Japanese management style has become, in some disciplines, avant-garde. Also, there are a horrific number of management reorganizations and personnel shifts due to the junk bond/buy-out, amalgamation frenzy. One of the fastest and most sure ways to destroy culture and dim prospects for continued legacy is by revolutionary (rather than evolutionary) reorganization. Time Warner and AOL failed miserably at recognizing this.

I have been in the discipline of business management for thirty—eight years and have been teaching college for seven (or eight) of those years. I have had the opportunity to study, first hand, innumerable companies. Overnight replacement of a high percentage of management personnel, overnight structural reorganization and the hiring of managers from competing firms with a history of changing jobs for a few dollars more creates mass confusion, cultural shock, and bureaucracy.

In all appearance and substance the new CEO wants to make a name for himself as fast as possible. He is under pressure to perform. This "fast recognition" parallels short term planning and goals. This speed—this compression of time—negates the ability to recognize and appreciate the intellectual excellence of the company—its employees.

Hickman and Silva address these issues in *CREATING EXCELLENCE*. For example, they directed their attention to Bausch and Lomb. Bausch & Lomb's instruments' group had at one time consisted of some thirty different product lines that competed against such successful giants as Hewlett-Packard. This loosely bound group of businesses had languished for almost a decade before Jim Edwards, an IBM whiz kid, rode to the rescue. The first phase of Edward's rehabilitation program was a wrenching *overnight* reorganization, creating four new divisions—three oriented to manufacturing and one dedicated to sales and service support for *all* product lines. In addition to the new divisions, Edwards brought aboard the matrix form of organization he had learned at IBM. The reorganization seemed brilliant because it united all the fragmented product lines under the direction of one business unit, thus taking advantage of economies of scale and share resources.

But, the loose-knit family at Bausch & Lomb didn't fall into step like the disciplined professionals at IBM, and Edwards found himself valiantly struggling to bind the family together with brochures and videotapes selling the new organization and mode of operation. Despite all his efforts, confusion blossomed, and the group grew demoralized. Before long the company announced a quarterly earnings drop of 32 percent, soon followed by Edwards' resignation. One former executive summed up the experience by saying, "Edwards didn't take the measure of the company, the employees, before he started." Apparently Edwards forgot for the moment that cultural change does not grow out of overnight reorganizations, policy directives, or matrix-style management.

The first question I would ask is what made Jim Edwards a whiz kid at IBM? Was it finance? Manufacturing? Sales? Production? Personnel? Was he just part of the overall matrix-style of organization at IBM or did he instill it there also? I am sure of one thing. IBM didn't install a matrix form of management style in a "wrenching overnight reorganization." It evolved through evolutionary common sense, keeping in mind people, product, and performance. And just because matrix "was in" at IBM doesn't necessarily mean it would work at Bausch & Lomb.

Maybe the group of Bausch & Lomb's businesses languished due to lack of incisive focus on customer needs therefore polarizing research and development plans for advancing the state of corporate technical art. Maybe they were satisfied at being second best. Who knows? It is these kinds of questions that must be answered, in time, before making organization changes.

Jim Edwards should have taken into consideration the culture of the company. How did the company establish its name and perpetuate it for so long? You find that answer in people; not organization. People will tell you what's wrong, not an organization chart that you assign personnel to. And by people, I mean employees, subcontractors, vendors, and customers.

Jim Edwards should have directed the analysis of Bausch & Lomb in the language of, and needs of, the customer before making changes. Customers in concert with management will communicate to an organization what is needed to compete and grow; needs are fulfilled by employees! One does not draw an organization chart and detail it with positions and names. It is the *function* of—the *detailed responsibilities* and accountabilities of—employees that dictate organization—not the other way around. If Bausch & Lomb's different product lines served different customers, why did they have to be shoved into *one* style of management? It is impossible for different customers, with different needs, to be serviced by the same sales and service personnel. The personnel do not speak the same language when they served different product lines. It is impossible to develop the rapport needed for what? The recognition and appreciation or expert knowledge!

Jim Edwards didn't take the time to ferret out, recognize, and appreciate knowledge and excellence in people.

McDonnell Douglas, Long Beach, California Division (manufacturers of the MD-80, MD-11, and C-17), had an unprecedented top-to-bottom reorganization February 13, 1989. It was an overnight organization! Does that sound like our whiz kid!

Years have passed and strong negative feeling remain among some Douglas employees to the reorganization in primarily the way in which changes were implemented. The reorganization included a complete restructuring of management and implementation of new work procedures throughout Douglas, based on the corporation's Total Quality Management System (TQMS). This is a new aerospace buzzword! I need not go into details for this dissertation. TQMS can be very effective with proper planning; and coincidentally, with personnel thoroughly trained to understand the tenets of TQMS' responsibility and communication. It can't be done overnight.

The reorganization eliminated approximately two-thirds of the company's top management positions. The reorganization occurred during a particularly critical time for Douglas because the company faced a large backlog of commercial aircraft orders; management and manufacturing capabilities could ill-afford additional stress. Douglas officials' argument isn't that major changes were long overdue, as the company was faced with growing demand for its products, but the officials continued finding it hard to understand the manner in which the reorganization was implemented: the severity, suddenness, secrecy, its immediate company-wide scope, the screening techniques, and in general, its impersonal manner. Corporate management in St. Louis planned the reorganization in the basement of one of the executives who was later to become president of Douglas Aircraft. After the planning in the basement was done in secrecy, they called all the employees together in a hangar in Long Beach and made the announcement that everyone was fired and all new positions were open to anyone *thought* qualified. What happened to expert knowledge? What's this "anyone who thought" sophistry?

One of the greatest weaknesses of the reorganization is the way the company treated people. One of my friends said some of the best managers left the company. "They lost some of the 'right stuff' and they didn't have to."

Today managers I personally know continue to criticize the screening process used to select the new slate of managers through role-playing sessions, peer review, and evaluation by subordinates. One person called the sessions, in which a small group of managers, evaluated by an observer, was given a problem to solve "amateurish" and "superficial."

"It was devastating to morale," my manager friend said. Experience and track record were not given enough weight. People who proved themselves over many years were knocked out by a two-hour evaluation run by a bunch of college kids.

The selection process has placed a large number of managers in new jobs across the company. As one manager said, "They are smart people, but they are in jobs they don't know how to do." Whitehead, in *AIMS of EDUCATION*, said " . . . Men who possess both culture and expert knowledge in some special direction . . . . give them the ground to start." Evidently management in St. Louis didn't read or know their Lessons from History. Officials inside and outside the company said they would have preferred to see the reorganization occur in an evolutionary, rather than a revolutionary manner, concentrating initially in specific areas that needed the attention most; such as the established MD-80 production program.

The corporate office in St. Louis should have worked with Douglas personnel in making the changes, rather than impelling a plan on the company.

Other aerospace companies are evaluating and beginning to implement TQMS' concepts within their organizations, but they often tend to be evolutionary in nature. Industry officials add that implementing a sudden, company-wide reorganization that cut management positions by one-half is not a prerequisite of the Total Quality Management concept.

When Douglas made the numerous re-organizational changes in personnel, I, as a manufacturer's representative and subcontractor representing four different companies at Douglas, vehemently opposed the plan. I conveyed to management personnel and my marketing and sales colleagues my belief that Douglas was destroying the basic culture of the company and they would find it extraordinarily difficult to regain their status in the aerospace industry whether it was commercial or military and that the company would unquestionably experience significant financial loss.

I couldn't talk without trying to do something about it. So I wrote the president of Douglas a letter; there were lessons to be learned from history, e.g. Jim Edwards at Bausch & Lomb. I said, "Organization changes should not be made without precise knowledge of an employee's history of performance; tasks should not be assigned without subjective and objective planning." I also wondered how could one person, followed by a group of persons, unite for the promotion of a common aim with no common cornerstone from which to start? I wanted the president to think evolution. I thought the place to start would be with the MD-80. I wanted senior management to think accountability. I wanted them to think eye-to-eye contact; contact with the customer and supplier. I wanted them to think incentives. Excerpts from the letter to the president are as follows:

"—and my sense of urgency now directs me to accept the responsibility and contact you myself. I have been calling on Douglas for over 20 years representing a number of clients. I even had an office at Douglas for four years. I was the Yugoslavian Representative for their offset program.

—indeed, I am well aware of the TQMS reorganization through personal and personnel association and articles in *AVIATION WEEK, AEROSPACE DAILY, QUALITY TIMES* and the office of the Douglas AFPR. Sir, it would be ill advised of me to find fault without offering a suggestion on how to strengthen a vital part of your organization. Therefore, I would like to suggest, starting only with the MD-80 Series and MD-11, the formation of a separate profit center entitled the McDonnell Douglas Purchasing Corporation. This separate profit center would be staffed only by incentive oriented professional purchasing and follow up personnel. The Purchasing Corporation would offer the following:

> All salaried personnel
> A profit sharing plan
> Number of hours worked each day concomitant to tasks to be accomplished
> Concentration on exchange of value versus low price
> Increased productivity
> Reduced overhead

Open lines of communication

Strengthening of the subcontractor base

Improved commonality of requirements

Flexible management in that experts would pulse in and out as needed

Absolute accountability of engineering changes

Elucidation of the basic tenets of leadership, responsibility and accountability

A dynamic new "make or buy" decision plan whereby the profit—oriented corporation would take advantage of hundreds of years of subcontractor experienced management working in collective tune with the new corporation's purchasing personnel."

The President was kind enough to answer my letter. I respect that; he was too busy to meet with me.

April 21, 1990—"McDonnell Says It Lost $84 million on Douglas Programs," by Ralph Vartabedian (Times Staff Writer)

"McDonnell Douglas disclosed Friday that major production problems continue to dog its Douglas Aircraft unit in Long Beach where transport aircraft programs lost $84 million on sales of $1.1 billion in the first quarter."

"The Company is attempting to recover from a massive reorganization that was intended to address the Douglas operation's longstanding losses over the past two decades, but employees in recent interviews said severe morale problems and lack of training are evident at the factory."

There are indications, through buyers I am working with, that management is growing increasingly concerned that the cultural—revolution isn't working out as planned.

In reference to the letter sent to the President, I suggested the separate commercial aircraft procurement profit center as a starting point for cost control and a complement to TQMS.

In my opinion the TQMS ill-advised revolution at Douglas eliminated many experienced managers in specific disciplines who knew how to "walk the floor." 'A Walk the Floor' management style allows for constant CONCEPTIONS for better work methods, personnel rapport, cost savings participation, innate increase in quality, and personnel with exacting PERCEPTION of the reasoning behind communication directives. It is a communication of RESPONSIBILITY with concomitant acceptance of ACCOUNTABILITY from the ground up. It is pure TQMS by evolution.

In lieu of total program control, it was suggested, along with "walk the floor" management style, a change in philosophy to common commodity and/or work center control that offers continued program authority with cost advantages of increased efficiency in production and procurement.

EXAMPLES:

Project (program) office (profit center) control of concept, design, engineering, sales and business management

Procurement (profit center) control supporting all commercial aircraft programs

Manufacturing/Production (profit center) control; i.e., fabrication and assembly

In essence, the program office is the customer authorizing the procurement and production at an agreed upon price based on the scope of work defined.

I think the Douglas reorganization broke the back of the employees. It has broken the back of the MD-11 and the MD-12. It had also, for a long period of time, tentatively broke the back of the C-17.

Let me digress for a moment from Douglas and talk about Texas Instruments. I have been calling on two of their divisions in Texas for one year as of this writing. I was impressed that I always had a place to park in clearly marked area of vendor parking. I was impressed with the fact that every phone was answered immediately with courtesy and with knowledgeable people. The receptionist was convivial; she made me, a subcontractor, feel at home! The purchasing and engineering personnel made appointments and were punctual. There was always a place to sit either in the lobby or in their offices for confidential discussions. There were private telephones available to make calls both inside and outside the plant, and each manager and buyer assisted in making sure I met the next buyer or engineer according to my appointment schedule. I was overwhelmed with their graciousness, technical expertise, and willingness to understand that, although I was an "outsider," I represented part of the team. I sensed something else: all engineering management and purchasing personnel had an air of confidence, mental strength, and cultural stability in their job and the company's position in the industry.

Douglas Aircraft Company is the antithesis of Texas Instruments. They don't pay attention to the little things. As a subcontractor on two current programs, I had, during one year, worked with 10 different buyers and eight engineers on the C-17 program and fourteen different buyers and nine engineers on the MD-80. Two buyers recently moved to a new building but had no phones on their desk, and a secretary refused to deliver messages saying she "was not in the messenger business." Phones go un-answered, Douglas personnel park in supplier slots, and receptionists could care less about the exchanged communication between sales personnel and buyer. In the purchasing lobby several years ago, when I wanted to send a buyer a very important piece of information, a receptionist told me that there were no interdepartmental envelopes and that I would have to find my own method of transmission.

I know many dedicated, knowledgeable individuals at Douglas. This dissertation has no reflection on them. In fact, we discuss it; and, as individuals, we "grin and bear it." But collectively, it has seriously damaged the foundation of the company.

We talked about Dewey earlier. In his RECONSTRUCTION *in* PHILOSOPHY, Dewey said, "A flame is not merely something which warms or burns, but is a symbol of the enduring life of the household, of the abiding source of cheer, nourishment and shelter to which a man returns; this marks the difference between bestiality and humanity, between culture and merely physical nature; because man remembers, preserving and recording his experiences."

Remember earlier I said individuals, not organizations, create excellence. If there is no abiding cheer—no nourishment—no shelter to return to—there will be no excellence.

McDonnell Douglas, teamed with General Dynamics, lost the A-12 Navy Attack Aircraft. It was canceled by the Secretary of Defense for massive cost overruns and poor management!

McDonnell Douglas, teamed with Northrop, lost the competition to Lockheed, General Dynamics, and Boeing for the Advanced Tactical Fighter for the U.S. Air Force.

McDonnell Douglas, teamed with Bell Helicopter, lost the competition to Sikorsky and Boeing for the Light Helicopter Program for the Army. Well why go on, there is no McDonnell Douglas anymore!!

Someone—somewhere—maybe some one thing—is "remembering, preserving, and recording his experiences"—doesn't want to return. The abiding source of cheer, nourishment and shelter has been snuffed out. A fighter is designed to obtain air superiority, but it will be useless without a trained pilot. It's the team that gains superiority.

The fighter is a cultural development in the sense that there has been stability in personnel, growth in management, and promotions based on experience and contribution. The evolution of the F4F, F5F, F6F, F7F, F8F, F9F to the renowned F-14 at Grumman Aircraft Corporation came through the amalgamation of engineering disciplines handed down over a period of years; the continuation of esthetic and intellectual excellence.

The fighter pilots that "teamed" with these famous Grumman planes won the Pacific War. The pilots weren't bomber pilots one day, transport co-pilots the next and fighter pilots the next. That kind of personnel juggling would be insane—particularly in a war. The USAF tried other, untrained at the time, cargo and bomber pilots in Vietnam. It was a disaster in that, after a transition course to the new (to the pilots) F-4 and F-105, they were assigned to combat wings in Vietnam. These pilots could not contribute to the "abiding source of cheer, nourishment, and shelter." They had no team mentality.

Wasn't Douglas in a war—a non-lethal war—to dominate—aircraft sales? Its earlier described reorganization caused management to lose control. New managers, with no experience, with new, ill defined responsibilities, had to concern THEMSELVES with what THEY had to do to survive. They had no understanding where the decision-making authority resided and how to generally comply with the orders of that authority. No organization can function unless that is totally understood. There must be a headman and he must be obeyed. There must be an experienced flight leader—in war and in business.

In the confusion at Douglas there was no window of opportunity to even think of culture; there were no collective experiences to pass on. There was no "expert knowledge to give anyone the ground to start from . . ."

In the TIME/LIFE book, *MAN and the ORGANIZATION*, a case of history is made in the year 1919, when General Motors was suffering from the inflation that followed World War I, a threatening depression, and worst of all, for want of an effective command structure, corporate confusion.

Alfred Sloan, an experienced 43year old president of one subsidiary drafted an "organization study" proposing "a principle of coordination without losing the advantages of decentralization." I don't know if Sloan ever heard of "TQMS" but he did know that attacking classic problems of an organization vary from culture to culture and he did not want to destroy the intrinsic culture prevalent throughout all of General Motors. Douglas' overnight reorganization, totally ignoring what history had to offer, destroyed the company's intrinsic culture; management judgment was over zealous by four inappropriate letters—TQMS. Cultural strength and management is an evolutionary development, not an overnight, revolutionary, unstable upheaval.

Cultural demise, as I mentioned at the beginning of the chapter, can happen in ways other than revolutionary reorganization. Remember, we mentioned culture came to mean general state of intellectual, material, and moral development.

Northrop Corporation had a proud cultural heritage to uphold. The company is known for the development of the first night fighter, the first all weather jet fighter, and the flying wing. In addition, Northrop developed and mass-produced the U.S. Air Force's first supersonic jet trainer.

But management has lost sight of their moral development as they have been accused by the government of falsifying test results on the production of parts for a marine aircraft and guidance systems for a missile.

Northrop was part of the team that lost the Advanced Tactical Fighter. Northrop's Ventura Division recently had their "Tacit Rainbow" air-breathing missile canceled due to poor quality control and management.

I see no foundation for cultural growth in these stories. I see no stability. I see total lack of control. Employees read the newspapers. How can a company develop culture out of chaos?

To me culture is based on historical performance and communication— "transmitted from generation to generation—." The foundations of mathematics were so well laid by the Greeks that our children learn their geometry from a book written for the schools of Alexandria two thousand years ago. Modern astronomy is the natural continuation and development of the work of Hipparchus and of Ptolemy; modern physics of that of Democritus and of Archimedes; it was long before modern biological science outgrew the knowledge bequeathed to us by Aristotle, by Theophrastus, and by Galen.

If the foundations of these great sciences contributed so immensely to the mental growth and culture of man, why would present day management allow the deterioration of employee mental growth and culture?

Because they don't understand! They think small! They move in revolutionary terms! For culture certainly means something quite different from learning or technical skill. It implies the possession of an ideal, and the habit of critically estimating the value of things by comparison with a theoretic standard. It takes time evaluate and compare and it's impossible to find the right standard if one is in too much of a hurry.

Perfect culture should apply a complete theory of life, based upon a clear knowledge alike of its possibilities and of its limitations.

A note: The former Vice President of Materiel at McDonnell Douglas (at the time of my letter to the President) was of great assistance to me in my writing of such letter.

TIME PATIENCE &
THE LESSONS OF HISTORY

"When you can't change the direction of the
wind—adjust your sails."

Dad

"Time," wrote the famous American philosopher-idler Henry David Thoreau, "is but the stream I go fishing in." Each of us—with the help of parents, grandparents, friends, teachers, historians, and others—go fishing in that stream. And we usually come up with what we knew, or strongly suspected, was already there. One of the purposes of any book of history is to make it possible for us to go fishing and come up with some surprises.[1]

I went fishing for 1927, the year I was born. That's the year Babe Ruth hit 60 home runs; and Lindberg flew the Atlantic. What a surprise to learn, also, what history gave us in 1927. It was the year when Trotsky was expelled from the Communist Party, when "*SHOW BOAT*" opened in New York, Sigmund Freud published *THE FUTURE OF AN ILLUSIUON,* and Thornton Wilder, *THE BRIDGE of SAN LUIS REY.* Also, Pavlov did his work on conditioned reflexes, Al Jolson starred in the epoch-making 'talkie' *THE JAZZ SINGER*, the German economic system collapsed, and the Harlem Globetrotters basketball team was organized.[2]

The word "history," for me, could not be easily defined. According to *FUNK & WAGNALL's*, history is a "systematic record of past events." The definition did not give me enough substance in trying to relate philosophy and the record of events in which man has taken part.

In continuing my studies though, I learned that *PHILOSOPHICAL* history considers causes and events—and resulting consequences. Those words gave me

---

[1]   Boorstin, D.J., *HIDDEN HISTORY*, Vintage Books, New York, 1989, pg. 56
[2]   IBID

logical support in developing my thought process about time and what could be learned from history and philosophy. It is an empathetic process for me. I am infused with the subjects. I seem to be more aware of, and sensitive to, what is being offered. I vicariously participate in the feelings, thoughts and experience of others from the past; a magnificent way to learn. I firmly believe philosophy gives us more than records, or something in writing for the purpose of preserving memory or facts.

I believe philosophers left man an intellectual bridge allowing application of the power of perception and thought to the lessons of history. The search for the "bridge" doesn't come easy. Man is enlightened about his past through history; his materialistic past through the scientific study of ancient cities, relics, artifacts, etc. Man's spiritual enlightenment comes through studies of leaders such as Mohammed, Buddha, and Christ and contemporary analysis of past culture such as the DEAD SEA SCROOLS. Not everyone gains equally in knowledge or mastery of subject but history helps establish a base from which to start. A business man, or woman, can be an "archaeologist" by searching for and studying philosophical history, and in so doing, develop insight and awareness as a foundation for attempting to understand and solve personal and business problems.

The Greek word philosophy translates to "the pursuit of wisdom" or better yet, for me, "a search for a general understanding of values and reality by chiefly speculative rather than observational means." and Sophia translates to wisdom. Philosophy however, has a much wider range of application (see the Greek philosopher Pythagoras below) than the modern English translation "pursuit of *wisdom*."

Wisdom in its broadest and commonest sense denotes sound and **anxiety free** judgment in the conduct of everyday life. This may or may not be accompanied by intellectual acuity and/or a broad range of knowledge. It involves a mental grasp of things or—insight. Wisdom does not worry so much about fact but the means and ends of a practical, common sense life.

There is always room for insight whenever mental agility can be exercised; in mechanical arts, in business, and in practical affairs. Pythagoras (Sixth Century B.C.), a curious combination of mathematician and religious seer, seems to have found in philosophy the guide to a practical life. Pythagoras saw *insight* as knowledge based on contemplation. In an athlete he recognized it as trained skills; in a businessman it seemed to be practical shrewdness combined with a perception of fact—or cognizance.[3]

In studying the lives of philosophers insight became a catalyst to me. In business I found that in trying to understand the wider range of application of wisdom I slowed down and started to think through problems. I began to realize the more 'time' I took to combine the theoretical and practical analysis of a problem, more avenues to lucidity and understanding opened. Theory took me on a circuitous, single-minded route. Practicality took me to people. As an example, you can study

---

[3]   Paraphrased from *Great Treasury of Western Thought*

and learn from texts numerous theoretical applications of a marketing and sales plan, but it will never be practical until a through, incisive, customer oriented marketing analysis serves as a conduit to write the plan in the language of, and needs of, the customers it is destined to serve.

One does not need the cost and time of writing a plan if you walk into a house of ill repute. The dollar bill (of a specific denomination) does all the talking—how much for how long. But even houses of ill repute have potential for growth. It all depends on word of mouth, market appeal, performance, quality, true value, and ultimate satisfaction. It is the ladies of the house that are taught to communicate pleasure and fulfillment. It is called "house of ill repute" only because of the nature of the business.

If a salesperson writes a clear-cut, penetrating and perceptive sales plan and takes the time necessary to know his or her potential customer (remember the plan is written in "language and needs" the potential for growth presents itself after the first sale. The only difference between your potential and what is stated above is the 'language' of the dollar bill offers a quicker, favorable development.

I studied *MEDITATIONS* by Marcus Aurelius and found a friend. He injected in me a solution for a tranquil heart and a life more free from agitation and disturbance. *Aurelius* told me not to worry about things—there is nothing happening today that hasn't happened thousands of times in the past. "How ridiculous and what a stranger he is who is surprised at anything that happens in life. All things from eternity are of like forms and come around in a circle, and that it makes no difference whether a man shall see the same things during a hundred years or two hundred, or an infinite time."

A trustworthy prescription for intellectual agitation!!!

In Pythagoras, I nurtured another friend. When confronted with a matter of uncertainty, Aurelius told me to give Pythagoras a call and invite him to dinner to discuss how he sees insight as affecting intellectual growth. At the same time ask him to relate time and its effect on the transfer from the theoretical to the practical.

Let me digress. Too many managers apply the theory—"if it works for them—it will work for us." Nothing could be further from the truth. A manager with that thought doesn't respect time—time to learn—time to train—time to understand. As an example, in retail sales (Super K-Mart, Nordstrom, Wal-Mart, Costco) and other successful marketing management and sales/merchandizing programs revolve around the interrelationship of people—customer sales personnel, quality of goods, value, buyer, manager. The highly professional and continuously highly trained sales person and manager and buyer remain basically the same. It is the customer that changes—almost daily. You can have all the pretty stores in America (K-Mart is going through a revolution of prettiness as I write this) or you can have a revolution in management and stockholder meetings as was Sears in the immediate past. And all the stores can have low prices, and no waiting in checkout lines; but if you can't presage the needs of the customer, all the prettiness and low prices mean nothing.

Wal-Mart's growth is purely evolutionary based around their phenomenal relationship between store personnel and customer. It's the customer that dictates in incisive buying, management planning and sales training. Wal-Mart is always out in front while the others play catch-up.

There is a lesson to be learned here. I don't see Wal-Mart as an entity that buys and sells. They fulfill. I see them as *excelling* in merchandizing (right product, right time, right customer, right price) with a powerful grip on the *logical* association between market research, developing marketing and business plans. Wal-Mart is in the continuous process of developing new product and services, coordination of manufacturing and quality, delivery of product on time to match planning, and marketing, and effective advertising and selling through their store personnel— fulfilling the customers' needs and desires.

I quoted Boorstin in the first paragraph on page one. In another chapter entitled, The Intimacy of *GIBBON's DECLINE & FALL OF THE ROMAN EMPIRE*, Boorstin says, "He (Gibbon) spoke to me from and for a period of history. But in the years since Gibbon first spoke to me, he has come to say something more. He has become a more *personal* historian and hence more intimate, both in what he said and in what I hear.[4]

Now you understand why I invited Pythagoras to dinner. Think of the thrill of inviting Socrates and Plato also, to visit and having a discussion on something that broadens your intellect. Plato would probably say, "Let's give Aristotle a call." You can't imagine how willing they are to contribute. What a learned person you will be!!!

It will take time and it won't be easy, but nothing worthwhile is.

"It is the critical moment that shows the man. So when the crisis is upon you, remember that God, like a trainer of wrestlers, has matched you with a rough and stalwart antagonist. 'To what end?' you ask. That you may prove the victor at the Great Games. Yet without toil and sweat this may not be!"[5]

The Golden Sayings of Epictetus

Most problems affecting personal relationships and business performance are usually driven by profound differences in personality and philosophy. Ralph Waldo Emerson left a thought that can help the way you seek reason and truth in conducting the affairs of everyday life. I have quoted Emerson in the past and I'll probably do it again. "Do you know," asks Emerson, "the secret of a true scholar? In every man there is something wherein I may learn of him; and in that I am his pupil."[6]

---

4   IBID; page 54

5   The Golden Sayings of Epictetus, *The Harvard Classics* edited by Charles Eliot, LL.D., Grolier Enterprises Corp., Danbury, Conn., p. 173

6   *The World's Great Thinkers*, edited by Saxe Commins & Robert Linscott, Random House, New York

Marcus Aurelius said, "Both nature and human nature are determined by casual law, and the wrongs and insults that other men inflict on us are, therefore, as inevitable as the tides. The wise man will understand this inevitability and not waste his substance in futile indignation or fear. He will conform himself to nature's laws, recognize that passion is a symptom of ignorance, free himself from emotional attachments and resentments, and live as far as he can the life of a 'passionless sage'."[7]

Pythagoras is also telling us that insight, in a successful businessperson, is one who combines the thoughts of Aurelius and the practicality of Emerson. The businessperson profits by understanding surrounding circumstance. Sagaciousness realizes that a problem is a question for discussion and settlement—or a matter of uncertainty requiring further light to discover the truth. Taking action requires the input of people. There is no time to find fault or verbally blame.

Finding the problem, planning a solution and carrying out the plan takes what? TIME!

How did the study of philosophy help me?? Certainly many learned philosophers, speaking through Socrates, helped me during my flight test career. But those days are gone—in everyday thought, but not in everyday practically. In my profession as a marketing consultant I discovered that I must try to understand the wider range of application of wisdom and take a hard look at things (people and circumstances and reality) as they really are. I had to be honest with myself. I wasn't a panacea and I didn't have all the answers. Collective experiences helped, but each marketing problem creates its own perplexing nuance; and it would be ill advised to rush in and try to find a short-time solution to show management how accomplished I thought I was.

The reason companies engaged my marketing analysis and sales planning services had, naturally, marketing and sales problems. Problems such as lack, or loss, of market share without understanding 'why'; the deprivation of too many competitive bids, failed product line, poor training, sales inefficiency (wasting time due to lack of fully understanding the customers' needs,) inability to identify market niche and customer. Also, and most important, a lack of a detailed and up to date marketing plan always accompanied by the concomitant business plan.

I don't call on buyers. I call on a man or woman to form a relationship that will, in time, make his or her decision to purchase a unit(s) from me (my company) that will add to the company's technical and economic competitive position. If a salesperson is trying to sell everything "on the block" he or she doesn't have the time to develop a professional business and social rapport. And by social I don't mean dinners, and drinks, and sports' tickets, theater tickets, etc. I mean knowing where the buyer went to school, his time with the company, his wife's name, all the kids, attending Little League games, hot dogs for the whole team after a win, etc. It's fun, it's honest, and it offers the opportunity to meet wonderful people.

---

[7]   *The Meditations of Marcus Aurelius*, translated by George Long, International Collectors Library, Garden City, N.Y.

In every case there is a goal; but it is always a matter of time to think through a plan. There is always the determination of how to *use* time effectively. And, most important, it was imperative for the client to understand the number of man-hours (time) it would take me to lay the foundation for making his or her business more successful in the marketplace. I can't tell you how many times I have heard, "Let's hurry, my ass is in a jam here. We 'gotta' get the job done."

Since we are talking about time, let's take little more of it try understand what we are talking about.

When we see the most famous equation of the 20th century, $E=Mc^2$, the relationship between energy and mass, we immediately think of Einstein.

It was around 1871 that, most scientists, Maxwell, Faraday, Ampere, agreed that light was a form of electric and magnetic interaction, but nobody could understand how it got from place to place. Everyone believed that some sort of medium (aether) was necessary to support the transmission of electric and magnetic forces until Einstein did away with it all. Einstein explored the aether puzzle with his friends for TEN YEARS, first at the ETH (Eidgenossiche Technische Hochschule) in Zurich from 1895-1900, and then at the Swiss patent office in Bern from 1901 to 1905. It was at this time when Einstein proposed relativity.[8]

Einstein didn't do it alone. He worked with others like Maurice Solovile, Conrad Habicht, along with Mileva Maric, Marcel Grossman and Mike Besso. Einstein studied Michelson, Morley, Mach and Galileo. And Einstein benefited from:

Vieta (1580)	Algebraic Notation
Stevinus (1585)	Decimals
Napier (1614)	Logarithms
Gunther (1620)	Slide Rule
Descartes (1637)	Analytic Geometry
Pascal (1642)	Adding Machine
Newton (1665)	Calculus
Leibniz (1684)	Calculus
Loventz (1800)`	System of Equations

I am working with friends like Aurelius, Emerson and Pythagoras. I am studying Drucker and Von Clausewitz, and Swift and Thomas Peters. I am benefiting from *GREAT TREASURY OF WESTERN THOUGHT* and the four volume *THE ENCYCLOPEDIA OF PHILOSOPY*.

The point I am trying to make is that anything worthwhile takes dedication and time. Einstein took ten years to think problems through. He was smart enough to call on other professionals for help. You, also, can research other's thoughts and

---

[8]   Joseph Schwartz & Michael McGuinness, *Einstein For Beginners*, Pantheon Books, New York, 1979, p.65

experiences to learn from the Lessons of History. Einstein did, Truman, a great student of history, did, and Hannibal, dead two thousand years, set an example at Cannae (216 BC) for Schlieffen in WWI. Cannae, an ancient town in Southern Italy, was the site of Hannibal's decisive defeat of the Romans. The encircling technique he perfected, regarded as a masterpiece of tactics, won him the battle and 10,000 prisoners. In William Hillman's book, *HARRY S. TRUMAN, IN HIS OWN WORDS*, (published by Bonanza Books, N.Y. 1984) Truman said, "There is nothing new in the world except the history you do not know."

Like the four-minute mile, flying faster than sound was long thought to be beyond human achievement. The problem lay not in attaining sonic speed, around 760 miles per hour at sea level, considerably less in the cold air of high altitudes, but in overcoming the unexpected things that happen to planes as they approached that speed. The trusted laws of aerodynamics seemed suddenly to go haywire; planes experienced loss of control, severe shaking or buffeting and a tendency to nose over as if in a stall. The phrase "Sound Barrier" was coined to describe the problem, as though there were some invisible wall in the sky. Finding a way through that wall took aircraft designers deep into studies of the physics of sound and into unexplored aerodynamic realms.[9]

Then one day in 1947, almost 40 years after the Wright Brothers, man broke the "Sound Barrier." Uncountable dollars were spent, many test pilot lives lost, thousands of designs tested, millions of man-hours expended. But so spectacularly have they succeeded that now the sound barrier is a mere threshold to an age beyond.

In understanding a span of 40 years, isn't it worthwhile for management to study product evolution, competition and customer? Isn't it actually more rewarding to understand the benefits from failure—sins of commission—and strengthen resolve as a result? Isn't it worthwhile to take the time to plan sales, or merchandising, or advertising campaigns in the same vein? Isn't winning the first purchase order and planning fundamental corporate growth based on the language of and needs of the customer, a mere threshold to an age beyond? Why is management always in a hurry—always wanting to change things? Short term goals is short term thinking?

In studying the wealth of knowledge philosophers left us, I learned to exercise my curiosity by asking myself, and others, "How come?", "What if?", "What about?" and "Do you think if we did this—?" You honestly must understand and be prepared to take the good with the bad. There is no good without bad. Just as there is no up without down or left without right.

Will Durant gave me an enormous lift in his book, *THE STORY OF PHILOSOPHY*.[10] Durant's introduction, "On the uses of Philosophy," speaks of life having meaning; "But so much of our lives is meaningless, a self-canceling vacillation

---

9   H. Guyford Stever, James J. Haggerty and the Editors of Time-Life Books, *FLIGHT*, Time-Life Books, New York, 1965, p. 176

10   Will Durant, *The Story of Philosophy*, Simon & Schuster, New York, New York, 1927, p. 1

and futility; we strive with the chaos about us and within; but we would believe all the while that there is something vital and significant in us, could we but decipher our souls. We want to seize the value and perspective of passing things . . . We want to know that the little things are little, and the big things big, before it is too late."

I find it difficult striving for continued personal satisfaction, but I understand what Durant is trying to tell me; that life at one's perceived best, is not an easy road, and one must try to make it better. Also, it is good to stop and examine the value of things and put them in proper view.

"The twentieth century has produced a world of conflicting visions, intense emotions, and unpredictable events, and the opportunities for grasping the substance of life have faded as the pace of activity has increased. Electronic media shuffle us through a myriad of experiences which would have baffled earlier generations and seem to produce in us a strange isolation from the reality of human history. Our heroes fade into mere personality, are consumed and forgotten, and we avidly seek more avenues to express our humanity. Reflection is the most difficult of all our activities because we are no longer able to establish relative priorities from the multitude of sensations that engulf us. Times such as these seem to illuminate the classic expressions of eternal truths and great wisdom comes to stand out in the crowd of ordinary maxims."[11]

Will Durant and Vine Deloria (see appendix) offer a bridge to decipher—to think in my own terms to determine how capable I will be in handling any crisis. I am like Mitya in *THE BROTHERS KARAMAZOV,* "One of those who don't want millions, but an answer to their questions."

All questions can't be answered, at least immediately. In the meantime, it is best to retreat into your self. "You want to be whole, to coordinate your energy by criticizing and harmonizing your desires; for 'coordinated energy' is the last word in politics—and ethics."[12]

Let's take another look at what I am saying. What I have learned!

When I look at myself, my life, my actions, my personal and business habits, the main ingredient is looking at my relationships with people. I look at all levels; from janitors to corporate executives, restaurant owners to busboys, private club top management to gardeners. I have come to learn that all men and women, regardless of economic position, race, education, relate to me on *my* terms. My terms are the terms I learned from Ralph Waldo Emerson, (1803-1882). He spoke in terms without decoration or qualification when he said, "In every man there is something I may learn of him, and in that I am his pupil." Emerson turned my life around. I don't have a restricting or modifying element for one category of individual vs another. The nexus of this thought process is that I have no room for bias that would

---

[11]   John Niehardt, *Black Elk Speajs*, Introduction by Vine Deloria, Jr., University of Nebraska Press, Lincoln, NE, 1972, p. xi

[12]   IBID Durant

allow wasted energy; and it opens my avenue for facing the truth and approaching everything with better judgement and wisdom. And what is wisdom? Wisdom is accumulated philosophic learning. It gives man the ability to discern inner qualities and relationships.

Maybe you, as many do, see things differently than I! That's OK, but I am basing my thoughts and actions on what I have learned from philosophy and the lessons of history. No matter the circumstances man must "stand tall" and face truth and reality. Plutarch, c.46-c.120, a Greek who wrote of the fall of Athens said, "As we would wish that a painter who is to draw a beautiful face, in which there is yet some imperfection, should neither wholly leave out, nor yet too pointedly express what is defective, because this would deform it, and that would spoil the resemblance; so since it is hard, or indeed perhaps impossible, to show the life of a man wholly free from blemish, in all that is excellent we must follow truth exactly, and give it fully."

If I call on a buyer or retail entrepreneur and exchange information for the purpose of *planning* to obtain market niche, I am conducting marketing analysis. If I call on a retailer with the right product, at the right time, for the right customer, at the right price and right management of inventory, I am merchandizing. And if my merchandizing effort is complemented by a targeted advertising campaign, I am classed as a brilliant marketing manager full of common sense. And if my vice-president of Marketing and Sales structures an organization based, not on the expectations of management gurus, but on fulfilling the needs of the customer—that's common sense.

The proliferation of "nothing down" and "how-to" books has introduced management, real estate, weight reduction, foreign currency, exercise, tennis, golf and love gurus to a gullible public of their something for nothing philosophy. What the authors promulgate is an effortless road to success. Millions of readers are looking for easy answers to complex questions and challenges.

Publishers have recently produced books that have created a minor revolution in contemporary management. They have succeeded (most are best sellers) in bringing to their readers the connection between contemporary management philosophies and our speed of sound pursuit for excellence.

In my opinion the authors failed to take the **time** to look within and recognize management includes concepts of customers, ambiguity, common sense, leadership, innovation, perception, intense planning, market analysis, etc., etc. These, notwithstanding their current popularity, are concepts that have been considered and analyzed ever since the evolution of who would manage and who would labor. Great thinkers have shared their ideas about these influences. To ignore these "starting points" would be tantamount to building a house without an architect. My architects are Aristotle, Augustine, Cicero, Voltaire, Descartes, Machiavelli, Santayana, et.

Don't get me wrong; I didn't quote Plato or Kant when meeting with people trained in engineering or business. Nor did I try to inject lofty speculations on the meaning of life in boardrooms or at power lunches. That would have been pretentious and counter-productive. I did, nevertheless, appreciate what and why the masters were saying and how to analyze as they analyzed and, most importantly, how wonderfully useful they were. In the "nothing down" and "how-to" books I couldn't find a book that provided a guide to the world's greatest minds coupled to the needs and aspiration of people doing and leading the world's work.

I have tried to address this need in a practical way—with examples of real life problems drawn from a variety of situations, and by using applicable quotations, experiences, and clarifications from philosophical writers.

I am a businessman who respects philosophy and scholarship. I don't believe there is any system, theory or inspirational message that provides an unwavering final solution to problems of mind and matter. Most of this material has been gleaned from a combination of my experiences and the experiences of others; whether or not those experiences occurred centuries ago—or weeks ago.

What I hope to do is to help people become the architects of their own working lives, and to live their lives more fully.

"To be a philosopher," said Thoreau, "is not merely to have subtle thoughts, nor even to found a school, but to so love wisdom as to live according to its dictates; a life of simplicity, independence, magnanimity and trust." We may be sure that if we can but find wisdom, all things else will be added unto us. "Seek ye first the good things of the mind," Bacon admonishes us, "and the rest will either be supplied or its loss will not be felt.[13]

Truth will not make us rich, but it will make us free.

---

[13]   *On the Story of Philosophy,* Durant

HOW MUCH LONGER WILL YOU GO ON

LETTING YOUR ENERGY SLEEP?

HOW MUCH LONGER ARE YOU GOING

TO STAY OBLIVIOUS OF YOURSELF?

DO NOT LOSE TIME IN CONFLICT

LOSE NO TIME IN DOUBT—

TIME CAN NEVER BE RECOVERD

AND IF YOU MISS AN OPPORTUNITY

IT MAY TAKE MANY LIVES

BEFORE ANOTHER COMES YOUR WAY

AGAIN!!!

BHAGWAN SHREE RAJNEESH

A CUP OF TEA

MARKETING ANALYSIS

In response to a youth's observation that "I am wise, for I have conversed with many wise men," Epictetus replied, "I, too, have conversed with many rich men, yet I am not rich." My studies of Epictetus, A.D. 60-138, left me with one resounding lesson; the importance of cultivating complete independence of external circumstances, the realization that man must find happiness within himself, and the *duty* of reverencing the voice of Reason in the soul. Believe me! It works.

I too has conversed with many marketing wise men either directly or empathetically through textbooks, yet I am not rich in knowledge as to, say, designing a perfect formula or plan for a market analysis. I think it was Cicero who expressed the thought that doubtless some philosophers have had all sorts of wisdom except common sense; so I am sometimes very philosophical about my responsibility to find out what is going on in the marketplace. Of course common sense entails the ability to make sensible decisions; it takes gumption, judgement, and wisdom. And what is wisdom? It is a deep, thorough, and mature understanding of that which will become to be known, or discovered, or perceived. It is knowledge about! And how do we gain knowledge about a territory, or knowledge about how to sell in the language and needs of a customer? Work! Hard work!

I do, however, know that my ken is marketing analysis. Large companies specialize in taking polls or surveys; I brainstorm with people, often starting out with only an idea of what I want to talk about and learn. But pretty soon, I'm asking very direct and pertinent questions in the language of the particular discipline I am in.

Consumer surveys are usually designed to determine whom the users of products are, with the sex, age, education, or economic status of a tremendous number of individuals taken in consideration. That action is called a survey. A survey does not provide the kind of information that allows a company or salesperson to sell in the language of the customer. I feel analysis is information obtained from exchanging one-on-one thoughts that provide part of a planning key.

An analysis allows flexibility—flexibility in communication by asking a lot of questions that either come to mind or are based on previous exchanges with communicants. An analysis also allows flexibility in observing, thinking through, and storing mental recommendations that later could become fact or fiction as the analysis proceeds.

THE MARKET ANALYSIS
THE MARKET RESEARCH

The essence of what we mean by "Marketing Research" is contained in Richard Crisp's definition of the term. Crisp has called marketing research "the systematic, objective, and exhaustive search for and study of the facts relevant to any problem in the field of marketing." The primary problem as far as I am concerned is developing and maintaining the highest percentage of market share.

However, there does not seem to be any universally accepted definition of the term. The American Marketing Association's interpretation used to describe the field is:

Marketing research is the inclusive term that embraces all research activities carried on in connection with the management of marketing work . . . .

It (marketing research) includes various subsidiary types of research, such as: (1) market analysis, which is a study of the size, location, nature, and characteristics of markets; (2) sales analysis (or research), which is largely an analysis of sales data; (3) consumer research, of which motivation research is a type concerned chiefly with the discovery and analysis of consumer attitudes, reactions, and preferences; and (4) advertising research, which is carried on chiefly as an aid to the management of advertising work . . . .

Marketing research is probably the key tool used by management in its problem solving and decision-making in the field of marketing. As such, marketing research is an aid to sound executive judgment and not a substitute for it. The aim of marketing research is to furnish as many as possible of the necessary facts upon which to base decisions.

Some years ago Professor McDonough observed where "Half the cost of running our economy is the cost of information. No other field offers such concentrated room for improvement as does information analysis."

But the method or the way the information is gathered plays the most important role because it is the analysis of that information—the proper kinds of information—that leads to fruitful decision-making and planning.

The more detailed and exacting the information is, the better the decision-making. That is not to say, however, that just because you have the best information you are going to make perfect decisions and lay out an impeccable plan.

Earlier I mentioned why an analysis was most important rather than a survey. Webster defines survey as follows: "to examine for some specific purpose; inspect or consider carefully; review in detail."

Analysis is defined as "a separating or breaking up of any whole into its parts so as to find out their nature, proportion, function, relationship, etc."

When the Pittsburgh Steelers are scheduled to play the New York Giants, an assistant coach or scout does not go to an earlier scheduled game and survey his upcoming opponent from the stands. Oh, the Steelers may send a man to watch a game for "some specific purpose—or to inspect or consider carefully," but the *planning* of the game plan is based on exchanging film so that an analysis can be made—"a separating or breaking up of the whole into its parts so as to find out"—how effective the pulling guard is, how the opponent defends against third and one, what formation defends against the shotgun, how effective the 4-3 or 3-4 is, etc. It is not one man watching a singular action; it is a coaching staff breaking down to find out and the coalescing their collective thoughts into an effective game plan. And if the plan breaks down early, the coach immediately makes the necessary changes to strengthen it. You see it every Sunday or Monday night during football season—the coach with his players gathered around working feverishly with a chalkboard or photograph. And the coach has 60 playing minutes at most.

Many sales managers today do not even have a basic plan because they do not realize or recognize the wealth of information that is available if they would just get out of the office and talk to people—look at some film—use some chalk. They don't have a marketing plan because they do not have anything to base it on—no knowledge about the territory, the customers, or their needs.

American businesses play their professional game every day. All sales management must focus and capture the action. But management must remain professional—focus on the players—not what is going on in the stands (although at times I'll admit it is a bit more exciting).

No two films of football games are alike; no two game plans are alike.

In marketing research no two tasks are exactly alike, nor is there any single procedure that can be followed in all investigations. The general procedure that follows is, however, applicable to most projects. Some of the steps listed here are inter-related, some overlap, and some are not needed in every project.

1. Define the objectives of the project and define the problem.
2. Conduct a situation analysis.
3. Conduct an informal investigation.
4. Plan and conduct a formal investigation.
   a. Determine the sources of information.
   b. Determine the methods of gathering primary information.
   c. Prepare information-gathering forms.
5. Analyze the information.
6. Interpret the information and prepare a marketing and sales plan. Follow up the plan.

I knew that sales and market research was just one of four categories of marketing research departments in a number of American companies. The others are advertising research, business economics and corporate research, and product research.

I investigated the categories of study under sales and market research according to the American Marketing Association and decided that I didn't have any argument with Stanton or the AMA. But many companies are not sophisticated and my analysis had to, at time, be unsophisticated or I would scare salesmen into telling their clients that I was some head-shrinking weirdo who was going to affect their job and territory. It is a matter of using common sense; a matter of spending a lot of time in the territory.

[Speaking of common sense, I recently read Thomas Paine's enormously successful pamphlet *Common Sense* published on Valentines Day, 1776. Paine argued that the colonies had outgrown any need for English domination and should be given independence. Evidently the colonists thought he made sense as the **Declaration of Independence** "was adopted July 4, 1776 by the Thirteen Colonies announcing the separation of those colonies from Great Britian and making them into the United States." (*THE COLUMBIA ENCYCLOPEDIA*, Coulmbia University Press, 1993.)]

I know as well it takes a lot of effort, time and money; also that expenditures pay off because of what more I had learned through a study by the American Management Association. The values of marketing and distribution research (analysis) are summarized by the AMA in *A Complete Guide to Market Research*. The salient facts follow:

Every practical businessman is bound to ask—and rightly so—"What am I to expect in the way of a return on the financial outlay for marketing research?" What better way to answer this question than by summarizing the answers most frequently given by other business men—men who have invested the "marketing research dollar" and have found the dividends fully as satisfactory, if not more so, than those from the "engineering design dollar" or the "laboratory dollar?"

1. An organization is enabled to build its marketing structure on facts, thus eliminating much of the inefficiency and waste incurred by distributive efforts based wholly on past experience, intuition and pure chance.

2. Marketing executives and sales personnel, as well as employees generally, are more confident of the soundness of operations and activities that rest on the bedrock of desirable and acceptable product or service, a favorable competitive position, and tested channels of distribution.

3. Major operating executives in the organization develop an understanding and appreciation of the product or service and of marketing methods in general, giving them a good reason to become "sales minded."

4. The findings of marketing research indicate the direction which technical research should take by providing concrete data on customer preference relating to composition, design or other attributes of the product or service.

5. Marketing research fosters goodwill, both in the consumer market and in the industrial market. As the activities become more firmly rooted in

scientific methodology and professional viewpoint, a cooperative spirit is introduced—between producer and consumer, between producers of complementary products, between producer and wholesaler, etc.—resulting in improved marketing methods for entire industries.

Because of these and other contributions, one executive has aptly characterized his company's program of marketing research as constituting an "insurance policy"—as one more vital means of insuring the survival of the individual enterprise in a dynamic economy which demands, above all, foresight and preparedness.

Charles F. Kettering has said that research is looking forward to see what industry may do when it can no longer do what it is doing. He also said that research is done in men's minds and not in laboratories, although laboratories may be necessary. And how does one get into a man's mind? By sitting down with the individual and going one on one. (the question answered by author)

The territory is my laboratory. A fighter ace cannot become such sitting at his home base; his lab or territory is the sky—a vertical plane. Mine is horizontal but there would be no difference; victory is sweet no matter the means as long as it is honestly attained.

In approaching an analysis of a market or territory, I also wonder if there is any historical data or guides to what my analysis would hold for the future of a company.

The history of a territory, if anything at all, is in the form of old sales reports or computer printout forms. The raw data remains the same, but man changes and I know I have to meet man in his own environment.

However, I also know that the "Historical aspect" was a rhetorical question because I remembered something about Barbara Tuchman, author of *THE GUNS of AUGUST, THE PROUD TOWER, A DISTANT MIRROR*, and other books. In a speech, Mrs. Tuchman remarked about sociologists assembling masses of statistics versus, and here are those words to remember again, common sense. I researched the speech and found a particular thought that made a dramatic difference in my attitude on market analysis and sales.

To quote:

"The commonest question asked by historians of laymen is whether history serves a purpose. Is it useful? Can we learn from the lessons of history?

When people want history to be utilitarian and to teach us lessons, means they also want to be sure that it meet scientific standards. This, in my opinion, it cannot do. To practice history as a science is sociology, an altogether different discipline which I personally find antipathetic—although I suppose the sociologists would consider that my deficiency rather than theirs. The sociologists plod along with their noses to the ground assembling masses of statistics in order to arrive at some obvious conclusion which a reasonably perceptive historian, not to mention a large part of the general public, knows anyway, simply from observation—that social mobility is increasing, for instance, or that women have different problems from men. One wish they would just cut loose someday, lift up their heads and look at the world around them."—or for sales managers to leave their desks and look at the territory around them. (by author).

Look at the world around them—herein lies the key—but a marketing manager or salesman doesn't have to look at the world around him—he just has to observe the happenings in his own territory and absorb the wealth of information available for the asking. And who better to ask than the purchasing agents or engineers or manufacturing managers or store proprietors who think about and look every day for more effective and efficient ways of doing business. These personnel would be only too happy to "brainstorm" pertinent questions. Is it not the marketing manager's job to match potential needs with his company's capabilities and performance? Of course it is; and that is why information gathered through an analysis of the territory provides rich information that flows with ideas on how to technically and economically structure a territory to produce its competitive best.

I want to return to Mrs. Tuchman's speech, to a portion relating to computers and quantification—and man; then I am going to quote from a marketing research test. See, after reading both, if you agree that the foundation for planning *any* analysis in *any* market is man. I want to make it clear for those reading this material to fully understand that analyzing a market is not recondite, abstruse, nebulous, scary, obscure, nor "gut-wrenching." Much to the contrary! It is an opportunity to work with, learn from, brainstorm with, plan with, and know—man.

Emerson put it quite succinctly: "Do you know the secret of the true scholar? In every man there is something wherein I may learn of him; and in that I am his pupil."

Mrs. Tuchman says, "If history were a science, we should be able to get a grip on her, learn her ways, establish her patterns, know what will happen tomorrow. Why is it that we cannot? The answer lies in what I call the unknowable variable—namely, man.

If marketing analysis was a science—and many educated, textbook-oriented, so-called sophisticated managers think it is—we should be able to "get a grip on her, learn her ways, establish her patterns, know what will happen tomorrow.

But the unknown variable, namely man, plays too significant a role; and the less we know of him, the further awry our marketing analysis and plans will be. Ask Ford Motor Company about a car called Edsel. Ask any manager about things gone wrong that were initiated according to the "game plan."

Mrs. Tuchman goes on to state that, "Human beings are always and finally the subject of history. History is the record of human behavior." As a sales manager (and here I mean a professional manager of sales personnel, not someone who sold the most typewriters) one must fundamentally understand that human beings are the subject of any territory; their record of performance and behavior and the understanding of such is the key to territorial performance and behavior. A computer cannot generate this data, and sitting at your desk won't do it. You do not necessarily have to practice history. Practice performance!

Mrs. Tuchman continues;

"Human behavior is the most fascinating subject of all, but illogical and so crammed with an unlimited number of variable that it is not susceptible of the scientific method nor of systematizing.

I say this bravely, even in the midst of the electronic age when computers are already chewing at the skirts of history in the process called quantification. Applied to history, quantification, I believe, has its limits. It depends on a method called "data manipulation," which means that the facts, or data, of the historical past—that is, of human behavior—are manipulated into named categories so that they can be programmed into computers. Out comes—categories, hopefully—a pattern. I can only tell you that, for history, "data manipulation" is a built-in invalidator, because to the degree that you manipulate your data to suit some extraneous requirement, in this case the requirements of the machine, to that degree your results will be suspect—and run the risk of being invalid. Everything depends on the naming of the categories and the assigning of facts to them, and this depends on the quantifier's individual judgment at the very base of the process. The categories are not revealed doctrine nor are the results scientific truth.

The hope for quantification, presumable, is that by processing a vast quantity of material far beyond the capacity of the individual to encompass, it can bring to light and establish reliable patterns. That remains to be seen, but I am not optimistic; history has a way of escaping attempts to imprison it is patterns. Moreover, one of its basic (bits of) data is the human soul. The conventional historian, at least the one concerned with truth, not propaganda, will try honestly to let his "data" speak for themselves, but data which are shut up in prearranged boxes are helpless. Their nuances have no voice. They must carry one fixed meaning or another and weigh the results accordingly. For instance, in a quantification study of the origins of World War I which I have seen, the operators have divided all the diplomatic documents, messages, and utterances of the July crisis into categories labeled "Hostility," "Friendship," "Frustration," "Satisfaction," and so on, with each statement rated for intensity on a scale of from one to nine, including fractions. But no pre-established categories could match all the private character traits and public pressures variously operating on the nervous monarchs and ministers who were involved. The massive effort that went into this study brought forth a mouse—the less-than-startling conclusion that the likelihood of war increased in proportion to the rise in hostility of the messages."

Mrs. Tuchman's thoughts have a tremendous impact on my thinking about why personal contact is vitally important; the words I have underlined help me to understand more and more why it is important for sales management to know—of, by, and for the people.

I was speaking recently with a lady real estate agent from Colorado springs about a problem—a problem of selling the last "six big houses" in an exclusive area of the community. She had all sorts of data—computer printouts about what to sell the potential clients—square footage, closet space, storage, sizes of fireplaces, distance to shopping centers, etc.—all the data that competitive real estate salespeople would present also. She was in a dilemma because she didn't have anything "different to sell." I asked her how many homes she had sold in that area, and when she answered "eight" I told her, "You have at least eight times eight more reasons for a successful sale than your competitors." She was incredulous, and asked, "What gives you that idea; you don't know anything about the Colorado Springs real estate market." I replied, "You're right, but I do know people and if I were you, I would go directly to the eight owners you have sold in the past and ask the women of the households to have lunch with you, or invite yourself over for tea. Over a cup of tea I would learn from these women a whole new data bank—what they like about Colorado Springs; what its geographical position means to their travels; the airline and bus service; the neighbors; the churches, schools, and libraries; women's clubs and golf and tennis facilities; postal service; maid service and babysitters; and fifteen things she liked about the house you sold her—heating and sunlight, view, ease of cleaning, and not the *size* of the family room but how she fixed it up—and how she decorated and painted and landscaped. Also who her decorators were and how she liked the gardener, and on, and on."

Now she didn't have space and size to sell. She had a home to add new dimensions to a family's living enjoyment. No, I *don't* have a real estate license. But I *do* have common sense and I constantly search for wisdom from the minds of others.

"To be a philosopher," Thoreau once said, "is not merely to have subtle thoughts, nor even to found a school, but so to love wisdom as to live, according to its dictates, a life of simplicity, independence, magnanimity, and trust."

"We may be sure that if we can but find wisdom," said Durant, "all things else will be added unto us."

"See ye first the good things of the mind," Bacon admonishes us, "and the rest will either be supplied or its loss will not be felt."

In seeking out the minds and thought processes of potential clients in a territory, a well-trained and experienced market analyst will remember the objectives of what will be a very important but informal investigation. In an informal investigation, the person responsible for the study talks informally with consumers, dealers, and key men in the industry to get an impartial point of view and the "feel" of the problem.

The informal investigation carries no precise notion of the form the final analysis will take, but attempts by informal interview to crystallize the central problem. It is essential that any person employed in this type of investigation be especially capable of drawing out people who are interviewed and recognizing significant facts when they appear.

One of the primary objectives of the informal investigation is to obtain a "feel" for the market. Too often in marketing research work the researcher closets himself with his thoughts to decide which lines to pursue in the study. So much stress has been placed upon the importance of deciding on the exact purposes of an analysis that many persons will enter into it with no tools other than a good supply of paper and a pencil to plan the study. Such an investigation will often completely overlook unknown basic and significant facts, which are the duty of the marketing research to reveal. It is fated to fail.

In developing a genuine "feel" for the market, the informal investigation provides many fundamental and essential ingredients for marketing research. This type of study emphasizes the qualitative aspects of the problem rather than the quantitative. Thus, it ensures against taking too mechanical an approach to the marketing problems of a business.

While the first purpose of an informal investigation is to develop the hypothesis for the study, there is no specific technique for directly finding it. It evolves automatically as the investigation progresses. The hypothesis may enter the conscious thought of a market analyst at most unexpected moments—riding in a car or plane, while playing cards, or while discussing politics and business in Sacramento or Washington, D.C. One may lay awake at night and suddenly discover the lines to pursue in tackling the problem.

Refer to the next chapter, "FULL of the PROBLEM." If it can help a man win the Nobel Prize for physics, and help a naval aviator plan a more effective attack on Pearl Harbor, it can surely help you sell more houses, analyze the territory in the needs of the customer, and therefore write a dynamic marketing and business plan. I can't emphasize enough the importance of the written plan. It won't be perfect but you will never find out until you "hit" the territory. So a few mistakes have been made. Big deal! By recognition and immediate correction you will be far ahead of your competition and you will be the one responsible for making a BIG DEAL for your company.

FULL OF THE PROBLEM

Murray Gell-Mann, Winner
Nobel Prize for Physics

There is a detailed account in **BOOK II** of the trilogy about Socrates surprising me with a visit to my apartment soon after I resigned from my experimental test-flying career at Lockheed. He wanted to say good-bye, for the present. He brought with him a beautiful marble plaque with gold lettering. I offered him a seat; he looked very comfortable in my EXORNES leather lounge chair. We chatted for a while—you know—small talk. I served him a beer with some pretzels. We both knew it was time for him to go and leave me on my own. I kept looking at the plaque on his lap. Finally, he said, "Here, I want you to have this in memory of our friendship. Sorry I didn't have time to wrap it like a gift shop would. He then stood up and very carefully handed it to me. I gingerly took possession and started to read. The plaque, made of fine marble, told the story (see BOOK II) of the bold and courageous fighter pilots giving their all in the battle of Britain and Europe, in the skies over the Yalu, the Chorwon Valley in Korea, and in Vietnam. It stated:

WHEN WE FIGHTER PILOTS LEAVE
THE WORLD WILL BE A LESSER PLACE!

The narrative, in gold lettering, was of outstanding quality; a masterpiece. This—this personal badge of distinction filled me full of emotion. Tears were streaming down my face. I told Socs I would hang it in a place of honor. He was looking directly at me. His eyes were watering also but he continued to look me in the eye. Socrates then gave me a firm handshake, put his arms around me, and said, "I know you love me Suitcase, I love you too! But you can't have my Bud Lite!"

I laughed, but I knew what was coming. He said, "I must go. I just stopped by to give you a gift you well deserve" And with that, with his wings pinned to his toga, shining particularly bright, (see **BOOK** I) he turned and started toward the door. He was on his way to club Cloud Nine. And then he suddenly stopped, looked back at me, and said, "Remember that experimental test pilots' poem—by a Mr. Wilson?"

"Sure," I said. "I know it by heart. Why do you ask?"

"Not to worry;" Socs said. "Recite a few lines for me, please!"

"OK!" I said. "The first few lines are:

> 'As long as this is a free man's world, someone has to lead.
> Someone has to carry the ball in thought, and word, and deed.
> Someone has to knock on doors that never have known key. And,
> Someone has to see the things that the throng would never
> See.'

"OK! OK! that's enough," Socrates said. "Now, Jack, I want you to think about what I am going to say. You have resigned from experimental flying and are about to enter the world of business and free enterprise. I know you will continue your studies of philosophers and history. Think through your readings, my friend—and learn. Lean what the lessons of history have to offer. We learned together in your combat and testing. I want you to consider four other 'extensions,' as I call them, of history. They are time, legacy, culture, and planning. Time could not be compressed in taking the F-104 from experimental flight test to operational suitability. Lockheed's culture, the total product of human creativity and intellect, took decades. The legacy of Lockheed's test pilots was passed from one generation to another. And planning—that's the killer in most companies. Suitcase, always have a plan. In speaking of Mr. Wilson's poem, planning will be your key when you knock on doors that never have known one. I don't care if it is 'cold' calling, making a technically oriented presentation to a group of individuals, or writing a detailed business and marketing plan. You must be able to presage their thoughts. Incisive planning and market analysis allows you to speak of—and in the language of—Who?"

"The customer."

"Right! Nothing moves without a customer.

Something else! In writing the pilots' handbook, or DASH I, for the '104' what were you doing?"

"Well, let's see. In following your thought, I was writing a technically oriented and operationally suitable plan for pilots to study and stay alive."

"Right again! And as you learned more and more about the performance of the STARFIGHTER you continually updated the plan. Right?"

"You bet! I see what you are getting at, Socs. If I write a business and marketing plan, it has to be in the needs of the customer and as it is tested in the field, to stay ahead of competition. And, it *must* be continually updated."

"Correct. If the plan isn't updated in business, the business dies. So do pilots if you didn't do your job properly as an experimental pilot. It is pure, professional dedication to occupational responsibility. Anything less is unacceptable."

"I know of a Lt. General in WW I. He was from Australia. Planning was his ken—the extent of one's perception and understanding. He said, 'A perfected modern battle plan is like a score for an orchestral exposition where the various arms and instruments and the tasks they perform are their respective musical phrases. Every individual unit must make its entry precisely at the proper moment, and play in phase in the general harmony.'

War, musical composition, any business enterprise, and in particular marketing and sales—the success comes from a detailed plan.

Suits, sometime in the immediate future, look up a physicist by the name of Murray Gell-Mann. It won't be tough—he won the Nobel Prize for physics. See what he has to say about 'filling yourself full of the problem.' If you have a problem in marketing and sales fill yourself full of it. You *will* solve your problem but not without paying the price of time. You will learn then, the solution presents, for free, a plan far beyond what is normal or customary. The thoughts of Gell-Mann may not seem important in calendar years, but the historical significance is priceless.

And speaking of historical significance, Suits, check on a staff officer who served during the Napoleon campaigns. His name is Carl von Clausewitz. Think of Santa Clause with wits—Clausewitz! He was an intellectual of the highest order. Winning a battle in war depends on incisive planning and strategy. So does winning the battle for market share. He believed in freedom of thinking, emphasis on the creative action of the individual, and had disdain for formalism. I have been speaking of pure synergy here; test flying, war, philosophy, and free enterprise. Sounds like another Suitcase book! And I mean that as a compliment.

One more thought and then I *really* have to go. Catch the book about the attack on Pearl Harbor authored by a guy named Prange. Study the story about a Commander Genda; impatient, intractable, a maverick. Gee! You and Clausewitz and Genda would make a great trio—of trouble for your superiors.

But don't worry, Suits. You'll succeed in your world of business. Your gains through experience will give you knowledge and from that flows what?"

"Wisdom! Insight! And I hope the ability to make sensible decisions."

"OK! And if you make a decision what are you not going to be afraid of!"

"Making a mistake."

"Good! And what will making a mistake offer?"

"The opportunity to learn."

"Excellent! Put down in writing what you learn—I'll help you in your marketing and business. I promise I will be back to discuss the important elements. I will not rescue you from failure; a good way to learn. Know yourself, be honest with yourself, be honest with others. And I'll help you with your golf swing. I understand you have more ways to slice than a delicatessen counterman."

"You can't get to me, Socs. Even if you make fun of my golf game, I'll still welcome you back with open arms."

"That will be great, my friend. Speaking of open arms, give me another hug and shake my hand. I'm outta' here."

We shook hands, and slapped shoulders as we gave each other a hug. Socs turned away and was gone; but certainly not forgotten.

I look forward to every day now, knowing he'll show up when he thinks I need him. I'll continue to have a flight leader in my business life. He's in the fast lane now that he has his wings. Socs will lead me. We'll have some cloudy times but the brightness lies in facing adversity together.

MURRAY GELL-MANN

Soon after my meeting with Socrates, I stepped into a minefield for the pursuit of consecutive progressive achievement. In other words I went to work for an engineering company by the name of BXFS Aerospace, spending weeks and weeks in training and learning product. I had a new car, a salary, an expense account, and an engineering sales untrained mind. Naturally my engineering degree and consumer sales experience helped, but I realized I had much to learn. More on this later!

At the same time, I continued my studies of philosophy, history, and war; my favorite reading subjects. I also liked to look at picture books; you know, like PLAYBOY. I was intrigued about Gell-Mann. All I could find in the encyclopedia was his name under Nobel Prize winners; nothing about 'full of the problem,' or associations with the business community. I continued my research; one evening I got lucky.

Remember my female friend, the left-handed tennis player from SOCRATES 'N SUITS? OK! If you didn't read the book, she and I were toweling each other after a cool shower one night after tennis when her boyfriend, THE WHISTLER, sounded up. The guy never said much; all he did was whistle. Thank God! It gave me a chance to "Run Spot! Run!" Well, she was in town one Saturday and called to say she was going to play tennis with some friends, and could I have dinner with them afterward. "Of course," I said. "Where's THE WHISTLER?" I asked. "Oh!, hell," she said. "He ran out of tune a long time ago. And, by the way, he never knew you were there."

"He never knew I was there? He must have felt the sonic boom as I ran down the street at the speed of sound."

She laughed, told me the address and the time for dinner.

"I'll bring the wine," I said.

I hadn't planned to do anything that particular evening but since the library was close to where we were going to have dinner, I showered and shaved early and gave myself a couple of more hours at my literary foundation. I decided to take a new approach to my Gell-Mann dilemma. I asked the librarian if she had anything about solving problems. She asked, "Like solutions in math or physics?" I said, "More like business, and you used the word 'solutions.' Have anything on that?"

She looked through a long list but finally said, "I have a book here entitled *THE SEARCH FOR SOLUTIONS*. What do you think?"

I said, "I think I would like to marry you. Where may I find it?"

We laughed. I looked for the book by reading a lot of numbers and decimals, and then—there it was, *THE SEARCH FOR SOLUTIONS*, by Horace Freeland Judson, Holt, Rinehart, & Winston, New York, 1980.

I had found my map, outlining the road to the pot of gold!

In the book *THE SEARCH FOR SOLUTIONS*, a conversation with Murray Gell-Mann makes a great case about thoughts entering the conscious at unexpected moments. Gell-Mann, a theoretical physicist at the California Institute of Technology, won a share of the Nobel Prize in Physics in 1969 for his work on subatomic particles. In 1963, he first conceived the entities that may, after all, be the stuff that all other stuff is made of. He named the quarks.

When someone asked Gell-Mann where ideas come from, he replied (rather lengthily),

"We had a seminar here, about ten years ago, including several painters, a poet, a couple of writers, and the physicists. Everybody agrees on how it works. All of these people, whether they're doing artistic work or scientific work, are trying to solve a problem.

Any art that's worth the name has some kind of discipline associated with it. Some kind of rule—but it's not the rule of a sonnet or a symphony, or a classical painting, but even the most liberated contemporary art, if it's any kind of art at all, has some kind of rule. And the object is to get across what you're trying to get across, while sticking to the rules.

In our business, it is hard to find out what nature is up to, and there are all sorts of constraints—you have to agree with every-thing you already know, and you have to have a nice self-consistent structure, and so on. And so, when you have to account for something new—or in the artist's case, when you want to express yourself within the rules—you run into problems. And the problems at first seem difficult, and perhaps insoluble. And you work very hard trying to understand, trying to fill yourself full of the problem, just to know what barriers you're trying to crack.

And after that, further voluntary effort, further conscious effort, is not so productive. And at that point, what the shrinks would call the preconscious, I guess, seems to be more important. Processes that are outside awareness go on, which thrust up bubbles of ideas from time to time. And that can happen when you're driving, or shaving, or walking—anything.

One of my ideas came in a slip of the tongue. I was getting up at a seminar—one person had just put forward a theory, and I was explaining why his theory was wrong, why it didn't work—and while I was explaining it, I happened to blurt out the correct way to do it. Just a slip of the tongue! And I recognized immediately that the slip would solve the problem."

"What was that?"

"Oh, it was the idea of 'strangeness,'" Gell-Mann said. "I was intending to say, 'isotopic spin-three halves' and, instead, I said 'isotopic spin-one,' which for the particular kind of particle, was *unthinkable*. Unthinkable, but correct! Everybody had taken it for granted that the value was a half integer. And it wasn't. As soon as I mentioned an integral number, which nobody had thought of, I realized that the integral number was the answer."

Which led him to the name 'quarks.'

"Gee!" I said to myself "Gell-Mann's statement, 'You work very hard trying to understand, trying to *fill yourself full of the problem* smacks of sheer genius. Six words summing up what every man must undergo and endure in preparation for the possible recognition and solution to the advancement of the state of any art, be it science, music, literature, or business. And what a challenge in the competitive atmosphere of business today! To be able to expose oneself to complete saturation of a problem—trying to understand—trying to bear the weight—hoping the process bears fruit. It is a blessing, because every though you may fail at first, the persistence will pay off. And the rewards will be the Gell-Mann of the business/marketing community."

And the mental bubbling process occurs in war, too.

CMDR. MINORU GENDA

I purchased the book on Pearl Harbor as Socrates suggested. In a passage from G.W. Prange's *AT DAWN WE SLEPT*, the author lauds the diligence and persistence of a high-ranking Japanese militarist who employed this technique for producing ideas.

Erect as a lance, wiry as a steel spring, Rear Admiral Takijiro Onishi, Chief of staff of the Eleventh Air Fleet, was blessed with undaunted confidence, a forceful personality, and a husky physique. He never bluffed, and he walked tall—'the central figure in any environment.' He had a special genius for working out the details of tactical plans. Once he turned to a problem, he concentrated so intensely that he saw nothing except the task at hand.

Admiral Isoroku Yamamoto, Commander-in-Chief, Combined Japanese Fleet, in writing personal letters to Onishi dated January 1941 regarding the bleak international situation said, "The time had come for the navy to devote itself seriously to war preparations because a conflict with the United States and Great Britain is inevitable."

Yamamoto outlined to Onishi his operational plan to destroy the enemy's main force at Pearl Harbor.

Yamamoto had selected an excellent officer to test his idea. Besides enjoying his trust and confidence, Onishi was rated as one of Japan's few genuine air admirals.

Onishi was no intellectual. In fact, he had flunked his entrance exam to the Naval Staff College and never attended that school for future admirals. Nor was he original or imaginative. But what he lacked of those qualities he made up in diligent application and sheer driving power. Onishi was a very ardent person—nothing was impossible if one went forward with great spiritual determination. Just a few months under fifty when he entered the Pearl Harbor picture, Onishi had enough hard practical experience to deepen his knowledge, ripen his judgment, and give him a sound approach to aviation problems.

Onishi continued to work on the Pearl Harbor problem. One thing was certain—for a surprise attack on Pearl Harbor to be even remotely possible, it must ride the wings of Japan's Naval Air Arm. To elevate the basic idea, followed by breathing life into it, Onishi needed an honest and precise worker, a true flier with a sure grasp of air power's capabilities, and, above all, a daring thinker who originality boarded on genius. A tall order in anyone's Navy, but Onishi knew where to fill it. Early in February 1941 he dispatched a message to the Staff Officer for Air aboard the carrier *Kaga*, moored in Ariake Bay. This note requested Commander Minoru Genda to come to Kanoya at once about an urgent matter. Thus, Onishi took a dynamic step that was to have a profound and lasting influence on Yamamoto's project.

A photograph of Genda in his commander's uniform reveals a symmetrical face with regular, aristocratic features. Thick, level eyebrows, a straight nose, and a firm chin are dominated by piercing eyes, almost frightening in their intensity of expression. No one who ever looked into those eyes could forget them. At thirty-six, Genda was impatient with mediocrity, at ease only with perfection. Behind his keen dark eyes lay a razor-sharp mind that cut straight to the heart of any problem.

He radiated the pose and savoir-faire of a man who knows and loves his job. A Japanese Billy Mitchell, Genda was intolerant of those who did not share his idea. In the highly competitive naval staff college some thought him mad. Despite his classmates' opinions, he could not have been far out of his mind because he graduated second in his class.

In November 1938, Genda joined the staff of the First Carrier Division and also received his promotion to Commander. During the next several months he preoccupied himself with the use of carriers and their formation in battle—the second aspect of Gendaism.

'The First Aspect of Gendaism' was Genda's ideas on the use of fighters and carriers in combat. A fighter must have two outstanding qualities—maneuverability and speed—later exemplified by the famous ZERO.

In maneuvers since 1935 the Navy had dispersed its carriers, using them primarily to provide defensive air cover for the other fleet units that delivered the main offensive thrust. The Navy also theorized that scattering the carriers would deny the enemy a mass target. But this meant the Japanese would have considerable difficulty in gathering and organizing their planes for a simultaneous attack in great force on a given objective.

One evening Genda took time off to go to a movie. There on the screen he saw the U.S. Fleet at sea with four carriers sailing majestically in a single column.

Probably it was for demonstration, thought Genda. But the seed had taken root in his subconscious. Several days later, as he jumped off a streetcar, the lightning struck. "Why should we have trouble gathering planes in the air if we concentrate our carriers," he said to himself as he was running toward his office.

The rest is history. Genda's run was the forerunner of the carrier task force—and Pearl Harbor, December 7, 1941.

I will not learn anything more from Gell-Mann about "quarks" or from Genda about planning a surprise attack. But I did learn from them that they experienced the same thing after intense study of their individual problems. Eureka! Gell-Mann while getting up to speak; Genda while getting off a streetcar! How ironic!

But I will continue to learn from Onishi. He may not have been intelligent or imaginative, but he had experience and common sense. Enough common sense to know he needed a steel-strap mind to complement his plans. He stayed with the problem until he was certain he needed a man like Genda.

Genda was impatient, intractable, unforgiving and a maverick—a personality laid wide open for mistakes. I can't see anything wrong with that!

Captain Mitsu Fuchida, who led the attack against Pearl Harbor, said, "Genda was sometimes too willing, too risky in his judgment when he should have been more careful. Genda was like a daring quarterback who would risk the game on one turn of pitch and toss. He was a man of brilliant ideas. Sometimes, however, his ideas were too flashy and needed a practical hand for their realization."

What Fuchida had to say didn't bother Onishi. He knew two things:

Genda always set high standards of performance for himself.

A performance record must include mistakes.

That was the kind of thinking that went through Rear Admiral Takijiro Onishi's mind, circa 1941.

PETER F. DRUCKER
An acknowledged teacher and author in
matters of fundamental concern
to management

Was Peter Drucker thinking of Gell-Mann, who boldly stood up to correct a colleague? Was he thinking Fuchida who said Genda should have been more careful? Thirty-two years later, Peter F. Drucker wrote:

"The constant temptation of every organization is safe mediocrity. The first requirement of organizational health is a high demand on performance. Indeed, one of the major reasons for demanding that management be by objectives and that it focus on the objective requirements of the task is the need to have managers set high performance for themselves.

This requires that performance be understood properly.

Performance is not hitting the bull's eye with every shot—that is a circus act that can be maintained only over a few minutes. Performance is rather the consistent ability to produce results over prolonged periods of time in a variety of assignments. A performance record must include mistakes. It must include failures. It must reveal a man's limitations as well as his strengths. And there are as many different kinds of performance as there are different human beings. One man will constantly do well, rarely falling far below a respectable standard, but also rarely excel through brilliance or virtuosity. Another man will perform only adequately under normal circumstances but will rise to he demands of a crisis or a major challenge and then perform like a 'true star.' Both are 'performers.' Both need to be recognized. But their performances will look quite different.

The one man to distrust, however, the man who never makes a mistake, never commits a blunder, never fails in what he tries to do. He is either a phony, or he stays with the safe, the tried, and the trivial.

A management that does not define performance as a batting average is a management that mistakes conforming for achievement, and demoralizes its organization. The better a man is, the more mistakes he will make—for the more things he will try."

In my experiences, such as the confrontation at Lockheed, (detailed in SOCRATES N' SUITS, **BOOK II**) most managers do not welcome a maverick like me for fear it would hurt their position in the company, or the company's position in industry. They are more worried about the 'political' implications than what a 'Genda' (or a Simpson) can do for the division or corporation. That is because most managers spend more time worrying about their political position than taking the time necessary to fully understand their responsibilities and how they should be held accountable. They think of the problems the man may possibly cause rather than the opportunities he open up to increase the value of the organization.

In my future college classes and lecture series as a professor, I asked the students (most of whom are in the business world desiring to learn more) if they believe their manager fully understood his duties and responsibilities. In eight years of teaching, more than 90 percent of the students not only answered in the negative, but were miffed because they were given a responsibility without the concomitant training or performance standards. Management did not take the time to organize their personal or professional relationship. Drucker says, "It is folly to ask workers to take responsibility for their job when the work has not been studied, the process has not been synthesized, and the physical information tools have not been designed. It is managerial incompetence."

ALPHA BAKER CHARLIE DRUG CO., INC.

I was walking down 'The Strand' in Manhattan Beach one lazy Sunday morning looking for a volley ball game when I ran into an old friend—a druggist who owned his own store.

"Dan my good man," I said, "I haven't seen you since the glory days of Panchos. I remember it was hard for a girl to say 'no' to you. You kept holding them for further questioning."

He laughed.

"You're right, Suitcase," he said as we shook hands and exchanged pleasantries. "But I finally found one that knew all the answers and I married her. I guess it has been sometime since I last saw you. I also sold the store; I sold it to the president of ABC DRUG CO. He offered me a job as vice president for business development. He wants to strengthen the divisions we have and find other arenas for growth. It was a proposition I couldn't turn down. I'm working just as hard—maybe harder—but I don't have to worry as much. I used to worry so much I often wondered what kind of wine went with fingernails."

"Well, you haven't lost your sense of humor. I'm happy to know that."

"Speaking of happy, Jack, you look like you're enjoying life. What have you been up to? I understand you have a successful maintenance business but aren't you doing some aerospace sales too!"

"You're pretty darn close, Dan," I said. "I sold the maintenance business a year ago and I am now representing four aerospace companies and have also done consulting to a real estate and credit life insurance company.

"What kind of consulting?"

"Dan, no matter the company it's all the same; it's almost universal. Companies offer product or services but many really don't know their customer, or how to sell in their customers' particular needs and language. Very few write detailed marketing and business plans. Even if they do, they do not keep them up to date. Dan, they don't spend enough time to comprehend market potential so management loses sight on assigning accountability and responsibility to sales personnel? I'm just a few years out of test flying but the lessons of history are common sense lessons although all are usually written in blood—or red ink. Let me ask you. Would I take a new fighter up for the first time without a plan or be aware of what to expect?"

"Of course not!" Dan said.

"Anyhow, one man's loss is another man's gain and I guess that encapsulates how I make my living. It was rather a long answer to your question but I do marketing analysis by talking to potential customers and develop a detailed business and marketing plan from there.

Dan asked, "How do you know what questions to ask?"

"I don't when I start but it makes sense to read about and study the particular discipline. I first establish a harmonious mutual understanding as to why I am conducting the analysis. I also point out that I am conducting an analysis, not a survey because in a survey questions are presaged and "yes" or "no" or "fill in the blanks from #s 1 to 10," does not offer the nexus for an effective plan. Surveys are usually conducted that feed you information after the fact!

I ask a lot of questions about sales, knowledge of customer and sales personnel, service, satisfaction with sales coverage, warehousing, distribution, communication, merchandizing, and organization. After I make six or eight calls I begin to learn to ask the proper questions of the customer in his language and needs. With the right answers, I can write a plan to market and sell in his language and needs. It's damn hard work, but it is worth it."

"You know, Jack, maybe it's fate that we chanced running into each other this morning. Or, I could use the word fortunate! Sir Francis Bacon once said that chiefly the mold of a man's fortune is in his own hands. I was thinking as you were talking and I have an idea. Maybe we could use six hands—yours, mine, and the hands of Able Baker Charley's CEO, Edward Martinelli. You see, we are having a hell of a time with the president of one of our divisions. It's in the pet supply business. The president of the division is telling us he is getting 60% of the market but when we ask 'what market' he can't come up with an answer, nor can he tell us what the potential is for gross sales in a particular (salesman's) territory"

"Look," Dan continued as he looked at his watch, "I have to go, you have a volley ball game. Neither one of us has a pencil so phone me Wednesday or Thursday at corporate headquarters in Century City. I'll set a time for you and me to meet Martinelli. I'll brief him on our meeting today and tell him what you are doing. We'll see if my idea works."

It was ten thirty on a Thursday morning when Dan and I stepped into my Martinelli's fashionable office. We were so high up in that office building I was sub-consciously looking for my oxygen mask. If anyone said Mr. Martinelli walked around with his head in the clouds, they were right. They were real clouds!

Dan introduced me. We shook hands; firm handshake, neat and trim in appearance in his tailored suit, and as he asked me to be seated I took notice; he was alert and lively in his movement and mannerisms. Dan must have briefed him well because after offering me coffee or a 'coke' he said, "I understand you have an experienced background in marketing analysis and sales; and, as a test pilot, you are used to thinking on your own."

"Yes, Sir," I said.

"How did you like test flying?"

"It was a challenge, Sir, but I have found in the business world mistakes are a little more forgiving. I am speaking about harm to the body, of course."

"Of course! Do you make mistakes?"

"Yes, Sir."

"Good! And please call me Edward. Dan may have told you I have a president of one of my divisions that I think is making a big mistake. Pet supplies, I'm not talking food, but everything else a pet would need such as brushes, collars, harnesses, soaps, powders, etc., etc. The president also purchased a tropical fish warehouse full of fresh water and seawater exotic and tropical fish. From what I have learned it appears to me to be a big business but none of our salesmen are trained to sell tropical fish and I am damn interested in getting a fair return on our invested capital. As far as pet supplies he keeps telling me he is capturing more than 60% of the business but I think his gross sales are only moderate compared to what, I feel, they should be. Trouble is, no one seems to be able to get his arm around the total market.

So, Mr. Simpson, I only have two questions. Would you like another 'coke', he said with a smile, and do you think your analysis of the market could give me an answer?"

"Well, Sir," I said, "No thanks for the 'coke' and I would be lying to you if I were to answer "Yes" to the second question. But I have the ability to try, and I am sure I can come up an idea of how to go about it. Dan and I will put together a six-month contract. If my idea doesn't show any progress by the end of three months, I'll agree to a termination. And I might as well tell you now, since living in Los Angeles, I haven't been near a pet store."

Mr. Martinelli sat at his desk and looked at me for what seemed like an eternity. I looked at him. In a second he was on his feet, picked up a pencil, studied it, tossed it back on the desk, looked up, and said, "You have a deal. At least you're honest. Work the contract out with Dan. And keep him informed. I'll pass the word on to Jim Johnson that you are going to do an analysis for me at his division and for everyone to make you feel at home. Any questions?"

"No, Sir."

"OK! You talk to Dan and Dan will talk to me. I'm not looking for anything fancy in your reports. I just want some straight answers to my questions about market. What the heck are total sales in California? Dan told you we have a sales office and warehouse in San Francisco, didn't he?"

"Yes, Sir, he did."

"What percentage of this unidentified market are we getting, or more importantly, what are we missing?

Well, I could go on and on. Just use your head and experience and see what you can find out. And—thank you for coming in."

"Yes, Sir. A pleasure meeting you Mr. Martinelli."

We shook hands. I did an 'about face' and walked out of his office closely followed by Dan. We walked into Dan's office, he put some papers he was carrying on his desk and said, "Let's go to lunch."

During lunch, a plate of Angel Hair pasta for Dan and a Club sandwich for me, I said, "You told me when we met you had an idea in talking to Mr. Martinelli about me. It evidently worked. What was that?"

"I frankly told Edward we needed someone that would be totally unencumbered, could be on his own, could think on his own two feet, and above all, wouldn't be hassled by anyone from the company—corporate or division. I told him we needed a fresh new look with no constraints or evaluation of (your) background in specific marketing and sales in Able Baker Charley's disciplines. Simpson's been on his own both in flying and as a sales rep. Remember, Sir," I reminded him, "the turning point of WWII in the Pacific was won by our Naval aircraft sinking four Japanese carriers. The whole plan of battle was the idea of an admiral with a destroyer, not carrier, background. He didn't even know how to fly. That's all I said."

"Dan," I said, "It worked and I thank you for it. The heat is on me. Maybe I should go down to San Diego and talk to a destroyer captain."

We laughed, finished our meal, made arrangements for our meetings, agreed on a contract, and departed company.

"Now what will I do?" I said to myself, in my car, in the buildings' underground parking. I just sat there and thought. "You have no experience when it comes to pet supplies, but you *do* know Socrates told you experience is granted only to those who surrender themselves to direct observation of or participation in events as a basis of gaining knowledge. If you want knowledge of the business there is no time like the present. It's only one thirty in the afternoon, so turn the ignition switch and go observe and participate. That means call on the division's retailers in a professional act of participation, and observe what's going on at division headquarters in relation to this "60% of the market share" business."

I found myself, heading west. At the corner of Pico and Sepulveda, I stopped at a red light. On the far southwest corner I saw a phone booth. I was lucky to be in the left lane. When the light changed I made a left turn, moved to the right and into a liquor store, laundry, billiards, hamburgers and hot dogs 'for sale' mini shopping mall. I parked, walked to the corner and grabbed the YELLOW PAGES. Under the titles PET SUPPLIES and TROPICAL FISH I looked up four retailers in the local area, made notes of the locations. ABLE BAKER CHARLEY's professional, respected, in-experienced—klutz, was about to make his first dog, cat, fish, bird, and turtle, sales analysis call.

The first retailer offered pet supplies only—that is, no tropical fish. The proprietors were two very nice ladies. I told them of my meeting with Mr. Martinelli and I was sure he had not as yet had the chance to talk to Mr. Johnson, the PET SUPPLY DIVISION president, his sales manager, or, in particular, the salesperson covering this particular store. I told them why I was there and I certainly didn't want to offend the salesperson but I said, "I'll be sure he finds out, I have a lot to learn, and would they mind me asking them a few questions."

The ladies said, "Yes, of course, we will be happy to answer what questions we can."

Well, we three shared as much information as they could give me. Since this was my first 'low pass' I wasn't sure if I was asking the incisive kinds of questions that would lead to maximizing a plan to sell in the language of the customer. I didn't realize it at the time, but as I stood there soaking up all the information I could, I was filling myself full of a number of problems that I knew nothing about at the time, but were playing an important factor in paralyzing the growth of the company. I was far from being a Gell-Mann or a Genda, but I was beginning to focus on the need to think in terms of what old Socs told me—'direct observation and participation in events as a basis for gaining knowledge.'

I called on three more retailers that afternoon with the same modus operandi. All the proprietors were very convivial and felt free to answer my questions. Yes, the salesperson was very knowledgeable about pet supplies but didn't press the sale of tropical fish. Yes, they were receiving "more than 50% of their sales; the salesperson could walk into the store and replenish stock on the shelves as they deemed fit." Yes, they were very dependable; "could set my watch every other Wednesday afternoon between 1 and 2pm." And, "Yes, deliveries were very dependable as is Mr. Ryan (the salesperson). He has been calling on my store for the past twelve years; give him as much business as I can. Hell, Mr.—, I'm sorry, what was your name?"

"Simpson."

"Hell, Mr. Simpson, he knows all my kids; sends them a birthday card. No, we don't sell much in the tropical fish arena, but Mr. Ryan has plenty to do by just keeping our shelves properly stocked."

So that is how it went my first day. The "Mr. Ryan" was calling on the stores in his territory every other week without fail. He was dependable, knew his business, and was welcome to walk in and replenished shelves. He always had good shelf space, and received at least 50% or more of the business. Also, the deliveries were on time, and everybody knew each other; it was one happy family.

There was one thing, however, that kept popping up. I stored the information I gained in the back of my mind. The PET SUPPLY DIVISION of ALPHA BAKER CHARLEY spent a ton of money on a tropical fish warehouse and wholesale distribution center but Mr. Ryan wasn't selling any fish. And I was on a fishing trip to an empty lake as far as Mr. Martinelli's query; "Percentage of *what* business"?

I spent two of the next three weeks making calls on the division's customers early morning and evening (no startling news) plus I spent many hours on working days at the division office. The president, Mr. Johnson, was 'friendly' but with the look of "what does this asshole, me, know about the pet supply business?" I can't blame the guy. I was vicariously attacking his fiefdom; since he was doing well above average in sales he couldn't understand what I was doing there in the first place. I met the sales manager and all the sales and warehouse personnel. I took a third day, a Saturday, and went to sales meeting. This is what I learned:

The organizational structure made the warehouse manager directly responsible to the President and the sales manager responsible to the warehouse manager. An organizational mistake I failed to comment on—at the time.

The President had no former experience in any kind of wholesale or retail operation. His position was the result of 'family orientation.' I considered that none of my business.

The sales manager was appointed to his position because he was the man who generated the most sales. He started with the company as a salesman in a county that turned out to be, in a relatively short period of time, the fastest growing county in the state. The increase in population brought an increase in pets with a need for pet supplies. It got to the point where he was taking orders more than he was selling. But I had to give him credit; he was a hard worker and was always at certain store on a particular day and time every other week. When he became manager he made sure his sales personnel followed that same pattern. Another fatal flaw that went completely over my head—at that time! He also had his sales personnel report to the warehouse offices every morning to turn in their sale records from the previous day. I innately knew that was an ill-advised practice but I didn't know enough of the details to say anything.

The sales manager spent an inordinate amount of his time during the day working with the warehouse manager making sure the delivery trucks were loaded properly so the goods were delivered on time with the properly fulfilled orders. He wanted complete customer satisfaction. No argument with that! Yet!

The sales meeting I attended was more of an exchange of information on more efficient writing of reports, the importance of customer relations, dependability, markdowns of certain items, effective territorial coverage, and a not too informative discussion on the sale of tropical fish. I made a comment, to myself, that markdowns are usually accompanied with a reason, usually associated with a 'merchandizing' plan. There is a big difference between marketing, sales, and merchandizing. Oh, sure! One can read about the difference in textbooks, but later in this chapter you will read of a powerful example of just what the difference is, accompanied by a rational ground, or motive, to kick competitions' rear end.

So, if you'll excuse the expression, at *this* time I was a fish completely out of water. I knew the organizational structure was wrong. I knew the sales manager was not managing sales. I knew the sales personnel were wasting their time reporting to the home office every morning, but who would dare open his mouth with a 60% rate of market share. I knew the company was not selling many tropical fish. I couldn't answer why they spent so much money on a fish warehouse with no expected rate of return on capital expended. I couldn't answer any of my own questions on 60% of *what* business. I was full of a problem that I couldn't find a foundation for. I did not have the slightest idea of what kind of material was needed as a basis to start solving it.

I was beginning to think I was my own problem!

I reported to Dan and the word came back to keep trying.

As a representative for other companies, particularly aerospace, the market was known. The total dollars funded by Congress for a weapon's system was published in the budget or, in my case, AVIATION WEEK. An excellent business and marketing plan spelled out what percentage of the market a particular company was expected to capture based on knowledge of product, competition, price, quality, delivery, and a continued evaluation of a product's advancement in the state of the art. To me, the more flawless the original business and marketing plan the sooner misconceptions or mistakes will be discovered and corrected. Thus, a continuous drive to keep the company and its reputation number one in its field.

A marketing plan must be written and continually updated by experienced sales personnel who "have been there, done that." As far as I knew there was no business plan or marketing plan for the PET SUPPLY DIVISION.

One of the definitions of WAR, according to Webster, (*WEBSTER'S NINTH NEW COLLEGIATE DICTIONARY*), MERRIAM-WEBSTER, INC., Publishers, is "a struggle, or competition, between opposing forces for a particular end or result.

I consider the constant *corporate* campaign for capturing a defined market share—WAR. Therefore, in my view, in a sales territory, there is a never-ending 'competition between opposing forces for a particular end or result.' However, there can be no positive result for *any* campaign without a plan based on knowledge of the opposing sales force and the corporation they represent.

Carl Von Clausewitz in his classic, *ON WAR*, states, (modified somewhat by the author) "By the word 'information' we denote all the knowledge which we have of the enemy (sales force) and his country (corporation); therefore, in fact, the foundation of all our ideas and actions.

A great part of the information obtained in war is contradictory, a still greater part is false, and by far the greatest part is of a doubtful character. What is required of an officer (VP Sales) is a certain power of discrimination, which only knowledge of men and things and good judgement can give. The law of probability must be his guide. This is not a trifling difficulty even in respect of the first plans, which can be formed in the chamber outside the real sphere of war (capturing market share). But it is enormously increased when in the thick of war itself one report follows hard upon the heels of another; it is then fortunate if these reports, in contradicting each other, show a certain balance of probability, and thus themselves call forth a scrutiny. It is much worse for the inexperienced (salesperson) when accident does not render him this service. One report, then, supports another, confirms it, magnifies it, finishes off the picture with fresh touches of color, until necessity in urgent haste, forces from us a resolution which will soon be discovered to be folly; all those reports having been lies, exaggerations, errors, etc. In a few words, most reports are false, and the timidity (by reason of lack of knowledge, or information) of men acts as a multiplier of lies and untruths. Sales reports made up of lies and pure fictional guessing. This difficulty of seeing things correctly, which is one of the greatest sources of friction in war, and sales management, make things appear quite different from what was expected.

I saw myself as a vicarious Carl Von Clausewitz lecturing to a group of corporate executives, marketing management, and field sales personnel. What I sermonized about information in war bears distinct relevance to information in the market place.

However, the time had arrived to declare war on myself and use the cutting edge of my sword to solve my problem. My strategy could not continue with a cloud of doubt or lack of knowledge in reference to my responsibility. I needed intact, unblemished, beneficial information. I couldn't wait for Socrates to suggest to me information on 'the problem-solving criteria' as he did with advising on the book about Gell-Mann and Genda. I said to myself, "Simpson, you know you're under the gun, but trying to compress time is the antithesis of what is needed in this case. Your library at home has numerous books on marketing analysis and research. READ! STUDY! THINK! And TAKE YOUR TIME!" I also said, to myself, "The hell with the retailers the PET SUPPLY DIVISION sales personnel are calling on. I'll make arrangements with PACIFIC BELL to send me THE YELLOW PAGES from the Valley, all of Los Angeles County, Orange County, and San Diego County."

Well, I did just that! I had more books than an 'A' student in his fourth year of college. Reminds me of the story of a father telling his friend, "My son saved me a fortune in books this year." His friend asked, "How's that?" The father answered, "He flunked out last year!"

"Yeah," his friend said, I know what you mean. My daughter flunked sex education."

"Sex education? How'd that happen?"

"Damned if I know. Know anyone who has a used crib for sale?"

In any event, I started with the Valley and continued through San Diego. I opened the pages to the headings of PET SUPPLIES, TROPICAL FISH, and ACQUARIUM SUPPLIES. I randomly circled the names of retailers, numbered them from 1 through 150, and then placed the numbers on street maps I had obtained from AAA. I then started an exhaustive analysis. Also, sales calls had to be made for my aerospace clients, so every planned call for The PET SUPPLY DIVISION was a call around them. Thus my strategy allowed me to meet retailers; I knocked on doors from 6 to 7:30AM or 8 to 10PM. I cleaned a lot of bid cages or shoveled (small shovel) a mass amount of dog shit (thank God they didn't sell elephants). The proprietors' appreciated my being there and talked to me; and I listened. I learned the PET SUPPLY DIVISION sales personnel were not calling on a number of retailers that seemed to be doing a larger volume of business than the stores the division personnel were presently calling on. Some retailers were of limited square footage offering only pet supplies; there were others with large stores who sold both pet supplies and tropical fish. Still, others concentrated mostly on tropical fish. A male, in 95% of the cases, having raised tropical fish as an avocation nurtured his knowledge into a vocation. I didn't know it at the time but this would be one of the key factors that helped the PET SUPPLY DIVISION boom and turn key personnel, on specific occasions, from salesperson to merchandiser. Some bigger stores carried pet supplies, fish, *and* aquariums with the concomitant accessories such as pumps, filters, 'frog men' with air hoses, sand, multi-colored gravel, castles, and the ever-present sunken ship with treasures of silver, diamonds, and gold chalices embedded with rubies and sapphires. Tropical fish love to swim in that kind of environment.

I started to feel pretty good about what I was doing. I had a system, as crude as it was, and I was objective. And talking to owners early in the morning, having regular sales with aerospace purchasing, engineering, and quality control personnel meetings during the day, and at night cleaning up behind pets, was exhaustive.

In my studies I learned half the cost of running our economy is the cost of information. No other field offers such concentrated room for improvement, as does information analysis.

But the method or the way the information is gathered plays the most important role because it is the analysis of that information—the proper kinds of information—that leads to fruitful decision-making and planning.

The more detailed and exacting the information the better the decision-making! That is not to say, however, that just because you have the best information you are going to make perfect decisions and lay out an impeccable plan.

I have always believed an analysis is more important, and more full filling, than a market survey. An analysis allows the luxury of asking questions directly to the needs, and language, of the customer. If you speak the customers' language you will learn more about gathering information you hadn't considered. Remember Socrates explaining to me the difference between "knowledge of" and "knowledge about"? If you want to know about your customer and how the company can best serve him, conduct a marketing analysis. It allows more incisive query; this will develop into a more incisive business and marketing plan.

In a survey the questions are asked in a way to confirm or deny a premonition; it's to inspect or carefully consider that which is contemporary. I have been inspecting and carefully considering the PET SUPPLY DIVISION. I have "knowledge of" the retail aspects of the marketplace but I don't know "anything about" it. That is, enough to put together a plan—yet!

I mentioned in the past, and I'll mention the following again in the event "full of the problem" may be one of your first chapters.

When the Pittsburgh Steelers are scheduled to play the New York Giants, an assistant coach or scout does not go to an earlier scheduled game and survey his upcoming opponent from the stands. Oh, the Steelers may send a man to watch a game for "some specific purpose—or to inspect or carefully consider," but the *planning*—the *game plan*—is based on exchanging film so that an analysis can be made—"a separating or breaking up of the whole into its parts so as to find out"—how effective the pulling guard is, how the opponent defends against third and one, what formation defends against the shotgun, how effective the 4-3 or 3-4 is, etc. It is not one man watching a singular action; it is a coaching staff breaking down the action to find out and then coalescing their collective thoughts into an effective game plan. And if he plan breaks down early, the coach immediately makes the necessary changes to strengthen it. You see it every Sunday or Monday night during football season—the coach with his players gathered around working feverishly with a chalkboard. And the coach only has 60 minutes. Many sales managers today do not even have a basic plan because they do not realize or recognize the wealth of information that is available if they just get out of the office and talk to people—look at some film—use some chalk.

American businesses play their professional game every day. All sales management has to do is focus and capture the action. But management must remain professional—focus on the players—not what is going on in the stands.

No two films of football games are alike; no two game plans are alike.

But many companies are not sophisticated and my analysis had to, at times, be unsophisticated or I would scare salesmen into telling their clients that I was some head-shrinking weirdo who was going to effect their job and territory. It is a matter of using common sense; a matter of spending a lot of time in the territory.

About three and a half months into my 'term of agreement' with Mr. Martinelli and Dan, I had made about forty calls. I knew a number of facts but zero knowledge of the size of the market and in particular, by what category. The question, "Percentage of *what* market?" was driving me nuts!

Romeo! Romeo! (Socrates) Where art thou?

What the hell! It was 2pm on a hot Friday afternoon so I decided rather than fight the long, agonizing, freeway-jammed trip to my home in the desert, I would hit the driving range for an hour. After that bit of relaxation, I would *then* face the mental conflict of too much rubber and metal in not enough free space. The driving range was just off the east/west Hwy. 60 so I decided I would give the traffic a chance to "lighten up" and when it did so, I would pack my clubs and be on my way. Besides, I had to straighten out my drives. I was still angry with Socrates for telling me I had more ways to slice than a delicatessen counterman. What the hell does Socrates know about playing golf? If he hits the ball at all he probably hooks it. That way, he could spend his whole day with hookers, and his wife wouldn't even give it a second thought.

Anyhow, hitting a few golf balls would give me a chance to think! The history of a territory, if anything at all, is in the form of old sales reports or computer printout forms. The raw data remains the same, but man changes and I decided I would have to meet man, and woman, in his or her own environment.

However, I also knew that the 'historical aspect' was a rhetorical question because I remembered something about Barbara Tuchman. I would imagine you know of her; author of, *THE GUNS OF AUGUST, THE PROUD TOWER, A DISTANT MIRROR* and other books. In a speech, Mrs. Tuchman remarked about sociologists assembling masses of statistics versus, and, here are those words again, common sense. I researched the speech and found a particular thought that made a dramatic difference in my attitude on market analysis and sales.

To quote: "The commonest questions asked of historians by laymen is whether history serves a purpose? Is it useful? Can we learn from the lessons of history?

I, for one, think so! "When people want history to be utilitarian and to teach us lessons, that means they also want to be sure that it meets scientific standards. This, in my opinion it cannot do . . . to practice history as a science is sociology, an altogether different discipline which I personally find antipathetic—although I suppose the sociologists would consider that my deficiency rather than theirs. The sociologists plod along with their noses to the ground assembling masses of statistics in order to arrive at some obvious conclusion which a reasonably perceptive historian, not to mention a large part of the general public, knows anyway. They know it simply from observation—that social mobility is increasing, for instance, or that women have different problems from men. One is to wish they could just cut loose someday, lift up their heads and look at the world around them—or, as I would suggest, for sales managers to leave their desks and look at the territory around them.

I added that last thought about sales managers getting off their rear-ends. Look at the world around them—herein lies the key—but a marketing manager or salesman doesn't have to look at the world around him—he just has to observe the happenings in his own territory and absorb the wealth of information available for the asking. And who better to ask than the purchasing agents or engineers or manufacturing manager or store proprietors that think about and look every day for more effective and efficient ways of doing business. Is it not the marketing manager's job to match those needs with his company's capabilities and performance? Of course it is; and that is why incisive information gathered through an analysis of the territory provides rich reception of knowledge that flows with ideas on how to technically and economically structure a territory to produce its competitive best.

I am learning that analyzing a market is not in any way, "recondite, abstruse, nebulous, scary, obscure, or 'gut-wrenching'!" Much to the contrary! It is an opportunity to work with, learn from, brainstorm with, plan with, and understand man; friend and foe alike. It's just like planning a combat mission.

If history were a science, we should be able to get a grip on her, learn her ways, establish her patterns, know what will happen tomorrow. Why is it that we cannot? The answer lies in what I call the unknowable variable—namely, man . . .

If marketing analysis was a science—and many educated, textbook oriented, so-called sophisticated managers think it is—we should be able to 'get a grip on her, learn her ways, establish her patterns, know what will happen tomorrow.

But the unknown variable, namely man, plays too significant a role; and the less we know of him, the further awry our marketing analysis and plans will be. Ask Ford Motor Company about a car called EDSEL. Ask any sports manager about things gone wrong that were initiated according to the 'game plan'."

If I were a manager of sales, I would fundamentally understand that human beings are the nexus of *any* territory. Their record of performance, and behavior, is the key to territorial performance and behavior. A computer cannot generate this data, and sitting at you desk won't do it. You do not necessarily have to practice history. Practice *performance*.

I was speaking recently with a lady real estate agent from Colorado Springs about a problem—a problem of selling the last 'six big houses' in an exclusive area of the community. She had all sorts of data—computer printouts about what to sell the potential clients—square footage, closet space, storage, sizes of fireplaces, location and conveniences of new kitchen equipment, etc.—all the data that competitive real estate salespersons would also present. She was in a dilemma because she didn't have anything 'different to sell.' I asked her how many homes she had sold in that area, and when she answered "eight" I told her, "You have at least eight times eight more reasons for a successful sale than you competitors." She was incredulous, and asked, "What gives you that idea; you don't know anything about the Colorado Springs real estate market." I replied, "Your right, but I do know people and if I were you, I would go directly to the eight owners you have sold in the past and ask the woman of the household to have lunch with you, say, at the Garden of the Gods Club; or invite yourself over for a tea. Over a cup of tea I would learn from these women a whole new data bank—what they like about Colorado Springs; what its geographical position means to their travels; the airline and bus service, the neighbors, the churches, schools, and libraries; also women's club and golf and tennis facilities; postal service; maid service and babysitters; and fifteen things she liked about the house you sold her—heating and sunlight, view, ease of cleaning, and not the *size* of the family room but how *she* fixed it up—and how *she* decorated and panted and landscaped. Also ask her how her decorators were and how she liked the gardener; and on, and on.

Also, how many of your competitors belong to the "Garden of the Gods' Club?"

My friend said, "I don't think any of them do."

"Well," I said. "I think you are letting a particularly excellent asset slip through your sales presentation. Why not take your potential homebuyers to the club for tea and offer them an incentive. If they buy the home, part of the package will be a year's social membership to the club."

Now she didn't have just *space* and *size* to sell; my lady real estate salesperson now had a new dimension, something I would call 'aesthetic authenticity'; she could speak with truth about other refined and cultured dimensions in addition to what 'brick and mortar' offered. She offered a home with new, well-proportioned beauty to a family's living enjoyment. No, I don't have a real estate license. But I do have common sense and I constantly search for wisdom from the minds of others. I also didn't have real estate license when I used 'the lessons of history' on a condominium project in Denver. It was completely in the doldrums with real estate agents sitting around waiting to talk to unqualified buyers. Nothing was selling at the time. I closed the on-site sales office and stopped all advertising in the newspapers. That type of sales and advertising made the real estate firm I was consulting to just like every other real estate firm. I didn't want to be like every other real estate company. But with a new sales plan in effect we sold the place out! However, that's another story.

My friend sold all the houses.

After practicing my golf, I started east on Hwy. 60 and hit traffic. And it was at a *complete* stop! I didn't move for fifteen minutes. I wasn't in a traffic *jam*; I was in traffic peanut butter—LAURA SCUDDERS Old Fashioned jam—the kind with the oil on top where you have to stir it at about ½ rpm; I finally started to move about that fast. My car was transformed into a turtle. After about another ten minutes we started to move a little faster. I was doing at least 15 mph.

I was settling in to a steady pace when the reason for the tie-up was revealed. The California Transportation Authority was building a cloverleaf tying our east/west California Hwy.60 into the north/south Interstate Hwy.15. I had been held up by a clean up crew! As I passed by the crew, I noticed they were starting to put their tools in a small warehouse; clearing the roadway for the weekend. I started thinking how the north/south Hwy. 15, by tying in the 60, and farther north the east/west Interstate Hwy.10, was to be southern California's main artery to Las Vegas. All of a sudden I stopped thinking! I suddenly started talking to myself! And then I yelled, "I GOT IT! I GOT IT! I GOT IT! I have the answer," I said. "I have the answer! To the PET SUPPLY DIVISION problem! And it will work! I'm sure it will work!"

I pulled off the road into an area giving me freedom from any on rushing traffic. I had filled myself full of a problem and now I was going to mentally review what got me excited about solving my dilemma. "OK!" I said to myself. "We have the problem of defining market share. No one at the division has any idea. They say they are getting 40 or 50%. It has been my problem to answer the question, '40 or 50% of *what* market'?"

I continued thinking and taking notes. I have been cleaning dog crap and papering birdcages while talking to the proprietors. They have been talking to me but I didn't have anything incisive to ask and it was neither my position as a rep, or my business, to ask what their gross sales were. But just now, as I passing the 60/15 interchange and I saw men putting their tools away in a warehouse, the thought struck me. I'll go back to these men and ladies plus about 100 more store owners and tell them we are thinking about building a warehouse in their geographical area and ask the question, 'What do you think you're gross sales will be in three years?' And I'll bet myself ten bucks that they will answer, "Well, 'right now,' or 'this fiscal year which ended such and such,' or 'so far this year,' we are doing, or did XXXX dollars worth of business." It fits in perfect! I couldn't ask them a question like that before but the word warehouse is the key. Damn! And it was Socs who told me to read about Gell-Mann and Genda. EUREKA! And if I didn't stop to practice my golf swing I would have never seen those men putting away their tools.

"EUREKA! A word associated with Archimedes. It means 'to discover'. He discovered a method for determining the purity of gold, or something like that. The story as told is, he was asked by Hiero II, a Greek Sicilian ruler, to determine whether his crown was pure gold or was alloyed with silver. Archimedes was, like me, perplexed. He filled himself full of the problem. Then one day, observing the overflow of water in his bath, he suddenly realized that since gold is more dense (i.e., has more weight per volume) than silver, a given weight of gold represents a smaller volume than an equal weight of silver. A given weight of gold would, therefore, displace less water than an equal weight of silver. Delighted at his discovery, he ran home without his clothes, shouting 'Eureka,' which means 'I have found it.' He found that Hiero's crown displaced more water than an equal weight of gold, thus showing that the crown had been alloyed with silver or another metal less dense than gold. Hiero II was one angry ruler.

"Eureka! In this case, I will increasing the range of one's information or understanding. I will now be able to write a marketing and business plan based on the range of information that will be coming directly by those most effected. Think of how client and I will progress. Progress is in the nature of things. But one must—what?"

"Be the flight lead."

"Correct!" Socrates, once told me, "not only does each man, or woman with the desire to lead, advance from day to day, but mankind as a whole constantly progresses in proportion as the universe gets older. The essence of man as a rational being, as some historian put it, is that he develops his potential capacities by accumulating the experience and their information of past generations. What did we say was most important at the beginning of each of the trilogy's?"

"That a lot of our learned discussions will be based on philosophy and the lessons of history!"

I was thinking about my life, since placing that collect call—what—almost thirty plus years ago—has been characterized by luck or good fortune. Socrates is my wingman; a sidekick devoid of any hypocrisy or pretense. Here I am, thinking about a close friend who was possibly the greatest teacher of all time, yet man enough to follow the Sophists' (professional teachers) lead in turning away from the study of the cosmos and concentrate on the case of the human being. But unlike the way the Sophists discoursed about the human being, Socrates wanted to base all argumentation on objectively valid definitions. To say, 'Man is the measure,' is saying very little if one does not know what 'man' is. Socrates' discourse moved in two directions—outward, to objective definitions, and inward, to discover the inner person, the soul, which for Socrates, was the source of all truth. Such a search was not to be conducted at a weekend lecture, but was the quest of a lifetime.

I read somewhere—don't remember where or when—that having an older personal or mental company is like relaxing under the shade of a tree on a hot summer day. I'm a lucky man.

The next morning, before breakfast, I called Dan and told him of my discovery. It took us about an hour to determine what I could tell the owners, or managers, of the stores without lying about the timing or location of the warehouse. I told the men and women the company was thinking about better distribution with several service centers around Los Angeles, but it depended on an incisive analysis of growth.

After breakfast I got on the phone to a number of proprietors I had previously called upon. All of them recognized me right away and were all very convivial. A compendium of the conversions over the phone is as follows:

"Good morning Mr. Such and Such, this is Jack Simpson from PET DEALERS and I . . . . "

Oh! yes, Jack, you're the one doing the marketing analysis that helped me clean up my shop. By the way, no other salesperson has ever volunteered to do what you did. What can I do for you?"

"I was glad to assist you. Mr. Such and Such, I had a thought yesterday and I think it's a good idea. But, in order to make it a practical one, I need your thoughts and some specific information. The added knowledge will help PET DEALERS do a better job of planning to serve you and other shop owners. The idea involves a warehouse. Let me say first we want to be honest as there is nothing yet in concrete, but if PET DEALERS constructed a warehouse in your geographical area because of our cognizance of growth, what kind of business do you think you will be doing three years from now?"

"Well, let's see, you have seen my store. Right now, I'm doing close to my forecast—about $65,000 per year, so in three years I'll certainly be doing #80,000 or more."

"YOU HAVE SEEN MY STORE," he said. My mind was racing! "Therein lays the answer," I said to myself as I thanked him. I could now scrutinize the nature, amount, and quality of merchandise, pet and aquarium supplies, and tropical fish. Combining this with knowing the gross sales of the store combined with a reasonable forecast would help solve the problem of "getting my arms" around gross sales and answer the question for PET DEALERS, "60% of what sales." The owners of the other three stores that I telephoned that morning, all answered my warehouse thought in the same manner—"Right now, I'm doing $100,000 so in three years I hope to be doing—mmmmm, let's see, $130 to $140,000. As you know, it depends on the increase in population and competition. But hell, Mr. Simpson, you know that!" (PET DEALERS wasn't calling on him).

I said' "Yes, Sir, I realize that and I guess part of my analysis will be finding out who is building what and where. Most likely I'll have to keep my eye open for information on shopping malls. Your store is located in one. It evidently helps."

"Of course it does." He laughed as he said, "People get their fish from the super market to eat and then stop in buy some from me as a present for the kids."

A mamma and papa store, located along a boulevard, were doing $40,000 and expected to reach $50,000, but as they said, "The store is paid for, all the kids are out of school, we watch our pennies, we're happy, and our home is upstairs." (PET DEALERS was getting 55% of their business.)

The next was a shocker! A man who raised tropical fish as an avocation was now in charge of {hired by three doctors) a tropical fish enterprise doing $400,000 a year and expected the gross to grow to $650,000 to $700,000. And PET DEALERS wasn't calling on him.

I was excited! My mind was racing and my left hand was scribbling. I had the beginnings of a whole marketing, sales, advertising, merchandising, transportation, training, and communication plan in front of me. Also, another thought fell into place. How to increase the sales of fish and capture a specific return on capital invested. Can you imagine? Three men, working for California transportation in an occupation diametrically opposed to selling dog soap or tropical fish, happened to be putting their tools away in a warehouse. In that paradox, was the key to PET DEALER'S financial growth.

"Jack," I said to myself, "You know the old saying; 'LUCK FAVORES THOSE WHO ARE WELL PREPARED!'"

I am going to follow my original plan, that is calling on the pet supply owners in the early mornings and evenings surrounded around engineering sales calls on my aerospace accounts. I have about 140 left now, so I expect to have a business and marketing plan ready for briefing to Mr. Martinelli and Dan, plus the President of PET SUPPLIES, in about twelve weeks.

REPORT TO MR. MARTINELLI, DAN,
AND THE PRESIDENT OF PET DEALERS

Three months had passed; I was ready. I had made 141 more analysis calls that covered Southern California's geographical area from the San Fernando Valley north of Los Angeles down to San Diego. I also made fifteen calls in the San Francisco territory and had spent time with their sales manager. Sharp man! A former car salesman! But his hands were tied because the President of PET DEALERS insisted the sales managers' report to the warehouse managers who reported to the President.

Every proprietor shared with me their growth plans in dollars based on their gross for the present time. I think the better way to examine and understand the knowledge obtained, and what decisions I made based on that knowledge, can best be grasped by comprehending the accompanying, rather simple X-Y chart.

I was invited by Martinelli to make my presentation to the San Francisco satellite office of PET DEALERS. I had been keeping in constant touch with Dan and had mentioned I was going to suggest some changes in management and sales responsibilities and accountabilities. I said to Dan, "I am going to suggest a new organizational chart based on the needs of the customer and growth of PET CEALERS, not on the President's idea of what an organizational chart should look like." That's a mistake many managers make; they put an organization chart together before they know the needs of the customer. An organizational chart should be as functionally close to, or supported, in the needs of the customer. It should belong to the customer as a utilitarian tool stressing the value of reality. "You know the adage, or brief statement of principle, 'value added',' Dan. No one should be in an organization unless their effort can be directly associated with adding value of product *for* the customer. The company mans an organization chart *for* the customer. Assigning an employee without up to date, well-refined responsibilities, is a move toward disaster. I was in the Air Corps and USAF. They speak of 'Table of Organization.' It's an organization to support a particular effort in war. In the theatre of combat operations, if it is not manned properly, people get killed. If you want to get killed in business, have an organizational chart a drawing of boxes to suit an executive's ego."

I also told Dan we needed a Director of Sales with the sales managers of both the Los Angeles and San Francisco offices reporting to him. I had chosen the Sales Manager from the San Francisco office because as a former car salesman, married, two children, was settled down and he was anxious to try something new. And I had some new ideas. Another thought was a draw against commission; as a car salesman he was familiar with what I had in mind. The sales personnel would not be put in a financial bind because they all financial obligations but I now knew what their territory should produce in gross dollars. They were going to be forced to call on the most productive accounts. It costs just as much time, and energy, to make a sales call on a store grossing $50,000 as it does $250,000 and more. With freedom of choice and an incentive on total sales, it would not take a salesperson long to define his own territory rather than the sales manager doing his thinking for him. And PET DEALERS and the sales personnel would make more money.

The meeting in San Francisco was important so I decided to fly up the night before, settle into a hotel room close to PET DEALERS, prepare myself for the presentation, AND, be on time for the meeting. Even in Los Angeles, if I had an early meeting in the Valley (I was living in an apartment in Newport Beach during the week) or San Diego, I always left the night prior to the assembly so as to be refreshed, prepared, and on time. The most unfavorable words in *any* person's vocabulary are, "Sorry I'm late!"

When I went to dinner, I took the map and the 'X-Y' chart out of my briefcase. I leaned the map up against two water glasses and then opened the 30"x30" chart and laid it on the table. I wanted to review a dramatic disclosure of PET DEALERS' supply business not formerly known or realized. My coverage was from the San Fernando Valley all the way south through LA, Long Beach, Orange County, down through Oceanside continuing south to San Diego.

The 'X' axis is numbered from 1 to 150 with the number 1 at the top-150 the bottom. The numbers represent to number of sales analysis calls. The 'Y' axis; the numbers, representing anticipated gross sales in three years, start at $50,000 and out to $750,000. I looked at the overall chart," Stores 1 through 12 represent an average, in three years, of $545,000 each or $6 and 1/2 million; 98% tropical fish and associated provisions—aquariums, pumps, etc. PET DEALERS' sales personnel have not called on them. Now the next 13 through 50! Thirty seven stores with an average forecast of $395,000 or a total of $14 and ½ million! That's a year! They represent 65 to 70% tropical fish and the other pet supplies. And we are only calling on about 30% of 'em. I looked at the next index, or group. The stores numbering 50 to 100 are averaging, or will average in three years, $220,000, times 50 stores represents $11,000,000. And guess what! PET DEALERS is getting less than 40%

of the business but it is mostly in pet supplies; no fish. And in stores number 100 to 150 PET DEALERS is writing orders for more than 55%, but in retail outlets (of pet supplies only) averaging less than $100,000. So what does that tell me?

It tells PET DEALERS is capturing 50% of a $5,625,000 market with the average number of stores times the average gross, what is the marketing and business plan for the average 32 million a year market that the company is hardly touching? Also, how did the company arrive at the decision to purchase and warehouse tropical fish without knowing the potential market and what return could be expected on capital expended?

My strength in analysis really started when Socrates told me to read about Gell-Mann. He came along just when I needed him. I must put Genda in there too! But I think Socrates hit it on the head earlier when we spoke of fate—that things in general are believed to come to be as they are, or events to happen as they do. It's like opportunity to me. It's being prepared to grab it as it passes by or rears up in the form of a favorable circumstance.

At the meeting in the Board Room in the morning, when I asked the two questions concerning the marketing plan and the tropical fish purchase, there was silence—and I mean dead silence. I didn't want to embarrass anyone but I wasn't being paid to speak softly or carry a limp stick. So I continued and said, "This is what PET DEALERS must do." I didn't say, "What I thought they should do."

I continued, "I'll take the top twelve and write out a sales and business plan, with a specific advertising plan, with the thought of enlarging the number to fifty. The first thing is to face reality! PET DEALERS is losing a potential of $27 million a year as outlined on my limited analysis; information that is fact! There is no reason why, if done properly, you gentlemen can't capture at least 13 to 14 million. I am going to suggest that PET DEALERS buy out two minimum gross, tropical fish retailers. Why? Because these are men whose avocations changed into vocations! These men would be perfect salesmen; they can talk the language of the customer, they would quickly understand their needs, they would gain their customers' trust. And most importantly, PET DEALERS could tie in an advertising/merchandising program to expand their sales base, in this particular category. Merchandising is having the right fish, salt water and fresh water, at the right retailer, at the right time, to the right customer, at the right price. And speaking of timing, PET DEALERS can turn those two salesmen into merchandisers with incentive advertising on particular weekends."

First, let's me assume that management agrees with my plan to literally buy out the two men. They agree! We reach a fair price! After orientation with PET DEALERS' operating procedures and familiarity with all personnel, they will be assigned 20 stores each. They take a month or so to develop a rapport with the owners. Hell, they speak their language from first hand experience not only from running their store but what it takes to be an effective salesman. If a company wants to hire a good salesperson, talk to a buyer.

These men know how to accept responsibility to increase orders for the fish and concomitant supplies. They can set their own schedule as to needs, follow the ordering procedure, *except*, no reporting to the office in person every day. Let them call in their orders to an order desk. The organizational change will make the warehouse manager (of tropical fish) responsible for getting the orders delivered correctly and on time. This will no longer be the sales manager's responsibility. The salesmen will also commit to a sales plan, in writing, giving management a fair appraisal of what they think they can do, in gross sales, the first three or four months. They know a retailer is doing a certain gross sales. I have already given the dollar amount to them. What percentage can they capture if PET DEALERS supports them with price, quality, delivery, and effective communications? Also, no more cars; they will be driving station wagons. Why? This is where the merchandising/advertising plan comes into to being.

We all know merchandising is having the right product, etc., etc. First, understand this is just a program for the 40 stores; it will give us the company a chance to measure the effect of the advertising/merchandising program; the advertising will be local complemented by handouts. The salesmen, through the knowledge of the proprietors, will be told what are the best fish to have available at the particular time—Easter, Christmas, 4th of July, summer vacation—whatever. Advertising will stress the particular species of fish for on sale, and bargain prices for aquariums, pumps, etc. The salesmen become merchandisers by having product in their station wagons to start the weekend and then continually re-supply by driving back and forth from the warehouse to the proprietor delivering product; right time, cost, and customer. During the same period of time, they also gauge the effectiveness of the advertising. In my opinion it is a great way to learn the 'conduct of developing a territory' by understanding proper strategy, and tactics. Von Clausewitz talks all about it in his book—pages 172 and 173. Clausewitz says, "The division into tactics and strategy is now in almost general use, and every one knows tolerably well under which head to place any single fact, without knowing very distinctly the grounds on which the classification is founded. But when such divisions are blindly adhered to in practice, they must have some deep root. We have searched for this root, and we might say that it is just the usage of the majority that has brought us to it."

According to our classification, therefore, tactics is the theory of the use of military forces in combat. Strategy is the theory of the use of combats for the objet of the War.

This is where the word synergy pops up. "Tactics, I said to myself, "is the use of trained sales forces in combat for market share. Strategy is the use of management and sales personnel theory, or marketing and business plan for the object of the war.

I thought of Socs. PET DEALERS', through information and an effective marketing analysis, gained its present 'deep root' through knowledge *about*—not knowledge of—but knowledge *about* their customer and his needs. I didn't know it at the time but I now see our strategy as the use of proprietors' knowledge providing us (PET DEALERS) the tactics for use of our sales personnel in combat thereby gaining a significant percentage of sales in the territory. I am not saying everything works exactly this way, but I will say, through adhering to the concept—thinking through the importance of what strategy and tactics means to business will put a company far ahead of its competition. And what comes next? A marketing and business plan; along with mistakes that will be made! So what do you do? You write it out again! And then you continually fine-tune until the combination of word power and manpower has a rate of closure on your competition at MACH 2.

And then it's time to really get serious; you ask, and listen, and plan, and change, and test, and strategize, and try again. And it's OK to fail because your momentum will keep you ahead of your rival—your antagonist. As a sales manager you'll feel like General Patton. He loved combat and he knew how to win. How? Because he was a *student* of history! He read, and absorbed, and studied, and planned, and tested, and learned from mistakes, and pushed forward and never looked back. And he WON!

On the 701st page of Stanley P. Hirshon's, *GENERAL PATTON, A SOLDIER'S LIFE,* Hirshon wrote, "In evaluating Patton one fact stands out. By any standards he was an extraordinary tactical commander, perhaps, as Admiral Hall suggested, 'The greatest master of quick tactical movement that World War II developed.' Among his great assets were his imagination and his ability to visualize the entire battlefield."

Patton was a voracious reader of history and empathetically lived with Ulysses S. Grant's running the Confederate batteries at Vicksburg and George Washington's crossing the Delaware at Trenton. He fought alongside the Greeks, Alexander at Tyre, and the Roman legionnaires. No one cared more for his soldiers than George Patton— always out in the cold and rain with them, seeing that they had the best food and medical attention; listening, listening, listening, listening, talking their language. I am learning from Gell-Man and Genda. I am taking what Socrates and philosophy and the lessons of history have taught me, and applying the knowledge to free enterprise.

"Well, everything I have said makes sense; good judgement on my part, and it's a practical way to launch the company's plan for growth. Notice I say "launch"—like a warship being launched. After building, by blueprint, the ship, after sliding down the skids (or ways) is suitable to float in a harbor. But many months of additional work must be done to make it fully capable of fulfilling its mission profile. Then, it must pass rigid sea trials before taking the war to the enemy. What I have learned indicates the company, if they agree with you, will do the same thing. I will hand them the blueprint, they will launch their salesmen, they will use my first idea for the marketing/ advertising plan, put it to trial, learn from mistakes, try again and then continue to apply it to all segments of the California territory. The sales war will be taken to the enemy and PET DEALERS will develop into a powerful company."

Now, when looking at the lower half the 'X' axis and the left end of the 'Y' axis, the company is spending a lot of money for a minimum return. Sure, the salesmen are garnering 50%, and I give them credit, but sales management, in the meanwhile, has let the greater volume of business pass them by. It's simple! The sales manager was too pre-occupied with the responsibility of delivery that shouldn't have been his, and his men are far too structured with rules and regulations that they are not given the opportunity to think on their own. For example, one store was selling $400,000 in tropical fish while the salesman was calling on a 'Mom and Pop' within a half mile away. That is because, as I understand, the sales manager was proud to tell everyone he always knew where his salesmen where. The first thing that hits me is the cost of sales. The company was spending the same amount of dollars to capture 50% of $50,000 while $400,000 was being ignored.

So, I will have to sell management on the idea of covering the 'Moms and Pops' by inside sales and mail order. It just costs too much money to put a salesperson on the street these days. Of course, the sales personnel who have devoted years of time and energy to develop a personal rapport should continue to personally call, but their time cannot interfere with their responsibility for their other territory's growth.

All of management was stunned by my report. So much time and energy and money wasted over a period of three years let alone the lack of planning for the return on capital invested in tropical fish. The organizational chart didn't even make sense. Accountabilities and responsibilities, as defined by the chart, deterred growth rather than complement it. There was no marketing plan; no business plan. The sales manager's zeal and pride in knowing where his salesmen were all the time allowed a multi-million dollar growth in sales pass PET DEALERS like a jet passing MODEL T Ford. And the biggest sin, was allowing competition to get a stronger foothold when it shouldn't have happened.

My in-depth marketing analysis changed all that! Sales personnel were assigned a specific territory with a specific number of stores with a specific knowledge of what the territory was producing in gross sales. The salesperson was directed to capture, to start with, his or her 60% only now it was 60% of hundreds of thousands of dollars instead of $50,000 or $80,000. And, in time, with the right advertising and merchandizing assistance, it was deemed to capture 65 or 70% of a half of a million. With the right incentives and commission on sales, the sales personnel could make thousands of dollars more a year. The two tropical fish salesmen got rich AND taught the others how to sell. I don't have to go into details, but with the new transportation, the marketing and business plans, the beneficial communication links to customer and home office, the advertising, the merchandizing, the electronic placing of orders, the professional use of the salespersons time, incentives, and recognition of actual growth, everything worked out very well.

What made the PET DEALER'S problem work out so well?

Part of 'getting into' or filling myself 'full of' the PET DEALERS' problem was looking to history.

Let me talk about von Clausewitz."

In his Book One, *ON THE NATURE OF WAR*, von Clausewitz wrote a chapter entitled INFORMATION IN WAR. I wanted to learn his view on the importance of information and how it should be handled.

What did I learn?

I learned we should trust only certain information; that we must always be suspicious. During our first sales meeting I was suspicious of the sales manager's ability to grasp the over-all situation he was in. He was acting just like a man who "sold the most" of something without analyzing how he did it. It wasn't his ability to sell as much as being in the right place at the right time—Orange County. He didn't understand the pure responsibility of a manager of sales. He shouldn't have allowed himself to be reporting to the warehouse manager. Warehousing is after the fact; sales management should prepare before the fact.

Clausewitz also said that most reports are false, and the timidity of men acts as a multiplier of lies and untruths. I didn't think that to be true in the case of PET DEALERS but one must consider a very good point as to why a marketing analysis 'in the language of the customer' is so important. No man or woman is going to present you with an untruth if he understands the reason for the analysis represents potential gain.

Something else! When you hear the words, 'We hold these truths to be self evident that all men are created equal, etc., etc. what goes through the readers mind?"

We all know those words are from the DECLARATION OF INDEPENDENCE; Thomas Jefferson's words. Probably one of, if not, *the* most profound documents ever written by man!

How about the MAGNA CARTA? From history I learned it is the most famous document of British constitutional history; issued by King John under compulsion from the barons and the church. The barons rebelled, but they weren't declaring independence from the king. They only wanted to get some relief from taxes and other devious tricks used by John for underhanded purposes.

The MAGNA CARTA was basically an agreement while the DECLARATION OF INDEPENDENCE was just that—a bold announcement of breaking away from English rule even while a couple of hundred or more of British ships were banging away at New York and landing thousands of troops. I mean, the DECLARATION started with the words, 'When in the course of human events, it becomes necessary to dissolve the political bands that have connected them with another—' Corporations have human events too! Always be prepared to dissolve whatever bands deemed necessary. Politics in some companies are so deeply imbedded it would take a tank car of H_2SO_4 to dissolve.

But I didn't bring up the above subjects to play a word game of discursiveness. I want to speak of the lessons of history and pass on to you something I didn't know.

Did you know that Jefferson borrowed readily from his own previous writings, particularly from a recent draft for a new Virginia constitution?"

Yes! Jefferson also drew from a declaration of rights for Virginia, which appeared in the Pennsylvania Evening Post on June 12. It had been drawn up by George Mason, on of the most affluent of the colonial planners, who wrote that "All men are equally free and independent, and have certain inherent natural rights—among them are enjoyment of life and liberty.' And then there was a pamphlet written by the Pennsylvania delegate James Wilson! It was published in Philadelphia in 1774, that declared, 'All men are, by nature equal and free: no one has the right to authority over another without his consent; all lawful government is founded on the consent of those who are subject to it.'

What have I based *my* thoughts and conversations on? Research, Gell-Man's thoughts, what I learned from philosophy, and the lessons of history! I am not saying that Jefferson, or Mason, or Wilson, is going to jump out of the walls and make me a pre-sager of things to come. Their history of performance does, however, offer me a chance to empathetically THINK and WRITE (a business plan) along with them.

But then Mason, Wilson, John Adams—no less than Jefferson, were, as they all appreciated, drawing on long familiarity with the contribution of the seeds for later development of the works of the English and Scottish writers and philosophers. We are talking John Locke, David Hume, Francis Hutcheson, Plato, Milton, Aristotle, Thucyydides, or such English poets as Defoe. If they can do it, why can't I? Who says they won't give me seeds for later development!

They were also very familiar with Cicero. I was wondering, at first, where Socrates was taking me with this. But I understand, now, where they were coming from. Marcus Tullius Cicero, was one of the greatest Roman orators; famous also as a politician and philosopher. His philosophical works include *De amicita*, about friendship, *De oficiis*, on duty, and another on a dialogue of the good. You can thank him, in part, for the three parts of your government—executive, bicameral legislative, and an independent judiciary. Here we are seeing, again, what history has to offer.

Cicero also said something that Jefferson grabbed on to:

"The people's good is the highest law."

So think about this. Jefferson took all of what history had to offer. He thought, and cogitated, and deliberated, and meditated, and reflected. And then he sat down and wrote, and brought forth a full and formal declaration announcing the separation of the Thirteen Colonies from Great Britain and making then into the United States. The CONTINENTAL CONGRESS had produced the most important of all-American historical documents.

What made Jefferson's work surpassing was the grace and eloquence of expression. Jefferson had done superbly and in minimum time.

I have something in mind as I write this. I am thinking that the CONTINENTAL CONGRESS and Jefferson's immortal DECLARATION gave the reader, and others, and me, a solid foundation for freedom of private business to organize and operate for profit in a competitive atmosphere without interference from government beyond regulatory principles. What bothers me, and I am seeing it in today's time, is too many men and women do not appreciate what time, and meditating, and reflecting, combined with the beautiful thoughts of what philosophy has in waiting, and willing, to present to us. Philosophy says, "Here! Take this; it's a gift from all of us with our collective experiences." Without understanding that, we are missing the opportunity of a lifetime. They are missing the chance to bloom like a bouquet of beautiful flowers in mind, leadership, pleasurable communication, and success. And in not offering it to themselves, they miss the occasion to offer it to their employees.

Think of this! If an entrepreneur learns to speak the language and needs of his customers, why can't he, or she, learn to speak the language and needs of employees?

Synergy! Defined by Webster as 'working together"—"combined action or operation"!

And just think! All we have to do is gather great books like flowers, arrange them in a common sense order, read them, and then THINK about how you, he or she, will bloom like the flower you just picked. Start leading, enjoy pleasurable, truthful, dynamic ideas with yourself and employees, and grow to offer a better and more powerful nexus to the dynamics of free enterprise.

A MARKETING & BUSINESS PLAN

The following is an actual marketing and business plan the author wrote to the senior executive for a company that had been in business for a number of years. It was determined by my marketing background, study, filling myself "full of the problem", experience in market analysis, and common sense, or as Samuel Smiles says, "common experience wisely improved." The analysis was complemented by Mr. Banker; his technical expertise was invaluable.

We learned the company had been selling to the wrong customer for years.

TO: John Banker, Senior Vice President
FROM: John J. Simpson
SUBJECT: A MARKETING PLAN OUTLINE

John, clearly, pulling together a marketing plan requires a great deal of time and effort. And by issuing EFI's formal blueprint for the business, you are exposing yourself to some substantial personal risks; that is, the marketing plan provides top management with a yardstick against which the plan's originators may be judged.

BENEFITS OF MARKETING PLANNING
The Need for Businesses to Plan

Provides a clear marketing action plan for the coming year.

Establishes priorities.

Sounds a call to action to other departments that must support marketing programs.

Sets forth measurable business goals against which marketing performance may be judged.

Establishes a base for follow-up planning.

Enables top management to examine the assumptions behind the profit and loss statement.

Provides a vehicle whereby the marketing department can sell new and innovative programs to top management.

Provides for marketing continuity during personnel changes.

Forces a discussion of contingencies and unknowns.

Enables corporate planners to test the marketing plan for consistency with corporate strategy.

Obstacles to Marketing Planning

Lack of needed information.

Forecasting problems.

Problems in coordination.

Lack of commitment by top management.

Time pressures.

The Organization

How does EFI conduct self-examination? Clearly, there are a variety of levels that account for vital sections of a complete analysis. The financial picture of a company is obviously a factor that has the potential to alter marketing planning dramatically.

The financial resources and capabilities, as given in the income statement and balance sheet, should be examined first. What are the company's gross and net profits? Are there sufficient available resources from cash flow, liquid assets, or borrowing capabilities to support the marketing program? What is the status of current operating facilities? Is there sufficient plant capacity? Are there sufficient quality control methods? What are capital equipment needs?

An examination of EFI should include an evaluation of perceived competitive strengths and weaknesses of each of the following items versus the known competition:

Product and product quality.

Breadth of product line.

Delivery.

Prices.

Sales force capability.

Advertising.

Sales promotion.

Service capabilities.

MARKET ANALYSIS

Market Size

Market potential.

Market forecast.
Sales potential.
Sales forecast.
Market share.
Determining market size.
Sources of Information for Market Size Analysis
Analysis of Market Size
Total size, growth, trends.
Analysis of components.

BUYING PROCESS

Distribution channels

The marketing plan should include a diagram of the channels of distribution showing the evolution of an EFI sale and percentage of total sales going through each channel—roll bond, weld overlay, dataclad, dynaclad.

The incisively defined customer purchase process.
Who is involved in the purchase process?
What criteria do people use to select EFI's product?
What EFI product is the customer aware of?

Market analysis should include a measurement of consumer awareness of various products. If the consumer is unaware of a product, it indicates a need for heavy advertising and sales promotion. Trade magazines often conduct awareness studies for industrial products. In reference to sales promotion and advertising, EFI learned from a meeting that the perception of explosive cladding is available only through DuPont and there has been no way to contact EFI. Also, the perception that cladding takes too long and costs too much.

DEVELOPING MARKETING STRATEGIES
Target Market Selection and Market Segmentation

Selecting a target market is perhaps the most crucial decision the marketing manager must make. Choice of a target market has implications for the product, which must be designed to meet customer needs; the distribution strategy, which must provide for making the product available at locations and at terms acceptable to the target customer; pricing, which must be consistent with the target customer's economic and psychological needs; and promotion strategies, which provide for delivery of the right message to the right people at the right time.

Examination must be made of petroleum, chemical, pulp and paper, and pharmaceutical combined with regional (Houston, West Coast, Gulf States, North East, etc.) potential by market analysis.

Plans for a Sales Campaign

Promotion the benefits of Dynaclad directly to the customer should be implemented. Examples:

The one-on-one sales call on the management of Red Hill Geothermal, Inc. whereby EFI could be willing to accept the responsibility of the purchase order. This for reasons of expeditious delivery of material thereby keying on time delivery.

Accepting responsibility for roll forming—re: Benicia Fab.

Direct sales presentations to the customer on benefits of cladding versus weld overlay—re: IOCO, Chevron, Burnabe, and TEL.

Product Benefits

IMPLEMENTING THE MARKETING PLAN

Organizing for the Marketing Planning Process

Functional organization.
Geographic organization.
Product management organization.
Determining responsibility.

Can the person accomplish the task directly, or does he or she have subordinates who can do it?

Is the task sufficiently important so the person will give it the appropriate attention?

Does the person have the time available to accomplish the activity?

Does the person have experience with successfully completing similar activities?

Factors Influencing Implementation of Marketing Programs:

Recognizing and diagnosing a problem.
Assessing the level where the problem exists.
Implementing plans.
Evaluating results.

Is there a clear marketing theme, strong marketing leadership, and a culture that promotes and provokes excellence?

Is there sub-functional soundness in the company's marketing activities? Are the selling, distribution, pricing, and advertising functions well managed?

Do the marketing programs of EFI integrate and deliver marketing activities in a focused fashion to various customer groups?

How good is marketing management at interacting with other marketing related staff, such as sales; other functions in the company; and the customers and trade?

What monitoring efforts are used by management to inform itself about not only its own moves, but also customer and prospect groups?

How good is management at allocating time, money, and people to marketing tasks?

How is management organized, both to do marketing tasks and to deal with customer interactions? Are there easily accessed organizational doors open to the customers and the trade?

THE BUSINESS PLAN: WHY AND HOW

Having lost sight of our objectives, we redoubled our efforts.
Old Adage

Define the Product:
What does the product do?
Whom does it serve?
Physically, what is the product?
What is its value to the customers? Why do they buy it?
Can the customer use it immediately? Is training necessary?
Will the customer have to change the way he or she does things to use the product?

Define Your Goals:
Define what you want to achieve from the business plan process:
Improved cash flow?
Improved profit?
Expanded market share?
A specific level of annual revenues?
Seed funding?
A public offering of shares in your firm?
Specified personal profit realized?

Analyze the Management Team

Have you previously prepared a detailed business plant? Do you follow it? How often is it updated?

Are sales volume, revenue, and expenses as high as you expected them to be? If there are variances, what is the cause?

What financial shape is your firm in? Do you periodically run short of cash? Are taxes paid? Are loans current? Are payables current? How do basic ratios look?

How happy are your customers? Do they recommend your product or service to others? Do they have complaints? How do you or your firm act on complaints? Do customers want changes in the product, or do they want a new product altogether?

How happy are your employees? Is the employee turnover rate higher or lower than the average for your industry and area? What comments are obtained from employees during exit interviews?

How often do employees contribute operational improvements or product suggestions? Are they enthusiastic contributors or, for example, do they think that the weekend is the best part of the week?

How does your product or service measure up against the competition? What are you doing about any competitive weaknesses or opportunities?

How effective is your marketing? What is your market share? What is the return on your marketing budget? What is the response to advertising? Do queries and sales leads come from sources you anticipated, or are unexpected responses being received? What is being done to capitalize on these opportunities? Is the marketing expense per unit sold and as a percentage of the total budget reasonable in comparison with other firms in the same industry?

How are your operations doing? Have you done everything possible to minimize costs at all levels in the firm? Are improvements in your methods or technology possible? What would their costs and benefits be?

Analyze What is Needed Internally:

Analyze What is Needed Externally:

DEFINE THE PRODUCT AND THE MARKET

"Cheshire Puss," Alice began, "would you please tell me which way I ought to go from here?" "That depends on where you want to get to," said the Cat.

Lewis Carroll

Define Your Product:

If you are developing a product, and plan to write a business plan, then a clear, comprehensible product definition will be important to your plan's development. Consider this statement made by a principal in a large venture capital firm: "Whenever I get a business plan in which the founders weren't able to clearly describe their product, I think maybe they don't know. The plan goes in the wastebasket." Thus, an effective product definition is crucial to your business plan.

The product definition will do more than influence the various audiences for your business plan. It will become the basis for your marketing literature and will affect the rate at which your product penetrates its market. You should, therefore, spend as much time as necessary writing this description. It should be short, easy to read, and make the major points with a minimum of rhetoric. Unless you are sending the plan to someone who is a specialist in your area, assume that you are writing for the layperson. The jargon that you and your co-founders are accustomed to will have to be replaced with words that non-specialists can understand. If this is impossible, then very careful, clear definitions of all technical terms must be provided. If the list of definitions gets too long, the description is probably too technical. In that case, you may want to consider enlisting the help of a professional writer.

Topics to Include in a Product Description:

Many topic areas can be included in a product or service description, depending on your industry and the type of product. In the list below, we suggest a simple set of general categories of information that should be included.

What does the product do?
What is the product?
Who are the customers?
What makes this product different?
How complex is the product from the user's point of view?
Can the product be tried with little risk?
What are the results of using the product?
Why will the customer buy the product?
What type of training is required to use the product?
What regulations are relevant to the use of the product?

Define the Market

Who are the customers?
How do you know these customers want or need your product or service?
How did you, or how will you, set the price?
How do you know the customers will pay your price?
How did you determine the market share you hope to achieve?
What might prevent you from reaching your sales goals?
Where are the customers located?
How can you tell the customers about your company and your product?
How can you get the product to the customer?
What customer service is required?
Who are your competitors now?

THE AUTHORS OF THE PLAN

"If, in order to succeed in an enterprise, I were obliged to choose between fifty deer commanded by a lion and fifty lions commanded by a deer, I should consider myself more certain of success with the first group than with the second."

Saint Vincent De Paul

Analyze the Skills of EFI's Management Team:

Who develops the product?
Who makes it?
Who sells it?
Who services it?
Who must manage the money?
Who must be the leader?
A Review of Skills is Difficult—But Crucial

General List of Management Skills:

President or Chief Executive Officer.
Product Champion.
Financial/Treasurer.
Financial/Controller.
Marketing Specialist.
Sales Manager/Staff.
Research and Development Manager/Staff.
Product Manufacture or Service Delivery Manager.
Customer Service and Maintenance Manager.
Overall Planning, Budgeting, and Control Skills.

Customize the List
Inventory Existing Skills
Using a Matrix to Compare Available Skills to Needs

OUTLINE OF A BUSINESS PLAN COMPLEMENTING EFI'S DETAILED MARKETING PLAN

A new or updated Business Plan does not necessarily command attention to new product development or new markets. The first order of business is concentration on and development of the present product that is the backbone of EFI's reason for being in business.

If EFI desires to succeed with continuing product development and an unrelenting to grow to the number one position in the marketplace, a detailed Business Plan must reflect perfectly good business opportunities (detailed in Marketing Plan), with a well trained, reasonable management team, and the promise of an ample return on investment.

Planning should encompass continuing improvements in management teams, approaches, services, products, research, quality, marketing analysis, and innovative sales planning.

THE COMPONENTS OF A BUSINESS PLAN

The Business Plan outline:

Table of Contents
Executive Summary
The Management Team
The Product
The Market for the product
Marketing Plan
Operational Plan
Financial Analysis
Objectives and Milestones
Controls and Reporting
Ownership and Equity
Appendices

In today's marketplace EFI faces a number of business related growth oriented problems. EFI faces aggressive competitors, dealing with a marketplace that is continually changing with regard to such factors as consumer wants, government regulations, raw material prices, constant refining of organizational structure, new marketing and sales concepts, etc., etc. The preparation of EFI's formal marketing plan can be of substantial value.

NEVER LIE! NEVER CHEAT! ALWAYS FACE REALITY!

A detailed, honest marketing plan gives a corporation an exceptional chance to face the truth about where the company has been and what the future holds for continued growth! Free enterprise gives the entity a chance to make mistakes and recover, but actions taken must be generated through a detailed marketing and business plan. Everyone commits an act or thought that unintentionally deviates from what is correct, right, or true. Recognition and subsequent correction of the deviation increases rate of performance and as a result, the company will find itself leading the league in its particular discipline!

Jack Simpson
The Simpson Co.

THE BACON LETTUCE &
TOMATO RECEPTIONIST

I was assisting the marketing and sales departments of a corporation on introducing a new product for potential customers. The corporation with whom I was under contract was a very good company; smart, experienced executives, an organization chart designed that exhibited detailed accountabilities and responsibilities, sound fiscal strength, a marketing and business plan and a high percentage of market share in two categories. I was hired to assist in the third category (new product).

Two sales personnel had been assigned to assist me in the development of an in-depth marketing analysis. We took our time, talked to a number of what we thought were potential clients. We asked and learned what was expected of the company and product; particularly price, quality, and if successful, what would be the particular demands on our company for JIT—just in time delivery. To be successful, what would the company do in strengthening distribution on peak days, weeks, or months? Would the company strengthen its sales force with more corporate sales personnel, or would sales be through manufacturers' representatives or warehousing distributors?

This is not a chapter designed to fill you full of the work, information gathering, analysis, and planning necessary to make the third category successful. You will learn from a myriad of chapters throughout this book. Yes, after 18 months we were moving along nicely based on the management of our corporate analysis and planning but, suddenly, we ran into a stumbling block. A powerful secretary/receptionist at a company that we thought had great potential, let it be known that one of our most effective salesman had insulted her and she wanted nothing to do with him or the company. We had to, for the time being, respect her opinion but we also had to talk to the personnel under "her control." They were important, influential department managers of Quality, Manufacturing, and Purchasing.

We had a meeting; I am sure the so-called insult was a misunderstanding. I suggested to my boss since I was not an employee maybe I could at least get her to meet with me personally in order to try to straighten the situation out. He agreed; he said, "OK! Mr. Suits, see what you can find out."

I had absolutely no idea what I would say; I just picked up the phone and called. I *did*, however, determine that I would not mention anything about the past. I just said, "If I may, I would just like to talk to you about what I believe would subjects beneficial to both of our companies. I only know only one thing, Ms. Jones. I have never called on a company without first going through purchasing."

Ms. Jones was a very nice lady. She said, "I'll be happy to see you Mr. Simpson, but first you will have to give me a little time for lunch."

I said, "Well then in about an hour or hour and a half?"

Ms. Jones said, "Oh no! I only have a sandwich and ice tea or "Coke"."

I said, "Sounds good to me. I can see a store from my phone booth that advertises 'sandwiches.' I'll grab a sandwich and ice-cold milk. The tuna fish or the one piled high with roast beef looked good. By the way, what kind of sandwiches do you enjoy?"

"Oh! I like toasted cheese, or turkey and cheese, but my favorite is bacon, lettuce and tomato."

"Sounds good to me," I said. "See you inside an hour. And, Ms. Jones, I appreciate your time."

When I walked into Ms. Jones office, I was carrying a bag and asked, "Where can I put the contents of this bag I am carrying?"

She said, "I—I—don't know? What is it? Pah—pah—put in on the table near the Xerox. What is it?"

"It's your favorite!" And I started to pull out a loaf of white, a loaf of rye, a pound of bacon, a container of ripe tomatoes, a head of lettuce, a jar of mayonnaise, a jar of dill pickles, a pond of butter, small containers of salt and pepper, and a "Coke." I said, "Now you won't have to leave the office for your favorite sandwich. But you'll have to cook the bacon at home."

Dumfounded! Amazed! Shocked! Appall! You pick a word! You name it! Ms. Jones was speechless! The first thing she did, after gaining her composure, was call the secretary from another office and said, "Come see what a gentleman just brought me!" The first thing noted was there were six secretaries gathered around laughing their small rear ends off. The BLT caper spread like wildfire! They would have given me the company; nothing had ever approached what I had done.

I won't go on, and I'll skip the details but a few meetings later Ms. Jones said, "It is probably just as much my fault as Mr. Laughlin's. Please tell him to call me and we'll work things out. I had not said a word. Our third category (product) sold, in time, more profitable goods and services to that particular company as any in the corporation.

The story I have told above is true!

SELL THE CHAIR

I have mentioned numerous times to sales personnel, to students when teaching night classes at Orange Coast College, and in this book, that all sales should be "in the language of, and needs of," the customer. Nothing defines this more than merchandizing! Merchandizing must offer right product at the right time, at the right place, at the right price, and to the right customer. I think that all sales personnel should incisively know the difference between marketing, sales, and merchandizing and what incisive role advertising plays. My mother's mother died when my mom was in the sixth grade. She had to drop out of school and raise seven brothers. She married my Dad, had five children, played expert, competitive bridge, had a great sense of humor, and when she tired of the country club life went to work at an exclusive woman's store. And after a few years my mother became director of merchandizing!

My mother didn't know textbook sales, or sales engineering, sales management or marketing, but she was one of the greatest merchandisers in the history of the store. Why? Because she knew people, how to make friends; she walked the floor, talked to customers, listened, and learned. If a customer wanted a dress for a bride and dresses for the maids of honor, my mother had an innate talent for knowing what the bride and her friends needed. And where was Mom the day the girl married? At her home helping the bride and her bridesmaids dress. The word spread like a wave covering sand on a beach. It wasn't long before the store had a whole floor devoted to "love and marriage." Don't they go together like a horse and carriage? Frank Sinatra thought so!

I don't care what kind of a salesperson you are—and associated with what discipline—marketing, sales engineering, direct sales, manufacturers' representative, warehousing distributor, wholesaler, whatever! You must know the customer and speak their language. This is the reason I think merchandising is the toughest of all. You almost must presage the buyers' thinking and risk thousands of dollars if you do not meet the tenants of good merchandizing because most merchandizing sales are a result of instant decision-making.

Selling THE CHAIR takes a different and difficult kind of salesmanship. It's tough! It takes time-consuming research, precise definition of potential customer, outstanding planning, important timing, person-to-person salesmanship, and absolutely no "taking of orders." The salesperson must WORK for "THE CHAIR".

"Must be a hell of a CHAIR," you say. "It is! It could make the difference between a huge profit or big loss if not sold properly." "WOW!" you say. "Wha—where is this so important CHAIR?"

Well, I am using THE CHAIR as a symbol of THINKING! Let's say, for example, it is sitting in your banquet facilities, your conference centers, and/or your meeting rooms in a hotel where you are a sales executive. It is sitting in any area in your hotel, or gathering halls where people congregate to have a party to celebrate—weddings, anniversaries, reunions, and in particular, the time between December first and New Year's Eve!

This whole "CHAIR" thing started after I played tennis one morning with a close friend and general manager of a beautiful hotel in Newport Beach, California. I don't know exactly how we got around to the subject but my friend was concerned about return on capital investment. He said, "for example, the owners of this elegant, eye appealing edifice spent millions on their conference centers and banquet facilities to attract the kinds of people that would want to be surrounded by tasteful richness of design. But when they attend, let's say a Christmas party or anniversary or wedding party, we seemingly are not able to attract the dollars along with it."

I said, almost immediately, "That's probably because, and I'll bet a dollar on it, your sales department, or catering department, are taking orders instead of selling. Your hotel may be likened to a real estate company selling homes by the hundreds in the Newport Beach, Huntington Beach, and Laguna Beach; cities located near, or on, the water. SEA! SAND! SUNSHINE! That is why the whole area is so much in demand. People are lining up to buy a home. The real estate agents are so busy taking orders they are not learning how to sell. It's the same with your hotel. I'll bet everyone is talking about it's beauty and at the same time telling their friends they will be surprised at how cheap it is to throw a party."

"Now I will ask, what kind of party? Is it for a group of very nice people like Baptists or Mormons or The Salvation Army who don't drink alcoholic beverages? Or, is the party for fighter pilots or legionnaires or a political party the members of which start drinking when they first get to the party and don't stop until it's over?"

"Let's say, for example, there are 100 chairs at the Baptist party and the bill per chair amounts to $35.00. The hotel has grossed $3500.00 dollars. If the chairs were available for fighter pilots the bill per chair would probably be $100.00 or more. Hell, they expect that! So now we are talking $10,000 dollars. The BIG question is, how do you separate the Baptist from the fighter pilots. To me the answer is market analysis—precise definition of potential customer.

Stop and think! In the Christmas season, you have thirty days. Let's say you have 500 chairs a night for 30 days. That's what?? 15,000 chairs! Do you want to sell them for $48.00 dollars and gross $720,000 or for $100.00 and gross $1,500,000?"

The value to your hotel is THE CHAIR! The marketing department and the food and beverage department must get together and lay out a definitive marketing and business plan. It may take a couple of years to "fine tune" it, but anything less is not acceptable!

SELL THE SIZZLE

The three words written above are not mine. They are coined from a very successful salesman by the name of Zig Ziglar. I hope I got that right! It has been years since I read his book but I wanted the reader to know. I think the name of the book was entitled, SELL THE SIZZLE, NOT THE STEAK!

Anyhow! My wife and I FINALLY decided we wanted to sell our home and move to Oregon to be nearer the kids, but particularly the grandson. One boy was recently sent to the Riverside area to attend advanced training sessions for Mercedes Benz' master mechanics. We drove over to have dinner on two occasions and on the way home, that was it! My wife misses the boys and her grandson, so the decision to sell was as easy one.

You will read in a chapter, "Filling Yourself Full Of The Problem," on how I was instrumental in assisting a real estate company (I do not have a real estate license) in selling ALL condos in a new housing project about ten miles west of Denver. The project was against fierce competition plus the cost of land, labor, material and money was "sky high."

Oh! The place was beautiful! Flags were flying in the breeze, balloons were tugging at their tie-down string, and real estate agents were available and only too happy to assist in showing personnel the models. The company also had pages and pages of advertising. There was just one problem; nothing was being sold!

Let's get back to my home! I asked for a meeting with our real estate agent and insisted, in nice way, I did not want the advertising of our home mixed in with the hundreds and hundreds of others in the REAL ESTATE SECTION of the Sunday paper. I said, "We are not selling a house; we are selling a MILLION DOLLAR view with a home and I want your agents to think the same way. The trouble with most agents in a booming real estate market is they get used to taking orders and forget how to sell. And I want every potential buyer to go through you. And I want them pre-qualified! I don't want to try to run your business because I understand you are one of the best but I want no "lookie loos."

I told our real estate agent I would write an idea for her marketing department to review. I did just that! They said they would think about it! Here it is!

YOU KNOW! I WAS JUST THINKING!

Here I am sitting at the edge of my gleaming, big swimming pool' with Jacuzzi, looking over what many people have told me is one of the most beautiful views in Orange County. One person told me the other day, "Jack, you have a magnificent, million dollar view." I said, "Well, I never thought of it in dollars, because it's your heart that tells you what something is worth. You've been there; like a baby's smile, a dog lapping you face, a warm and sensual kiss from your loved one. Even helping a "little old lady from Pasadena"—in tennis shoes—across the street!

But come to think of it you're right! From my new upper deck, you can see from Disneyland to Laguna. In fact, you can see the Disneyland fireworks every night and on the 4th of July you can watch a minimum of 10 cities with their fireworks' display. From the new lower deck, the view is no less beautiful. One can even see Catalina, that is, on a clear day! That's about 30 miles!

I AM OFFERING TO SELL THE VIEW!

Two very large bedrooms, one a Master, with bath, each having access to the deck through new double pane sliding glass doors with screens! Also there is a new three-speed ceiling fan. Another bedroom with access to another bath plus fan, new window and screens. The hallway and stairs, with new recessed lighting, takes you to the living room large enough for two table tennis tournaments. It has a gas log fireplace with controllable recessed lighting highlighting, to the ceiling, 16ft. of beautiful marble. The downstairs bedroom (or den) with bath has access to the pool through the same type of sliding glass and screen as the master bedrooms. Or, you can access the pool through a door in the bathroom. There is a shower just inside so one can "clean up" before entering the home. There is also a door from the den to a three-car garage. A new garage door is installed. The dining room with table seats 10 with a chandelier that Louis the XIV would have loved but he's of the 1600 vintage; so, my feeling would not be hurt if you wanted a change. There is a long wide covered entrance with new lighting and double doors opening into a marble hallway taking you to the family room; same thing—access to the new patio, with view through sliding glass doors with screen. There is also a gas log fireplace. There is a recently refurbished kitchen with dining area. A few have discussed taking down the wall between the family room and kitchen. That would increase the view, making one believe as a passenger on the GOODYEAR blimp!

Complete landscaping surrounds the house with new pipes and valves and sprinklers; the slope in back is completely landscaped and there is room in the side yard for a set of swings and such for children. The whole lot is fenced; just ask my dog.

Since the buyer would be new to the area, I'll assist your "settling in" by providing maid service, pool service, landscaping services (all under present contract,) for a year after signing of the purchase agreement. None of the above mentioned personnel have missed their assigned day for ten years. I'll give you the name of our home improvement and electrical contractor. I'll also buy you a subscription to USA TODAY for a year.

The price is $1,395.000; $1,000,000 for the view; $395,000,00 for the home. Appointments, preferably to couples, or a bachelor that invested in the GOOGLE IPO, should be timed to see the home in daylight but late enough to see a major part of ORANGE COUNTY light up before your eyes.

If interested in a change of lifestyle please contact—!

I am going to talk to my real estate agent about no pictures of the home; I just want to show—THE SIZZLE!

Today is the middle of August, 2005! I wrote the ad in early October, 2004. The view and the house sold on my wife's birthday in January, 2005. Our real estate agent did a terrific job! The buyer said he bought the view!!!

TACTICS/STRATEGY & HISTORY

John Von Neumann, American mathematician, was the founder of the mathematical theory of games. A game consists of a set of rules governing a competitive situation in which from two individuals, or groups of individuals, choose strategies designed to maximize their own winnings or to minimize their opponent's winnings. The rules specify the possible actions for each player, the amount of information received by each as play progresses, and the amounts won or lost in various situations.[14] John Von Neumann would have made an outstanding Marketing Manager.

The secret to game theory, war games, war, business maximization and sales competition is choosing the right strategy and the proper use of "the amount of information received." Herein lies the nexus of corporate growth by maximizing winnings through proper use of marketing analysis.

To maximize winnings and minimize opponent's wings, a leader in addition to being a great planner, must have awareness, must be able to manage all activities to accomplish objectives, must understand strategy and tactics and must have effective communication links. And he must define, in detail, the responsibility and accountability of all commanders—managers (executive heads).

I've been doing a little research with a thought in the back of my mind. I was wondering what different management and marketing experts have to say about awareness, and strategy and tactics, and objectives and responsibility, etc. Since I am combining the research of philosophy and the lessons of history with my own experiences in marketing and business consulting, I thought I would divide the schools of thinking on these subjects into two categories—the historical versus contemporary—and bridge the two through time. The outline looks something like this:

---

[14]   Edited by William Harris and Judith Levy, *THE NEW COLUMBIA ENCYCLOPEDIA*, Columbia University Press, New York, 1975, p. 1042.

HISTORICAL	BRIDGE OF TIME	CONTEMPORARY THOUGHT & DISCIPLINE
"Great Treasury of Western Thought" Adler & Van Dorn		"Management" Drucker
"On War" Carl Von Clausewitz Howard & Paret		"Competitive Strategy" Porter
"Two Centuries of Warfare" Chant, Holmes & Koenig		"Selling" Thompson
"A Book of Five Rings" Musashi		"Passion/Search for Excellence" Waterman, Peters, Austin

The reason I refer to accounts of war is because modern, total war, calls for the regimentation and coordination of peoples and resources. The use of fighting forces as instruments in war became a scientific art with the development of strategy and tactics. The way in which war is carried out is governed by the principles of strategy and tactics, by the type of weapons employed, and by the type of communication and transportation facilities available.[15] The same principles and thought processes also apply in competitive business.

TACTICS

The discipline of a soldier is formed by exercise rather than by study; the talents of a commander are appropriated to those calm, though rapid, minds, which nature produces to decide the fate of armies and nations: the former is the habit of life, the latter the glance of moment[16]

On 5 December 1757, Fredrick the Great of Prussia attacked an Austrian army at Leuthen, Silesia. The odds were heavily against the Prussians, who were outnumbered by nearly three to one. The Austrian position was, furthermore, a strong one, squarely blocking the Breslau Road, Fredrick's main line of advance. The Prussian plan was simple enough. Fredrick intended to make a feint against

---

15   Ibid, p. 2929

16   Gibson, *DECLINE and FALL OF THE ROMAN EMPIRE*, LIII.

the Austrian right while the main weight of his army, swinging south of the Breslau Road, struck the Austrian left.

The oblique order tactic was used to perfection by Fredrick the Great at Leuthen, but both the Austro-Russian forces and Napoleon attempted to use a variation of the tactic at Austerlitz in 1805. The outflanking of the enemy by a single envelopment approach is itself a variation on the double envelopment tactic use at Cannae, (Hannibal, 216 BC).[17] It is best used when one flank is inoperable because of difficult terrain, or if, in the case of Desert War (North Africa) of 1941-42, and Desert War No. 2 (Saudi Arabia etc. of 1992) one flank is covered by water.

FIGHTER TACTICS OVER THE YALU RIVER
KOREA, 1950-1953

Communist MiG-15 fighters patrol at high altitude to the north of the Yalu. On seeing the approach of American bombers at a lower height, they dive south over the river, accelerating the whole time, make one firing pass at the bombers and then continue their dives to cross back over the Yalu and so into friendly air space at very low level.

American counter-tactics are similar in concept. American fighters patrol south of the river at high altitude and wait for the MiGs to make their foray over the river. Once the Sabre pilots see the MiGs start to dive, they too dive, hoping to intercept the Communist fighters before they can fire on the bombers and to chase them as far as the river 'border.'[18]

LOSSES

Total Sabres Lost—78
Total Sabre Kills—810

There are lessons of history to be learned here. Tactical planning focuses on the implementation of those activities specified by a strategic plan. Tactical plans are typically more short-term, focusing more on current and near-term activities that must be completed to implement overall strategies. Resource allocation is a common decision area for tactical planning.

Two examples of tactical planning was, in the case of selling the condos in Denver, to first convince potential buyers of town houses the importance of understanding the effect of pricing on land, labor, and material. And my brother, from "Big Brothers", needed the advantage of the other workers introducing him to the personnel manager.

---

[17]   Parenthesis by Author

[18]   Ibid, p. 451.

"The conduct of war consists in the planning and conduct of fighting. If fighting consisted of a single act, no further subdivision would be needed. However, it consists of a greater or lesser number of single acts, each complete in itself, which are called "engagements" and which form new entitles. This gives rise to the completely different activity of planning and executing these engagements themselves, and of coordinating each of them with the others in order to further the object of the war; one has been called *Tactics*, and the other *Strategy*."[19]

I am now going to change three words—for war I'm going to say capture of market share; for fighting I'm substituting the word marketing and an engagement is "communicating an exchange of information with customer."

The conduct of capture of market share consists in the planning and conduct of marketing. If marketing consisted of a single act, no further subdivision would be needed. However, it consists of a greater or lesser number of single acts, *each complete in itself*, which are called "communicating an exchange of information with customer" and which form new entitles. This gives rise to the completely different activity of planning and executing these exchanges of information themselves, and of coordinating each of them with the others in order to further the object of capturing market share. One has been called tactics, and the other strategy.

Would Clausewitz qualify as a brilliant marketing executive? Read on! Tactics teaches the use of armed forces in the engagement; strategy, the use of engagements for the object of the war.

According to my substitution, then, tactics teaches the use of trained salesman in communicating an exchange of information with customer; strategy, the use of communicating this exchange for the object of capturing market share.

In continuing my research of Clausewitz on strategy, I came across a more detailed analysis of what strategy really is and its effects on many aspects of what success is all about. I am directly quoting from pages 177, 178 and half of 179 from Clausewitz *ON WAR* and rather than substituting words, I'll outline them now and the reader can actually substitute as he reads and grasp the relationship between strategy in war and strategy in capturing market share.

Engagement—for the purpose, we'll use sales call
War—capturing market share
Fighting Forces—salesmen in the field
Strategist—sales or marketing manager or vice-president, sales and marketing
Government—Office of CEO
Army—sales or marketing department
General Headquarters—office of Vice President or Marketing Manager

---

19 Carl Von Clausewitz, *ON WAR*, Princeton University Press, Princeton, New Jersey, 1976, p. 128.

Prince or General—company executive responsible for market share

Turning an opponents Flank—outmaneuvering competition in one of many ways

OK! Here we go!

Strategy is the use of the sales call for the purpose of capturing market share. The marketing manager must therefore define an aim for the entire operational side of capturing of market share that will be in accordance with its purpose. In other words, he will draft the plan of capturing of market share and the aim will determine the series of actions intended to achieve it. He will, in fact, shape the individual campaigns and, within these, decide on the individual sales call. Since most of these matters have to be based on assumptions that may not prove correct, while other more detailed orders cannot be determined in advance at all, it follows that the marketing manager must go on the campaign himself.

Detailed orders can then be given on the spot, allowing the general plan to be adjusted to the modifications that are continuously required. The marketing manager, in short, must maintain control throughout.

This has not always been the accepted view, at least so far as the general principal is concerned. It used to be the custom to settle strategy in the capitol, and not in the field—a practice that is acceptable only if the office of the CEO stays so close to the marketing department as to function as general in the office of the marketing manager.

Strategic theory, therefore, deals with planning; or rather, it attempts to shed light on the components of capturing market share and their interrelationships, stressing those few principles or rules that can be demonstrated.

The reader may recall, from the first three chapters of *SOCRATES 'N SUITS,* **BOOK I**, that vitally important matters are involved in a combat mission. Capturing market share demands the same unusual mental gifts that are needed to keep the whole picture steadily in mind.

A corporate vice president can best demonstrate his innate capability by managing a campaign exactly to suit his objective and his resources, doing neither too much nor too little. The same can be said for a flight leader in combat. But the effects of this innate capability show not so much in novel forms of action as in the ultimate success of the whole. What we should admire is the accurate fulfillment of the unspoken assumptions, the smooth harmony of the whole activity, which only becomes evident in final success. The final success can be measured in a mission completed and/or the complete success of capturing market share.

Everything in strategy is very simple, but that does not mean that everything is very easy. Once it has been determined what capturing marketing share, or capturing air superiority, is meant to achieve, and what it can achieve, it is easy to chart the course. But great strength of character, as well as great lucidity and firmness of mind, is required in order to follow through steadily, to carry out the plan, and not to be thrown off course by thousands of diversions. Take any number of outstanding men, some noted for intellect, others for their acumen, still others for boldness or tenacity of will: not one may possess the combination of qualities needed to make him a greater than average marketing executive or fighter wing commander.

It sounds odd, but everyone who is familiar with this aspect of capturing market share will agree that it takes more strength of will to make an important decision in strategy than in tactics. In the latter, one carried away by the pressures of the moment, caught up in a maelstrom where resistance would be fatal, one presses boldly on. In strategy, the pace is much slower. There is ample room for apprehensions, one's own and those of others for objections and remonstrations and, inconsequence, for premature regrets. In a *tactical* situation (trained salesmen in a territory exchanging value with customer) one is able to see at least half the problem with the naked eye, whereas in strategy (exchanging value for objective of capturing market share) everything has to be guessed at and presumed. Conviction is therefore weaker. Consequently most GENERALS, (corporate VP's) when they ought to act, are paralyzed by unnecessary doubts.

Let us reflect again on history. What else did Frederick the Great possess that made him successful against the Austrian army at Leuthen?

I didn't know the answer at first, and then one day eight months ago (I was still researching this chapter) at the experimental test pilot symposium, three former Lockheed experimental test pilots and I had a "wee small hours in the morning" discussion. The discussion was about the XF, YF and F-104A flight test program and the number of planes and pilots lost. During the course of the conversation someone said I was very lucky. "Yes," I said, "I was lucky, but I was always prepared for the worst and I never let myself get involved beyond my mental and physical ability to recover." I remember one of the guys paying me a compliment. He said, "Suitcase, you were a wise man." There was the key to Frederick the Great.

What is really admirable is the King's *wisdom*: pursuing a major objective with limited resources, he did not try to undertake anything beyond his strength, but always just enough to get him what he wanted. This campaign was not the only one in which he demonstrated his judgment as a general. It is evident in all the three wars fought by a very wise and great King.

Wisdom is oft-times nearer when we stood than when we soar.
Wordsworth, William (1770-1850)
The Excursion, III, 231

Wisdom attempts nothing enormous and disproportioned to its powers, nothing which it cannot perform or nearly perform.
Emerson (1803-1882)
The Conservative

TIMING IN STRATEGY

In *A Book of Five Rings*, the author Musashi says, "There is timing in everything. Timing in strategy cannot be mastered without a great deal of practice."

Timing is important in dancing and pipe or string music, for they are in rhythm only if timing is good. Timing and rhythm are also involved in the military arts, shooting bows and guns, and riding horses. In all skills and abilities there is timing. A fighter pilot and military commander must know this. A marketing and sales executive must know this.

There is timing in the whole life of the warrior, in his thriving and declining, in his harmony and discord. Similarly, there is timing in the way of the merchant, the marketplace, the way of merchandizing, and in the rise and fall of capital. All things entail rising and falling timing. Much depends on the knowledge and analysis of competition. If one is planning to sell in the language of the customer one needs to know the "body language" of the competition. This is the main thing in strategy. It is especially important to know the background timing. Otherwise your strategy will become uncertain.

You win in battles with timing by knowing the enemies' timing, and thus using a timing which the enemy does not expect. This, in turn, demands detailed planning.

I, the author, can give a perfect example, through experience, why timing and planning is critical for capturing market share. I ask the question, "When does a sales representative turn his or her self into a merchandiser? And, for what reason! The answer is in plain view at the end of this chapter.

Now let us research what Drucker has to write about strategy or strategic decision-making, or strategic planning.

Planning what *is* our business, planning what *will* it be, and planning what *should* it be, has to be integrated. What is short range and what is long range is then decided by the time span and futurity of the decision. Everything that is "planned" becomes immediate work and commitment.

General Electric calls this work "Strategic Business Planning." The ultimate objective of the activity is to identify the new and different business, technologies, and markets that the company should try to create long range. But the work starts with the questions, "What is our present business?" Indeed, it starts with the questions "Which of our present *business* should we abandon? Which should we play down? Which should we push and supply new resources to?"

This may sound like semantic quibbling and, to a point, it is. But the confused semantics have led to confused thinking. They have tended to paralyze strategic decision-making rather than to mobilize for it. They are largely to blame for the failure of many large companies so far.

What was it that Clausewitz said? "Strategy is exclusively concerned with engagements and with the directions relating to them. Unlike other areas of life it is not concerned with actions that consist only of words, such as statements, declarations, and so forth. But words, being cheap, are the most common means of creating false impressions."

To obtain results from elaborate planning efforts, Drucker goes on to say that it is important for the manager to know what strategic planning is not: It is not a box of tricks, a bundle of techniques.

It is analytical thinking and commitment of resources to action.[20]

Strategic planning is not the application of scientific methods to business decision. It is the application of thought, analyses, imagination, and judgment. It is responsibility, rather than technique.

Strategic planning is *not* forecasting. It is not masterminding the future. The future is unpredictable.

Strategic planning does not deal with future decisions. It deals with the futurity of present decisions. (see the following two page "story of the secretary—my strategic plan) Decisions exist only in the present. The question that faces the strategic decision-maker is not what his organization should do tomorrow. It is, "What do we have to do today to be ready for an uncertain tomorrow?" The question is not what will happen in the future. It is, "What futurity do we have to build into our present thinking and doing, what time spans do we have to consider, and how do we use this information to make a rational decision now?"

Strategic planning is not an attempt to eliminate risk. While it is futile to eliminate risk, and questionable to try to minimize it, it is essential the risks taken be the right risks. The end result of successful strategic planning must be capacity to take a greater risk, for this is the only way to improve entrepreneurial performance. To extend this capacity, however, we must understand the risks we take. We must be able to choose rationally among risk-taking courses of action, rather than plunge into uncertainty on the basis of hunch, hearsay, or experience, no matter how meticulously quantified.

"If a man will begin with certainties, he shall end in doubts; but if he will be content to begin with doubts, he shall end in certainties."

Francis Bacon (1561-1726)
Advancement of Learning

The Japanese are acutely aware or conscious, through their experiences and hard work "in the trenches," of America's curious addictions to corporate grand strategy."

I am going to quote an article from Fortune, but first an excerpt.

"The Japanese are ever distrustful of 'concepts,' for in their view an idea that *focuses* attentions does so at the expense of peripheral vision."

---

[20]   Peter F. Drucker, *THE PRACTICE of MANAGEMENT*, Harper & Row, New York, 1954, pp. 122. 123.

Years earlier, about 200, Clausewitz speaking of the elements of strategy said, " . . . it would be disastrous to try to develop our understanding of strategy by analyzing (these) factors in isolation . . ."

FORTUNE's four part series, from ten or so years ago, "New Management Strategies," traced the dominant strategic concepts of the Seventies, such as the experience curve and portfolio theory, and outline a new generation of ideas that seems destined to satisfy the satiable American appetite for such material. But why do we, as compared with the Japanese, for example, make such a big fuss about strategy in the first place? Why was an entire decade's worth of managers swept away by concepts that in the final analysis have been found quite misleading? Why do we stand ready to accept the "new wave" concepts of the Eighties with undiminished enthusiasm?

Our strategy fetish is a cultural peculiarity. We get off one strategy like the French get off on good food or romance. There's something masculine about it too—and high status. It seems fitting that corporate leadership concern itself with strategy. Not surprisingly, the $multi-million-a-year management-consulting industry has latched onto "strategic concepts" as the best potion for arousing corporate chieftains since firewater.

Bruce Henderson, founder of the Boston Consulting Group and guru of corporate strategists, recently published his second book, *Henderson On Corporate Strategy*, now in its fifth printing. It was given to a number of Japanese executives and solicited their reactions. Their response was consistent. While not dismissing it out-of-hand, they wondered what all the fuss was about. To them it seemed obsessive and overly intellectualized.

Their reaction wasn't surprising. During the Seventies most major U.S. consulting firms opened offices in Japan. Their expectations, based on the vast Japanese appetite for American control systems and technology, was that clients would flock to their doors. Instead, Japanese clients kept them at arm's length, confining them to narrow studies and intelligence gathering on U.S. and European competitors. The consultant's strategic concepts, so enthusiastically embraced in the U.S., were received with courtesy and veiled skepticism in Japan. Any literate Japanese manager could look about him and identify dozens of Japanese companies that had defied strategic concepts and succeeded brilliantly. In musical instruments, for example, a mature industry facing stagnation as birthrates in the U.S. and Japan declined, Yamaha should have classified its products as "cash cows" and gone on to better things. Instead, beginning with a negligible share of the U.S. market, Yamaha plowed ahead and destroyed the dominance of well-established U.S. competitors.

The Japanese view our excitement over strategy as we might regard their enthusiasm for Kabuki or sumo wrestling. They study our habits, not with the intent of cultivating a taste for them, but for insight into our culture and our vulnerabilities. The Japanese are ever distrustful of "concepts," for in their view any idea that focuses attention does so at the expense of peripheral vision. In their judgment, it is peripheral vision that picks up changes in the customer or technology or competition, and so is the key to corporate survival over the long haul. They regard our propensity to be guided by strategic formulas as a weakness.

The Japanese don't reject concepts such as the experience or curve or portfolio theory outright; they regard them as a stimulus to perception. They also strive to ferret out the "formula" of their concept-driven American competitors and exploit our inflexibility. YKK's success in zippers against Talon (a Texton division), and Honda's conquest in the motorcycle field over Harley-Davidson (then an AMF subsidiary), are sobering illustrations.! Both American conglomerates were wedded to the portfolio concept and regarded these as products to be milked rather than nourished and defended.

The consultants are academics that invented strategic concepts. They say the theories were never intended to be mindlessly applied in setting a strategic direction. Most would also agree that there is a widespread tendency in American corporation to misapply concepts, to become obsessed by a magic formula, and to ignore the marketplace, the customer, and the problems of execution.

The Japanese avoid these pitfalls by avoiding master strategies. In our recent awe of things Japanese, most Americans forget that the original products of the Japanese automotive manufacturers badly missed the mark. Toyota's Toyopet was square, sexless, and mechanically defective. It failed miserably, as did Datsun's first several entries into the U.S. market. More recently, Mazda miscalculated badly with its first rotary engine and nearly went bankrupt. Contrary to myth, the Japanese did not, from the onset, embark on a strategy to seize the high-quality small-car market. They manufactured what they were accustomed to building in Japan and tried to sell it abroad. Their success, as any Japanese automotive executive will readily agree, did not result from a bold insight by a few big brains at the top. On the contrary, success was achieved by senior managers, humble enough not to take their initial strategic positions too seriously. What saved Japan's near-failures was the cumulative impact of "little brains" in the form of salesmen and dealers and production workers, all contributing incrementally to the quality and market position these companies enjoy today. Middle and upper management saw their primary tasks as guiding and orchestrating this input from below rather than steering the organization from above along a predetermined strategic course. It's the inverted triangle of the Nordstrom department stores. (by author)

The Japanese triumphs should lead us to re-examine the roots of our folklore about strategy. Most graduates of business schools over the past 15 years have been exposed to the case of TIMEX—used in the classroom to demonstrate the power of strategy. The case describes TIMEX emerging from World War II as a mass producer of fuses and timing mechanisms for bombs and projectiles. Seizing on its ability to produce semi-accurate timekeeping devices, the story goes, it repackaged them as wristwatches and revolutionized the world watch industry.

Such is the folklore. In truth, TIMEX was in despair at the end of World War II as its government contracts ended. From the bowels of the organization came the suggestion that the company might peddle the riveted-together timing devices as watches. Having no alternative, TIMEX tried; prototypes were produces and a small sales force was recruited to sell them through traditional channels. The jewelers, who make a sizable income from watch repair rejected the notion of a cheap watch that could be used for a while and thrown away. As a last gasp for survival, TIMEX tried drugstores, which liked the idea of a new novelty item. Only gradually did TIMEX come to embrace its role as a mass producer and marketer of watches and a revolutionary force in that industry.

The "TIMEX strategy" has been sold to us as a "big brain" strategic coup. In fact, it conforms more closely to the iterative Japanese process of trial and error. A whole generation of business school graduates has been (and continues to be) exposed to what amounts to a pedagogical deceit. TIMEX is used to teach the folklore of what our corporate culture wants to believe rather than as a powerful illustration of how a success story evolved from experimentation and paying attention.

In recent months a number of observers have been nibbling at the edge of our managerial addiction to strategic concepts. McKinsey & Co. studies of excellent companies point inescapably to the conclusion that long-term success does not lie in concepts. It depends on an organization's ability to pool the small incremental improvements and insights of the "antennae" of the organization—its salesman and engineers and workers—to keep an edge on the competition. This dissenting point of view was stated forcefully eighteen months ago in, *Managing Our Way To Economic Decline,* an award-winning article in the Harvard Business Review by William J. Abernathy and Robert H. Hayes, both professors at the Harvard Business School: "These new (strategic) principles, despite their sophistication and widespread usefulness, encourage a preference for (1) analytic detachment rather than insight that comes from 'hands-on' experience, and (2) short-term cost reduction rather than long-term development of technological competitiveness. It is the new managerial gospel, we feel, that has played a major role in undermining the vigor of American Industry."

STRATEGY BY HINDSIGHT

The Japanese don't use the phrase "corporate strategy." They think more in terms of "strategic accommodation," underscoring their belief that corporate direction evolves from an incremental adjustment to unfolding events. Rarely, in their view, does one leader (or a strategic planning group) produce a bold strategy that guides a firm unerringly. Far more frequently, the input is from below. It is this ability of an organization to move information and ideas from the bottom to the top and back again in continuous dialogue that the Japanese value above all things. As the dialogue is pursued, what in hindsight may be called "strategy" evolves.[21]

I have researched six marketing and sales texts on the subjects of strategy, objective and tactics. Only one text addresses all three topics in one chapter. Thompson does it under the section entitled "Planning and managing sales effort."[22]

Thompson states, "Modern management defines an *objective* as 'what you are trying to accomplish—the end result you are striving for.' *Strategy* becomes a plan, a method, a sequence of activities structured to accomplish a specific objective or *objectives* in a specified period of time." *Tactics* are the "means or techniques through which the plan is according to.

If we re-read Clausewitz's *Concept Of Strategy*, plus my substitutions of words, we find that if you want to "win the war" in the marketplace, an executive must understand objectives, strategy and tactics. But he must first understand the customer and answer the question, "Does he have the product the customer needs?"

Thompson goes on to say, "Although these definitions are relatively clear-cut, the student in marketing frequently is confused about how these terms apply in the business situation, because they are used differently at various levels of management. Also, there is much overlapping of 'objectives' and 'strategy' as well."

Corporate objectives are concerned with return on investment, growth rate of profits, share of the market, survival, and so on. Specific corporate objectives are generally established by the chief executive officer. This is done in cooperation with his executive staff. The president, of course, reports to a board of directors, and sometimes his corporate objectives are modified by the board of directors. Objectives are, in a sense, carried out by the overall organization process with the company's vice-president or executive being the first link in the process. Each Vice President or executive heads a specific section of a company's operation; for example, finance, production, marketing, research, or the divisions producing major products.

Often, from the president's viewpoint, what vice-presidents do to accomplish corporate objectives is 'strategy.' But what is part of the strategy to the president is an objective for the vice-president involved and for his section of the company.[23]

OBJECTIVES AND THE SALESPERSON'S VIEWPOINT

There are several reasons why an understanding of managing by objectives is critical to a salesperson's role as a market manager.

---

[21]　Richard Pascale, *FORTUNE*, January 25, 1982.

[22]　Joseph Thompson, Ph.D., *SELLING, A BEHAVORIAL SCINNCE ANALYSIS*, McGraw-Hill, New York, 1973, pp. 93-115.

[23]　Ibid.

An objective is like a compass. If you don't have one, you may not be able to tell where you have been or where you are going. Many individuals have a low level of aspiration unless they know what they are trying to accomplish and why.

An objective to a salesman is like a crossbar to the pole-vaulter. If he doesn't have one, he really doesn't know how high he has jumped.

Without objectives, it is difficult to assess results. Objectives help avoid that lost feeling of just drifting, because with objectives an individual can better determine the consequences of his actions.

Through objectives and planning in terms of facts of the marketplace (a complete territorial analysis), the salesman has the raw materials from which to develop a strategy—his plan. And again developing strategy to accomplish objectives calls for planning.[24]

I think any business or military organization, to be successful, must rise above or transcend the inclination to analyzing factors in isolation. Through an innate awareness of consciousness—a consciousness honed in the marketplace or in the trenches—will come the realization that nothing in itself is the answer—thoughts and feedback begin to interconnect by—what did we say before—the CEO being close to the sales department.

Only by my awareness do I know myself, and the thoughts going through my mind as I pound on doors in the marketplace and fill myself full of the problem. I know this consciousness of the marketplace will lead to judgments on which I'll have to stand against the others who haven't been there—and I'll stand by my convictions.

And I will be able to consciously (and conscientiously) do a better job of planning than my competitors.

Tolstoy says, "Consciousness is a source of self-cognition quite apart from an independent of reason—through this reason man observes himself, but only through consciousness does he know himself."

Knowing yourself comes from experience—exposure—study—understanding. In the case of decision-making in war or business the strength of conviction is a quality leaders must have.

And there is never any excuse for ignorance. If I, the general, or sales manager do not know what is going on in the front lines or in his territory, the responsibility to find out is his and his alone.

"All ignorance is either ignorance of things or of the limits of knowledge."
Kant (1724-1804)

Kant continues; "If my ignorance is accidental and not necessary, it must incite me, in the first case, to a dogmatical inquiry regarding the objects of which I am

---

[24]   Ibid.

ignorant; in the second, to a critical investigation into the bounds of all possible knowledge."

In one case of a company asking me for advise, I was at first ignorant of why the CEO thought market share was far more than being reported, and, I was also, ignorant at the time, as to how I was going to find out if market share was or was not accurate. I'm not a Patton—or Napoleon—but I can act as a result of understanding their actions. They knew they had to be close to the front line. The same thing is necessary in answering the question, "Why lack of market share?"

I won't go into a lot of detail but (see Chapter "Full of the Problem") I made twenty-seven cold calls on retailers before I was asking the right questions to the right people. I was asking questions "in their language."

I was starting to learn a lot about the market, but I could not find a lead to market share—until one evening, after weeks of filling myself "full of the problem"—I was in backed up traffic on the Pomona Freeway—the answer came to me. I was in stalled traffic, watching workers from the highway department store their tools in a warehouse.

I said to myself, "That's it!!! During my next series of inquiring conversations and observations with retailers, I'll ask the owner or manager where he expects his business to be in gross dollars in three years as my client expects to build a warehouse in his area to better support his operation."

For the next 100 calls, without fail, every retainer said, "Well, let's see, this year I'll gross x dollars in sales, so in three years I should be doing such and such."

In six months I knew more about market share according to commodity than my competitors and even the Association the retailers belonged to. And my strategy and planning "in terms of the marketplace" made the company a giant in its field.

The strategic planning was, in essence, a gift of the marketplace, and, in a way of thanks, I knew exactly how to structure the organization. Also, many managers may not think as I, but the thanks came by way of the customer. Because by structuring properly, my service to him made him more competitive in the marketplace.

Therefore, the company witnessed an extraordinary increase in the number of goods sold—or merchandized; there is a difference.

My planning and decision-making encompassed the following—with the customer in mind:

> Organizational structure
> Hiring qualified Sales Personnel
> Training
> Assigning specific, identified territories with knowledge of market; knew
> what expected percentage to capture
> Proper warehousing
> Distribution/frequency of delivery, Transportation,
> Communication

Marketing, Selling, Merchandizing, Advertising
Fiscally sound incentives, Growth, Return on capital

I mentioned above that there is a difference between selling and merchandizing; there is a difference between marketing and selling too, but that is so fundamental it won't be discussed here.

The difference between selling and merchandizing is a matter of timing and needs of the retailer/consumer. A salesman will sell to a retailer; the retailed will sell to the consumer.

But if you link advertising with desire to move the right product to the right people, at the right place, at the right time, for the right price—that's merchandizing.

And advertising ties in more effectively to merchandizing than marketing or selling because of the ability to measure results in a more telling fashion.

The salesman in the field is more closely tied to the retailer during a merchandizing phase than a selling phase. The salesman must be present to support—during this time he is vicariously a merchandiser—providing right product, at right price, to right *retailer*, etc.

"Pay attention to your Market," is a truism. But many consultants continue to be amazed at how few strategists talk to the sales force, make customer calls themselves, or field complaints from buyers.

"I appeal to common observation, which has always found these artificial methods of reasoning more adapted to catch and entangle the mind, than to instruct and inform the understanding."

John Locke (1632-1704)
An Essay Concerning Human Understanding

John Locke! "I appeal to common observation—" A philosopher, offering, about 350 years ago, appealing to common sense, for me. Ah! The lessons of history!

THE STORY OF THE SECRETARY IN ST. LOUIS WHO WOULDN'T ARRANGE A MEETING

I am sure she was a very nice lady; most corporate executive secretaries are. But some do, at times, get a little bit haughty and over protective of their domain. This woman had the barbed wire and electrical current.

I was calling—let's say her name was Ms. Bongo Drums—from Los Angeles to a particular aerospace company in St. Louis seeking an appointment with a particular executive. I deemed the executive to be in trouble on a large overseas contract because someone was lying to him. I knew from experience a particular man was making too strenuous an effort to secure unearned, at the time, money. I thought fraud and deception was prevalent. The only way I could be sure was to call personally on the executive and explain what I thought were serious flaws in the contract.

I called Ms. Bongo Drums to seek an appointment. When she asked what the meeting would be in reference to I told her, in all due respect, the subject was of a confidential nature and it was in the best interest of Mr. Tuttle to meet with me.

She said, "Wrong! I can't tell Mr. Tuttle a man is flying in from California to speak to him on a confidential matter. Do you know how many men and ladies try to pull the wool over my eyes in a week with a phony story just to try to sell something to Mr. Tuttle?"

"Ms. Bong Drums, I don't care how many. I only know I have a responsibility to brief Mr. Tuttle and I would appreciate you asking him when we could meet."

I called four times from Monday through Thursday. I was told: He's in a meeting! Mr. Tuttle is out to lunch! Mr. Tuttle has been called to corporate. He left early to give a speech at Rotary. He will not return! He has executive personnel from XYZ Company this morning through lunch! Etc., etc., etc!

I called on Friday from my ranch in Springville. Mrs. Bongo Drums answered the phone. I said, "Ms. Drums, this is Mr. Simpson. I am now located 3 and 1/2 hours north of Los Angeles International. I am going to leave here Monday morning at 4:30AM. I am going to drive one hour to Bakersfield and catch a 6:15AM United Express to LA. I am then going to catch a TWA flight to St. Louis arriving at 2:50PM. I will then take a cab to your executive office building. If I do not have an appointment with Mr. Tuttle, I will walk out to the grass on the side of your building and set up camp as I have done a hundred times at my ranch. I will have a sleeping bag, a Coleman stove and lantern, bottles of water, a steak, a can of beans, and some bread. And I will STAY there, Ms. Drums, until I meet with Mr. Tuttle. If you desire, send him down; I'll split my steak with him."

"Now I know your aerospace police, the sheriff, the local police, and probably the National Guard will throw me in jail. But before they do, I will tell them I was there because of the refusal of a particular individual to offer me a time to meet with Mr. Tuttle. Now, Ms. Bongo Drums, if you think I am kidding, don't give me the courtesy of a meeting. Have a nice week end!"

When I walked into the executive office building, I had a visitor's pass ready and a company security officer waiting to escort me to the 8th floor. Mr. Tuttle was waiting. After an hour and a half of straight talk, he said, "Mr. Simpson, I can't thank you enough. I will call all personnel involved, cancel the contract, and tell everyone they are not to talk to Mr. Such and Such again.

I caught a late flight for LA. I wrote to Ms. Bong Drums and thanked her for setting up the meeting.

What I have just told you is a true story!

Until one is committed, there is hesitancy, the chance to draw back, always ineffectiveness. Concerning all acts of initiative (and creation), there is one elementary truth, the ignorance of which kills countless ideas and splendid plans: that the moment one definitely commits oneself, then Providence moves too.

All sorts of things occur to help one that would never otherwise have occurred. A whole stream of events issues from the decision, raising in one's favor all manner of unforeseen incidents and meetings and material assistance, which no man could have dreamed would have come his way.

Scottish Himalayan Expedition*
A GUIDE FOR THE ADVANCED SOUL, Susan Hayward

INITIATIVE/PERSEVERANCE

The man
Who wins may have
been counted out several times,
but he didn't hear
the referee

H. E. Jansen

After the Korean War I was assigned to North American Aviation because of experience gained as a fighter pilot and maintenance test pilot in Korea during the war and in southern Japan after the war. In addition to my combat missions, I flew many additional hours as an instructor in the "replacement training unit" and also, flew squadron test flights after minor airframe repair from combat damage, and/or an engine change.

When it looked like the war was due to end, I was transferred to southern Japan as a pilot to test fly all F-86 Sabre Jet aircraft that were overhauled due to enhanced flight time, and minor and major war damage. There were the fighters from the 4th, 51st, 18th, and my own famed 8th fighter wing. Each wing had about 75 aircraft.

While in southern Japan, I learned from the North American technical representative stationed at my Japanese base, that Air Force test pilots could be assigned to aircraft manufacturers like North American Aviation, located at the International Airport, in Los Angeles. I was excited about the possibilities so I took the initiative, with help from Bill, NAA's rep, and working through my own command with blessing from the Commanding Officer, wrote to the Commanding Officer of the Air Force Plant Representatives' office in Los Angeles and asked for the assignment. His answer arrived within a very short time. He, Col. Bill Barns, indicated that the Air Force "Table of Organization" allowed for the assignment of a rated (pilot) First Lieutenant but he could not ask for me by name. He did state, however, that, "I could use his letter in any way I deemed necessary for me to gain the assignment."

Now, I was a little excited! Could this happen to me?? I received permission from my commanding officer to take a short leave of absence and I flew to every air base in Korea and Japan and talked to every Commanding Officer, Operations Officer, Maintenance Officer, and Wing Commanders I had known, or flown with. I showed them Col. Barns letter and respectfully asked for their help. Soon the plant representative's office at North American Aviation was inundated with letters of recommendation. Colonel Barns was saying, "Who is this guy?"

My perseverance changed his thinking. He went to Washington and asked for me by name. I reported to Colonel William Barns on January 10, 1954. It was the beginning of an extraordinarily rewarding career in aviation that continues to this day.

I want you to know, before I had received an answer, many of my fellow pilots treated my thought with derision—even to the point where I was beginning to have self-doubt. The consensus was that every pilot in the Air Force with a hell of a lot more experience than I would be after that test pilot assignment. You?? They would say! At North American—famous for the WWII P-51 and Gen. Dolittle's North American B-25 raid on Tokyo? And, also, Simpson, the Korean Sabre Jet! You! Living like a civilian in Southern California! There ain't no way, Simpson, no way, "yer' wastin' yer' time."

I blocked their unfavorable comments from my mind and continued to think only of the rewards. In addition, I could never know without trying. But I remember reading a book where John Stuart Mill (1806-1973) who wrote, "The initiation of all wise and noble things comes, and must come from individuals; generally at first from some one individual. The honor and glory of the average man is that he is capable of following that initiative . . ."

I said to myself, "Screw my distracters."

HUMAN GREATNESS

My letter to the plant representative, plus my visit to the air bases seeking letters of recommendation, put me on an uninterrupted course. I was committed. I was determined to persevere.

In his famous printed and bound work, *ON WAR*, Carl Von Clausewitz, speaks of perseverance by comparing an architect, a doctor and a general.

Are you not an architect for your foundation of lifestyle? Do you not prescribe the principle governing the affairs of your life? Are you not the one in charge?

"In war, more than anywhere else, things do not turn out as we expect. Nearby they do not appear as they did from a distance. With assurance, an architect watches the progress of his work and sees his plans gradually take shape! A doctor, though much more exposed to chance and to inexplicable results, knows his medicines and the effects they produce. By contrast, a general in time of war is constantly bombarded by reports both true and false; by errors arising from fear or negligence or hastiness; by disobedience born of right or wrong interpretations, of ill will, of a proper or mistaken sense of duty, of laziness, or exhaustion; and by accidents that nobody could have foreseen. In short, he is exposed to countless impressions most of them disturbing, few of them encouraging. If a man were to yield to these pressures, he would never complete an operation."

When I first received the answer to my inquiry advising me to use the letter in any way I saw fit, my first stop was in Tokyo seeking an appointment with the Air Force Chief of Personnel (assignments).

I still remember "that" Lt. Colonel. The first thing I noticed; he didn't have any wings pinned to his left chest! He read the missive then looked at me over the top edge of the page and took action intended to evoke contemptuous laughter. "Who the Hell?? Do you think I could sort you out, here, in Tokyo, and put you above thousands of pilots wanting an assignment like this??"

I said, "Yes, Sir."

He said, "Why?"

I said, "Because I'm the only one of the thousands that has a letter."

He asked, sarcastically, "What am I going to do—read a letter every time someone wants a juicy assignment?" I didn't say a word but under my breath I said to myself, "Prick!"

The colonel wouldn't help me. I asked for and received my letter back.

"PERSEVERANCE in the chosen course, is the essential counterweight."

By trying to understand what Von Clausewitz has to say, man will, in my opinion, enhance his determination to follow through on any commitment or duty and follow a course of action that is demanded of one. You are the General! The buck stops with you regardless of "reports, true or false, errors arising from fear, etc., etc." You are free the moment you do not look outside yourself for someone to lean on.

"PERSEVERANCE, working in the right direction, grows with time, and when steadily practiced, even by the most humble, will rarely fail of its reward. Trusting in the help of others is, under some circumstances, of comparatively little use."

I was approached at one time by the vice-president of marketing for a large industrial packaging firm located in south central Los Angeles. The packaging firm, which specialized in corrugated boxes of all sizes, shapes, and strengths, had been very successful in the industrial and commercial marketplace, but were interested in a program that would, in time, capture a large share of the aerospace packaging field.

The vice-president of marketing for this particular company had no contacts with the aerospace purchasing profession and asked me if I would help him establish contacts and lay out a marketing plan to capture this aforementioned share.

We met two or three times but nothing progressed at all for about six weeks, and I asked the vice-president what the delay was. He told me that the gentleman (the president) he had been working under for a number of years, didn't believe in consultants, didn't believe he needed any help, and thought that he could make inroads into aerospace by using his present sales staff under the direction of the vice-president.

My vice president said, "Jack, I'm going to tell you what I told the boss."

"Sir, I wish to tell you a story. I want to follow the same focus as does the President and CEO of All Nippon Airways. Don't look at me that way. I read this in FORTUNE a couple of months ago. Seriously, I think aerospace requirements will teach us quality. And with quality comes the ability to effectively compete at higher prices. The president of All Nippon said, 'We knew we couldn't compete on quantity, so we are focusing entirely on quality. We are constantly listening to our customers—what they like, what they don't like, and what they want. We listen and we respond.' You know our sales have been increasing lately and this guy Simpson specializes in marketing analysis and he knows the aerospace market."

Of course, I knew this could not possibly happen in a short time because it takes years to develop a rapport with purchasing personnel of any territory, let along aerospace. So, I took the initiative and suggested to the vice-president that I would be happy to call the president of his firm and seek an appointment. He gave me his "OK" so I made the telephone call, introduced myself, and for the next 15 minutes, listened to an emotion packed fulmination by this man who said he had been in business for 50 plus years, was 70 years old, got to the office every morning at six o'clock, had developed a business from nothing, and he didn't think that he needed any help from anyone outside his company.

I could have, at that time, forgotten the whole program, but there was something this man had said over the phone that jogged my consciousness. He had said "six o'clock in the morning."

I got up the next morning at three-thirty and drove from Newport Beach to south central Los Angeles to find the warehouse where his office was located. I did find a "dough-nuts" shop. I remember that particular morning—pitch black—raining very hard—unfamiliar territory—it took me a while to find it. When I did, I had to laugh. I reminded myself of Sam Spade—hands in my trench coat pockets, collar pulled high, rain dripping from my hat. Here I was standing outside a warehouse under a 150watt bulb, seeking shelter under the eaves of the roof, waiting for a man I had never met to come to work.

At about five minutes to six, a four-door Pontiac, driven by a chauffeur, came around the corner and pulled up in front. The chauffeur got out, looked me over very carefully, walked around and opened the door of the car, and a 70year old man egresses. He looked startled! Before he said a word I stretched my sleeve, looked at my watch and said, "Well, I'll be darned, you do get here at six o'clock in the morning. My name is Jack Simpson. Are you buying the coffee? I have the 'dough-nuts'."

What else could the man do but invite me in, share with me the tasks of making coffee, and finally, saying, "Okay, what's it going to cost me and how long is it going to take?"

I worked for that man for more than two years helping his vice-president do his planning and sales, etc. He became one of my great friends, and for many years he couldn't wait to tell every person he ever met about this young "sales guy" that met him at six o'clock in the morning at his warehouse, checking to see if he got to work on time. I know one thing—no one else ever did!

Perseverance provides the means to take all of life in stride. Talent is worthless unless you work unflaggingly in developing it. And speaking of possible failure, I take umbrage with Rene Descartes, mathematician and philosopher.

Descartes, (1596-1650) is often called the Father of Modern Philosophy. He did for metaphysics (a division of philosophy that is concerned with the fundamental nature of reality and being) what Francis Bacon (1561-1626) did for science. He gave it a new method, the method of systematic doubt.

In his deliberation, for example, on "Freedom of the Will," Descartes' dilemma centered on the problem on how God could be responsible for human error! Since God would not deceive us, we can know that our "clear and distinct" ideas are true. How, then, can we ever be in error? Descartes' answer is that our will runs ahead of our certain knowledge, we anticipate conclusions instead of abstaining until we can perceive clearly and distinctly what the truth is; and thus, we abuse our free will. "We can, and should, avoid making a decision," Descartes says, "whenever the truth of the manner is not clear."

I totally disagree!!

I couldn't perceive clearly and distinctly what the truth was in my ability to become a fighter pilot, survive combat, and two life threatening crashes as an experimental pilot?? I saw nothing ill advised in anticipating my conclusion—you're darn right I could perceive clearly—by self-reverence, self-knowledge, and self-control complemented with initiative and perseverance. Read again the aphorism opening this chapter—"Until one is committed . . ." If I had followed Descartes' thinking, I would have never known the pure thrill of flying.

Every time I make a sales call, I anticipate another conclusion in the form of a purchase order. I am not providing a buyer a catalogue of ideas; I am providing specific product information and service to fill his or her needs. Why shouldn't they buy from me? If Descartes was my sales manager I'd never make the decision to call.

If I make a decision, I'm ready to face the truth. Yes, I could have died in combat or experimental flying, but that is the price you may have to pay for setting high goals and standards.

Sure, I could have lost a purchase order, that's the price you pay for learning how to be more economically and technically competitive for the next bid. How do you know there will be a next time?? That is what perseverance is all about.

You don't have to take as "gospel truth" everything you read, even from men of acclaimed reputation. However, but you will never learn what you perceive to be true until you commit to challenge.

Anyhow, let's get back to my warehouse friend. It was a challenge to meet the man; a challenge to see if my mind perceived, properly, as the thought unrolled and if probability would become fact—that this wonderful, elderly man would undoubtedly love the idea of my challenging him at 6AM—and that he would probably tell his friends about it for years to come. Both turned out to be true.

I have a California teaching credential. I had asked the business curriculum administrator of Orange Coast College if I could be a guest speaker at some of their sales and marketing classes. I was told that I would have to obtain my credential. I did so, but found out that was the easy part.

It took me two and a half years of calling, recalling and calling again on the head of the business department. Finally, after the fourth try, I was not only given the opportunity to teach, but was requested to help the college outline a detailed curriculum for the business sector with emphasis on marketing and sales. I taught evening classes for seven or eight years.

Maybe if I was given the immediate opportunity to guest lecture, I would have missed the rewards of planning the curriculum based on my business experience. I also knew I was teaching what businessmen needed to enhance their career. Personal perseverance can be rewarding to others, also.

One of the boys I helped raise through Big Brothers had graduated from high school, started night school, engaged to be married, and had no job because, and let this be a lesson, he quit an unfulfilling job before he got a new one.

This is not to say he had not worked hard all through high school and during night school, but he just had not found the kind of job that would give him the stability he felt he would need to get married.

One evening I had dinner with him, and he told me about a job opening he had read about in the local paper. He called the company and was told there were many, many applicants and they would start interviewing the next day at 10:30AM. The job was as an apprentice in a printing shop, and my little brother was very much interested in this because this particular printer specialized in high school yearbooks. During the course of the original conversation with the potential employer, my little brother was told that if he was the successful applicant and had any artistic talent, he could, as a maturing employee, draw cartoons or caricatures that were sometimes needed in yearbooks. He was very excited about the potential and said that he was going down the next day at 10:30 for an interview.

I said, "Wrong! I want you to get up tomorrow morning at five o'clock, shower, dress properly, and drive down there and be standing in front of that printing shop by no later than six o'clock. Every time a worker goes into the plant, I want you to ask for the personnel manager or the particular gentleman who's going to do the interviewing. As always, as craftsmen prepare for work, they sit around with a cup of coffee. They will start saying, 'I wonder who that kid is out there waiting to see Mr. Jones. Jones probably won't get in until 8:30 or 9 o'clock. There is no sense of him standing out there in the cold. Why don't we bring him in and when Jones comes in, we'll take him in and introduce him.'"

"Now," I continued, "when they take you in to introduce you to Mr. Jones, look him in the eye and shake his hand, as I've taught you, and tell Mr. Jones that you got up at five o'clock this morning to come to the plant and you've been waiting for three-and-a-half hours to meet with him. Tell him there is no sense in him conducting interviews at 10:30 that morning because, and start taking your tie off, you are ready to go to work for him right now. Then say, 'The only way I could prove to you that I was ready to go to work was by doing what I did this morning.'"

I told my little brother that if he did what I said, he would get the job. I told him that of the potential 100 or so applicants, no one would think of doing what I wanted him to do. And I told him something else. That personnel manager will hire you because he won't be able to wait to tell his business associates about this kid "that showed up at six a.m." I also told him I knew he had little money and if he did as I suggested, I would pay his rent for three months. "It will give you a chance to catch up," I said.

Every word I said came true. My little brother got up at five o'clock, kept asking for Mr. Jones, the workers took him in, bought him a cup of coffee, introduced him to Mr. Jones, he told him he wanted the job and Jones put him to work that morning. I didn't know it until later, but my little brother even took his lunch. Now that is pure positive thinking. Combine that with initiative and perseverance and what do you have? Dynamite!

But the most important thing to come from the experience was that for many, many years I had been calling for my little brother and his other friends at his orphanage. I would gather them around and talk about subjects like self-discipline, being a gentleman, work ethics, etc. The boys thought, oh, Jack Simpson was just another old guy that had a lot of thoughts and suggestions and regulations and funny sayings. But nothing ever made any sense to them, because they really hadn't been given the opportunity to put reality to the test.

It only took about five minutes for my little brother to spread the word at the orphanage on how he got the job.

The next time I went to the orphanage to pick up the boys for dinner, one boy ran out to me and after we greeted, said, "Gee, didn't you notice anything different?" I said, "To be honest, no." He said, "Didn't you see how I looked you in the eye when I gave you a firm handshake?" Another boy said, "Look how I shined my shoes," and a third said, "Maybe you ain't so dumb after all."

"Perseverance pays in many ways. There needs all the force that enthusiasm can give to enable a man to succeed in any great enterprise of life. Without it, the obstruction and difficulty he has to encounter on every side might compel him to succumb; but with courage and *perseverance*, inspired by enthusiasm, a man feels strong enough to face any danger, to grapple with any difficulty."

In the Bible, praises are given, not to the strong man who "taketh a city" but to the stronger man who "ruleth his own spirit."

> "This stronger man is he who, by discipline, exercises a constant control over his thoughts, his speech, and his acts. Nine-tenths of the

vicious desires that degrade society, and which, when indulged, swell into the crimes that disgrace it, would shrink into insignificance before the advance of valiant self-discipline, self-respect and self-control."

"Self-reverence, self-knowledge, self-control, these three alone lead life to sovereign power."

Tennyson

I don't care if you are the Pope, The President of the United States, the President of General Motors, a famous doctor, lawyer, physicist, astronomer, whatever—there ii no stronger man than by my "little brother" from "Big Brothers" because he exercises constant control over his speech, his acts, and his thoughts.

AN ADDENDUM

The young gentleman I speak of worked at the print shop for three years; didn't miss a day. At the same time he went to night school, graduated as an engineer and is today the senior designer (CAD/CAM) for a technically oriented specialty instrument company. Now married with four children, this fine gentleman, whom I met in the 6th grade, was an orphan; he never knew his mother or father.

He has never complained about a thing!

THE SIDE VIEW MIRROR CAPER

I DON'T KNOW IF "CAPER" IS THE RIGHT CHOSEN WORD. WHAT HAPPENED TO ME WAS NOT NECESSARILY PRANCING ABOUT IN A PLAYFUL MANNER. BUT YET, I COULD SAY IT WAS A CAPRICIOUS ESCAPADE BECAUSE I DID SOMETHING STUPID. AS FAR AS I WAS CONCERNED IT WAS IMPULSAIVE AND UNPREDICTABLE.

I HADN'T MET, AS YET, EITHER OF TWO BEAUTIFUL FASHION MODELS WHO HAD BREAKFAST AT A RESTAURANT WHERE I ATE TWICE A WEEK OR SO. BUT IT DID GET TO THE POINT WHERE WE AT LEAST SAID "HELLO" ONCE IN A WHILE.

THEN, ONE DAY, I WAS INTENSIVELY WATCHING ONE OF THEM LEAVE THE RESTAURANT AS I WAS BACKING UP MY NEW CADILLAC SEVILLE. SINCE MY INCREASE IN SCOPE WAS DIRECTED MORE TOWARD THE BEAUTIFUL LADY THAN WATCHING WHAT I WAS DOING, I TORE THE SIDE VIEW MIRROR COMPLETELY FROM THE CAR BY HITTING IT ON A CONCRETE PILLAR. THE PILLAR DID NOT MOVE; THE MIRROR DID!

SO I ACTED AS ANY ARDENT, ANXIOUS, SOLICITOUS, THIRSTING, FIGHTER PILOT WOULD DO. I RAN OVER TO CATCH HER AND SAID, "LOOK WHAT YOU DID TO MY CAR. LOOK AT THAT MIRROR!"

SHE STOPPED AND EYED ME WITH A LOOK OF INQUISITIVE QUESTIONING, YOU KNOW, LIKE I WAS NUTS! SHE SAID, "WHAT ARE YOU TALKING ABOUT? IT'S NOT MY FAULT YOU DON'T KNOW HOW TO BACK UP YOUR CAR."

I IMMEDIATELY SAID, "YES, IT IS! IF YOU DIDN'T HAVE SUCH PRETTY LEGS I WOULD'T HAVE HAD MY EYES ON YOU. SO THE ONLY WAY YOU CAN MAKE AMENDS IS TO HAVE LUNCH WITH ME."

SHE SAID, "NO! NO! NOT LUNCH—OR DINNER! BUT I'LL HAVE BREAKFAST WITH YOU—SHE STOPPED TO THINK—ON FRIDAY MORNING." MY NAME IS JOANNA."

I SAID, "DYNAMITE, JOANNA. 8:AM! AND EAT A BIG DINNER."

SHE SMILED AT ME—BEAUTIFUL TEETH! SHE THEN TURNED AND WALKED TOWARD HER CAR.

SHE BROUGHT HER GIRL FRIEND MARY ANNE; THAT WAS OK WITH ME. I HAD BREAKFAST WITH BOTH, OR EITHER, FOR A NUMBER OF WEEKS. AND THEN ONE DAY, THEY WERE GONE.

IT'S A TRUE STORY; EVERYTIME I LOOK IN MY SIDE VIEW MIRROW, WHILE BACKING OUT OF A PARKING SPACE, I THINK OF JOANNA AND MARY ANN.

THAT WAS BMWD—BEFORE MY WIFE DAGMAR—ABOUT 1975!

FAILURE IS SIMPLY THE OPPORTUNITY TO BEGIN AGAIN, THIS TIME MORE INTELLIGENTLY!

Henry Ford, *TIME*
INSIDE BUSINESS,
December, 2004

How many more must fall? EACH MONTH seems to bring the sound of another giant crashing to earth. Enron, WorldCom, Global Crossing, Kmart, Polaroid, Authur Anderson, Xerox, Qwest. They fall singly. They fall in groups. They fall with the heavy thud of employees laid off, families hurt, shareholders furious. How many? Too many; **257** companies with **$258 billion** in assets declared bankruptcy last year (2001), shattering the previous year's record of **176** companies and **95 billion**.

Why do companies fail? Their CEOs offer every excuse in the book: a bad economy, market turbulence, a weak yen, hundred-year floods, perfect storms, competitive subterfuge—forces that are very much outside their control. A close study of corporate failure suggests that, acts of God aside such as Sept. 11, most companies founder for one simple reason: **managerial error**. (**bold** type—author)

FORTUNE
May 27, 2002

In the past forty years I have represented (my ken—marketing analysis, and management/engineering sales) a cross section of industrial, commercial, service oriented, and aerospace companies large and small. Today, three large aerospace companies, one "next level" aerospace company, three former leaders in aerospace landing gear, flight controls, and mechanical actuating systems, a leader in supplying a safety device to nuclear power-plants, a division of a large drug distribution corporation, a large real estate company, a business jet distributor, a helicopter service corporation, a planned recreation division of a Las Vegas hotel, and two corporations with presidents consumed in greed as they purchased one company after another with no detailed plans for amalgamation. These corporations are no longer part of the free enterprise system. They are gone! Defunct! Vanished! Dead! So are the millions of dollars wasted on frivolous expenditures such as an ornate fountain in the president's reception area on the 25th floor, a personal chef and dining room, and a personal jet aircraft. But so are the employees! And their savings plans! And their health insurance! And their retirement dollars!

My experiences with the above named situations are no different from what I read in *TIME, FORTUNE, THE WALL STREET JOURNAL,* and *FORBES.* The failures start with one main reason; management stops minding the store; they soon grow soft with what they think is success. They get bigger cars, join country clubs, and begin competing with friends as to who can bring the youngest, prettiest girls to surreptitious dinner parties. In time, since they aren't paying strict attention to the business at hand, egregious errors in judgment appear; management assignments soon start to flow to personnel totally incapable of managing the responsibilities and accountabilities of the particular department or discipline assigned. Divisions of the company and then the corporation itself, starts to lose money. So, what do they do? They can't give up the club or the buxom blonde. Next? They cook the books!

In the paragraph above I said—"grow soft with what they think is success." Success as defined by *WEBSTER'S NINTH COLLEGIATE DICTIONARY* is "a degree or measure of succeeding." Also OUTCOME, RESULT, the attainment of wealth!

My meaning of success is—"Here's a guy who worked his tail off all his life, attained his specific goal of satisfaction, sold or closed his company with honor with enough cash or equivalent assets to live a life of leisure of his choosing. No one can measure success in anyone else's terms other than his own. Certainly degrees of success can be measured by many means such as on Wall Street alone, but the degrees are fleeting and ephemeral. Success is the totality of, as *WEBSTER* says, OUTCOME!

FORTUNE, May 27, 2002, reads, "Let's acknowledge that, yes, failures usually involve factors unique to a company's own industry or culture. As Tolstoy said of families, all happy companies are alike; every unhappy company is unhappy in its own way. Some go out in blinding supernovas (Enron). Others linger like white dwarfs (AT&T). Still others fizzle out over decades (Polaroid). Failure is part of the natural cycle of business. Companies are born, companies die, capitalism moves forward. Creative destruction, they call it."

It was roughly this sentiment that Treasury Secretary Paul O'Neill was trying to convey when he said that Enron's failure was "Part of the genius of capitalism." But aside from sounding insensitive, O'Neill got one thing wrong. Capitalism's true genius is to weed out companies that no longer serve a useful purpose. The dot-coms, for instance, were experiments in whether certain businesses were even viable. We found out: They were not! Yet many recent debacles were of companies that could have lived long, productive lives with more enlightened management—in other words, good companies struck down for bad reasons. By these lights, Arthur

Andersen's fall is no more part of the "genius of capitalism" than the terrorism of Sept. 11 was part of the "genius of evolution."

By "failure," we don't necessarily mean bankruptcy. A dramatic fall from grace qualifies too. In the most recent bear market, for instance, 26 of America's 100 largest companies lost at least two-thirds of their market value, including such blue chips as Hewlett-Packard, Charles Schwab, Cisco, AT&T, AOL Time Warner, and Gap. In the 1990 bear market, by contrast, none did according to money management firm Aronson & Partners. The sheer speed of these falls has been unnerving. Companies that were healthy just moments ago it seems, are suddenly at death's door.

But this impression may be misleading. Consider, for instance, a certain Houston institution we've heard so much about. There was no one moment when its managers sat down and conspired to commit wrongdoing. Rather, the disaster occurred because of what one analyst calls "an incremental descent into poor judgment." A "success-oriented' culture, mind-numbing complexity, and unrealistic performance goals all mixed until the violation of standards became the standard. Nothing looked amiss from the outside until, boom! It was all over!

It sounds a lot like Enron, but the description actually refers to NASA in 1986, the year of the space shuttle *Challenger* explosion. We pull this switch not to conflate the two episodes—one after all, involved the death of seven astronauts—but to make a point about failures: Even the most dramatic tend to be years in the making. At NASA, engineers noticed damage to the crucial O-rings on previous shuttle flights yet repeatedly convinced each other the damage was acceptable. Companies fail the way Ernest Hemingway wrote about going broke in the *The Sun Also Rises*: gradually, and then suddenly!

What undoes them in the familiar stuff of human folly: denial, hubris, ego, wishful thinking, poor communication, lax oversight, greed, deceit, and other *Behind the Music* plot conventions. It all adds up to a failure to execute. This is not an exhaustive list of corporate sins. But chances are your company is committing one of them right now.

As an entrepreneur the idea of family, friends, and business associates knowing you are working 20 hours a day six or seven days a week sounds good, but to me it sounds as if you are not planning your time properly. I don't care who you are or what business you are in, you can't accept all the responsibilities at once. Planning is the key; a key to unlock the secrets of how to use, efficiently and effectively the **only** asset you and your business has. And that is—**TIME!**

In *TIME AND THE ART OF LIVING*, author Robert Grudin states, "Experts at time management will give would-be achievers the following hints. Grudin goes on to list 12 hints, but for the purpose of this chapter I am going to list only four.

- Refuse, politely but decisively, to accept involvements that would distract you from the purposes you value.

- Seek advise from experts, but otherwise avoid projects whose success depends on the charity or competence of others.
- Work much and regularly, but rest and exercise as much and as regularly as you work.
- Ensure that very important activity receives a large and uninterrupted period of time.

In the continual review of your marketing and business plan (see end of chapter) you will find you have no time to accept distracting involvements.

When I was given the responsibility to analyze a market for the purpose of writing a plan, I hired experts who had more knowledge than I in a particular discipline. They could speak the market language of the companies we called on looking for answers and ask incisive questions and listen intently to their answers. Their answers to the many questions offered the nexus for my marketing and business plan. I paid them well for an agreed to period of time. I trusted them and while they were gathering information relevant to the matter at hand, I went about other factors that needed to be systematically studied in order to create an effective plan. (see chapter on MARKETING & BUSINESS PLAN)

The most effect of "work much and regularly" is directly proportional to the consequence of the efficacy of the plan.

Very important activities will receive large and uninterrupted periods of time if you plan your time properly. The time belongs to you; you meter it out to fit the periods needed.

Since I mentioned time belonging to the entrepreneur, I'll mention how I handle it.

When I call for an appointment to meet ANYONE, I always suggest to the secretary or individual the time. For example, I say, "I am free from 9am to 10:30. Is that convenient for him (or you.) If the answer is negative I say, "What does his (or your) time look like this afternoon about three or how about tomorrow morning at eight? I'll bring the do-nuts! I could fill a whole week or two with appointments built around **MY** time. AND!! If it looked like I would possibly be a minute late, I would always call, even if it meant pulling off the freeway to find a phone. I would say, "It looks like I may be a few minutes late, will that be inconvenient for Mr. Jones (or you)? Every time I would get the same answer. "Thank you for calling. Take your time. I have plenty to do until you get here."

My office was in the trunk of my car. I received my messages through voice mail. Correspondence was under the firm control of a brilliant secretary! She could take dictation, regarding my day's activities, as fast as I could talk. She worked from her home in the evenings when she returned from work at an aerospace company. I had all the corporate letterheads of the companies I represented at her home and I had enough trust in her to let her sign my name. It worked beautifully. It saved me time from going to "the office." I paid her a fair price per letter, and it got to the point when I wanted to thank someone for their time (which I ALWAYS did,) I would just say, "Here's his name and address; you know what I want to say."

Speaking of "thank you letters," I had an appointment with an executive I had talked to earlier about a contract I was very much interested in. When I called, the secretary, she said, "Oh! yes, Mr. Simpson. Mr. Jones will be out shortly." I waited! And waited! The secretary called the receptionist and told her to tell me he was on his way. When Mr. Jones got there we sat down and started to talk. He knew my interest and was taking notes. I suddenly realized why it took him longer than usual to meet me in the reception area. He was taking notes on the back of a SIMPSON COMPANY envelope—the envelope that, a few weeks earlier, contained my "thank you" letter. He was late because his secretary was looking for my correspondence.

I did not have control of my business; I had a constant **GRIP** on it. If I didn't keep up to date with the constant changes in the business community, both technical, operational, plus competition with its economic and potential crushing aspect, it would not have been long before I would not have had a business.

I chose my clients carefully; if a potential client wanted my collective experience with the desire to have me represent them, they had to pay for my time either by retainer or a retainer against commission. If a company "paid" for my time, they "paid" attention to what I had to say.

Anyhow, in reference to the gentleman taking notes on the SIMPSON COMPANY envelope, I won the contract. Sales expense? A 28-cent stamp! Sometimes, also, it's the little things that count!

One day I received a call from a gentleman in West St. Louis. He was the vice-president of a large sheet metal fabrication corporation. He had gotten my name from a purchasing manager from an aerospace company. He told me his name and said, "Mr. Simpson, I am looking for a representative in the Los Angeles, San Diego areas, and your name was given to me. Would you be interested?"

I said, "Well, Mr. Springwater (he was ¼ TACOMA Indian with a Masters Degree in mechanical engineering,) I am flattered, but we will have to discuss many subjects on this matter, although I am free to do so as I have no conflicting clients at this time. What do you have in mind?"

Mr. Springwater said, and I am paraphrasing, "Why don't I send you some brochures and a tape outlining our capabilities and satisfied customers, and you can let me know what you think; if you think there is any business on the west coast, maybe we can work out a deal.

"Mr. Springwater," I said. "Hundreds of companies can send me pictures and tapes, but that doesn't tell me anything except you have pretty pictures and tapes. The buyers and purchasing management personnel from every aerospace company with which I am familiar, see brochures all the time. They will want to know, as I will, what is your management, your quality, your production control, your manufacturing engineering, your on-time deliveries, your financial status, and your desire to invest in programs over the long term. But, rather than discuss these things over the phone, now, let me talk to a few people and I will call you in a week or so and lay out the foundation for potential growth for MISSOURI SHEETMETAL and MANUFACTURING on the west coast. There may be one problem though."

"What could that be?" he asked.

"Mr. Springwater," I answered. "I am sorry but I do not work on commission. If we agree on the plan I send you, you will have to pay for my time with a consulting fee, or a fee against commission. But you and I can consider that matter in due time."

He didn't say anything for a few seconds, and then he said, "OK! I'll wait for your plan and take it from there."

The plan I sent Mr. Sprinwater was as follows:

Mr. Springwater to visit the L.A. area for three and ½ days with personal calls, with me, on purchasing, engineering, and quality personnel. Calls, by appointment, are to be made from 9:00am until 4:00pm on Tuesday through Friday morning with business meetings at lunch and dinner at local, but first class restaurants. Lunches will be with purchasing managers, dinners will be with aerospace executives in each discipline; purchasing, engineering, and quality. Mr. Springwater will be host and a few wives may be present at dinner.

Mr. Springwater will make any presentation he thinks necessary to these professionals. That is, specific talks to the men depending on responsibility—quality, engineering, and procurement.

The men will be very much aware why Mr. Springwater is hosting the above-mentioned meetings. Many questions will be asked; these men would like to give MISSOURI SHEETMETAL and MANUFACTURING an opportunity for business if they are convinced the try is worth it.

THE SIMPSON COMPANY will have all hotel reservations, restaurant reservations, transportation, and communication responsibilities covered. The cost of the hotel will be defrayed by MISSOURI SHEETMETAL through a billing by the SIMPSON COMPANY. Mr. Springwater will be met at the plane on arrival. After a short meeting at TWA's AMBASSADOR CLUB his baggage will be transported to the hotel by a SIMPSON COMPANY employee while Springwater and Simpson travel to their first Tuesday morning appointment. The reverse will hold true on Friday morning. Mr. Springwater's baggage will be transported to the airport while Simpson and Springwater travel to their business meeting(s) and luncheon. After arriving at the airport for the flight to St. Louis, Mr. Springwater will be given his baggage check and seat assignment in the TWA AMBASSADOR CLUB where Mr. Springwater and Mr. Simpson will discuss the future of their relationship.

We agreed on a contract I had in mind. A fee for six months followed by a fee against commission, **after** I met with the personnel Mr. Springwater and I had met during the intensive three and a half days. He said, "Simpson, I'm going back to St. Louis and get some sleep. I'm too old to follow you around. But I see what you did!

In a little over three days with ten meetings, four lunches, and three dinners they sure known who the hell we are. Lockheed, North American, Douglas, and TRW offer much potential. If they are as positive as I think they are, we have a deal.

Well, they *were* positive. Mr. Springwater and I worked together for six years. It was a great account—for both of us. That is an account I had a **grip** on.

Many companies fail, both the principal and the sales representative, because of the lack of belief in each other, communication, lack of a method for exchanging information, to and just plain sloth. Mr. Springwater met the men I worked with, and he flew me to St. Louis to meet his personnel. It works!

A note:

The Simpson Company "employee" I speak of in this and other potential contracts plus visits from, at the time, present clients, were always bright, scintillating, articulate, stewardesses. If my present or potential client were flying to L.A. on TWA I would hire a TWA stewardess. If flying on American I would hire an American stewardess. If United, a United stewardess, and so on. They were always my friends and I could count on them. They knew their way around the airport, hotels, and how to make men, and their wives, feel at home. Upon arrival we always made our collective plans at the airline's VIP lounge. They knew how to handle baggage, hotel check-ins, seat selections and any requests the client might have had.

I paid them well, and it worked for both of us.

"The current emphasis on reengineering essentially means changing an organization from the flow of things—to the flow of information.

Peter F. Drucker
HARVARD BUSINESS REVIEW
May-June 1993

How many times in this **BOOK III** of a Trilogy have I said, "Speak in the 'language of" and the 'needs of' the customer? Remember in **BOOK I** when I made a fool of myself on my first mission? Socrates spoke to me about this by telling me, "Suitcase," you knew **of** the capabilities of the F-86, and you knew **of** the enemy, and you knew **of** the tactics and strategy before being in combat, but you didn't know a damn thing **about** the F-86, the enemy, and tactics when it came to fighting for your life in war."

I learned to speak the 'language of' and the 'needs of' the customer when I was selling for someone else. But when it came time to be in business for myself and learned to get a grip on things, there was suddenly a demand or prerequisite—it was like combat; "of" wasn't good enough.

I had to know more "about." I had to think in terms from the flow of things—to the flow about information!

A dramatic example of what we learn from the lessons of history!!

Learning more "about" meant learning more about me, defining my business, my experiences, my responsibilities, my accountabilities, my ability to plan, my ability to set and meet goals, my growth patterns, my financial needs, the company's financial needs, my information gathering plans and needs, my ability to understand and be knowledgeable of TIME, my ability to understand and pre-sage problems, and above all, to understand the need to learn to be competitive—in a resolute and honest manner.

I learned to be a better businessman by writing, in detail, a business and marketing plan and then reviewing it almost monthly. This was my nexus, my center, my core to success.

Without it, would be my Waterloo!

Think again, or study more of the lessons of history. I say think of Darwin.

"Darwin?" you say.

"Yes!" I say. "Darwin gave us a theory of the origin and perpetuation of new species of animals and plants that offspring of a given organism vary, that natural selection favors **the survival of some of these variations over others**."

In my business I was constantly aware of competition and the survival of some of my clients ability to continue to compete; the various means they used to try to beat down my client. They tried it on the POLARIS program, they tried it on HOOVER, they tried it at North American, Columbus.

They failed!

And Lo! And Behold! I was reading a new book over the last weekend. It is entitled *The World Is Flat*, by Thomas Friedman, a *Los Angeles Times* editorial writer.

Friedman contends that Americans is coming decades will have to cope with a kind of economic **Darwinism**: "You want constantly to acquire new skills, knowledge, and expertise that enable you constantly to be able to create value—(read my chapters; An Exchange of Value and Listen, Learn, Think, then Sell) something more than vanilla ice cream. You want to learn how to make the latest chocolate sauce, the whipped cream, or the cherries on top, or to deliver it as a belly dancer—in whatever field you endeavor."

'Nuff said!

SELF-INDENTITY / RELIABILITY
ATTRIBUTES OF AN INDIVIDUAL
THAT MUST BE **EARNED**!

"Self-reliance is like a flash-light; no matter how dark it gets, it will help you find your way." My Dad told me that one when I about 8 or 9 years old. He told me I was getting old enough to accept responsibility around the house—emptying the trash, cutting the grass, keeping the furnace hot with coal, and emptying the ashes. My Dad only spoke once! I started accepting responsibility!

When I was eleven years old I got a paper route. It wasn't given to me; I followed our paperboy for six months pestering him about taking over when he was ready to give it up. One day he said, "In two weeks!" Maybe it was "those rainy days and Mondays that always got him down." I had thirty-five customers that expected their papers to be delivered, on time, Monday through Friday evenings, rain, sleet, snow, bitter cold, blistering heat, no excuse; plus early Saturday afternoons, and early Sunday mornings. My gross—nine dollars and eighty cents a week! My Profit? Too little to remember!

The paper route presented me an opportunity to actually experience—reliability.

My Dad told me a few months after I started my route that the reliability of a person is measured to a great extent by the promptness with which he meets all appointments and fulfills all obligations regardless of the personal inconvenience of hardships encountered. He must learn not to assume obligations or make promises that he cannot fulfill. Obligations or promises must be fulfilled; not because of any reward for performance or punishment for non-performance, but merely because his word has been given.

As this story of my paper route unfolds, I think the reader will understand what knowledge I gained from this learned man who seemed to have uncanny insight as to how I could mentally grow by just giving me things to think about. I was then up to me to accept the responsibility of keeping thirty-five individual families happy; every day! Seven days a week! Thirty + days a month! And, twelve "cold as hell," "hot as hell," "raining like hell" "windy as hell" "snowing like hell" months a year! I am asking myself, "Are you worthy of being relied on?" "Does your self-identity give you a strength of character?" I answered my own question. "Damn right"!

A Man's Character is the reliability of himself!
His reputation is the opinion they have formed of him;
Reputation is from other people.
Henry Ward Beecher
1813-87
American orator, lecturer

Ralph Waldo Emerson Said, "There is a time in every man's education that he must take himself for better or worse as his portion; that though the universe is full of no good, no kernel of nourishing corn can come to him but through his toil that plot of ground which is given to him to toil. The power which resides in him is new in nature, and none but he knows what that is which he can do, nor does he know until he has tried."

I wonder if Emerson knew I was going to get a paper route?

One Saturday morning in early spring (Saturday papers were usually delivered my noon), my Dad invited me to go to a Pittsburgh Pirate baseball game. He said, "Fold your papers and jump in the back of the car. We will get them delivered in a hurry and still get to the game on time." We delivered the papers in short order! I had, as I said earlier, thirty-five customers.

On the way to the ball game my Dad said to me, "There's something I do not understand."

I said, "What is that?"

Dad said, "I saw you delivering a paper to one particular house, you would then skip three houses, deliver another paper, skip a couple more houses, deliver a paper, deliver one or two paper to an apartment house when there must be at least 15 tenants and so on. If you're going to use all that time and energy, why have you not stopped at the houses in between to ask those people to become your customer?"

I said, "I don't know, I guess I'm sort of always in a hurry to finish my route; I didn't think about it."

He said, "I'll tell you what I'll do. You tell Mr. Spector (he was my distributor and area manager) to give you 10 extra papers every day for a week, then skip a week; then ten every day during the third week, then skip a week; then ten more the fifth week, etc., until you reach a cycle of eight weeks. As I see it, you will have received 280 extra papers. I'll pay for all of them. What I want you to do is start leaving a paper every evening, early Saturday afternoon, and Sunday morning at those potential customers we skipped. During the second week, knock on their door and ask them if they liked the convenience of the delivery and if they wanted to become a steady customer. Then do the same the third week and so on. You're geographical territory won't get any bigger so concentrate on what you have been assigned."

After eight weeks, out of forty potentials, I signed up thirty-one; I now had 66 customers.

Most of my customers had a reliable source for a paper such as a newsstand or retail outlet so they asked me questions like, "Will you be dependable?" "Can we rely on you?" "Will you be able to handle delivery in the snow and rain?" And, "Don't promise me you're going to be able to deliver and then give me some hard luck story when you don't." Even Mr. Spector wondered if I could assume the obligation to pay for all the extra papers when collections were not always that easy.

I told my new clients they could depend on me but they could always ask "that customer over there" and pointed to someone I had been delivering to. I convinced Mr. Spector that he should take a chance on me and, besides, my dad had purchases 280 extra papers and that if I got in trouble he would help carry me over.

After about six weeks I divided the route into three sections and convinced the delivery van to place 22 at three intersections. Of course my dad helped. He met the driver at each intersection soon after he agreed and gave him a case of ice-cold "Rolling Rock" beer.

It was early August and very hot, muggy, and with daylight savings, it seemed the damn sun would never go down. I went to my dad and said I really appreciated the fact that he helped me with the growth of my route, but I now needed a wagon to help me carry the load of all the papers. He turned and looked me in the eye and simply said, "If you need a wagon, looks like you'll have to save your money and buy it?"

I was stunned! I saw myself lugging those papers forever! His answer made me extremely angry; I thought he would help! I said to myself, "Ok! you cheap so and so, if that's the way you are going to be—I will. I'll save my money—I'll show you!"

Therefore, for the next five months including struggling through the fall and January winter, I continued to haul the papers on my back, and saved week after week what little money I could. I raked leaves, washed cars, shoveled snow, took care of coal furnaces for neighbors without kids, wheel barreled coal from alleys to basement windows, and helped a man caulk every window in his house. Of course I was busy but I had my Saturday afternoons and was free after about 9am on Sundays.

Dad never said a word except to acknowledge I was "working pretty hard."

Finally! I had enough money to buy the cheapest wagon SEARS & ROEBUCK had to offer. I then went to my dad and asked if he would take the time to drive me downtown to get the wagon. On the following Saturday evening we went down to SEARS and I pointed out to the salesman the box that contained the small tin wagon I now had the money to pay for. Damn! I hated things that came in a box! Still do!

As I reached into my pocket for the money, my dad said, "Hold it! Keep your money in your pocket. There's your wagon on the other side of the showroom." I looked over and there was the biggest, most beautiful, double wheeled, wooden sided, magnificent wagon that any company in the country could ever build; and probably cost ten times the money I had saved. The wagon was all put together—ready to go. What I didn't know at the time was that my dad had called SEARS earlier and planned it all. I'll never forget what he said as long as I live—"All I wanted you to do was prove to me you wanted a wagon bad enough to save for it."

What can I say? In my dad's own way he had taught me the practical meaning of reliability—to endure the great effort of saving money with the promise I made to myself to buy the wagon; thanks to him, I was becoming mentally tough.

At least I thought so! Every Sunday morning the alarm went off at 4:30 AM. One particular Sunday I looked outside, and there must have been six inches or more of snow on the ground. Gees! A howling blizzard, with the winds driving the snow parallel to the ground! I decided no one could be moving in weather like that, so I went back to bed. Now remember, I was on the third floor. In less time than it took me to curl up in my sheets, blanket, and comforter, my bedroom door was thrown open, the light was switch slammed on, and there was my Dad, a six foot, two inch Attila the Hun, standing over me. He said, "Get your tail out of that bed! NOW! There are a lot of people out there who have sons fighting the war in Europe and Japan, protecting people like you, your sisters, and your mother, and me. And you are the one that holds the key to their communication with them in the paper you are committed to deliver, on time, so they may read it on their way to work in the steel mills and machine shops. So, make up your mind! Are you going to be held accountable in seeing that they get their vital communication? If not, give up your paper route. And as he backed out, my Dad shut off the light and closed the door—let's say with enthusiasm.

Naturally, it took me about five seconds to get dressed and "out of there." I remember it was tough going that Sunday. I couldn't use my wagon because of the snow and the delivery truck could only drop the papers at on place. So there I stood in front of 66 thick Sunday papers. With my strap and bag I could only carry about 8 at a time; I had to make a decision! I sat down in the snow and pulled all of the bull shit advertising and other crap and carried only the real news. I made the paper about a third of its weight until I could carry 22 at a time. It was about 5:20 AM so I had to haul ass. I then decided that although it would take me three individual round trips, I would deliver the paper to only those houses where I knew the men worked in the mills; I had a pretty good idea who they were. I would also deliver to only the houses with their lights on. I would get the others later!

Well, it took me about six hours; that was OK, I missed Sunday mass. But every customer received his paper; and no one complained. I think they thought the "middle stuff" (that I expertly removed) didn't make it to the publisher because of the storm. And from that Sunday on, and I am talking sixty-seven years, I have never stepped back from a responsibility. I have realized what responsibility means and how people (management) should comprehend accountability once a particular responsibility is assigned.

As a result of accomplishing what was for me an enormous task at 11 years old (in 1938 daily papers were three cents; Sundays, 10 cents; so my collection from each customer was 28 cents per week). My commission was a few cents. I vowed that from that time on I was going to be my own man. If I wanted anything done, I would do it myself. If I wanted anything of value, I would buy it myself.

So I worked. And as I got older (I gave up my paper route at 15 and a half) I worked in a drug store, delivered special delivery mail for the Post Office, worked as an office boy for a paper company after school and finally (before service in WW II) as a laborer at J & L Steel—for 87 cents per hour.

I was learning reliability; learning to be loyal, confident, ambitious, proud—I was slowly mastering self-control and discipline. And I made a lot of mistakes!

I am not saying this to be boastful—these qualities sort of went with the territory. It was the exposure of working for others that brought it about. And, occurring in company with work was a gain in self-identity because all of a sudden I was not afraid to make a mistake.

I learned in my early reading a thought from John Oliver Hobbes. "Men heap together the mistakes of their lives, and create a monster called—Destiny."

SELF-IDENTITY

"My self-identity is in my mind, in my thinking, doubting, feelings, perceiving, imagining, and desiring. I am, essentially, 'A thing that thinks'."

Descartes

Self-identity begins with a flash of insight—moment of pride, a moment of vanity, a moment of embarrassment—your moment of pride because you have just been praised, moment of embarrassment when you can't remember a friend's name. This is all being part of yourself—your identity.

I can't remember who said the above;
And I can't take credit!

But I have honestly set the standards for my own self-identity. It used to be a problem trying to decide which side or position I should take, but I soon determined that flexibility played a role in some instances whereby standing firm was better in others. It seems that as time went on and I learned more of myself, I didn't care what other people thought about my identity. I was not going to change my personality to meet everyone's criteria for liking me, or the way I thought. You win some and lose some; there is nothing wrong with a firm stance as long as you do not do anything to purposely hurt anyone. Besides, I very much like to be alone. The authors of the hundreds of books I have read (or in the process of reading) are my friends. If you peruse my library you'll meet many brilliant guys of intellect and experience.

Arthur Schopenhauer, 1788-1860, German philosopher, presented the bias of his own temperament and experience (his celebrated philosophy of pessimism) with such clarity and skill as to gain eventual recognition as one of the great philosophers.

Schopenhauer was a loner; not many friends, and never married. But he had a great mind; free to think; to use the powers of the mind; to conceive ideas; to draw inferences; make judgments. To me, that's pure luxury.

As I said, I like to be alone, but I am not a loner. However, for twenty years I lived in a 400 sq. ft. cabin on top of a hill, with an outhouse, on a 180 acres ranch in central California. I had no running water; no electricity; no phone; no neighbors; I survived, happily, on a Coleman stove, a Coleman lantern, a Ben Franklin fireplace, an outdoor Bar-B-Que built in rocks, a battery powered radio, and two 55 gallon drums of water; one for the (cold) shower, and one for the flush toilet. The outhouse was named "The Plush Flush," and the ranch, "MUM'S THE WORD."

I had my books, light from my lantern, complete solitude, Beethoven (FM, 91.5, Bakersfield) on the battery powered radio, and the limited noise of the perking of the coffee pot, the crackling of the fire, and the rain on the roof.

In the summer, if I had visitors, male or female, we showered in our birthday suits. In the winter, we had the country club followed by a laugh and giggle at the Springville Inn. Not too long ago I visited Springville. In seven years the population soared by 27 people to a total of 1027 individuals. That town was so small the fire department used Water-Pics to put out fires.

Anyhow, I'm glad I read some of Schopenhauer. In *Our Relation to Ourselves*, he wrote, it is natural for great minds—the true teachers of humanity—to care little about the constant company of others; just as little as the schoolmaster cares for joining the gambols (skip about in play) of the noisy crowd of boys that surround him.

The mission of these great minds is to guide mankind over the sea of error to the haven of truth—to draw it forth from the dark abysses of a barbarous vulgarity up into the light of culture and refinement. Men of great intellect live in a world without really belonging to it; and so, from their earliest years, there is a perceptible difference between them and other people. But it is only gradually, with the lapse of years, that they come to a clear understanding of their position. Their intellectual isolation is then reinforced by actual seclusion in their manner of life; they let no one approach who is not in some degree emancipated from the prevailing vulgarity.

I am not an intellectual although I love my isolation or seclusion; at the same time I do not prejudge any one who approaches me. I had two Mormon missionaries approach me one day while I was putting up a barbed wire fence. I offered them coffee or a "Coke". That was an honest mistake! But when they started to talk to me about religion, I said, "Gentlemen, I respect you and your missionary enthusiasm, but I believe I am capable of making up my own mind about what particular God I serve, if any. I believe in minding my own business, and thinking in my own terms about the affairs of religion and State. I also believe "the better the day, the better the deed." Now, if you would like to grab a hammer and wire stretcher—." They were very personable as they decided to leave.

And now, speaking of not hurting anyone, I feel free to think in terms with Socrates.

Socrates, when reminded that he should prepare for his trail, answered:
"Thinkest thou not that I have been preparing for it all my life?"
"In what way?" asked a friend
"I have maintained that in which me lay," Socrates answered.
"How so?" another asked.
"I have never, secretly or openly, done a wrong unto any," Socrates answered.

Gaining self-esteem and self-respect are tough assignments; it is not supposed to be easy. But think of the potential reward of enhanced pleasure of living by simply taking on the assignment of reading philosophy about the building blocks of man, and allowing yourself the company of some of the world's great minds. The classics (*THE HARVARD CLASSICS & GREAT BOOKS OF THE WESTERN WORLD*) were often thought to be nothing more than books on education. On the contrary! They sought to teach us how to pass from *esse* to *bene esse*, from "being" to "well being," to use Aristotle's famous phrase for the task of politics. But politics, as Aristotle knew, led us to contemplation; to the consideration of the right order of things.

Freud thought that philosophy had no immediate influence on the great majority of mankind and it interested only a small number even of the thin upper stratum of intellectuals, while all the rest found it beyond them. Freud thought philosophy behaved itself as if it were a science.

In *The Story of Philosophy*, (Simon & Schuster, New York, 1928) Durant's thoughts were that philosophy seemed always to lose ground to science. This is because philosophy accepts the hard task of dealing with problems not open to the methods of science; problems like good and evil, beauty and ugliness, order and freedom, life and death.

As soon as a field of inquiry yields knowledge susceptible of exact formulation it is called science.

Science is analytical description. Philosophy is synthetic interpretation.

My thoughts, as I keep Freud's and Durant's view in mind, is that the advancement of any scientific state of the art is based on careful consideration of historical knowledge coupled with contemporary study and experience. The atom bomb fits that category, and the cure for infantile paralysis, and breaking the sound barrier.

Philosophy would, therefore, for me, behave itself like a science in that in order for me to advance *my* state-of-the art, intellectually and philosophically, I look to history. Einstein did, Dr. Jonas Salk did, NACA (National Advisory Committee Aeronautics) did, so why shouldn't I—or you?

So, maybe only a small number of intellectuals *are* studying philosophy. I find that good news in that those individuals will take, empathetically, the scientific route, and "combine careful consideration of historical knowledge, etc.," and advance the state (mental capacity) of anyone's mind willing to accept the challenge to learn more. In all probability someone(s) will leave a great legacy and allow man to further recognize the reality of being able to understand his self better and, hopefully, live in a more desirable world.

One can actively involve experience and thought interwoven with the lives of philosophers and try to understand their common sense reasoning. Philosophy purifies the will. But philosophy is to be understood as experience and thought, not as mere reading or passive study. The more you study, the more you try, the more you will approach self-reliance in thought, speech, and action.

If one can experience the knowledge and reflection in terms with Schopenhauer, the gain in self-identity and reliability is surprising. You'll now be doing things without worrying about what other people say. Understanding philosophic reasoning. Combined with experience forms courage and perseverance and builds strength enough to face any danger or difficulty.

"To believe your own thought, to believe that what is true for you in your private heart is true for all men—that is genius. Speak your latent conviction, and it shall be the universal sense; for the inmost in due time becomes the outmost, and our first thought is rendered back to us by the trumpets of the Last Judgment. Familiar as the voice of the mind is to each, the highest merit we ascribe to Moses, Plato and Milton is that they set at naught books and traditions, and spoke not what men, but what *they* thought. A man should learn to detect and watch that gleam of light which flashes across his mind from within . . ."

Ralph Waldo Emerson
GREAT TREASURY of WESTERN THOUGHT

Many times I have had gleams of light—I call them flashes of thought—race across my mind. I learned from reading Emerson that too many men dismiss, without notice, their thoughts because it is theirs. "In every work of genius we recognize our own rejected thoughts."

I remember once in reading about International Harvester's Problems—debt, new president, union problems, loss of market share, etc. At the same time I was reading where the Japanese heavy equipment manufacturer, Komatsu, was trying to make an in-road into the United States market. I thought crossed my mind; since it would cost Komatsu millions of dollars to set up a marketing and distribution network in the United States, why not team with International Harvester's existing sales and distribution network. Komatsu could pay International Harvester the monies saved and those monies could be used to re-strengthen the company. I thought it was such a good idea. I got on the phone and made a cold call to a vice president of International Harvester in Chicago. I told him I had a "Gleam of Light" and during a trip to the East within the next few weeks, I would like to discuss it with him. He said, "Ok, you're a gutsy guy; if you're willing to pay your way, I'll listen."

Well, I *did* meet with the vice president. He like the idea but it was something they had already been exploring. He very much appreciated the fact that I would take the time to run this type of thought by him. Although this particular idea of mine did not come to fruition, the next one was extremely rewarding.

I learned that an aerospace company I was familiar with was having trouble with one of its prime subcontractors. The subcontractor had qualified a mechanical actuator servo system for a drone but proceeded to have production, quality control, and financial problems. I called the aerospace company and made an appointment with the program manager an informed him about another subcontractor I was working with. I told him my company was in the servo, mechanical and hydraulic, disciplines and wondered if they might consider us. He informed me they might consider us but as a new subcontractor we would have to build and quality our unit to the prime contractor specifications. We both knew this would impose a severe test of dollars, time, and management strength. It would delay production of the drone that was already behind schedule.

I, therefore, suggested to the program manager that instead of spending time and money, why not strengthen the present source? He asked how that could be done. I said I was sure my company had the capability to product the unit and, in addition, provide fiscal, quality assurance, and management integrity. I added, "We may even buy it."

The program manger said, "Well, Jack, you can go ahead and try, but it is not within my right and power to advise my present subcontractor of your thoughts. If it works, you will relieve us of a lot of worry. I'll give you two weeks, but I don't think it will work."

I immediately called the president of the company I was doing business with as a consultant and offered the thought that his company should be the one to team with, or purchase the servo system; they certainly had the capability. The president and I had considerable discussions. He called a board meeting; it was agreed that I should pursue the idea.

Every board member was wondering how I could possibly get the president of the actuator servo systems company, who I didn't even know, to agree to the situation. I said the only was I could find out was to get on the phone and ask. I had to look up the area code and number, and after six different tries, the president of the company picked up the phone in his office one evening. After I explained whom I was and what I thought we could do, he said, "Your call could not have been more fortuitous."

The rest is history. We acquired the company, added the management structure needed to make the program successful and, as a division, it has become the flagship of the aerospace company.

Another consulting contract was awarded to me in addition to paying me for the time to assist in putting the merger together. I did not take a finder's fee. I took remuneration in the form of an additional contract so I would be present during the transition and production.

Personnel from three companies were relying on me; taking a finder's fee and leaving would have, in my opinion, been morally wrong.

"Man must act and speak what he thinks now—in hard words—and tomorrow speak what he thinks in hard words again, though it contradicts everything he said today. 'Ah, so you shall be sure to be misunderstood.' Is it so bad then to be misunderstood? Pythagoras was misunderstood, Socrates, Jesus, Luther, Copernicus, Galileo, Newton and every pure and wise spirit that ever took flesh. To be great is to be misunderstood.'"

Philosophy: Who Needs It
Ayn Rand, Bobbs-Merril, New York

I can give a classic example of being misunderstood. Many pilots from Wright Field and the Tactical Air Command would visit a particular company I worked with to study the mock-up and mission profile of a new fighter being developed. They would then offer constructive criticism.

The big wheels, so called "marketing executives," from corporate would call and ask what restaurant we were going to in the evening so they could "come down an join us to assist in the sales process."

I would tell the executives that if they wanted to participate they should join us during the day and learn from the discussion; and besides, I had already made plans to take the pilots to a cocktail party and barbecue at one of the local beaches. I was asked if there would be women at the party. I said, "Of course, what fighter pilot wouldn't want women around?"

Talk about being misunderstood. I was accused of bad judgment, lack of professionalism, giving the company a bad name, and immature in my entertainment philosophy.

What corporate did not know is that I had carefully orchestrated these kinds of parties. Most of the airline pilots living at the beach were former Air Force, Navy or Marine pilots with combat experience. I asked these men and their girlfriends (who were flight attendants) to host the party for my visiting pilots and myself. I naturally paid for the party out of my expense account. The reason for having the pilots attend the party was it gave me an opportunity to have experienced pilots cross fertilize all ideas associated with what is most needed in a new fighter with both air-to-air and air-to-ground capabilities. In the ensuing days I would spend a lot of time with my friends from the beach and learn what they had learned from my guests so that my company could do a better job of marketing in "the needs of" and "the language of" the customer. It is amazing the information I found out. The information that helped us sells the airplane to the United Status Air Force.

Upper management expected me to fulfill **their** needs and communicate **their** thoughts—the antithesis of what is good for the company and customer. To satisfy the customer is the mission and role of every company. The nature of customer satisfaction is acute and penetrating and by its own evolution will bring fundamental disagreements and misunderstanding. I think disagreement is beneficial; it is a means toward assertion and self-reliance. I lost my battle and in short notice was "out the door!!" Corporate management in their myopic tunnel vision and self-importance thought they were too good to mingle at the "beach level." And on top of that, not one of them had ever flown a fighter.

"Thus, it is good for men to be roused into action and stiffened into self-reliance by difficulty, rather than to slumber away their lives in useless apathy and indolence. It is the struggle that is the condition of victory. If there were no difficulties, there would be no need of efforts; if there were no temptation, there would be no training in self-control, and but little merit in virtue; if there were no trail and suffering, there would be no education in patience and resignation. Thus, difficulty, adversity and suffering are not all evil, but often the best source of strength, discipline and virtues."

CHARACTER
Samuel Smiles, A.L. Burt Co.
New York

A SUPPLEMENT

I consider myself a lucky man; truly loving great parents, loving family, I'm educated, served my country in two wars, fighter pilot, experimental test pilot, never a day without work, fired from a couple of financially sound management positions (too much of a maverick, I was told), started my business, as a janitor, at $300.00 a month, met many lovely ladies, fine men, a professor of marketing and sales at a community college (night school), married, at sixty, after going steady for seven years, a magnificent lady, and finally, after 78 years, I guess I could consider myself an overnight success although I am still consulting three days a week and finishing my third book. Keeps me out of trouble!!

It's hard for me to explain, but not one day has gone by during the evolution of my life that hasn't presented me with my share of problems; join the crowd! But I have never complained because I didn't feel I had the right to. Marcus Aurelius, 121-180, told me nothing happened to me that didn't happen to tens of thousands of other men before me. "Besides," he said, "most of the trouble you got into is probably that of your own doing. So, my friend, don't complain, accept the responsibility, and get out of it yourself!"

I believe "Mr. Free Enterprise (MFE)" picks up on men like me and throws us troubles just to put us to a test. "MFE" wants us to fail ONLY if we don't stand up, dust ourselves off, and start all over again, and again. Success, after potential failure, is an endowment well earned, and "MFE" takes heed. He then coalesces all of what he has learned from us to "dish out" certain business situations characterized by difficulty, and when those selected potential failures stand firm and succeed, the whole cross-section of business succeed; we are then given our gift—it's called America.

There are plenty of experienced men and women willing and able to assist in the achievement of something desired, planned, or attempted in any category of discipline—business, art, medicine, music, etc. All one has to do is open a book!

A book offers direct one-on-one personal knowledge derived from participation or observation with a willingness to share. One can keep a book by his or her side, take it on a trip, a vacation, or a class discussion. Empathetically, one is speaking directly from experience. A book is a convivial associate.

One of the big drawbacks from completely understanding one's self is the constant anxious uneasiness about what other people think of you. I was watching, for the third time, the movie *OPEN RANGE* a few nights ago. Annette Benning was hurrying from her home to a bar in this very small western town to help her wounded true love, Kevin Costner. Women did not go in bars. Everyone from the town was outside—farmers, cattlemen, the town's businessmen, wives, the women of ill repute, young boys and girls, persons passing through. He, Kevin Costner, was sitting on the bar nurturing his damaged leg and when he saw *his* true love come in the bar he said, and I am paraphrasing, "I am sorry to do this to you. The whole town is out there seeing you walk in to see me."

Ms. Benning turned and perused the crowd and said, "I don't *care* what people think."

My kind of lady!

We can all learn to be like that; it will open your heart and soul to greatness that, by the way, is a constant struggle.

I say learn because it does take time to be your own person, to learn to laugh at yourself and with others, to never laugh at someone, to learn to speak only good of someone, or not at all. Remember what Emerson said, "In every man there is something I may learn of him, and in that I am his pupil."

Jack "Suitcase" Simpson
Early Fall, 2005

SUCCESS ISN'T PERMANENT,

AND

FAILURE ISN'T FATAL!

Mike Ditka

WHAT ARE YOU DOING HERE?—A

One of my clients, a company specializing in electro-mechanical actuators received a bid from an aerospace company located in Ventura County. The company had received an order from the United States Air Force for hundreds of Unmanned Combat Aerial Vehicles (UCAV) to be used primarily for reconnaissance, but also as a combatant by utilizing "stations" (connecting mechanisms) under its wings to hang a particularly lethal missile. That particular phase of the "weapons' system" was classified.

I am not going to go into all the perturbations and states of discomposure about meeting the demands of the customer; engineering drawings, size, weight, engineering changes, quality, configuration management, manufacturing, production, statistical process controls, subcontractor management, acceptance testing, etc., etc. I had to spend my time developing a business minded rapport with the senior buyer. Of course the demands of the company came through him and although it kept me very busy, the fallout added strength to a developing rapport between the two of us.

One morning I called the buyer and asked if I could bring our Chief Project Engineer and Quality Control Manager for a meeting with their counterparts to discuss pertinent features of the actuator and the quality control standards we expected to use for manufacturing and processing. Mr. Roberts (his name was Harold Joseph Roberts, but he liked to be called "Joe") suggested I have an early meeting so he could kept informed of the results as he was taking several days off to travel to another contractor.

The four of us had a fruitful meeting and afterward I invited the four gentlemen to lunch and told them on our way out I would stop and quickly brief Mr. Roberts on the results of the meeting. I asked him if he would join us for lunch as he was busy and we could give him the details of our meeting over a soup and sandwich. I was somewhat surprised when he said, "Yes, I'd be glad to and I appreciate you filling me in with the details as I am hastily preparing for my trip."

During lunch the four gentlemen filled Mr. Roberts in with the details. He told us frankly that we were considered number one from a technical and quality point of view, but that was all he could say because there were price and performance figures still under considerations.

When Mr. Roberts returned from his trip I asked for an appointment to meet with him on the 2nd day of the following week. He agreed and during our meeting he said that we were very technically strong but that the contract would amount to hundreds of thousands of dollars and the company wanted to make sure they awarded the purchase order to the right subcontractor. He asked me if I was going to stay in the area for the evening and I told him that I was going to call on another prime contractor in Santa Barbara the following morning and had planned to spend the night at the local Holiday Inn. Surprisingly, he asked me if I liked to shoot pool and I said, "Oh sure I would like to, but I'm not very good at it."

Well, to make a long story short, I met several of his friends, we had a couple of games of pool and an enjoyable dinner together and I might add, he made sure he paid his own way. This "professional socializing" continued for several weeks. In that time I found out from engineering that my company was selected but nothing further came of it. One evening before I left to go to the hotel, I asked him (I was now call him Joe) what time he arrived at work in the morning. He said, "You know Jack, since I'm single I get up early to work out and after a quick shower, I'm usually at the office by 6:30 AM." He volunteered that getting to the plant early gave him a parking place near the entrance to the building and in that way he didn't have to go in through the rear entrance. The guard always unlocked the front door for him.

So, that evening when I went to the hotel I asked for a 4:30 AM call. I got up, showered, shaved, had a small bite to eat, got in my car and drove to the plant with the intention of meeting Joe. When his car drove up, I pulled beside him. We both stopped about the same time; we rolled down our windows. With a startled look Joe asked, "What the heck are you doing here?" I looked him right back in the eye and said; "Joe, we both know we have the responsibility of meeting a very tough schedule. I will be personally responsible to you for our company's performance and I'm not here today leaving until you give me a purchase order." He stared at me for a very long time. "Okay!" he said, "You'll have to park in visitor parking. I'll meet you at the entrance and we'll talk it over."

I left 3½ hrs later with a very large (in dollars) purchase order. That was the day one of my test pilot friends was killed at Edwards Air Force Base. Of course, I will never forget it. I haven't forgotten "GI Joe" either. We are still friends to this day.

I called him "GI" because he did everything by the book; a trait that I admired in him.

One day—brought eng quality chief design eng looked good had lunch had to stay over asked me about pool very honest and bright man but knew how to smile etc

WHAT ARE YOU DOING HERE?—B

I was under contract from a very big aerospace company from Canada. Their specialty was judicious electronics, radio, and radar, particularly in the Canadian Air Force and the United States Air Force Strategic Air Command.

One day I got a call from my sales manager inviting me to Montreal to review and discuss a new product. The only thing he would tell me was the fact that they thought of it as a break through in several aircraft instruments such as those reporting altitude, air speed, RPM, fuel quantities and selected pressures. It sounded good to me so I immediately made my reservations and arrived three days later.

My ken, as you have read in **BOOK III**, is marketing analysis. My Canadian client wanted me to peruse both the civilian and military aircraft manufacturers to see what they thought about the new instruments' potential. I will not go into many details regarding my analysis, but I was able to convince a United States Army Helicopter Manufacturer to give my Canadian Corporation a request for proposal (RFP) for selected instruments on a new helicopter.

Again, the details of the RFQ and our subsequent response, including my Canadian Corporation's trip to Southern California does not have to be detailed. But two particular aspects that should be mentioned are the describing of our aptitudes and skills. Also, the prime contractor's trip to Montreal to resolve a myriad of questions about the new instruments and whether or not we, as a subcontractor, would have the time to qualify to Army specifications.

It is not important for me to mention more details of the potential contract as we were not selected. An enterprise with years of experience was chosen because of the reliability factor, and I must say they in all fairness, they were technically responsive. The prime contractor, although they were impressed with our proposal, basically said they couldn't take a chance.

As time went on, I kept asking a few of my friends at this particular aerospace company about how my competition was doing. I began to get word on more than one occasion that the chosen contractor was way behind schedule because of some of the Army requirements were new to them also.

One afternoon on the way home from a meeting at this particular prime contractor, where I asked a number of "pointed" questions, I called my sales manager at his residence and told him to take a chance and go ahead and build the instruments as if we had been chosen. You have assembled a number of prototype instruments so do what you can to loose? Just match the requirements as if you were under contract. I think I have found a way to put us in good light in the event our competition fails. Please let me know when the instruments are ready.

Well, they listened to me and my Canadian Corporation built a set of instruments. About six weeks passed and the aircraft was now going through pre-flight testing and they did not have necessary instruments, so I volunteered ours. I called the program manager and told him we would be happy to deliver them to the plant; they were very pleased. I gave them a time that they would arrive at my home by special delivery. Today that company is known as Federal Express.

The day for delivery arrived and they were not there. I called the program manager and promised to have them in his hands the following day. They did not arrive. So I got up at 3:30 AM the next day and drove to Culver City and stood at the guard gate of the entrance to the plant and waited. The program manager showed up at 6:30 and said. "What are you doing here?" I told him the only way I could prove to him that I was honest in saying the instruments had not arrived, was by telling him in person. He was very much impressed that I would do something like that but told me everyone was on edge and we, collectively, could be in a lot of trouble. He then asked, "What are we going to do next?" I told him the instruments would probably be there when I arrived home this particular afternoon, and if he could arrange to have them accepted by Quality Control at Palomar (the flight test facility) I am sure they're working day and night and I would deliver the instruments that evening. I also told him, after looking at my watch, it was 10 o'clock Eastern Standard Time, and I would also call my plant and have them send to the chief instruments' engineer and the installation specialist to San Diego. I said, "I will pick them up tonight, take them to Palomar, so in three days everything should be under control.

All I can say is that the instruments' engineer, the installation specialist, and I spent the next five days and nights working around the clock. No! the engineer and specialist from our plant worked around the clock and I delivered coffee and doughnuts, submarine sandwiches, cokes, and lots of pizza and Kentucky Fried Chicken—round the clock.

Our instruments performed flawlessly during the "operational suitability" test flights. Our competition's contract was cancelled and the contract was given to my company.

That was a long time ago.

I see the prototype test pilot every year at the Society of Experimental Test Pilots' symposium. To this day the production instruments are still flying with precision and reliability.

What lessons have we learned from "What Are You Doing Here?"

Well, I learned that believing in your self and product is fundamental. Never take anything for granted. Always develop rapport based on honesty and integrity. Always know your competition; don't ever, ever, put them down! Purchasing personnel are forever having trouble with sub contractors on delivery and quality. If your supplier is heading for the same type of trouble, tell the buyer immediately and ask for assistance. You company will be held in high esteem for telling the truth. THINK! If the prime contractor assists your company and the team collectively solves problems, purchasing will not want to have the problems all over again by giving your item to another company. Don't be afraid to get your hands dirty. Walk the floor with shipping and receiving personnel. Know the personnel in the quality labs testing your product. If the coffee truck arrives "outside the gate" at 6AM, be there, introduce yourself, and buy the men and women a cup of coffee and a do-nut. Learn! Put what you are learning to good use.

REMEMBER! you are a professional sales person. You are the company you represent. Be CIRCUMSPECT at all times. Do not allow for an edge giving your competition a reason to vilify you. And please remember the adage, "In every man there is something I may learn of him, and in that, I am his pupil."

THERE IS NO DISCIPLINE

IN THE WORLD

SO SEVERS AS THE

DISCIPLINE OF EXPERIENCE

SUBJECT TO THE TESTS OF

INTELLIGENT DEVELOPMENT

AND DIRECTION.

DEWEY

EXPERIENCE AND

EDUCATION, II

YOU MUST HAVE BEEN A BEAUTIFUL BABY 'CAUSE BABY, LOOK AT YOU NOW!

Yes, she was a beautiful baby, but she was now a more beautiful airline stewardess.

The time was late 1952. I was in gunnery at Nellis Air Force base in Las Vegas having graduated from flight training as a jet fighter pilot and assigned to the 8th Fighter Bomber Wing in Korea. I was at Nellis on a 10 week TDY (temporary duty) to learn to shoot guns and drop bombs from the F-80 *SHOOTING STAR* and the F-86 *SABRE JET.*

I met, and became friends with, a fighter pilot who had graduated in a class before me. He was having trouble! He was afraid of the F-86. The base operations officer assigned him a T-33, the advanced jet trainer we all learned to fly in advanced pilot training. He was to tow the sleeve for gunnery missions and fly personnel for instrument—refreshing courses.

He was in love with the beautiful stewardess. He asked her to marry him and asked me to be his best man. We both said, "We would be honored." Well, I said I'd be honored. I don't know what she said but whatever came out of her mouth was in the form of "yes!"

So, she gave up flying for, at that time, *Bonanza Airlines.* They had a beautiful, but small, wedding and honeymooned at an elegant new hotel in Scottsdale, Arizona.

My friend soon returned to Nellis and his lovely bride assumed the duties of housewife. But he was soon re-assigned to McDill AFB in Tampa, Florida. Several of the guys, and gals, and I, had a happy luncheon for them at the Desert Inn and threw rice and cheered as they headed for Florida in his new Oldsmobile convertible.

But the friendships, and smiles, and scintillating adventures always have some chicken shit way of bringing unhappiness. Four weeks had not gone by when I learned my friend had been killed in a T-33. A broken hearted, depressed, joyless, lonely lady, after a heartwarming military funeral, got back in the convertible, drove to Las Vegas, and asked *Bonanza* for her job back. They were glad to oblige. I was, at that time, in Korea.

As described in **BOOK I,** I returned from Korea in November of 1953 and reported to North American Aviation, in Los Angeles, as an air force test pilot. It was January 10, 1954.

I don't know how we got together; I knew her Mother lived in Pasadena and I was in the Manhattan Beach phone book. She called; we talked, had a truly great reunion over dinner, and as you can see, even with sand on her beautiful face, she was a knock out. She was still in love with the memories of her late husband.

After spending the next day on the beach followed by dinner at Panchos, she returned her rental car and took a *Bonanza* flight back to Las Vegas. That was the last time I saw her. Soon thereafter, however, I flew to Nellis in the new TF-86F (see **BOOK I).** Her "roomies" said she had tran

ity; long forgotten by me!

Gee! That was 51 years ago!!

NOTHING IN LIFE IS TO BE FEARED,

IT IS ONLY TO BE

UNDERSTOOD!

MARIE SKLODOWSKA

MADAME CURIE

MY FUNNY VALENTINE

SWEET COMIC VALENTINE,

YOU MAKE ME SMILE WITH MY HEART

YOU LOOKS ARE LAUGHABLE

UNPHOTOGRAPHICAL

YET YOU'RE MY FAVORITE WORK OF ART

WELL, MY STEWARDESS FRIEND WAS MY FAVORITE WORK

OF ART. AND I DON'T LAUGH AT THOSE LOOKS! ACTUALLY,

I THINK SHE IS QUITE PHOTOGENIC! YES, SHE SENT ME HER

SWEET, COMIC VALENTINE. AND I HAVE BEEN SMILING

FOR THE PAST 30 YEARS!!!

LIFE IS GREAT, ISN'T IT???

FOR ME, IT IS ALL BASED ON REALITY AND TRUTH!

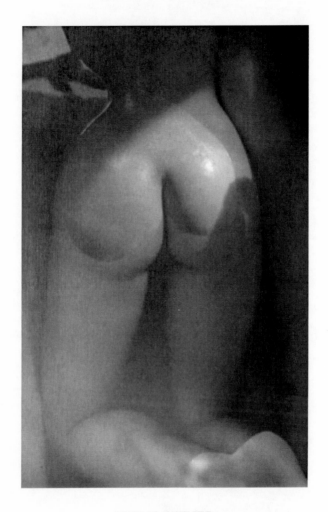

LIFE IS EITHER

A DARING ADVENTURE—

OR NOTHING.

Helen Keller

YOUR TIME INCREASES

IN VALUE

WHEN YOU SHARE

ITS PRODUCTIVITY

WITH OTHERS!

GEORGE HALL

Edwards Brothers Malloy
Thorofare, NJ USA
March 26, 2013